Music Coding and Tagging

SOLDIER CREEK MUSIC SERIES

Richard P. Smiraglia, Series Editor

Number 1. *Music Subject Headings*, by Perry Bratcher and Jennifer Smith. 1988

Number 2. *Music Coding and Tagging*, by Jay Weitz. 1990

Music Coding and Tagging

MARC Content Designation for Scores and Sound Recordings

By Jay Weitz

Soldier Creek Press
Lake Crystal, Minnesota
1990

Printed in the United States of America

First Edition

Library of Congress Cataloging in Publication Data

Weitz, Jay, 1953-
    Music coding and tagging : MARC content designation for scores /
by Jay Weitz. -- 1st ed.
       p.   cm. -- (Soldier Creek music series ; no. 2)
    Includes bibliographical references (p.
    Includes index.
    ISBN 0-936996-36-6 : $35.00
    1. Cataloging of music--Data processing. 2. Cataloging of sound
recordings--Data processing. 3. MARC System. I. Title.
II. Series.
ML111.W35 1990
025.3'48--dc20   90-9776
                                           CIP
                                           MN

Soldier Creek Press

Nancy B. Olson, President
Edward Swanson, Editor-in-Chief
Sharon Olson, Managing Editor

Postal Drawer U, Lake Crystal, Minnesota 56055 USA

For Esther

... something like beloved plus friend divided by two ...

— Robert Musil
The Man Without Qualities

Table of Contents

List of Illustrations

Preface

Music Coding and Tagging arises from a perceived need for a manual detailing the coding and subfielding conventions that allow the Machine-Readable Cataloging (MARC) format to communicate bibliographic information for scores and sound recordings. To my knowledge, no such tool has been published since Ruth Patterson Funabiki's and Karl Van Ausdal's *Music OCLC Users Group Tagging Workbook and Reference Manual* (Newton, Mass.: Nelinet, 1980). In the decade since, the MARC format, the cataloging rules, and the formats of sound recordings in particular all have undergone extensive change. The time seems ripe for a new guide through the computerized thicket.

In some respects the challenges posed by scores and sound recordings resemble those of other bibliographic formats, but in many details they are quite different. *Music Coding and Tagging* does not attempt to address every field and tag, but it does consider many of the fields commonly used in music records (plus a few not so commonly used) from a music-specific point-of-view. The *Descriptive Tabulation, Library of Congress MUMS Format Data: MUMS Music Records* (1987) was invaluable in this selection process. It was used to ensure that all of the most common, and a fair sampling of the more obscure, subfield orders and possibilities were covered. Where possible, examples are drawn from actual music records; where appropriate, special applications found in the cataloging of music are considered. *Appendix A* briefly lists the music-related fields that either no longer are valid in the USMARC format or that are reserved only for pre-*AACR 2* use.

Although the extensive examples that illustrate the use of each field and subfield appear mostly in OCLC format, the guidelines for input are just as valid for users of RLIN or WLN, or any other MARC-based system. The widespread use of, and my own familiarity with, the OCLC-MARC format conspired with reasons of space to limit most examples to the single format. However, because the placement and spacing of subfield delimiters is the only major field-level difference among the three formats, I felt that this limitation would be acceptable to most users. *Appendix B*, which explains the different field input practices of these three bibliographic systems, precedes the full record examples.

These full-record tagged cataloging examples, which constitute *Appendix C,* are derived largely from Library of Congress MARC music cataloging. A representative selection of records is formatted as they would appear in OCLC, in RLIN, and in WLN. Because this is not a cataloging manual, facsimiles of title pages, disc labels, and the like purposely are not included. Their inclusion would falsely imply a leap from the item being cataloged directly to the machine-readable cataloging record without the intervening steps of descriptive cataloging, subject cataloging, and authority work, none of which is covered in this manual.

All of the full-record examples and most of the individual field examples (except where noted) reflect *AACR 2R* cataloging practices, as this manual aims to address current rather than retrospective bibliographic input. (Guidance on the input of old LC control numbers in field 010 and the list of obsolete and pre-*AACR 2* fields in *Appendix A* are notable exceptions.) Of course, most of the same coding and tagging advice applies to pre-*AACR 2* input as well. If there is enough demand for it, perhaps a future edition of *Music Coding and Tagging* can cover retrospective input more explicitly.

It must be recognized that the authority file from which headings are taken is dynamic, with thousands of headings being changed each week. Every effort has been made to keep the headings current, but the forms found here should not be considered authoritative.

Although numerous people helped on this book, the responsibility for any errors is solely my own. Neither cataloging nor inputting is an exact science, and reasonable catalogers and inputters certainly can disagree about specific practices. By all means, readers and users of this manual should bring to my attention any and all inaccuracies, lacunae, and further questions that could be addressed in any future revision.

Acknowledgments

Thanks go out to all of those people who had a hand in making this book possible. First, thank you to Nancy Olson, Edward Swanson, and Richard Smiraglia, who transformed some idle chatter at the 1988 Music Library Association Annual Meeting in Minneapolis into a proposal for this volume. Thanks again to Richard Smiraglia and Edward Swanson, my official editors, and to Esther Silverman, my unofficial editor and official wife, for their patient, insightful, and good-humored advice (particularly in setting me straight about the which/that distinction, ~~that~~ which I never recall having learned in grammar school). Extra special thanks to Esther for her unfailing faith in my abilities and her support in all things.

My OCLC colleagues Rosanna O'Neil and Glenn Patton, and my former OCLC colleague Joan Schuitema (now at Northwestern University), deserve special thanks for plowing through each and every page of the manuscript, pointing out errors, questioning my judgment, and generally making sure I didn't make a complete fool of myself. Without their collective and individual wisdom and experience, this book would have been considerably less clear and less accurate than it is.

Without the aid of Ruth Sawyer of the OCLC Pacific Network and Carol Carr of Whitman College in Walla Walla, Washington, I might not have been able to include WLN examples. Thanks again to Richard Smiraglia for help with the RLIN records.

Also, I must thank my managers at OCLC, Carol Davis, Liz Bishoff, and Tom Sanville, who generously allowed me the time and resources to accomplish this task and didn't complain too much when other work stood neglected. In addition, my thanks to all of those people in the Online Data Quality Control Section (especially our ever-patient secretary Cheryl Bers) and elsewhere at OCLC, in LC's Music Section (Fred Bindman, Deta Davis, Richard Hunter, Harry Price, David Sommerfield, Kenneth Valdes, and Steve Yusko, in particular), and in the library world who, wittingly or un, provided examples, questions, and answers.

To Albert Maag and the Capital University Library staff and to Thomas Heck and the Ohio State University Music/Dance Library staff, I am indebted for generous access to their collections.

Finally, thanks to the OCLC Online Computer Library Center, the Research Library Group's Research Library Information Network, and the Western Library Network for the use of their bibliographic records, and to the Library of Congress as the source of the cataloging.

Foreword

The MARC music format[1] has revolutionized the cataloging of music and sound recordings. The frustrations of Harvard Music Librarian Mary Lou Little, whose sound recordings catalog in the late 1960s had become so seriously flawed that it provided little assistance to users, have resulted in a set of complex data coding requirements that meet national and international standards, and in the rapid and enthusiastic embrace of automated cataloging techniques through the music library profession. A remarkable invention in and of itself, the format has been the catalyst for the construction of two magnificent network data bases that now provide bibliographic control of much of the nation's printed music and sound recordings collections.

Little's project began with the format that already had been approved for use with book cataloging. To it she and her staff added content designation for specifically music related elements of the bibliographic record. The Library of Congress willingly took over the maintenance and further development of the proposed format, and in consultation with the Music Library Association (MLA) developed a series of drafts, and eventually in 1976 the first published version of the music format.[2]

At the behest of music librarians everywhere the music format was rapidly implemented in networks across the United States. Music librarians had become severely frustrated by this time because many of their institutions already had converted book and serial cataloging from manual to automated techniques, and many had been illegally inputting score cataloging into the OCLC database utilizing the books format.

OCLC was the first to implement the music format in 1978. OCLC's implementation, and in particular their indexing routines, was well advised by an ad hoc committee of the Music Library Association (MLA). Following the formal implementation of the music format on OCLC, this committee mutated into what has become the largest and most influential of specialized music organizations devoted to bibliographic system use, the Music OCLC Users Group (MOUG). In the absence of any plan for implementation of the format at the Library of Congress, MOUG conducted content designation workshops, devised the first tagging manual, commissioned studies of OCLC music users and their needs, and generally provided the collegial support needed by the hundreds of music librarians who had set out to build a national bibliographic network. RLIN, the shared bibliographic network of the Research Libraries Group, implemented the music format in 1980. WLN implemented the music format in 1984, completing the third node of what has become a tremendous bibliographical source for the music field. The Library of Congress did not begin even small scale-use of the music format until 1985.

Now the format is maintained at the Library of Congress with the advice of the American Library Association's MARBI (Recording of Bibliographic Information in Machine Readable Form) committee. The Music Library Association has a formal liaison to the MARBI committee. In MLA, discussion of developments take place in its Bibliographic Control Committee, which has permanent representation from its Subcommittee on the MARC Format. Recent developments have produced an integrated draft of the USMARC format, in which all specialized fields will be available for use in any type of record, meaning that when format integration is implemented, music catalogers will be able to catalog music serials (for example) without having to choose one or the other format.

The complexities in the music format will be clear from a careful reading of this book. It is useful for those wading through those complexities on the job to remember that all MARC formats are essentially communication formats. That is, they exist to communicate bibliographic data from automated systems to users, and from one automated system to other automated systems. Perhaps the clearest indication of this purpose is the set of small differences in the input requirements for the various networks and the Library of Congress. Each has defined its implementation of the format in terms of its own priorities and objectives. These differences are small and usually are frustrating only to system managers who must import and export MARC records (and perhaps briefly to those who move from system to system in their work).

As Jay Weitz explains in this book, cataloging music and sound recordings using the music format must be thought of in terms of content designation. That is, the complete cataloging must be prepared (or at least thought out) according to existing standards for descriptive and subject cataloging. Only then is the format used as a framework for designating the content of the bibliographic record for machine readability, manipulation, and information retrieval.

Several questions of purpose have arisen about the music format and are beginning to be discussed in various format maintenance circles. These have to do with overlapping usages of various fields, such as field 028 (Publisher's Number for Music), which is used in three ways: 1) as a means of storing control data; 2) to generate printed descriptive notes; and 3) to generate indexed access points. Another such question arises in consideration of the field 505 (Contents), which was designed to generate a printed formatted note, but which has become a useful source of information retrieval (albeit uncontrolled) in systems that provide keyword searching of bibliographic records. Subject access problems are apparent in the continuing discussions of the usefulness of fields 045 (Time Period of Content), 047 (Form of Composition), and 048 (Number of instruments or voices). These fields were designed as control fields to provide useful means of subject retrieval that could not be accommodated effectively with Library of Congress subject headings. The fields are difficult and time-consuming to encode, and structurally their placement in separate unlinked fields could lead to a high number of false drops were they actually used for retrieval. However, they have been very useful for the generation of music-specific indexes, such as those produced by the Institute for Jazz Studies at Rutgers University. These problems, among others, will have to be addressed not only by those responsible for format maintenance, but also by those responsible for the design of descriptive and subject cataloging techniques.

Weitz begins this volume with an introduction to content designation of music cataloging using the MARC music format. In his introduction he explains the complex of standards that are reflected in the entire USMARC format, discusses the origins of the music format, and explains the conventions he uses throughout the book. In the main text he explains the use of each segment of the format (fixed, control, and variable fields), the latter in convenient tag groups (1xx, 4xx, etc.). Each field explanation is accompanied by input requirements for National level records, OCLC, RLIN, and WLN networks, and those used by LC. The book includes three appendices, the first two of which illustrate obsolete fields, and differences among the OCLC, RLIN, and WLN format versions. The third appendix, which occupies a large proportion of the book, is replete with coded examples of full bibliographic records for scores and sound recordings as they would appear in each of the three network databases. A bibliography of other tools useful for music cataloging and content designation appears at the end.

This is the second volume to appear in the *Soldier Creek Music Series*. Like the first volume, *Music Subject Headings*, this volume represents a unique desk tool for music catalogers and students of music cataloging. Also like the first volume, we at Soldier Creek Press hope that this volume will assist in detailed study of the music format, with the goal of improving its effectiveness for both technical services and information retrieval.

Richard P. Smiraglia
Editor, *Soldier Creek Music Series*

NOTES

1. I use this misnomer as a generic term to describe the series of versions of the format. The first version was a separate publication: Library of Congress, MARC Development Office. *Music: A MARC Format.* (Washington, D.C.: Library of Congress, 1976); later versions, updated quarterly, have been contained in: Library of Congress, Automated Systems Office. *MARC Formats for Bibliographic Data.* (Washington, D.C.: Library of Congress, 1980); and Library of Congress, Cataloging Distribution Service. *USMARC Format for Bibliographic Data.* (Washington, D.C.: Library of Congress, 1988).
2. For a detailed history of these developments see Donald Seibert, *The MARC Music Format: From Inception to Publication.* MLA Technical Report no. 13. (Philadelphia: Music Library Association, 1982).

Introduction

Cataloging by example is a practice generally frowned upon by catalogers because it falsely suggests that the theoretical and philosophical underpinnings of cataloging can be ignored safely. This volume is most emphatically *not* a cataloging manual and should not be used as such. It assumes that the cataloging process has been completed, and that the process of pouring the bibliographic data into the Machine-Readable Cataloging (MARC) format is about to take place. With few exceptions, the cataloging rules are invoked only to further clarify certain points, not to explain the finer elements of music cataloging. As such, knowledge of the *Anglo-American Cataloguing Rules,* 2d edition, 1988 revision (*AACR 2R*), and basic familiarity with the structure of the *USMARC Format for Bibliographic Data* (UFBD) are assumed.

Instead, this volume is an aid to coding and tagging MARC records for scores and sound recordings (musical and nonmusical, in spite of the title) *after* the actual cataloging is complete. Unlike cataloging by example, tagging and coding by example seem to be eminently sensible practices. So this volume is littered with examples at almost every opportunity. In most cases they are real examples from real bibliographic records, although occasional examples have been borrowed or invented to illustrate specific or obscure points.

MARC records comprise three intertwined elements: the record structure, based on the American National Standard for Bibliographic Information Interchange; the content designation, i.e., the codes and conventions that allow identification and manipulation of bibliographic data; and the record content, governed by such external standards as the International Standard Bibliographic Description (ISBD) (for our purposes, particularly those for Printed Music, *ISBD(PM),* and for Non-Book Materials, *ISBD(NBM)*); the *Anglo-American Cataloguing Rules,* 2d edition, 1988 revision (*AACR 2R*); and the *Library of Congress Subject Headings*.

Donald Seibert, in his quirky and delightful *The MARC Music Format: From Inception to Publication,* offered a brief history of the evolution of machine-readable cataloging of music materials from its book format antecedents and its Harvard birth in 1969 to its final publication in 1976. By 1980 the music format had been incorporated into the *MARC Formats for Bibliographic Data* (MFBD), which in 1988 was transformed into the *USMARC Format for Bibliographic Data* (UFBD). The evolution continues as "format integration" (best summarized as the extension of the validation of all data elements to all forms of materials) progresses, aiming for full implementation by the end of 1993. The process is detailed in *Format Integration and its Effect on the USMARC Bibliographic Format.*

Parallel to the development of this carrier of bibliographic information was the creation and growth of the bibliographic networks, cooperative ventures that amassed and distributed vast numbers of the bibliographic records created by their members. Each of the networks issues its own documentation (OCLC's *Online Systems* series of individual format documents, RLIN's *Bibliographic Field Guide,* and WLN's *Data Preparation Manual*), but rarely are they able to present the music-specific guidance that users often need. This volume's purpose is to supplement those documents with guidance and examples that relate specifically to tagging and subfielding records for scores and sound recordings.

Roughly following the structure of a bibliographic record, this manual first considers what I've called the "fixed fields," those coded elements from the Leader and the 008 field of the MARC record. Next are the "control fields," the coded data fields 007 and 010 through 048. Finally are the "variable fields" 1XX through 8XX. Obsolete and pre-*AACR 2* fields are listed in *Appendix A.*

Heading each section is a chart or series of charts, one for each field under consideration. These charts outline in simplified form the designation of each field, its standards for input, and its repeatability in the following formats: USMARC (UFBD); the MARC formats as modified in the documentation of the Online Computer Library Center (OCLC), the Research Libraries Information Network (RLIN), and the Western Library Network (WLN); and the 1982 draft of the Library of Congress *Music Online Input Manual* (MOIM). Following is an explanation of information contained in the charts.

UFBD: 000 (A/A) (Rep)

    000   Field designation in the *USMARC Format for Bibliographic Data*

    (A/A)   National Level Record/Minimal Level Record requirements

            M   Mandatory

            A   Mandatory if applicable

            O   Optional

    (Rep)   Repeatability (does not apply to fixed fields)

            Rep   Repeatable

            NRep   Not Repeatable

OCLC: 000 (R/R) (Rep)

    000   Field designation in the OCLC *Scores Format* and/or the OCLC *Sound Recordings Format*

    (R/R)   OCLC *Bibliographic Input Standards* (Level I full cataloging/Level K less-than-full cataloging)

            M   Mandatory

            R   Required if applicable or readily available

            O   Optional

    (Rep)   Repeatability (does not apply to fixed fields)

            Rep   Repeatable

            NRep   Not repeatable

RLIN: 000 (NR) (Rep)

    000   Field designation in the *RLIN Bibliographic Field Guide*

    (NR)   RLIN input standards

            R   Required

             NR   Not required

    (Rep)   Repeatability (does not apply to fixed fields)

            Rep   Repeatable

            NRep   Not repeatable

WLN: 000 (NR) (Rep)

    000   Field designation in the *WLN Data Preparation Manual*

    (NR)   WLN Encoding Level "r" input standards for retrospective cataloging

            A   Mandatory if appropriate

            M   Mandatory

            NR   Not required

    (Rep)   Repeatability (does not apply to fixed fields)

            Rep   Repeatable

            NRep   Not repeatable

MOIM: 000 (Rep)

    000   Field designation in the Library of Congress *Music Online Input Manual* (1982 draft)

    (Rep)   Repeatability (does not apply to fixed fields)

            Rep   Repeatable

            NRep   Not repeatable

    [Input standards from MOIM have not been included, as they were meant to correspond to the National Level Record/Minimal Level Record requirements now found in UFBD]

As an example, here is the introductory chart for Field 245:

245   Title Statement

UFBD: 245 (M/M) (NRep)
OCLC: 245 (M/M) (NRep)
RLIN: 245 (R) (NRep)
WLN: TIL (M) (NRep)
MOIM: 245 (NRep)

    Considered in the heart of each section is the proper use of the field(s), any indicators, and subfields. Where necessary, codes are defined. Examples illustrate proper use of individual codes and subfields, and, concluding most sections, entire fields. Because the writers of WLN documentation thoughtfully have incorporated the numeric equivalents of their own alphabetic field designations and indicator values, most textual references are made to these numeric values without fear of confusing WLN users.

    With only one major exception (punctuation in Field 505) and a few minor ones, descriptive cataloging issues are not addressed in this manual. Similarly, subject cataloging is not considered here, although tagging the resulting subject headings is. Useful tools for descriptive and subject cataloging, plus other aids for both cataloging and tagging, are listed in the bibliography.

FIXED FIELD ELEMENTS

Accompanying Matter

UFBD: 008/24-29 (M/O)
OCLC: Accomp mat (O)
RLIN: AMC (NR)
WLN: ACC MAT (NR)
MOIM: Box 06 (ACC MATR)

Up to six alphabetic codes describe the program notes and other accompanying text and material for sound recordings and scores. If more than six codes apply, choose those most important. Codes should be entered alphabetically and left-justified.

Only those types of accompanying matter deemed significant enough to be mentioned in the title or statement of responsibility (such as a preface or introduction), in a note (such as program notes or vocal texts), or in a subject heading subdivision (such as discographies or bibliographies) should be coded. However, reasonable catalogers might differ in their appraisal of the import of certain accompanying matter.

Except for code "s", which is used only in sound recordings records, the use of this field and the following codes is largely the same for both scores and recordings. Obviously though, the codes are somewhat music-oriented, so questions sometimes arise about applying them to nonmusical recordings. Differences and special applications are mentioned in the code list.

[blank] **No accompanying matter**
  Use this code also for any accompanying matter not significant enough to be mentioned anywhere else in the record.

a **Discography**
  Accompanying matter that includes a discography or other bibliography of recorded sound.

b **Bibliography**

c **Thematic index**

d **Libretto or text**
  Any printed transcript of a libretto or text. For sound recordings, use for transcriptions of either sung or spoken verbal content. For scores, use for words printed as text.

e **Biography of composer or author**

f **Biography of performer or history of ensemble**
  For musical sound recordings, use for biographies of any musical performers or ensembles. For nonmusical sound recordings, use for biographies of any performers (actors, narrators, etc.) or ensembles (theater companies, etc.)

g **Technical and/or historical information on instruments**

h **Technical information on music**
  Use for any instructions on performance of the music.

i **Historical information**
  Use for either musical or nonmusical historical information.

k **Ethnological information**

r **Instructional materials**
  Use for guides, teacher's guides, fact sheets, manuals, etc.

s **Music**
Use this code only in sound recording records when the recording is accompanied by a printed version of the music; do not use in score records.

z **Other accompanying matter**
Use for other kinds of accompanying matter not in the list. For recordings, use for general program notes that have been noted in the catalog record. For nonmusical recordings, use for any accompanying material that does not fit readily into other categories. For scores, use for general prefaces, etc. that have been noted in the catalog record.

Examples

504   Bibliography: p. 2.
        Accompanying Matter fixed field: b

500   Program notes and biographical notes on the performers (4 p. :
        ports.) inserted in container.
        Accompanying Matter fixed field: fi

500   Program notes by the composer and text with French translation
        on container.
        Accompanying Matter fixed field: di

500   Program notes by John Toll and harpsichord specifications on
        container.
        Accompanying Matter fixed field: gi

500   Includes thematic indexes and discography.
        Accompanying Matter fixed field: ac

Bibliographic Level

UFBD: Leader/07 (M/M)
OCLC: Bib lvl (M)
RLIN: BLT Position 2 (R)
WLN: BIB LV (M)
MOIM: Box 27 (BIB LEVL)

Bibliographic Level is a one-character code for the relationship of the item being cataloged to its constituent parts or to the item of which it is a constituent part.

a **Monographic component part**
A bibliographic unit physically contained in or attached to another, such that, in order to locate and retrieve the component part, the host item must be located and retrieved. The component part is monographic. A single cut on a sound recording and a single musical work in a score that contains a number of individual works are two examples. The bibliographic record for the monographic component part includes both fields that describe the component part, and data (a 773 Host Item Entry field) that identify the host item, a situation commonly referred to as "in analytics."

b **Serial component part**
A bibliographic unit physically contained in or attached to another, such that, in order to locate and retrieve the component part, the host item must be located and retrieved. The component part is serial. A regularly appearing column or feature in a periodical would be an example. The bibliographic record for the serial component part includes both fields that describe the component part, and data (a 773 Host Item Entry field) that identify the host item, a situation commonly referred to as "in analytics."

c **Collection**
A collection here is an arbitrarily compiled multipart set, put together by the cataloging agency for its own convenience. The cataloging agency does not consider the individual items to be of enough bibliographic importance to catalog separately. Published collections of works (such as an anthology of opera arias or songs) are *not* to be considered "collections" in this bibliographic level sense.

m **Monograph/Item**
A nonserial item, complete either in a single part (a single sound recording or score) or in a finite number of separate parts (a multivolume score or a multiple-disc sound recording).

s **Serial**
A bibliographic item issued in successive parts with some kind of chronological or numeric designation and intended to continue indefinitely. Periodicals, newspapers, annuals, numbered monographic series, and the journals, proceedings, etc., of societies are considered serials. The Library of Congress does not use code "s" for sound recordings or printed and manuscript music.

Type of Date Code

UFBD: 008/06 (M/O)
OCLC: Dat tp (M)
RLIN: PC (R)
WLN: DATE KY (M)
MOIM: Box 20 (DATE TYP)

Date 1, Date 2

UFBD: 008/07-14 (M/O)
OCLC: Date 1, Date 2 (M)
RLIN: PD (R)
WLN: DATE1, DATE2 (M)
MOIM: Box 21-22 (DATE 1,
DATE 2)

These three MARC fields work in tandem to identify the types of dates and the A.D. dates of publication, imprint, release, production, execution, recording, and/or manufacture associated with an item. Usually, this information is derived from the 260 field and from notes. The Type of Date Code is a single-character code specifying the kind of dates to be found in the Date 1 and Date 2 fields. Date 1 and Date 2 are each four-character fields designed to hold numerics representing the various dates. Except for codes "b" (used only in scores) and "p" (used only for sound recordings), these codes may be used in either score or sound recording records.

More than one Type of Date Code could apply to the same score or recording. Use the following tables of precedence for scores and sound recordings to determine which code to use when more than one code applies. Codes are listed in order of precedence.

For single-part items and multipart items complete in one year
- **b**   **B.C. date**
- **q**   **Questionable date (when Date 1 lacks digits in imprint)**
- **r**   **Reprint/original date**
- **s**   **Single date**
- **p**   **Distribution/production date**
- **q**   **Questionable date (*except* when Date 1 lacks digits)**
- **c**   **Actual/copyright dates**
- **n**   **Unknown date**

For collections and multipart items complete in more than one year
- **b**   **B.C. date**
- **q**   **Questionable date (when Date 1 lacks digits in imprint)**
- **i**   **Inclusive dates**
- **r**   **Reprint/original dates**
- **m**   **Initial/terminal dates**
- **q**   **Questionable date (*except* when Date 1 lacks digits)**
- **c**   **Actual/copyright dates**
- **n**   **Unknown dates**

Certain combinations of Date 1 and Date 2 are not dealt with in the following code explanations because the tables of precedence preclude them.

Codes

- **b**   **No dates given; B.C. date involved**

    Code "b" indicates that B.C. dates are associated with the item and that Date 1 and Date 2 will contain blanks. B.C. dates can be coded explicitly in field 046. Because recording and playback equipment were rather hard to come by back then, code "b" may be used for scores but not for sound recordings. The Library of Congress does not use this code.

c **Actual date and copyright date**

When an imprint contains both the release/publication date and a copyright date, the code "c" is used. Publication date is entered as Date 1, copyright date as Date 2.

Imprint dates	Code	Date 1	Date 2
1979, c1966	c	1979	1966
[1988?], c1975	c	1988	1975

i **Inclusive dates of the collection**

For archival collections that have inclusive dates, use code "i". Because such collections are considered unpublished, even if individual items are published, code "m" would be inappropriate. Date 1 contains the earliest year and Date 2 the latest year covered. Should the inclusive dates be represented by a single year, repeat that year in both Date 1 and Date 2. Where terms denoting a time period are used instead of actual dates, approximate the earliest implied date for Date 1 and the latest for Date 2. Missing digits in the first date are replaced by zeroes, in the second date by nines (unless the resulting date is later than the date of cataloging, in which case the date of cataloging should be recorded as the latest date). The Library of Congress does not use this code for sound recordings and printed or manuscript music.

Inclusive dates	Code	Date 1	Date 2
Sketchbooks, 1809-1812	i	1809	1812
1766?	i	1766	1766
18- - - 1809	i	1800	1809
19th and early 20th century	i	1800	1900
Field recordings, 1950-196-	i	1950	1969

m **Multiple dates**

A range of dates for a multipart item published over a period of time is coded "m" in Type of Date Code. Date 1 contains the beginning or initial date; for any unknown portion of this initial date, substitute zeros. If the entire initial date is enclosed in angle brackets (<>), Date 1 contains the first two digits of the given date plus two zeros; angle-bracketed single or double digits are replaced by zeros. Date 2 contains the ending or terminal date; for any unknown or angle-bracketed portions of this terminal date, substitute nines. Should the terminal date be unknown, for example, because the item is not yet complete, Date 2 is "9999". When an initial date is unknown, Date 1 is blank.

Imprint dates	Code	Date 1	Date 2
[1978-1984]	m	1978	1984
1985-	m	1985	9999
-1981	m	ƀƀƀƀ	1981
<c1977>-	m	1900	9999
1976 [i.e. 1969-1976]	m	1969	1976

n **Dates unknown**

AACR 2R requires that an imprint carry an actual or estimated publication date, so code "n" will be rare in *AACR 2R* records. Pre-*AACR 2* records might contain the designation "n.d." indicating no date. In this case, Date 1 and Date 2 would contain blanks.

Pre-AACR 2 date	Code	Date 1	Date 2
[n.d.]	n	ƀƀƀƀ	ƀƀƀƀ

p **Date of distribution/release/issue and production/recording session when different**

For scores, code "p" is not used, but for sound recordings its use is fairly common. When the release date of a sound recording differs from its recording date, code "p" is appropriate. Release date, found in the 260 field, goes in Date 1; recording date, often found in a 518 or other note, is placed in Date 2. When Date 2 is missing one or two digits (such as [197-] or [19- -]), substitute zeros to construct the earliest possible date. If the recording dates span more than a single year, record the earliest year in Date 2. When the date of issue (Date 1) is missing digits, Type of Date code "q" takes precedence.

Release date	Recording date	Code	Date 1	Date 2
[1974]	"A pungent sampling of satire from their radio shows of the 50's and 60's."	p	1974	1950
p1984	Nov. 16, 1943- May 29, 1947	p	1984	1943
[1981?]	Dec. 1979- Feb. 1980	p	1981	1979
p1983	March 16-18, 1981	p	1983	1981
1983	"Field recordings made between 1936 and 1968."	p	1983	1936

q **Questionable date**

When one or more digits in a date are missing (such as "19- -" or "197-?") or when a date is expressed as an uncertain date within a range ("between 1966 and 1971"), code "q" is used. For dates with missing digits, substitute zeros to create the earliest date for Date 1 and nines to create the latest date for Date 2. If Date 2 would turn out to be later than the year of cataloging, use the year of cataloging instead. With a range of dates, place the earlier date in Date 1 and the later date in Date 2.

Imprint date	Code	Date 1	Date 2
[19- -]	q	1900	1988 (year of cataloging)
[196-?]	q	1960	1969
[between 1945 and 1949]	q	1945	1949

r **Reprint/reissue date and original date**

A work that has been previously published or released receives "r" as the Type of Date. This information most often is found in a note; in a series statement or publisher's name that includes the word "reprint," "facsimile," etc.; in an edition statement; or in a double imprint. The date of the reissue or republication is placed in Date 1 and the date of the original in Date 2, if it is known. If there is evidence of previous publication but the specific date is unknown, do not guess at a date or supply an approximation; put blanks in Date 2. When multiple dates are associated with the original publication, record the earlier date in Date 2. When the date of reissue is missing digits, Type of Date code "q" takes precedence.

Sound recordings

Sound recordings are considered reissues when they are:
- issued with a new music publisher's number
- issued on a new label
- released in a new recording medium

An anthology recording that collects previously released material from numerous sources qualifies as a reissue. In all cases, the date of the reissue is put in Date 1. The date of the original goes in Date 2, if it is known; if not known, Date 2 remains blank. If the date of the original is actually a range of dates, the earliest date is Date 2.

Scores

Scores can be reprints, offprints, facsimiles of previously published editions, or some other kind of republication; *do not* consider *preprints* or *prepublications* to be reissues. A photoreproduction of a score is considered a reissue (photoreproduction date in Date 1, original date in Date 2) *unless* it is a copy of a manuscript never previously published. Scores edited or substantially altered from previous editions or reproduced from unpublished manuscripts or holographs are not considered reissues and are not assigned Type of Date Code "r". However, do consider a score a republication if its content differs from an earlier version only in the addition of such new material as an introduction, preface, afterword, etc. Microform reproductions of scores, with the original described in the 260 and the microform described in a 533 note, are considered republications; the date of the microform goes in Date 1; the date of the original goes in Date 2.

Imprint	Evidence	Code	Date 1	Date 2
p1983	"All selections previously released between 1968 and 1979."	r	1983	1968
[1984]	"Originally issued on the Capitol label."	r	1984	bbbb
[1985], p1979	"Reissue of: Meridian E77009 (1979)."	r	1985	1979
[1972]	"Reprint of the 1915 ed."	r	1972	1915
1976	"[Nachdr. d. Ausg.] Leipzig 1928."	r	1976	1928
1973	"Reprinted from the German ed., 1854-1857."	r	1973	1854
1979	"Da Capo Press music reprint series"	r	1979	bbbb
[1960]	"Reissued from Augener plates."	r	1960	bbbb
1779	533 Microfilm. ‡b New Haven : ‡c Yale University Photographic Service, ‡d [1985]. ‡e 1 micro-film reel ; 35 mm.	r	1985	1779

s   **Single known date/probable date**

Any known or conjectural single date of publication or release that can be represented by four digits is assigned Type of Date Code "s". This single date is placed in Date 1; Date 2 contains blanks. When they appear in conjunction with a date of publication, ignore dates of printing, impression, manufacture, or distribution; input such a date in Date 1 *only* when it is the sole date given. Where the date has been corrected by the cataloger, place the corrected date in Date 1, blanks in Date 2. Any date that includes a question mark or the qualification "ca." is recorded without qualification in Date 1; Date 2 is blank. These are considered "probable" dates, not "questionable" dates (i.e., Type of Date Code "s", not "q".)

Imprint date	*Code*	*Date 1*	*Date 2*
[1974]	s	1974	ƀƀƀƀ
p1988	s	1988	ƀƀƀƀ
c1983	s	1983	ƀƀƀƀ
[ca. 1960]	s	1960	ƀƀƀƀ
[1968?]	s	1968	ƀƀƀƀ
1972 [i.e. 1987]	s	1987	ƀƀƀƀ
c1980 (1983 printing)	s	1980	ƀƀƀƀ
1979 [distributed in 1980]	s	1979	ƀƀƀƀ
1953 printing	s	1953	ƀƀƀƀ
1961, t.p. 1963 [pre-*AACR 2*]	s	1961	ƀƀƀƀ
1980/81 [i.e. 1980?]	s	1980	ƀƀƀƀ
[1977 or 1978]	s	1977	ƀƀƀƀ

Descriptive Cataloging Form

UFBD: Leader/18 (M/M)
OCLC: Desc (M)
RLIN: DCF (NR)
WLN: CAT FORM (M)
MOIM: Box 36 (DESC CAT)

A single character indicates the conventions used to catalog a score or sound recording. In earlier years, other codes existed to signify other cataloging forms, but these have been invalidated and narrowed down to just three.

[blank] **Non-ISBD**

A record whose descriptive elements are not formatted according to the guidelines of the International Standard Bibliographic Description (ISBD) conventions is assigned code "blank." Among those cataloging rules that do not conform to ISBD descriptive and punctuation requirements (mostly because they predate ISBD) are: *Catalog Rules, Author and Title Entries* (1908); *A.L.A. Catalog Rules, Author and Title Entries* (1941); *A.L.A. Cataloging Rules for Author and Title Entries* (1949); and *Anglo-American Cataloging Rules*, 1st edition (*AACR 1*) (excluding the revised chapters).

a *AACR 2*

The *Anglo-American Cataloguing Rules*, 2d edition, 1988 revision, and/or other *AACR 2*-based cataloging manuals serve as the basis for cataloging in records coded "a". Among those manuals are:

- *Graphic Materials: Rules for Describing Original Items and Historical Collections*, by Elisabeth W. Betz (1982)
- *Archival Moving Image Materials: A Cataloging Manual*, by Wendy White-Hensen (1984)
- *Archives, Personal Papers, and Manuscripts*, by Steven L. Hensen (1983; 2d ed., 1989)
- *Bibliographic Description of Rare Books*, by the LC Office for Descriptive Cataloging Policy (1981)

Generally, these *AACR 2*-based manuals refine certain descriptive details but leave access consistent with *AACR 2* and descriptive form consistent with ISBD. Their use in the cataloging of a record is identified by the USMARC-assigned code in subfield ǂe of the 040 field. Code "a" indicates that the choice and form of entry for all access points conform to *AACR 2R*.

i **ISBD**

Punctuation and description in code "i" records follow ISBD conventions, but do not otherwise conform to *AACR 2* cataloging rules, particularly in the choice and form of access points.

- Scores cataloged under the rules of *AACR 1*, Revised Chapter 6
- Retrospective records with ISBD punctuation but pre-*AACR 2* cataloging
- Records that conform to *AACR 2* but contain headings incompatible with *AACR 2*

Records that would previously have been coded "p" (partial ISBD form) or "r" (provisional ISBD form) are now coded "i".

Form of Composition

UFBD: 008/18-19 (O/O)
OCLC: Comp (O)
RLIN: FCP (NR)
WLN: COMP (NR)
MOIM: Box 02 (FRM COMP)

The Form of Composition fixed field is a two-character alphabetic code that identifies the musical form or genre of a printed score, manuscript score, or musical sound recording. Codes are selected based on the titles and subtitles of the works themselves, on uniform titles, on subject headings, and on contents and other notes in the bibliographic record. The chosen code should apply to an individual work as a whole (that is, code a concerto as "co" and disregard the facts that the first movement might be in sonata form and the finale a rondo; code a suite as "su" and not for its constituent movements).

When only one form applies to a bibliographic record, code that single form in the Form of Composition fixed field. If two codes are appropriate and one of them is either "uu" (unknown) or "zz" (other), input only the other code, not "uu" or "zz". When more than one form applies (excluding "uu" and "zz"), code the fixed field "mu" (for multiple forms) and record the specific codes in the 047 field. Nonmusical sound recordings always are assigned the code "nn" (for "not applicable").

The definitions of many of these codes are extremely general and should not be taken as definitive. Reliable music reference sources such as the *New Harvard Dictionary of Music* or the *New Grove* that can offer historical context, background, and detail should be consulted when such aid is needed.

an   **Anthems**
Compositions for solo voices and/or choir based on sacred texts selected from such sources as the Bible or the Book of Common Prayer, designated anthems, antiphons, or magnificats

bt   **Ballets**
Music written to accompany a ballet performance

bg   **Bluegrass music**
Improvisational country music genre usually played on unamplified stringed instruments and featuring close, often high-pitched harmonies

bl   **Blues**
Popular music genre usually characterized by 12-bar phrases, three-line stanzas, and flatted "blue" notes

cn   **Canons and rounds**
Compositions employing strict imitation throughout

ct   **Cantatas**
Sacred or secular multimovement works for one or more voices with accompaniment and usually based on a continuous narrative text

cz   **Canzonas**
Instrumental music written in imitation of lute or keyboard transcriptions of French chansons and usually featuring repeated sections and contrasting treatments

cr   **Carols**
Traditional songs for Christmas or similarly joyful devotional occasions

ca   **Chaconnes**
Usually triple-time set of variations on a repeated succession of chords without a clear ostinato

cs   **Chance compositions**

Often called aleatory or stochastic music or music of indeterminacy, works in which some elements are left to the performer's choice or to random selection

cp   **Chansons, polyphonic**

Fifteenth- and 16th-century French vocal compositions featuring usually four- or five-part writing, either through-composed or using repeat forms

cc   **Chant, Christian**

Monophonic, unaccompanied liturgical music of the Eastern and Western Christian religions, including plainsong, Ambrosian, Anglican, Armenian, Byzantine, Coptic, Gallican, Gregorian, Mozarabic, Old Roman, and Syrian chant

cb   **Chants, other religious**

Monophonic, unaccompanied liturgical music of the non-Christian religions, including Buddhist, Hindu, Jewish, and Sufi chant

cl   **Chorale preludes**

Works based on Protestant chorales, usually written for organ

ch   **Chorales**

German Protestant hymn tunes

cg   **Concerti grossi**

Orchestral works that set a small group of solo instruments against the full orchestra, usually dating from the baroque era

co   **Concertos**

Compositions for solo instrument(s) and orchestra that are so named; if the subject heading "Concertos" is not appropriate to the work, do not assign this code regardless of its title

cy   **Country music**

Form of popular music derived from the folk, ballad, or swing styles of the United States West, Southwest, and Southeast

df   **Dance forms**

Music for individual dance forms except for mazurkas, minuets, pavans, polonaises, and waltzes, which have their own codes

dv   **Divertimentos, serenades, cassations, divertissements, and notturni**

Usually light, suite-like entertainments for small instrumental ensembles, consisting of a number of brief movements; use this code for instrumental music with any of these designations

ft   **Fantasias**

Use this code for any instrumental works designated fantasias, phantasies, fantasies, fancies, etc.; usually free-form instrumental works of improvisatory character

fm   **Folk music**

National, ethnic, or indigenous music, sometimes anonymous and orally transmitted, and the modern popular music genre that derived from it; use this code for folk-songs, ballads, work-songs, narrative songs, etc.

fg **Fugues**
Works featuring successively-entering voices in which one or more themes are developed using imitative counterpoint

gm **Gospel music**
Popular religious musical form derived from the slave songs, hymns, spirituals, call-and-response chants, and folk music of African-Americans

hy **Hymns**
Religious songs of praise, thanksgiving, or devotion

jz **Jazz**
Popular, originally African-American musical genre deriving from ragtime and blues, often featuring improvisation and syncopation

md **Madrigals**
Secular three- to six-part unaccompanied vocal works of the 16th and 17th centuries in imitative style

mr **Marches**
Works usually in strong rhythm, regular phrasing, and duple or quadruple time, originally suitable to accompany marching, but often more stylized

ms **Masses**
Musical settings of the religious service of the Roman Catholic or other Christian churches

mz **Mazurkas**
Polish folk dances in moderate triple meter

mi **Minuets**
Country dances of French origin in moderate 3/4 time

mo **Motets**
Unaccompanied polyphonic choral work usually based on a sacred Latin text

mp **Moving picture music**
Music written or compiled for a motion picture soundtrack or to accompany a silent film

mc **Musical revues and comedies**
Revues comprise a series of loosely related sketches, songs, dances, and skits; musical comedies tend to better integrate song, dance, and plot; may include some operettas

mu **Multiple forms**
Use only when more than one form code would be appropriate in the Fixed Field; the multiple codes are recorded in field 047; this code is not valid for use in the 047 field

nc **Nocturnes**
Often Romantic-era free-form character pieces, usually for piano

nn **Not applicable**
Use for any item that is not printed or manuscript music or a musical sound recording; will usually be used for nonmusical sound recordings; not valid for use in the 047 field

op   Operas
    Musical dramas consisting of songs and choruses with orchestral accompaniment; orchestral overtures and interludes; and either spoken, accompanied, or sung dialog; may include some operettas

or   Oratorios
    Usually sacred works for soloists, chorus, and orchestra, often narrative, but without scenery or action

ov   Overtures
    Most often, single-movement orchestral works intended to introduce an opera, oratorio, or play, but also includes independent works designated as overtures

pt   Part-songs
    Usually unaccompanied songs in two or more vocal parts with one voice carrying the melody

ps   Passacaglias
    Continuous variation in triple meter based on a clear ostinato; use for all kinds of ostinato basses

pm   Passion music
    Musical settings of the last days and crucifixion of Jesus Christ

pv   Pavans
    Slow, duple or quadruple meter dance of Italian origin

po   Polonaises
    Stately Polish national dance in triple meter

pp   Popular music
    Broad term for mostly 20th-century musical works composed in a style that requires improvisation in performance; "music in the popular idiom" rather than works that are "well loved;" use for works not covered in other "popular" categories such as bluegrass music, blues, country music, jazz, rock music, etc.

pr   Preludes
    Usually solo instrumental works, originally written as introductory pieces but later as independent character pieces

pg   Program music
    Music intending to depict a sequence of images or incidents, often suggested by the title and/or described in explanatory notes; use this code for all program music *except* symphonic poems

rg   Ragtime music
    Early jazz form, originally piano-based, that emphasized regular phrases, traditional harmonies, syncopation, and polyrhythm

rq   Requiems
    Musical settings of the Mass for the Dead

ri   Ricercars
    Usually instrumental works in which a succession of motifs is developed imitatively; some ricercars of the 16th and 17th centuries are nonimitative technical studies

rc **Rock music**

Popular music genre often featuring a heavily accented beat and usually played on amplified instruments

rd **Rondos**

Musical form in which a recurring section alternates with episodes of contrasting thematic material; also includes all instrumental rondeaux

sn **Sonatas**

Musical works usually for a solo instrument or a solo instrument with keyboard accompaniment, typically in three or four contrasting movements

sg **Songs**

Brief compositions for solo voice, usually accompanied

st **Studies and exercises**

Pieces designed to help students practice and develop technical skills on an instrument; use only for studies, exercises, etudes, etc., expressly intended for teaching purposes, not for "concert etudes"

su **Suites**

Instrumental works comprising a series of contrasting, usually dance-inspired pieces often in the same or related keys

sp **Symphonic poems**

Programmatic orchestral works, usually in a single, free-form movement; also called "tone poems"

sy **Symphonies**

Usually multimovement sonata-form works most often composed for orchestra

tc **Toccatas**

Compositions, typically for keyboard instrument, written in free style, featuring full chords, rapid runs, and (usually) imitative passages

ts **Trio-sonatas**

Baroque chamber works written in three parts and usually played on four instruments (two upper melody instruments, a bass instrument, and a keyboard as bass and thoroughbass realization)

uu **Unknown**

Use when the form and genre of the composition are unstated or unknown or are merely implied or understood; use when the subject headings actually reflect medium of performance (for instance wind quintets, string quartets) rather than form or genre; not valid for use in the 047 field

vr **Variations**

Compositions in which a stated theme is followed by modified restatements of that theme

wz **Waltzes**

Dances in moderate 3/4 time with the emphasis on the first beat

zz **Other forms of composition**

Use for genres or forms of composition specified in the work but not found in this list; use this code when the genre or form term used in the work also appears as a subject heading and is not merely a medium of performance statement (for instance incidental music, electronic music, fanfares); not valid for use in the 047 field

Examples

```
100 10   Soler, Antonio, ǂd 1729-1783.
240 10   Concertos, ǂm organs (2)
245 00   Six concertos pour deux orgues ǂh [sound recording] ...
650  0   Organ music (Organs (2))
```
Form of Composition fixed field: uu
> *[Although titled "concertos," these works were written for two organs and so do not conform to the definition of the concerto code (solo instrument(s) and orchestra)]*

```
100 10   Taylor, Koko.
245 10   Koko Taylor, Queen of the Blues ǂh [sound recording] ...
650  0   Blues (Music) ǂz United States.
```
Form of Composition fixed field: bl

```
100 10   Simons, Netty.
240 10   Design groups, ǂn no. 1
245 10   Design groups I : ǂb (1967) : for percussion (1 to 3
         players) ....
500      "The choice of instruments is left to the performers."
650  0   Percussion music.
650  0   Chance compositions.
```
Form of Composition fixed field: cs

```
245 00   Grwa mig mtho˙n ba kun ´ses : ǂb a collection of notations
         for chanting (dbya˙ns yig) and the drum (r˙na gra˙ns) for
         the rites of the ´Bri-gu˙n-pa tradition ...
650  0   Music, Buddhist ǂz China ǂz Tibet.
650  0   Chants (Buddhist) ǂz China ǂz Tibet.
650  0   ´Bri-gu˙n-pa (Sect) ǂx Rituals.
```
Form of Composition fixed field: cb

```
100 10   Avison, Charles, ǂd ca. 1710-1770.
240 10   Concertos ǂn (1744). ǂk Selections
245 00   Concerti grossi nos 4, 5, 8, 11 ǂh [sound recording] ...
650  0   Concerti grossi.
```
Form of Composition fixed field: cg

```
100 10   Tashiro, Mary Jane.
240 10   Dances, ǂm piano
245 00   3 dances for piano solo ...
505 0    Pierrette -- Spanish silhouette -- Ice caprice.
650  0   Piano music.
650  0   Dance music.
```
Form of Composition fixed field: df

```
100 10   Morricone, Ennio.
245 10   Once upon a time in America ‡h [sound recording] : ‡b
         original motion picture soundtrack ...
650  0   Motion picture music.
```
Form of Composition fixed field: mp


```
100 10   Dohn´anyi, Ern˝o, ‡d 1877-1960.
240 10   Legfontosabb ujjgyakorlatok
245 10   Essential fingerexercises : ‡b for obtaining a sure piano
         technique ...
650  0   Piano ‡x Studies and exercises.
```
Form of Composition fixed field: st


```
100 10   Chopin, Fr´ed´eric, ‡d 1810-1849.
240 10   Etudes, ‡m piano
245 14   The complete ´etudes ‡h [sound recording] ...
650  0   Piano music.
```
Form of Composition fixed field: uu


```
100 10   Vercken, Fran¸cois.
245 10   Fanfare en m´emoire de Claude Lejeune ...
650  0   Brass octets (Trombones (4), trumpets (4)) ‡x Scores.
650  0   Fanfares.
```
Form of Composition fixed field: zz

Format of Music

UFBD: 008/20 (M/M)
OCLC: Format (O)
RLIN: SCO (NR)
WLN: SCORE (M)
MOIM: Box 03 (SCORE)

The format of a music manuscript or an item of printed music is represented by a single-character alphabetic code in the Format of Music fixed field element. The item in hand and terms appearing in the physical description field (300), in subfield ‡s of the Uniform Title field (130, 240), in the title and statement of responsibility (245), and in notes (5XX) should influence the choice of code.

However, be aware that such terms as "choral score," "chorus score," and "vocal score" sometimes are used indiscriminately by publishers and should not determine which code to assign. Factors such as the presence or absence, and the fullness or reduction, of accompaniment in the item itself should decide. If an item consists of a score and parts, consider only the score when coding this element. The quoted definitions that follow are from *AACR 2R*.

a   **Full score**
The item is in full score format, "a series of staves on which all the different instrumental and/ or vocal parts of a musical work are written, one under the other in vertical alignment, so that the parts may be read simultaneously" (*AACR 2R*, p. 622) (see Figure 1). Although in common parlance a "score" is *any* kind of printed music, for cataloging purposes, a "score" must represent two or more instruments and/or voices. Works for a single voice or instrument cannot be rendered in score format (and should be coded "z"). Use also for popular music formats with two staves for piano and a separate staff for the vocal part, with or without guitar chords.

b   **Full score, miniature or study size**
"A musical score not primarily intended for performance use, with the notation and/or text reduced in size" (*AACR 2R*, p. 619) (see Figure 2).

c   **Accompaniment reduced for keyboard**
Solo voice and/or instrumental parts remain unaltered but the orchestral or instrumental ensemble accompaniment has been reduced (that is, arranged) for keyboard instrument(s) (see Figure 3). Included here are concertos and other concerted works whose orchestral accompaniments have been arranged for piano(s); piano-vocal and organ-vocal scores of operas; cantatas; and other works in the larger vocal forms. For popular music, this code should be used only in those rare cases when there is explicit evidence that the original accompaniment was for orchestra or other large ensemble, now reduced for keyboard.

d   **Voice score**
Vocal and/or choral parts are unaltered but any accompaniment has been entirely omitted (see Figure 4). Vocal and choral works that originally were written without accompaniment should be assigned other codes, as appropriate.

e   **Condensed score or piano-conductor score**
Orchestral or band music that has been reduced to only a few staves is assigned code "e". A condensed score gives "only the principal musical parts on a minimum number of staves, and generally [is] organized by instrumental sections" (*AACR 2R*, p. 617) (see Figure 5). A piano-(violin-, etc.) conductor score is "a performance part for a particular instrument of an ensemble work to which cues have been added for the other instruments to permit the performer of the part also to conduct the performance" (*AACR 2R*, p. 621).

g   **Close score**
Commonly found in hymnals, the close score format presents all the separate parts transcribed on (usually) two staves (see Figure 6).

TEHILLIM

Part I

Steve Reich

Figure 1: Example of *full score* format (format of Music fixed field element: a)

Figure 2: Example of *miniature or study size score* format (Format of Music fixed field element: b)

Figure 3: Example of *accompaniment reduced for keyboard score* format
(Format of Music fixed field element: c)

Figure 4: Example of *voice score* format (Format of Music fixed field element: d)

23

Figure 5: Example of *condensed score* format (Format of Music fixed field: e)

THE HYMNARY
BOOK ONE
HYMNS FOR WORSHIP AND PRAISE

1 Holy, Holy, Holy

NICÆA. 11. 12. 12. 10.

REGINALD HEBER, 1827

JOHN B. DYKES, 1861

1. Ho-ly, Ho-ly, Ho-ly! Lord God Al-might-y! Ear-ly in the
2. Ho-ly, Ho-ly, Ho-ly! All the saints a-dore Thee, Cast-ing down their
3. Ho-ly, Ho-ly, Ho-ly! Tho' the dark-ness hide Thee, Tho' the eye of
4. Ho-ly, Ho-ly, Ho-ly! Lord God Al-might-y! All Thy works shall

morn - ing our song shall rise to Thee; Ho-ly, Ho-ly, Ho-ly!
gold-en crowns a-round the glass-y sea; Cher-u-bim and ser-a-phim
sin-ful man Thy glo-ry may not see, On-ly Thou art ho-ly;
praise Thy name, in earth, and sky, and sea; Ho-ly, Ho-ly, Ho-ly!

Mer-ci - ful and Might-y! God in Three Per-sons, bless-ed Trin-i-ty!
fall-ing down be-fore Thee, Which wert, and art, and ev-er-more shalt be.
there is none be-side Thee Per - fect in power, in love, and pu-ri-ty.
Mer-ci - ful and Might-y! God in Three Per-sons, bless-ed Trin-i-ty! A-men.

Figure 6: Example of *close score* format (Format of Music fixed field element: g)

m   **Multiple score formats**

Often the case with band music, several types of scores (full and condensed, for instance) are issued together; these multiple formats are coded "m". *Do not* consider a score and part(s) to be multiple formats; code only for the format of the score.

n   **Not applicable**

Use this code when the item is not printed or manuscript music. All sound recordings will receive this code.

u   **Unknown**

The format of the item cannot be determined.

z   **Other than score format**

When none of the other codes is appropriate, assign code "z". Solo keyboard music (see Figure 7), music for solo voice, music for any solo instrument, works in graphic notation (see Figure 8), and works that consist solely of performance instructions receive this code. A solo part ("the music for one of the participating voices or instruments in a musical work" (*AACR 2R,* p. 620)) or a set of parts should be assigned code "z". For popular music, use this code when the item consists of two staves for piano with words printed between the staves, either with or without guitar chords.

PIÈCES DE CLAVECIN
(1707)

Elizabeth Jacquet de La Guerre
(1659 - 1729)

La Flamande

O.L. 93

Figure 7: Example of solo keyboard music, *other than score format* (Format of Music fixed field element: z)

CASSIOPEIA

GEORGE CACIOPPO

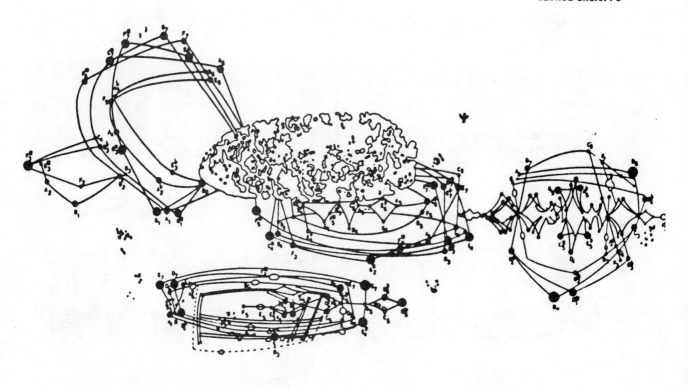

Figure 8: Example of a work in graphic notation, *other than score format*
(Format of Music fixed field element: z)

Language

UFBD: 008/35-37 (M/O)
OCLC: Lang (M)
RLIN: L (R)
WLN: LAN (System supplies from 041)
MOIM: Box 15 (LANGUAGE)

Languages are represented by three-character lowercase alphabetic codes as found in the *USMARC Code List for Languages*, based on the predominant language of the sung or spoken text associated with the recording or score. When only one language is associated with the item, that code is recorded in the Language fixed field. When multiple languages are involved, when the item is a translation, or when there is accompanying textual material, all applicable codes are transcribed in the Language code field (041) and the predominant language, if any, is coded in this fixed field element (it must also be the first code in subfield ǂa of the 041 field).

Never consider the language(s) of accompanying material (including program notes, prefaces, performance instructions, etc.), only the language(s) of the sung or spoken text, when trying to determine the predominant language of a musical work. If no predominant language can be determined, the codes are recorded in alphabetical order in the 041 field and the first is recorded in the Language fixed field. For translations, the language of the translation, not the language of the original, is coded as the Language fixed field element.

For musical compositions without sung or spoken text (purely instrumental works, electronic works) and for recordings that consist of nonverbal sounds (train sounds, birdcalls), RLIN and WLN users should code this fixed field "ƀƀƀ"; OCLC users should code this fixed field "N/A" (for not applicable).

When the number of languages involved exceeds six, code this fixed field "mul" (for multiple languages).

When the language of the item cannot be determined, or when the "language" content consists of arbitrary syllables, humming, or other human-produced sounds not associated with a language, use the code "und" (for undetermined).

The WLN system automatically transfers the first code in field 041 subfield ǂa or ǂd to the LAN fixed field during input into the Working File; the LAN fixed field does not appear on the WLN input screen but does appear on the edit screen.

For examples of the use of the Language fixed field element, see the section on Field 041.

Literary Text for Sound Recordings

UFBD: 008/30-31 (M/O)
OCLC: LTxt (O)
RLIN: Lit (NR)
WLN: LIT TEXT (NR)
MOIM: Box 07 (LIT TXT)

The textual content of a nonmusical sound recording is indicated by one or two single-character alphabetic codes. If only one code is recorded, it is left-justified and the second position is left blank. Two codes should be recorded in the priority order found in the code list. If more than two codes would be appropriate, only the two most important are recorded, in the code list order.

[blank]   **Item is a music sound recording**
All musical sound recordings are coded as two blanks (ƀƀ)

p   **Poetry**
Recorded poetry is coded "p"

d   **Drama**
Recorded plays and nonmusical dramas are coded "d"

f   **Fiction**
Recorded novels and short stories are coded "f"

k   **Comedy**
Spoken comedy routines are coded "k"

h   **History**
Any record of significant events is coded "h"; included are narrations, presentations, or re-creations that might overlap other codes (historical drama, historical poetry, etc.)

l   **Lectures, speeches**
Recordings of lectures or speeches (exclusive of conference proceedings) are coded "l"

o   **Folktales**
Usually anonymous stories in the oral tradition are coded "o"

c   **Conference proceedings**
Speeches, lectures, discussions, and sessions recorded during conferences or other meetings are coded "c"

i   **Instruction**
Instructional recordings, coded "i", include "how to" directions for accomplishing a task, learning an art, etc. (language instruction is coded "j")

j   **Language instruction**
Language instruction, coded "j", might overlap with other codes such as fiction, drama, or poetry; where appropriate, code for up to two in priority list order

s   **Sounds**
Coded "s", sounds include sound effects, natural sounds, birdcalls, nonmusical utterances, and vocalizations that might or might not convey meaning

a   **Autobiography**
First-person nonfictional readings about a person are coded "a"

b   **Biography**

         Third-person nonfictional readings about a person are coded "b"

e   **Essays**

         Readings of analytic or interpretive compositions that often deal with a subject from a personal point of view are coded "e"

g   **Reporting**

         Accounts of newsworthy events observed or documented and informative messages are coded "g"

m   **Memoirs**

         Personal, usually autobiographical, narratives are coded "m"

r   **Rehearsals**

         Any practice session for a nonmusical performance is coded "r"

t   **Interviews**

         Exchanges between questioner and subject are coded "t"

n   **Not applicable**

         Use when the item is not a sound recording; all printed and manuscript music is coded "n"

z   **Other types of literary text**

         When none of the other codes is deemed appropriate, code the item "z"

Examples

Literary Text fixed field: ƀƀ

```
245 10   Anne Sofie Otter sings H¨andel, Monteverdi, Telemann ‡h
         [sound recording].
             [A musical sound recording]
```

Literary Text fixed field: n

```
100 10   Chance, Nancy Laird.
245 10   Odysseus : ‡b a song cycle for solo voice, percussion, and
         orchestra / ‡c by Nancy Laird Chance.
500      Greek text with English translation: p. 3.
             [A printed score]
```

Literary Text fixed field: a

```
520      An autobiographical narrative, in which the author describes
         his experiences in Nazi concentration camps.
```

Literary Text fixed field: dh

```
520      Dramatizes events in the life of George Washington ...
```

Literary Text fixed field: e

```
520      Presents E.B. White reading On writing, and other essays from
         his collection One man's meat.
```

Literary Text fixed field: fb

    520   Following a brief introduction to her life and work, author
              Alice Walker reads her short story Nineteen fifty-five, which
              is a fictional account of the exploitation of Black music by
              white musicians.

Literary Text Fixed Field: gt

    520   In this 1982 radio broadcast, host Deborah Amos explores the
              controversy surrounding school prayer, focusing on the First
              Amendment's principle of church-state separation. Includes
              interviews, speeches, and journalistic analysis.

Literary Text fixed field: i

    520   Presents exercise instruction and music designed to assist a
              person wishing to improve the fitness of the entire body.

Literary Text fixed field: j

    520   Presents instruction in the reading of ancient Greek,
              including vowels, consonants, pitch accent, and poetic
              rhythm.

Literary Text fixed field: k

    245 10   Dick Clark presents Radio's uncensored bloopers ‡h
              [sound recording].

Literary Text fixed field: lc

    245 00   New bankruptcy law amendments of 1984 ‡h [sound recording] :
              ‡b ALI-ABA course of study.
    520   Speakers discuss jurisdiction and procedure, consumer
              amendments, and other substantive amendments. Includes a
              question-and-answer session.

Literary Text fixed field: o

    520   Three Gullah dialect stories offered by Samuel Gaillard
              Stoney ...

Literary Text fixed field: p

    520   Marianne Moore reads selections of her poems.

Literary Text fixed field: s

    520   Presents the sound of steam trains in adverse weather
              conditions and with mechanical difficulties as they attempt
              to pull freight and passenger trains.

Literary Text fixed field: t

    245 13   An interview with Elijah Muhammed ‡h [sound recording].

Literary Text fixed field: z

    245 14   The New Testament ‡h [sound recording] : ‡b King James
              Version.
    511 0   Read by Alexander Scourby.

Type of Record

This one-character code differentiates among the various types of materials cataloged using the USMARC formats.

Scores

For scores, two codes are used:

c **Printed music**
Printed music or microform of printed music; includes published facsimiles of manuscripts

d **Manuscript music**
Manuscript music, including microforms of manuscript music

Confusion sometimes arises because microforms do not constitute a separate type. Simply remember that any published score, whether eye-readable or microform, is "c"; this includes published facsimiles of manuscripts. Actual manuscripts and microform reproductions of these actual manuscripts (not facsimiles or other published versions) receive code "d". Treating actual manuscripts (not reproductions) under the Archival and Manuscripts Control format is an option when use of its special control fields is desirable, but that issue is outside the scope of this work.

Another area of confusion is works that straddle the border between book and score. Instructional materials (works in LC classes MT170-MT950, according to *Cataloging Service Bulletin* no. 21 (summer 1983), p. 59) that are predominantly music rather than "on musical topics" are to be considered scores. Sometimes the subject subdivisions that have been assigned to a work can be a hint as to its "score-ness." These guidelines might be useful:

Instruction and study	usually "a"
Methods	might be either "a" or "c"
Studies and exercises	always "c"
Orchestra studies	always "c"
Teaching pieces	always "c"

Hymnals, operas and their librettos, and song collections also can be puzzling:

Hymnals
- Hymnals with music, whether simple melody or full harmonization, are considered scores.
- Hymnals with text only and no music at all, as well as hymn text collections unrelated to a particular hymnal, are books.

Operas
- Publications of operas with words and music, whether full score, chorus score, vocal score, or aria collection, are scores.
- Opera librettos with no music are books.

Song collections
- Collections of art songs (Lieder, melodies, etc.) with words and music are scores.
- Collections of art song texts (sometimes with translations) without music are books.
- Collections of songs (national, patriotic, folk, political, etc., that is, those classified in M1627-M1998), either with or without music, are entered as scores.

Sound Recordings
    In most cases, the distinction between musical and nonmusical sound recordings is fairly obvious.

i	**Nonmusical sound recording**
j	**Musical sound recording**

However, in certain instances judgments must be made. Consider to be nonmusical sound recordings:

- Sound effects
- Birdcalls
- Physical exercise recordings (aerobics, workouts, etc.) that consist of spoken, shouted, sung, or chanted instructions over a musical accompaniment
- Stories read over incidental musical accompaniment
- Plays with incidental music

    Music instruction recordings ("how to play the ...") can straddle the border between musical and nonmusical in the same way that printed instructional materials can. Generally, if instruction predominates over musical content, consider the item nonmusical; if musical examples are the chief focus, consider the item to be musical.
    Filmstrips or slides with accompanying sound are usually cataloged in the USMARC Visual Materials format as projected graphics (Type code "g"), not as sound recordings or as kits. However, it is preferred that "read-along" materials be cataloged as nonmusical sound recordings with accompanying text.

CONTROL FIELDS

007　Physical Description Fixed Field

UFBD: 007 (A/A) (Rep)
OCLC: Scores (Microform): 007 (R/O) (Rep)
　　　Sound recordings: 007 (M/O) (Rep)
RLIN: Scores (Microform): 007MIC (NR)
　　　(Rep)
　　　Sound recordings: 007REC (NR)
　　　(Rep)
WLN: DFF (A) (Rep)
MOIM: 007 (Rep)

Encoded physical description information is contained in the 007 field. All the information is derived from the item itself, so no special research is to be done to determine correct codes. The field has a "tree" structure wherein the value of the first element determines the length of the field and the definitions of the subsequent elements. In the realm of music, the 007 field is used only for sound recordings and for music in microform.

Different systems display the field differently. WLN displays the field as a string of characters in a single subfield ‡a (as such, if the field is used, every position must be filled, so no WLN input standards are included in the charts that precede each position). In RLIN, the field takes the form of a line of mnemonic subfields. OCLC uses an alphabetic subfield for each data element.

Taken together, the 007 field has probably undergone more change over the years than any other single field in the USMARC format. In 1980 the field was restructured with the addition of two bytes at the beginning, allowing the first byte (General Material Designation) to determine the application of the remaining bytes. The evolution of recording technology necessitated the addition of new codes, particularly to accommodate compact digital discs. In 1987, 007/04 for Sound Recordings was redefined to apply only to playback channels, splitting the original capture and storage technique coding off to the new 007/13.

Indicators

Both indicators are blank.

Scores

For scores, the 007 field is used only for microforms. It is not used for sound recordings that accompany printed or manuscript scores. This field has not been defined for the physical description of printed scores or musical manuscripts. Microform scores are described here in much the same way as are other microforms, whether they are originals or microforms of previously published materials.

007/00　Category of material
　　　OCLC: ‡a (General material designation (GMD)) (M)
　　　RLIN: [General material designation does not display]
　　　WLN: 1st position (Category of material)

The broad category of material, microform (code "h"), is encoded in the first position. Any microimage of a score that appears on aperture cards, microopaques, microfilm, microfiche, or other microformat that is too tiny to be read with the unaided eye is considered a microform score. Microforms can be original publications or reproductions of previously existing materials.

007/01　Specific material designation (SMD)
　　　OCLC: ‡b (Specific material designation (SMD)) (M)
　　　RLIN: MMD (Microform material designator) (NR)
　　　WLN: 2nd position (Specific material designation (SMD))

The specific type of microform is designated here.

a　Aperture card
　　　A card, usually a punched so-called IBM card, with one or more rectangular openings for a piece of photographic film containing microimages.

b Microfilm cartridge

A strip of microfilm wound onto a single hub and encased in a protective container; one end of the film protrudes from the cartridge.

c Microfilm cassette

A strip of microfilm wound between two hubs and sealed in a protective container; analogous to a sound tape cassette.

d Microfilm reel

A strip of microfilm wound on an open, unenclosed reel.

e Microfiche

A transparent sheet of film with microimages arranged in a grid; it usually has eye-readable identifying information as a heading.

f Microfiche cassette

Not currently used in the United States.

g Microopaque

An opaque sheet of material with microimages arranged in a grid, much like microfiche; it usually has identifying information as a heading large enough to be read by the naked eye.

z Other microform type

Other types of microforms, for which none of the previous codes is appropriate, are found in proprietary automatic retrieval equipment. These include:

- microchip: very small sheet of photographic film
- microform scroll: very wide roll of photographic film
- microdot: tiny piece of photographic film with ultrahigh reduction ratio

007/02 Original versus reproduction aspect
OCLC: ǂc (Original versus reproduction aspect) (Do not use)
RLIN: OR (Original versus reproduction aspect) (NR)
WLN: 3rd position (Original versus reproduction aspect)

This byte was intended to specify whether the item was an original or a reproduction and is the only 007 element whose definition is uniform for all kinds of material. However, its usefulness has been the subject of continuing debate. Until the Library of Congress online system is able to accept a fill character here, it will code this position "u".

OCLC recommends that the subfield not be used. RLIN suggests inputting a fill character (?) in this position. WLN recommends the input of a fill character (|).

f Facsimile

The item resembles the original in all regards but is not an original.

o Original

The item is the original and is not a reproduction of any sort.

r Reproduction

The item is some sort of reproduction; it might or might not be in a form different from the original.

u**Unknown**

It cannot be determined whether the item is the original or a reproduction.

007/03**Positive/negative aspect**
OCLC: ǂd (Polarity) (M)
RLIN:**POL (Polarity (Microform)) (NR)**
WLN:**4th Position (Polarity (Microforms))**

Specifies the polarity of the microform.

a**Positive**

Dark images against a light background. Microopaques always are considered positive.

b**Negative**

Light images against a dark background.

m**Mixed polarity**

A microform with both positive and negative images.

u**Unknown**

A microform of unknown polarity. Some colored negatives appear positive when the original colors are unknown.

007/04**Dimensions**
OCLC: ǂe (Dimensions (Microform)) (M)
RLIN:**DM (Dimensions (Microforms)) (NR)**
WLN:**5th position (Dimensions (Microforms))**

Records the size of the microform item, not the dimensions of the images thereon. Only the most common measurements are included in the list of codes.

Microfilm (width)
a**8 mm.**
d**16 mm.**
f**35 mm.**
g**70 mm.**
h**105 mm.**

Microfiche and Microopaque (height × width)
l**3 × 5 in. or 8 × 13 cm.**
m**4 × 6 in. or 11 × 15 cm. (standard microfiche)**
o**6 × 9 in. or 16 × 23 cm.**

Aperture cards (height × width)
p**3 1/4 × 7 3/8 in. or 9 × 19 cm.**

Microforms in general
u**Unknown dimensions**
z**Other dimensions**

007/05	Reduction ratio range
007/06-08	Reduction ratio

 OCLC: ‡f (Reduction ratio) (O)
 RLIN: RR (Reduction ratio) (NR)
 WLN: 6th position (Reduction ratio code)
 7th-9th positions (Reduction ratio)

Reduction ratio, usually indicated on the microform itself, is the ratio between the dimensions of the original and the dimensions of the corresponding microimage. The initial position contains a one-character code representing the ratio range. The remaining three positions contain the specific ratio, optional except when the code is "e" for ultra high reduction. In OCLC and RLIN, hyphens are used for unknown digits in the reduction ratio; three hyphens indicate that the specific ratio is not recorded. In WLN, substitute fill characters for the hyphens. The value of the ratio is right-justified with leading zeros.

a **Low reduction ratio**
 Less than 16× or 16:1.

b **Normal reduction**
 16×-30× or 16:1-30:1; use for most common microfiche.

c **High reduction**
 31×-60× or 31:1-60:1.

d **Very high reduction**
 61×-90× or 61:1-90:1.

e **Ultra high reduction**
 Over 90× or 90:1; use of this code requires the recording of the specific ratio in the remaining three positions, for example: e150.

u **Unknown**

v **Reduction rate varies**
 Use when not all parts of the microform have the same reduction ratio.

007/09 Color
 OCLC: ‡g (Color) (O)
 RLIN: COL (Color (Microforms)) (NR)
 WLN: 10th position (Color (Microforms))

The color of the microform image is coded here. USMARC and RLIN stipulate that this field is mainly for archival use.

b **Black-and-white (or monochrome)**
 Use when microimages are in a single color, for example black-and-white (that is, black and transparent), blue-and-white (blue and transparent), etc. Microopaques are always monochromatic.

c **Multicolored**
 Use when microimages are in more than one color.

m **Mixed**
 Use when the microimages are combinations of monochrome and color.

u   **Unknown**

z   **Other**

007/10   **Emulsion on film**
      OCLC: ‡h (Emulsion on film (Microform)) (O)
      RLIN: EML (Emulsion on film (Microforms)) (NR)
      WLN: 11th position (Emulsion on film (Microforms))

Emulsion is the light-sensitive material coating the microform film surface. The type of emulsion determines proper storage, handling, and use of the microform.

     a   **Silver halide**
           A compound of silver and halogens. Silver halide microform, the most common commercial type, always appears black-and-white (black and transparent).

     b   **Diazo**
           Sensitized layers composed of diazonium salts that react with couplers to form dye images. The makeup of the diazonium compound and the couplers determines the color of the images, often black or violet.

     c   **Vesicular**
           The light-sensitive component is suspended in a layer of plastic. When exposed, optical bubbles or vesicules form, creating the latent image. Heating the plastic layer and allowing it to cool fixes the latent image and makes it visible, although until it is viewed through a microform reader, it does not appear to have much contrast. The most common colors of vesicular microforms are blue and beige.

     m   **Mixed emulsion**
           Results when, for example, microfilms with different emulsions are spliced together. Not to be confused with mixed emotions.

     n   **Not applicable**
           The microform has no emulsion. Because microopaques are not on film, they should be coded "n".

     u   **Unknown**

     z   **Other**

007/11   **Generation**
      OCLC: ‡i (Generation) (R)
      RLIN: GEN (Generation (Microforms)) (NR)
      WLN: 12th position (Generation (Microforms))

Generation indicates the microform's relation to its original images and might be a hint as to the quality of the reproduction.

     a   **First generation (master)**
           Camera master or COM recorder master. Used for all master films made on archival stock according to archival production standards, and stored under relevant standards formulated by the American National Standards Institute (ANSI) and the Association for Information and Image Management (AIIM). The RLG Preservation Committee adds that this code is used for preservation master microforms, first-generation camera negatives that are used only to create printing masters.

b   Printing master

A microform of any generation used chiefly for the creation of other microforms. This code is used for all masters not made and stored under archival standards. The RLG Preservation Committee prefers that storage standards be followed for printing masters, but it recognizes that taking adequate steps for maintenance of quality is sufficient.

c   Service copy

A microform made from another microform that is intended for use rather than for production of other microforms. In this category are included all microopaques. Most microforms in common use in libraries are service copies.

m   Mixed generation

A microform copy made up of a combination of film generations.

u   Unknown

007/12 Base of film
OCLC: ǂj (Base of film (Microform)) (O)
RLIN: BSE (Base of film (Microforms)) (NR)
WLN: 13th position (Base of film (Microforms))

The type of material used as the base for the film. USMARC, RLIN, and WLN stipulate the use of this field mainly for archival purposes.

a   Safety base

Relatively nonflammable film base that meets the ANSI standard for safety base. Often the microfilm itself will have the inscription "safety base" (or its foreign equivalent) or a small equilateral triangle at the film edge. Vesicular and diazo films are always safety base, as are silver halide films made in the United States since about 1951.

b   Not a safety base

Film base, such as nitrate, that does not meet ANSI standards for safety base film.

n   Not applicable

Item does not have a film base. Since microopaques are not on film, they should be coded "n".

u   Unknown

Examples

The following examples are all coded for the same item: a commercially available microfilm reel, positive polarity, 35 mm., normal reduction (25×), black and white, silver halide emulsion, on safety film.

OCLC coding example:
```
007      h ǂb d ǂd a ǂe f ǂf b025 ǂg b ǂh a ǂi c ǂj a
```

RLIN coding example:
```
MMD:d  OR:?  POL:a  DM:f  RR:b025  COL:b  EML:a  GEN:c  BSE:a
```

WLN coding example:
```
DFFǂa ǂhd|afb025baca
```

Sound recordings

For sound recordings, this field describes in encoded form certain physical characteristics of the recording. If the recording indicates that it is available in other physical formats, additional 007 fields may be constructed to describe them. Duration appears in coded form only in the 306 field, not in the 007. Use the sound recording Physical Description fixed field also for sound track film not intended to accompany visual images.

007/00 Category of material
> **OCLC:** ǂa (General material designation (GMD)) (M)
> **RLIN:** [General material designation does not display]
> **WLN:** 1st position (General material designation)

The broad category of material, sound recording (code "s"), is encoded in the first position. Any disc, tape, film, wire, or cylinder that contains sound vibrations for the reproduction of that sound, and paper rolls that have been perforated to represent the notes of a musical composition that can be mechanically reproduced, are considered to be sound recordings.

007/01 Specific material designation (SMD)
> **OCLC:** ǂb (Specific material designation (SMD)) (M)
> **RLIN:** RMD (Recordings material designator) (NR)
> **WLN:** 2nd position (Specific material designation (SMD))

The specific physical format of the sound recording is designated here. These correspond roughly to the SMDs outlined in *AACR 2R* rule 6.5B1.

d Sound disc
> A thin circular object on which sound waves, recorded as pulses or modulations, are incised or indented. Early discs were made of wax, aluminum, acetate, or shellac. Mass-produced analog discs nowadays are usually vinyl, whereas compact digital audio discs (CDs) are a combination of aluminum and polycarbonates.

e Cylinder
> A cylindrical object on which a continuous circular groove, representing sound waves, has been incised or indented. Early cylinders were tinfoil or wax; later mass-produced cylinders were plastic.

g Sound cartridge
> A container holding a single sound tape that runs as a single, continuous loop.

i Sound-track film
> A sound recording consisting of a narrow band usually along the edge of motion-picture film. Use this code for such a recording not intended to accompany visual images or when its accompanying role cannot be determined.

q Roll
> A roll (usually of paper) on which the notes of a musical composition are represented by perforations and from which the sound can be mechanically reproduced on a player piano or player organ, for example.

s Sound cassette
> A container housing a narrow (usually 1/8 in.) sound tape wound between two reels.

t Sound-tape reel
> An unenclosed reel of audio tape. Sometimes these are referred to as "reel-to-reel" or "open reel" tapes. Supply (feed) and take-up reels are independent of each other.

    w   **Wire recording**

        A round steel wire on which sound waves have been magnetically recorded.

    z   **Other sound medium type**

        Some material other than those listed on which sound has been recorded for reproduction.

007/02 Original versus reproduction aspect

OCLC: ǂc (Original versus reproduction aspect) (Do not use)
RLIN: OR (Original versus reproduction aspect) (NR)
WLN: 3rd position (Original versus reproduction aspect)

This byte was intended to specify whether the item was an original or a reproduction and is the only 007 element whose definition is uniform for all kinds of material. However, its usefulness has been the subject of continuing debate. Until the Library of Congress online system is able to accept a fill character here, it will code this position "u".

OCLC recommends that the subfield not be used. RLIN suggests inputting a fill character (?) in this position. WLN recommends the input of a fill character (|).

    f   **Facsimile**

        The item resembles the original in all regards but is not an original.

    o   **Original**

        The item is the original and is not a reproduction of any sort.

    r   **Reproduction**

        The item is some sort of reproduction; it might or might not be in a form different from the original.

    u   **Unknown**

        It cannot be determined whether the item is the original or a reproduction.

007/03 Speed

OCLC: ǂd (Speed) (M)
RLIN: SPD (Speed) (NR)
WLN: 4th position (Speed)

The playback speed of a sound recording is coded in this field.

Analog discs (in revolutions per minute)

    a   **16 rpm**

        Some recordings for the visually impaired, so-called "talking books," play at this speed.

    b   **33 1/3 rpm**

        Standard speed for what were once called "long-playing" (LP) discs.

    c   **45 rpm**

        Most "singles" (the 7 in. discs with the large holes) and many "extended play" (EP) discs are this speed.

    d   **78 rpm**

        The speed for most of the pre-LP, "shellac" discs.

e   8 rpm

>   Some recordings for the visually impaired, so-called "talking books," play at this speed.

Compact digital discs (in meters per second)

f   1.4 m. per sec.

>   The surface of a compact digital audio disc (CD) is scanned at a standard constant speed of approximately 1.4 meters per second although the actual rotating speed of the disc varies from about 500 rpm as the center is scanned to about 200 rpm toward the outer edge.

Cylinders (in revolutions per minute)

h   120 rpm

i   160 rpm

>   Blue Amberol cylinders, introduced in 1912 by Edison, play at this speed.

Tapes (in inches per second)

k   15/16 ips

>   Minicassettes often found in small half-speed portable cassette recorders usually run at this speed.

l   1 7/8 ips

>   Most standard cassettes use this speed.

m   3 3/4 ips

>   Standard tape cartridges and some regular, consumer and nonprofessional reel-to-reel tapes are recorded at this speed. Some unusual cassettes also have this speed.

o   7 1/2 ips

>   Some reel-to-reel tapes, both studio and nonprofessional, are recorded at this speed.

p   15 ips

>   Most studio and professional reel-to-reel tapes are recorded at this speed.

r   30 ips

>   Studio and professional reel-to-reel tapes occasionally, but rarely, use this speed.

All types of sound recordings

u   Unknown

>   Use for recording speeds that cannot be determined.

z   Other speed

>   Use for recording speeds other than those listed above.

007/04 Configuration of playback channels
OCLC: ǂe (Kind of sound) (M)
RLIN: SND (Kind of sound) (NR)
WLN: 5th position (Configuration of playback channels)

The configuration of channels for the playback of a sound recording (monaural, stereophonic, quadraphonic, etc.) is coded here. This information usually appears in the 300 subfield ǂb. When a recording does not clearly indicate its intended playback configuration (resulting in cataloging that does not have mono, stereo, or quad in the 300 subfield ǂb), this position may be coded as "unknown." However, in its records the Library of Congress often infers a channel configuration from the date of a recording, from aural examination, or from other evidence. Those coding this element may choose either road. No reference is made in this byte to the number of channels originally recorded or to the means (acoustical, electrical, or digital) by which the sounds were captured (which is treated in 007/13).

m   Monaural

All of the sound information is played back on a single channel. The recording must be marked mono, monophonic, monaural, single-track, one-track, or some equivalent.

q   Quadraphonic

The sound information is played back on four separate channels. The recording must be marked quad, quadraphonic, quadnaural, quadrasonic, four-channel, or some equivalent.

s   Stereophonic

The sound information is played back on two separate channels. The recording must be marked stereo, stereophonic, binaural, two-channel, or some equivalent. Use this code also for recordings that have been rechanneled, reprocessed, or enhanced to simulate stereo effect. These recordings usually include some designation such as "simulated stereo," "electronically enhanced for stereo," or "electronically reprocessed stereo."

u   Unknown

The configuration of playback channels is not mentioned on the recording and is therefore unknown. When a recording has no such indication, as is increasingly the case, one may code as "unknown" or follow apparent LC practice by inferring channel configuration from related evidence or aural examination.

z   Other configuration of playback channels

The configuration of playback channels is other than mono, stereo, or quad.

007/05   Groove width/groove pitch
      OCLC: ‡f (Groove width/groove pitch) (O)
      RLIN: GRV (Groove width/groove pitch) (NR)
      WLN: 6th position (Groove width/groove pitch)

The path cut by a stylus on an analog disc or on a cylinder is known as the groove. On analog discs, groove width is the size of the groove from wall to wall. On cylinders, groove pitch is the distance between the centers of the grooves in lines per inch. Information in this byte is found in textual form in the 300 subfield ‡b only when it is nonstandard for the type of recording. For cylinders, the number of grooves per inch sometimes appears in a general note.

m   Microgroove/fine

Most analog discs that have playback speeds of 16, 33 1/3, or 45 rpm are microgroove unless they state otherwise. Microgroove indicates about 225 to 300 grooves per inch. Cylinders with the speed 160 rpm are usually fine, around 200 grooves per inch.

s   Coarse/standard

Most 78 rpm analog discs, unless otherwise noted, are coarse grooved, containing 100-120 grooves per inch. Most 120 rpm cylinders are standard, about 100 grooves per inch.

n   Not applicable

Use this value when the item does not contain grooves. All compact digital discs (on which sound is encoded in pits and spaces) and all tapes (which store sound magnetically) are grooveless and are coded "n."

u   Unknown

z   Other groove width/groove pitch

007/06 Dimensions
      OCLC: ‡g (Dimensions (sound recordings)) (M)
      RLIN: DIM (Dimensions (sound recordings)) (NR)
      WLN: 7th position (Dimensions (sound recordings))

The diameter of discs and tape reels, and the length and width of cassettes, cartridges, and cylinders are coded here. This information should appear in the 300 subfield ‡c for all discs and tape reels, but is included for cassettes and cartridges only when the dimensions are nonstandard.

Analog discs and open reels (diameter in inches)
      a   **3 in.**
      b   **5 in.**
      c   **7 in.**
      d   **10 in.**
      e   **12 in.**
      f   **16 in.**

Compact digital discs (diameter in inches and centimeters)
      g   **4 3/4 in. (12 cm.)**

Standard tape cassettes (length × width in inches)
      j   **3 7/8 × 2 1/2 in.**

Standard tape cartridges (length × width in inches)
      o   **5 1/4 × 3 7/8 in.**

Standard cylinders (diameter × length in inches)
      s   **2 3/4 × 4 in.**

All types of sound recordings
      n   **Not applicable**
             Item is not a disc, reel, cassette, cartridge, or cylinder. Use for such things as piano or organ rolls and spools of wire.

      u   **Unknown**

      z   **Other**
             Use for discs, reels, cassettes, cartridges, and cylinders that have dimensions other than those listed above.

007/07 Tape width
      OCLC: ‡h (Tape width) (M)
      RLIN: WID (Tape width) (NR)
      WLN: 8th position (Tape width)

The width of the recording tape (in inches) in a cassette or cartridge or on a reel is encoded in this field. In *AACR 2R* records, the 300 subfield ‡c contains this information if the width is not the standard for the variety of tape. If no width is specified, assume the standard width for that kind of tape.

l   **1/8 in.**

> Most standard cassette tapes are this width.

m   **1/4 in.**

> Most nonprofessional and standard consumer reel tapes, some professional reel tapes, and most 8-track cartridge tapes are this width.

n   **Not applicable**

> Use when the item is not a tape and does not include a tape. This code is used for all discs, cylinders, wires, sound-track films, and rolls.

o   **1/2 in.**

> Some professional studio reel tapes and some 8-track cartridge tapes are this width.

p   **1 in.**

> Some professional studio reel tapes and some 8-track cartridge tapes are this width.

u   **Unknown**

z   **Other tape width**

> Use for tape widths other than those listed above.

007/08   Tape configuration
        OCLC: ǂi (Tape configuration) (M)
        RLIN: TC (Tape configuration) (NR)
        WLN: 9th position (Tape configuration)

Tape configuration indicates the number of recording tracks, the magnetic divisions of the width of tape read by the playback and recording heads, on a tape. Subfield ǂb of the 300 field in *AACR 2R* records contains the number of tracks when it is not standard for the type of tape. When cassettes and cartridges do not state a configuration, assume the standard; reels have no standard, so they should have a configuration specified or be coded for "unknown."

a   **Full (1) track**

> The full tape width is used for a single recording channel (monophonic).

b   **Half (2) track**

> Division of tape width into two recording channels.

c   **Quarter (4) track**

> Division of tape width into four recording channels. Most standard cassette tapes are 4-track unless otherwise noted.

d   **Eight track**

> Division of tape width into eight recording channels. Most cartridge tapes are 8-track unless otherwise noted.

e   **Twelve track**

> Mostly professional tape use.

f   **Sixteen track**

> Mostly professional tape use.

n   Not applicable

Use when the item is not a tape and does not include a tape. This code is used for all discs, cylinders, wires, sound-track films, and rolls.

u   Unknown

z   Other tape configuration

Use for numbers of tracks other than those listed.

007/09 Kind of disc, cylinder, or tape
OCLC: ǂj (Kind of disc, cylinder, or tape (archival use only)) (O)
RLIN: KD (Kind of disc, cylinder, or tape) (NR)
WLN: 10th position (Kind of disc, cylinder, or tape)

Indicates the kind of disc, cylinder, or tape, in relation to its place in the manufacturing process or outside of it. Most discs, cylinders, and tapes will be of the mass-produced variety. Other kinds of archival recordings (instantaneous, test pressings, masters, "fathers," "mothers," and so on) can be identified from accompanying documentation, labels, or secondary sources such as manufacturers' catalogs.

a   Master tape

Tape containing the final mix of sound (including all editing and processing) that is used to create a disc master for production of discs or a tape duplication master for the production of tapes.

b   Tape duplication master

Tape produced from a master tape and used to reproduce multiple copies of reel-to-reel, cartridge, or cassette tapes.

d   Disc master (negative)

Also known as a matrix, master matrix, or "father," this is a molded negative disc (with raised surfaces instead of the analog grooves or digital pits), used to create the positive "mother."

i   Instantaneous (recorded on the spot)

Nonprocessed, original recording of a performance or other sound event, usually existing as a unique copy, although the same event might have been recorded simultaneously on different tapes, discs, or cylinders, all of which would be instantaneous.

m   Mass-produced

Commercially or privately produced discs, tapes, or cylinders for distribution to the public. This includes limited pressings and limited issues. Mass-produced recordings usually have a label and/or container that includes the name of the issuing company, the issue number, and other bibliographic information.

n   Not applicable

Item is not a disc, cylinder, or tape. Use for sound-track film, piano and organ rolls, and wire recordings.

r   Mother (positive)

Positive disc formed from the negative "father" and used to make the negative stampers which press the discs for distribution.

s   Stamper (negative)

Negative metal mold, formed from the "mother" by electroplating, that is used to press discs for distribution.

t   **Test pressing**

A single finished disc or one of a limited number of finished discs pressed as trials to be examined aurally before mass production proceeds.

u   **Unknown**

Use when the type of disc, cylinder, or tape is not known or when it cannot be determined whether the item is mass-produced or instantaneous.

z   **Other**

007/10   Kind of material

OCLC: ǂk (Kind of material (archival use only)) (O)
RLIN: KM (Kind of material) (NR)
WLN: 11th position (Kind of material)

The type of material out of which both mass-produced and instantaneous discs and cylinders are fashioned is noted in this field.

a   **Lacquered**

Some early commercial discs and cylinders are made of acetate, as are some instantaneous discs and cylinders.

l   **Metal**

Some instantaneous discs are aluminum; the earliest cylinders are made of tinfoil.

m   **Metal and plastic**

Compact digital audio discs (CDs) consist of a thin layer of aluminum coated with plastic.

n   **Not applicable**

Item is other than a disc or cylinder. Use this code for all tapes, wires, rolls, and sound-track film.

p   **Plastic**

Most mass-produced 16, 33 1/3, and 45 rpm discs are plastic; most mass-produced cylinders also are plastic.

s   **Shellac**

Most mass-produced 78 rpm discs are shellac.

w   **Wax**

Some instantaneous discs and most instantaneous cylinders are wax.

u   **Unknown**

007/11   Kind of cutting

OCLC: ǂl (Kind of cutting (archival use only)) (O)
RLIN: KC (Kind of cutting) (NR)
WLN: 12th position (Kind of cutting)

Specifies the kind of incision made in a disc or cylinder to be read by the stylus or needle.

h   **Hill-and-dale cutting**

Also known as vertical cutting, this is found on all cylinders and some early discs. It requires the stylus to move up and down during recording and playback.

l   **Lateral or combined cutting**

Monophonic analog discs usually have lateral cutting, in which the stylus moves side-to-side. All quadraphonic and most stereophonic analog discs have both lateral and vertical, or combined, cutting.

n   **Not applicable**

Because they are pitted and not cut, compact digital audio discs (CDs) are coded "n". All tapes, wires, rolls, and sound-track film also lack cutting.

u   **Unknown**

007/12 **Special playback characteristics**
      OCLC: ǂm (Special reproduction characteristics) (O)
      RLIN: RC (Special reproduction characteristics) (NR)
      WLN: 13th position (Special playback characteristics)

This field is used only when special equipment, settings, or equalization are needed for proper playback of certain discs or tapes, not simply when these were used in the recording process. Subfield ǂb of the 300 field in *AACR 2R* records might include some of the information encoded here.

a   **NAB standard**

The National Association of Broadcasters playback equalization is required for some transcription recordings.

b   **CCIR standard**

The playback equalization standard of the Comité consultatif de la radiodiffusion (CCIR) is required for some transcription recordings.

c   **Dolby-B encoded**

Dolby-B is the standard Dolby noise reduction used on audio tapes. Commercial tapes with Dolby-B might simply say "Dolby" without further qualification or might have the "double D" insignia. Although these identifiers also might appear on commercial discs, this code never is used for mass-produced discs.

d   **dbx encoded**

Use for discs and tapes that indicate that dbx decoding is required for playback; if dbx was used for recording but standard playback equipment can be used, do not assign this code.

e   **Digital recording**

Use for all compact digital audio discs (CDs) and for special audio tapes (such as Sony PCM tape) that require digital playback equipment. Analog discs and standard tape recordings never use this code. If digital equipment was used during the recording but is not necessary for playback, do not use this code.

f   **Dolby-A encoded**

Only "master tapes" and other professional tapes clearly labelled "Dolby-A" should have this code. It never applies to mass-produced discs or tapes. Instantaneous tapes, especially cassettes, that are labelled "Dolby" are usually Dolby-B (see code "c").

g   **Dolby-C encoded**

Use only for tapes that specify that Dolby-C decoding is required. "Dolby" or the "double D" insignia without further qualification usually signifies Dolby-B (see code "c").

h **CX encoded**

Use only for recordings with pressing dates since 1981 that have the "CX" symbol. They might be labelled as being compatible with standard playback equipment.

n **Not applicable**

u **Unknown**

z **Other special playback characteristics**

Use for the "QS" quadraphonic reproduction process.

007/13 Capture and storage technique
OCLC: ‡n (Capture and storage technique) (O)
RLIN: CAP (Capture and storage technique) (NR)
WLN: 14th position (Capture and storage technique)

The means by which sounds were originally captured and stored is coded here. Any recording enhancements after the original capture and storage should be ignored.

a **Acoustic**

Most acoustical recordings predate the 1927/1929 period when electrical recording was developing. Live sounds were captured using an acoustical horn that directed sound vibrations to a diaphragm connected to a stylus. The stylus in turn engraved the vibration patterns directly onto a cylinder or analog disc, which became the master. This technique is sometimes referred to as mechanical recording.

b **Direct storage, not acoustical**

Recordings using microphones and other electrical equipment and stored directly on the surface of a disc. Before the availability of magnetic recording in the late 1940s, all electrical recordings employed direct storage. Nowadays, discs labeled "direct-to-disc" or some equivalent, use much the same method. Electromechanical recording is another name for this method.

d **Digital storage**

Electrical capture and digital storage usually is indicated by a phrase such as "digitally recorded" on the label or package and a similar note in the cataloging record. The original sound signal is sampled at small intervals and encoded in binary form on the original recording medium. Neither digital remastering, digital mixing, nor digital playback (which is coded in 007/12) implies digital storage of the original recording.

e **Analog electrical storage**

Electrical capture coupled with storage of the sound as pulses and modulations on a magnetic surface such as tape or wire was the method used for most recordings from the late 1940s until the advent of digital technology in the early 1980s.

u **Unknown**

The capture and storage technique cannot be determined.

z **Other capture and storage technique**

Techniques of capture and storage other than those listed above. Piano and organ rolls and any analog or digital sound recordings that originated as piano or organ rolls should be coded "other."

Examples

Compact Discs

For compact discs, the contents of this field should change very little as most of the information, save for the kind of sound byte and the capture and storage technique, is standard. Speed (1.4 m. per sec.), dimensions (4 3/4 in.), and the fact of digital reproduction all remain constant. In this example, the original capture and storage was made by digital means.

    OCLC coding example:

```
300     1 sound disc (69 min.) : ‡b digital, stereo. ; ‡c 4 3/4
        in.
007     s ‡b d ‡d f ‡e s ‡f n ‡g g ‡h n ‡i n ‡j m ‡k m ‡l n ‡m
        e ‡n d
```

    RLIN coding example:

```
300       ‡a1 sound disc (69 min.) :‡bdigital, stereo, ;‡c4 3/4
          in.
[007REC]  RMD: d OR: ? SPD: f SND: s GRV: n DIM: g WID: n TC:
          n KD: m KM: m KC: n RC: e CAP: d
```

    WLN coding example:

```
COL  ‡abc   ‡1 sound disc (69 min.) :‡digital, stereo. ;‡4 3/4
            in.
DFF  ‡a     ‡sd|fsngnnmmned
```

Analog Discs

For analog discs, the bytes for speed, kind of sound, and dimensions are those most likely to change from record to record. A commercial 12 in. stereo 33 1/3 rpm analog disc would be coded as such, with microgroove being understood. Unless an explicit note or the original recording dates indicate otherwise, assume the original capture and storage technique to be analog.

    OCLC coding example:

```
300     1 sound disc : ‡b analog, 33 1/3 rpm, stereo. ; ‡c 12
        in.
007     s ‡b d ‡d b ‡e s ‡f m ‡g e ‡h n ‡i n ‡j m ‡k p ‡l l ‡m
        n ‡n e
```

    RLIN coding example:

```
300       ‡a1 sound disc :‡banalog, 33 1/3 rpm, stereo. ;‡c12 in.
[007REC]  RMD: d OR: ? SPD: b SND: s GRV: m DIM: e WID: n TC: n
          KD: m KM: p KC: l RC: n CAP: e
```

    WLN coding example:

```
COL  ‡abc   ‡1 sound disc :‡analog, 33 1/3 rpm, stereo. ;‡12
               in.
DFF  ‡a     ‡sd|bsmennmplne
```

Coding for a commercial 10 in. mono 78 rpm analog disc assumes the standard, although unstated, coarse groove width. In this case, the original recording was made acoustically, early in the 1920s.

    OCLC coding example:

```
300     1 sound disc : ‡b analog, 78 rpm, mono. ; ‡c 10 in.
007     s ‡b d ‡d d ‡e m ‡f s ‡g d ‡h n ‡i n ‡j m ‡k s ‡l l ‡m
        n ‡n a
```

RLIN coding example:

```
300      ǂa1 sound disc : ǂbanalog, 78 rpm, mono. ;ǂc10 in.
[007REC] RMD: d OR: ? SPD: d SND: m GRV: s DIM: d WID: n TC: n
         KD: m KM: s KC: l RC: n CAP: a
```

WLN coding example:

```
COL  ǂabc   ǂ1 sound disc :ǂanalog, 78 rpm, mono. ;ǂ10 in.
DFF  ǂa     ǂsd|dmsdnnmslna
```

Cassette Tapes

Standard speed (1 7/8 ips), size (3 7/8 × 2 1/2 in.), tape width (1/8 in.), and track configuration (4-track) are omitted from the physical description of cassettes but should be coded in the 007 field.

OCLC coding example:

```
300      1 sound cassette : ǂb analog, Dolby processed.
007      s ǂb s ǂd l ǂe u ǂf n ǂg j ǂh l ǂi c ǂj m ǂk n ǂl n ǂm
         c ǂn e
```

RLIN coding example:

```
300      ǂa1 sound cassette : ǂbanalog, Dolby processed.
[007REC] RMD: s OR: ? SPD: l SND: u GRV: n DIM: j WID: l TC: c
         KD: m KM: n KC: n RC: c CAP: e
```

WLN coding example:

```
COL  ǂab    ǂ1 sound cassette :ǂanalog, Dolby processed.
DFF  ǂa     ǂss|lunjlcmnnce
```

Cartridge Tapes

Although standard tape width (1/4 in.), dimensions (5 1/4 × 3 7/8 in.), and track configuration (8-track) are not recorded in the physical description, they should still be coded in the 007 field.

OCLC coding example:

```
300      1 sound cartridge : ǂb analog, 3 3/4 ips, stereo.
007      s ǂb g ǂd m ǂe s ǂf n ǂg o ǂh m ǂi d ǂj m ǂk n ǂl n ǂm
         n ǂn e
```

RLIN coding example:

```
300      ǂa1 sound cartridge : ǂbanalog, 3 3/4 ips, stereo.
[007REC] RMD: g OR: ? SPD: m SND: s GRV: n DIM: o WID: m TC: d
         KD: m KM: n KC: n RC: n CAP: e
```

WLN coding example:

```
COL  ǂab    ǂ1 sound cartridge :ǂanalog, 3 3/4 ips, stereo.
DFF  ǂa     ǂsg|msnomdmnnne
```

Reel-to-reel Tapes

Supply the code for standard tape width (1/4 in.) when it does not appear in the physical description.

OCLC coding example:

```
300      1 sound tape reel : ǂb analog, 7 1/2 ips, stereo. ; ǂc
         7 in.
007      s ǂb t ǂd o ǂe s ǂf n ǂg c ǂh m ǂi u ǂj m ǂk n ǂl n ǂm
         n ǂn e
```

RLIN coding example:

```
300      ‡a1 sound tape reel :‡banalog, 7 1/2 ips, stereo. ;‡c7
         in.
[007REC] RMD: t OR: ? SPD: o SND: s GRV: n DIM: c WID: m TC: u
         KD: m KM: n KC: n RC: n CAP: e
```

WLN coding example:

```
COL  ‡abc   ‡1 sound tape reel :‡analog, 7 1/2 ips, stereo. ;‡7
            in.
DFF  ‡a     ‡st|osncmumnnne
```

Cylinders

Cylinders are assumed to be acoustic recordings.

OCLC coding example:

```
300      1 sound cylinder : ‡b 160 rpm ; ‡c 2 3/4 x 4 in.
007      s ‡b e ‡d i ‡e a ‡f m ‡g s ‡h n ‡i n ‡j m ‡k p ‡l h ‡m
         n ‡n a
```

RLIN coding example:

```
300      ‡a1 sound cylinder :‡b160 rpm ;‡c2 3/4 x 4 in.
[007REC] RMD: e OR: ? SPD: i SND: a GRV: m DIM: s WID: n TC: n
         KD: m KM: p KC: h RC: n CAP: a
```

WLN coding example:

```
COL  ‡abc   ‡1 sound cylinder :‡160 rpm ;‡2 3/4 x 4 in.
DFF  ‡a     ‡se|iamsnnmphna
```

Rolls

OCLC coding example:

```
300      1 piano roll.
007      s ‡b q ‡d z ‡e z ‡f n ‡g n ‡h n ‡i n ‡j n ‡k n ‡l n ‡m
         n ‡n z
```

RLIN coding example:

```
300      ‡a1 piano roll.
[007REC] RMD: q OR: ? SPD: z SND: z GRV: n DIM: n WID: n TC: n
         KD: n KM: n KC: n RC: n CAP: z
```

WLN coding example:

```
COL  ‡a    ‡1 piano roll.
DFF  ‡a    ‡sq|zznnnnnnnnz
```

010 Library of Congress Control Number

UFBD: 010 (A) (NRep)
OCLC: 010 (R/R) (NRep)
RLIN: 010 (NR) (NRep)
WLN: RID/CRD (M or system
supplied) (NRep)
LCN (Used only by LC or
other external sources)
(NRep)
MOIM: (010) (NRep)

The Library of Congress assigns a unique control number to each bibliographic record it creates in order to facilitate processing of the record. This Library of Congress Control Number (LCCN), or in some cases a "pseudo-LC control number" (distinguished by certain prefixes), appears in the lower right hand corner of LC printed cards and has taken various forms over the past century. In addition, the LCCN proper also might have appended prefixes, suffixes, and/or revision information. These aids in interpreting and correctly inputting LCCNs can be useful when transcribing LC cataloging copy or when an LCCN is encountered on a score or sound recording.

WLN practices for the LCCN differ somewhat from those for OCLC and RLIN. In WLN, when an LCCN is known, it serves also as the WLN record identifier and is input in the RID field; WLN records input without an LCCN have a WLN record identifier assigned by the system. The WLN system also automatically transfers suffixes, alphabetic identifiers, and revision information into the CRD field. At least one slash must precede these data for the transfer to take place correctly. The guidelines that follow are valid for the WLN RID field, except that RID has no subfield ‡z. WLN's LCN field is used only by the Library of Congress and other external sources and should not be input by WLN users.

Indicators

Both *indicators* are blank.

Old-Style Card Number Systems (June 1898 to November 1968)

Least consistent and most confusing were the various numbering systems predating most modern bibliographic automation, particularly those systems used before 1902.

Numbers assigned from June through August 1898 lack any indication of the year, consisting simply of an up-to-three-digit copyright number or a number with the prefix "C". As only 398 such records were issued during those three months, the chances of encountering any are exceedingly slim. In any case, they should be entered with the prefix "c98-".

On Printed Card	Enter As
100	c98-100
C-324	c98-324

From September 1898 to May 1901, card numbers were constructed using the month, day, and year followed by a serial number ("Oct. 18, 1900-216"). Because each week's output began again with the serial number "1," the numbers are not unique without the date. During December 1900, the cards appeared with the month and year followed by the serial number ("12-1900-245"). In 1912, new values for all of these numbers were established using the prefixes 98, 99, [0]0, and [0]1 for all such cards subsequently reprinted.

If the card was not reprinted, special tables published in LC's *Card Section Bulletin* no. 22 (December 1912 and reprinted in October 1914) must be consulted. When numbers such as these are encountered on cards that have not been reprinted and you don't have access to the aforementioned *Card Section Bulletin*, contact your bibliographic network or utility, or the Library of Congress Cataloging Distribution Service or Office for Descriptive Cataloging Policy. Someone will be able to translate the number into the correct form for input.

Between May and December of 1901, LCCNs appeared with a "1" and an alphabetic prefix other than "C." When these were reprinted in 1912, the "1" was dropped. Occasionally, the alphabetic "prefix" followed the number. All of these are entered with the year series "01" and up to three lower-case alphabetic characters as the prefix (regardless of its position in the original LCCN).

Pre-1912 Form	Post-1912 Form	Enter As
1-D-245	D-245	d01-245
1-F-245	F-245	f01-245
1-G-245	G-245	g01-245
1-I-245	IT-245	it01-245
1-Map-50	Map-50	map01-50
1-Music-25	Music-25	mus01-25
1-Rc-245	Rc-245	rc01-245
1-Z-245	Z-245	z01-245
1-300 Music	Music-300	mus01-300
1-308 Music div.	Music div.-308	mus01-308

LCCN styles gained a little more consistency from January 1902 through November 1968.

- alphabetic prefix (optional)
- two-character year indicator
- one-to-six-digit unique serial number
- supplement number (optional)
- suffix and/or revision information (optional)

Prefixes appear only in the old-style LCCNs. They always are entered in lower case and, if they have more than three characters, are shortened to three characters according to the following table:

Prefix on Card	Enter As
CA Dupl	cad
MicA	mid
Micp	mie
MicpA	mif
PhoM	php

A complete list of the alphabetic prefixes used in the old system can be found in the *Books: MARC Conversion Manual* and in the *WLN Data Preparation Manual*. Among those prefixes that might be found on old-style cards for scores, sound recordings, and related items are:

A	Cards printed from copy supplied by other American libraries, 1909-1968
AC	Cards printed for annotated cards for juvenile books, 1966-1968
C	Cards printed for Chinese entries cataloged by the Library of Congress, 1949-1968
HE	Cards printed for Hebrew entries cataloged by the Library of Congress, 1964-1968
J	Cards printed for Japanese entries cataloged by the Library of Congress, 1949-1968
K	Cards printed for Korean entries cataloged by the Library of Congress, 1951-1968
M	Cards printed for sheet music cataloged by the Library of Congress, 1953-1962
MA	Cards printed for sheet music from copy supplied by other American libraries, 1953-1961
Mic	Cards printed for microfilms cataloged by the Library of Congress, 1949-1968
MicA	Cards printed for microfilms from copy supplied by other American libraries, 1946-1968
Micp	Cards printed for microcards and microprints cataloged by the Library of Congress, 1953-1968
MicpA	Cards printed for microcards and microprints from copy supplied by other American libraries, 1953-1968.
MPA	Cards printed for sheet music from copy supplied by the Pan American Union, 1956-1968
NE	Cards printed for books published in the Near East or in the languages of those countries, 1961-1968
R	Cards printed for phonograph records cataloged by the Library of Congress, 1953-1968

RA   Cards printed for phonograph records from copy supplied by other American libraries, 1955-1968

SA   Cards printed for books published in Southeast Asia or in the languages of those countries, 1961-1968

Old-style LCCNs also might be full of other miscellaneous quirks, but there are standard ways to deal with them.

Do not input a slash followed by a numeral. These cards were prepared for a special edition of the 1904 ALA catalog.

On Printed Card	Enter As
4-5448/2	04-5448
3-14444/4	03-14444

Do not input a second hyphen followed by one or more numerals.

On Printed Card	Enter As
17-8859-60	17-8859
3-29453-4	3-29453
D-142-3	d01-142

Do not input a second hyphen followed by the letter "M" or any following numerals.

On Printed Card	Enter As
1-21-M2 Music div.	mus01-21
1-105-M2 Music div.	mus01-105

Do not input a single dagger (†) that follows an LCCN. The single dagger signifies less than the normal amount of revision.

On Printed Card	Enter As
3-3928†	03-3928
3-7584†	03-7584

However, a double dagger (‡) following an LCCN in the old, interim, and new systems is translated into the upper-case alphabetic identifier "L", indicating "limited cataloging."

On Printed Card	Enter As
M59-405‡	m59-405/L
62-5703‡	62-5703/L

Do not input an asterisk (*) that follows an LCCN.

On Printed Card	Enter As
Music-283 rev*	mus01-283//r
48-30275*	48-30275

Do not input the terms "Additions," "Exception," "Provisional," "Cancel," "Brief Cataloging," or "Unrev'd," that might follow the LCCN.

On Printed Card	Enter As
8-13021 Additions	08-13021
CA32-387 Unrev'd	ca32-387

Multiple alphabetic identifiers and suffixes in the old, interim, and new systems are input in the order they appear and are separated from each other by a single slash.

On Printed Card	Enter As
C62-2014‡/M	c62-2014/L/M
74-272231 SA MN	74-272231/SA/MN

Do not input the alphabetic identifier "CD," or the suffix "P".

On Printed Card	Enter As
64-7345/CD	64-7345
65-7097/MN/CD	65-7097/MN
10-35080 P	10-35080

Do not transpose an alphabetic prefix into a suffix. Prefixes (always input in lower case) are integral parts of their LCCNs and help make them unique identifiers. Suffixes (input in upper case), on the other hand, have no effect on the uniqueness of their LCCNs.

Interim Card Number System (December 1968 to January 1972)

Sometimes known as the "7" series because each LCCN under this system began with that numeral, the short-lived "interim" system utilized a check digit immediately following the "7". Hence, the first two numerals in an interim-system LCCN do not correspond to a date. Nor do interim card numbers have alphabetic prefixes. Instead, "alphabetic identifiers" appear below the card number on printed cards (although they usually were cut off when the cards were reprinted in the various National Union Catalogs) and are input as suffixes, separated from the LCCN by a slash. Multiple alphabetic identifiers are separated by a slash. The result is an LCCN with the following structure:

- initial digit (always "7")
- check digit
- hyphen
- one-to-six-digit unique serial number
- supplement number (never implemented)
- alphabetic identifier and/or revision information

Regarding "supplement numbers," it was LC's early intention that separate records would be created for supplements, indexes, and the like (items that for many years had been given "dashed-on" treatment). These would be linked to their parent records by having the same LCCN proper but with the extra supplement number. Because this idea was never put into practice, such numbers will not be encountered. Now such materials are cataloged separately and have their own LCCNs.

It was quickly recognized that the check digit was more trouble than it was worth and that the available numbers would soon have been exhausted, so this system was abandoned.

New-Style Control Number System (February 1972 to the present)

The current system by which the Library of Congress assigns LCCNs looks outwardly similar to the "interim" system, but eliminates the check digit. Instead, the first two digits reflect the year the LCCN was assigned, resulting in the following structure:

- two-character year designator
- hyphen
- one-to-six-digit unique serial number
- alphabetic identifiers or suffixes (optional)
- revision information (optional)

Like the interim system, the new system does not use alphabetic prefixes but does use the alphabetic identifiers that appear below the LCCN on printed cards (again, they usually are cut off when the card is reproduced in the *National Union Catalog*).

Alphabetic identifiers in both the interim and new systems are input as upper-case suffixes, separated from the card number proper by a slash. Multiple suffixes also are separated from each other by slashes.

Among those alphabetic identifiers that might be found on cards for scores, sound recordings, and related items are:

A	Printed from copy supplied by other American libraries
AC	Annotated card
C	Chinese
HE	Hebrew
J	Japanese
K	Korean
M	Music
MN	Book on music
NE	Near East
R	Sound recording
SA	South Asian
SC	Shared cataloging

Revision Information

Revision information is found either following the LCCN or in the area of a printed card just to the right of the guard hole, the printing symbol area. Most of the symbols here, having to do with the year of printing and the number of cards that were to be printed, are of little interest to anyone outside the Library of Congress and can be ignored. But when the term "Revised", the abbreviation "rev", and/or the bracketed symbol "r" followed by a two-or-three-digit number appears, it indicates that the bibliographic data have suffered some sort of indignity at some point during the card's lifetime.

Although both major and minor changes will cause LC to issue a corrected machine-readable record, only a major indignity will be reflected in a revision date. In the days before widespread automation, the Library of Congress defined "major" as anything important enough to warrant redistribution of a card set to its own catalogs. These now include changes to:

- content designation
- any access point (1XX, 240, 245 ‡a, 440, 6XX, 7XX, 8XX)
- extent of an item (300 ‡a)
- publication date (260 ‡c)
- LCCN
- ISBN (020 ‡a or ‡z)
- classification (050, 051, or 082)
- Descriptive Cataloging Form (Leader/18)

Transcribe revision information after the LCCN proper, as a lowercase "r" followed by any two-digit date code associated with it. Where multiple changes have been made to a record, the number of changes (a single numeral that may follow "rev") becomes the final numeral in the revision date. When it appears without intervening suffixes, revision information is separated from the card number proper by two slashes; separate it from suffixes by a single slash.

On Printed Card	*Enter As*
2-16966 Revised [r38b2]	02-16966//r38
R53-131 rev2	r53-131//r2
77-364971 77[r85]rev2	77-364971//r852
AC38-4114 rev*/M	ac38-4114/M/r

When working from an actual LC printed card or proof slip and the term "rev" appears without the lower case "r" and two-digit revision date in the printing symbol area, do not record it. However, remember that cards printed in the National Union Catalog often have their printing symbol area cut off. As a result, it might be wise to include such incomplete revision information (as a lone lowercase "r") when working with a card image missing the printing symbol area.

Pseudo-LC Control Numbers

Pseudo-LCCNs are control numbers structured like LCCNs but distinguished by certain prefixes. Music catalogers will rarely, if ever, have to input these pseudo-LCCNs, but they might encounter them occasionally. They are found mostly in two types of records: CONSER serial records authenticated by the Library of Congress, the National Library of Canada, and/or other CONSER participants, and records found in the various national union catalogs for which LCCNs do not exist. The CONSER prefixes are:

sc	Serials, CONSER Non-Canadian imprints not held by LC
sf	Serials, Form card LC records that have an entry in LC's Official Catalog but for which no printed card exists
ce	NLC English-language record for Canadian bilingual English-French publications
cf	NLC French-language record for Canadian bilingual English-French publications
cn	NLC English- or French-language record for Canadian unilingual or multilingual (other than English-French) publications
sn	All other CONSER records eligible for distribution in the MARC Distribution Service—Serials CONSER records with Authentication Agency Codes "nsdp", "nst", or "msc" in Field 042

Numbers with the prefixes "sc", "sf", and "sn" derive from three separate sequential lists. However, the same numbers are used for the English and French publications assigned the "ce" or "cf" prefixes; the prefixes distinguish the two records.

The prefixes for records without true LCCNs in the various national union catalogs are:

nuc   Record printed in the *National Union Catalog* for which no LCCN is available

scc   Record printed in the *Slavic Cyrillic Union Catalog of Pre-1956 Imprints* for which no LCCN is available

um   Record printed in the *National Union Catalog, Cartographic Materials* for which no LCCN is available

Subfield ‡z: Cancelled/invalid LC control number

The validity of an LCCN will not always be readily apparent, but there are a number of circumstances where putting the LCCN into a subfield ‡z would be appropriate.

- A new edition has been printed with the LCCN of an older edition; publishers often are remiss in this regard

- An item is cataloged separately but has been printed with the LCCN of the serial or set of which it is a part

- The LCCN has been printed in the item with a typographical error (that is, it differs from the LCCN found on an LC card or in an LC MARC record)

- The LCCN has been used by LC for a different item

- The cataloger has chosen to catalog as a single unit an item that LC has cataloged as separate works, or vice versa. This most often occurs when pre-*AACR 2* LC cataloging (linked by "with" notes) exists for separate works on a sound recording. If, under *AACR 2R*, the item were cataloged as a unit, the LCCNs for the separate works would go in subfield(s) ‡z

- The accuracy of the LCCN is in doubt for some other reason

Subfield ‡z is repeatable.

EXAMPLES OF LCCN ENTRY

On Printed Card	*Enter As*
49-19863 rev2*/M	49-19863/M/r2
HE67-1054/M	he67-1054/M
Music-20 Revised [r28c2]	mus01-20//r28
MicA55-542/M	mid55-542/M
73-219149 M rev 73 [r74c2]	73-219149/M/r74
59-18945 rev2‡/MN	59-18945/L/MN/r2

J62-1018‡	j62-1018/L
M55-1211 [a63r56c½]	m55-1211//r56
2-27984 rev*/M	02-27984/M/r
R57-840 rev4	r57-840//r4
85-750823 [r86] rev2	85-750823//r862
Micp63-14 rev	mie63-14//r
6-21694 Additions 2	06-21694
SA63-2046‡/MN	sa63-2046/L/MN
49-14656*	49-14656
M59-235	m59-235//r71
rev [r71b2]	

74-229011
    M
    74[r75]rev
	74-229011/M/r75

AC38-1276 Revised [r40c2]	ac38-1276//r40

024   Standard Recording Number

UFBD: 024 (A/A) (Rep)
OCLC: 024 (O/O) (Rep)
RLIN: 024 (NR) (Rep)
WLN: SRN (NR) (Rep)
MOIM: (not present)

Given the utter chaos of music publisher's numbers for both scores and sound recordings, a music cataloger cannot but be forgiven for harboring contradictory sentiments concerning any possible standardization of music identification. "Not another number!" must be one reaction. "If it is widely enough adopted, perhaps it can begin to impose some order" might be the other.

The 024 field has been set aside for the International Standard Recording Code (ISRC) or other standard music industry code for sound recordings. So far, it largely has been employed to hold the Universal Product Code (UPC) for sound recordings, that now-familiar, ten-digit, bar-coded number. The Universal Product Code Council administers the system for the recording industry.

International Standard Recording Code (ISRC)

In 1986 the International Organization for Standardization published its International Standard ISO 3901, the *International Standard Recording Code (ISRC)* (see Bibliography). Identified by the letters "ISRC" that precede it, this is a matrix-like number, attached to an individual recording throughout its entire lifetime. The document clearly states that the ISRC "is not to be used for the numbering of audio, visual, and audio-visual carriers." Its twelve characters are divided by hyphens into five parts:

- two-letter *country code*
  Codes identifying the country of residence of the first owner are derived from ISO 3166, *Codes for the Representation of Names of Countries*
- three-character *first owner code*
  Alphanumeric code for the producer of the recording
- two-digit *year of recording code*
  Last two digits of the year the recording process was finished
- three- or four-digit *recording code*
  Assigned sequentially by the first owner; four-digit codes 0000-2999 are for recordings with fewer than ten subunits; three-digit codes 300-999 are for recordings with more than nine subunits
- one- or two-digit *recording item code*
  If the recording code is four digits, the recording item code is one digit (0-9); if the recording code is three digits, the recording item code is two digits (00-99)

Transcribe ISRCs exactly as they appear, retaining the hyphens.

Universal Product Code (UPC)

The Universal Product Code is a ten-digit number printed in Optical Character Recognition (OCR) typeface beneath a bar-code symbol (see Figure 9). Three portions compose the UPC:

- a five-digit code representing the manufacturer
- a five-digit selection number code
- a one-digit product configuration code

The fifth digit of the manufacturer's code serves double duty as the first digit of the selection number. The final digit product configuration code indicates the format of the recording:

1   long-playing record (analog disc)
2   digital compact disc
4   cassette tape
8   8-track tape
0   other recording medium

Figure 9: Universal Product Code (UPC) from a sound type cassette.

Input the UPC without the hyphens and spaces that appear in its printed version. The digit that appears to the left of the Left Guard Bar Pattern (the Numbers Systems Designator, which is "0" for the recording industry), and the check digit that may appear to the right of the Right Guard Bar Pattern are both ignored.

Other Standard Numbers

Do not confuse the ten-digit UPC with the European Article Number (EAN), a bar-code symbol containing more than ten digits that is used by some European manufacturers (see Figure 10). EANs should not be input in the 024 field, as it has been defined only for U.S. UPCs and ISRCs thus far.

An International Standard Music Number (ISMN) has been proposed for printed music but no standard has been defined yet. International Standard Book Numbers (ISBN) do appear on some scores; they belong in the 020 field.

Indicators

The *first indicator* specifies the type of standard number being transcribed.

OCLC & RLIN	WLN	
0	I	**International Standard Recording Code (ISRC)**
1	U	**U.S. Universal Product Code (UPC) for sound recordings**

The *second indicator* is blank.

Subfields

‡a **Standard recording code**

Valid ISRCs and UPCs are transcribed here.

‡d **Additional codes following the standard code**

Sometimes, optional digits are added by the manufacturer to the right of the UPC proper as list price information (see Figure 11). These go in subfield ‡d.

‡z **Cancelled/invalid standard code**

Any cancelled (erroneously assigned) and/or invalid (incorrectly formatted) codes are in subfield ‡z.

Examples

```
024 0   NL-C01-84-1326-5

024 0   SE-T38-85-302-12

024 1   5151885101

024 1   7464331911 ‡d 02

024 1   4411413874 ‡d 02

024 1   ‡z 759923674
```

DIGITAL · STEREO 400 045-2

ARCHIV
PRODUKTION

3 259140 004523

ANTONIO VIVALDI
(1678–1741)

Le Quattro Stagioni
Die vier Jahreszeiten · The Four Seasons · Les Quatre Saisons

**La Primavera (Der Frühling · Spring
Le Printemps) op. 8 No. 1**
Concerto in mi maggiore (E-dur · in E major
en mi majeur) RV 269

☐1 1. Allegro	[3'15]
☐2 2. Largo e pianissimo sempre	[2'37]
☐3 3. Danza pastorale. Allegro	[3'36]

L'Estate (Der Sommer · Summer · L'Eté) op. 8 No. 2
Concerto in sol minore (g-moll · in G minor
en sol mineur) RV 315

☐4 1. Allegro non molto	[4'42]
☐5 2. Adagio – Presto	[2'15]
☐6 3. Presto	[2'43]

**L'Autunno (Der Herbst · Autumn · L'Automne)
op. 8 No. 3**
Concerto in fa maggiore (F-dur · in F major
en fa majeur) RV 293

☐7 1. Allegro	[4'48]
☐8 2. Adagio	[2'28]
☐9 3. Allegro	[2'59]

**L'Inverno (Der Winter · Winter · L'Hiver)
op. 8 No. 4**
Concerto in fa minore (f-moll · in F minor
en fa mineur) RV 297

☐10 1. Allegro non molto	[3'11]
☐11 2. Largo	[1'50]
☐12 3. Allegro	[2'43]

Simon Standage, Violino
The English Concert
auf Originalinstrumenten · on Period Instruments
avec instruments originaux · con strumenti originali
*Cembalo und Leitung/Directed from the Harpsichord by/
Clavecin et direction musicale/
Clavicembalo e direzione musicale:*
TREVOR PINNOCK

℗ 1982 Polydor International GmbH. Hamburg
Previously released as 2534 003

Printed in West Germany by/Imprimé en Al-emagne
par Neef, Wittingen · Made in West Germany

Figure 10: European Article Number (EAN) from a compact disc.

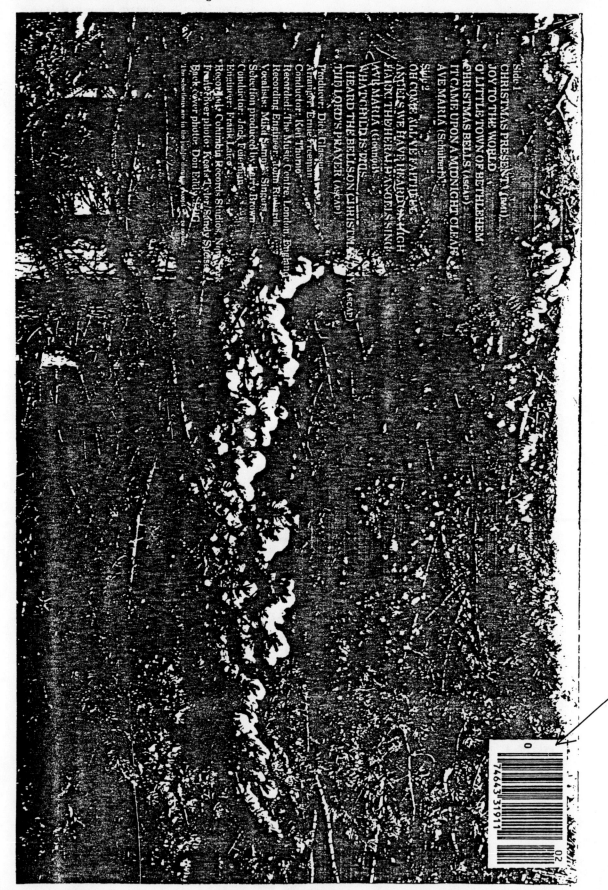

Figure 11: Universal Product Code (UPC) with additional codes following the standard code.

028   Publisher Number for Music

UFBD: 028 (A/A) (Rep)
OCLC: 028 (R/R) (Rep)
RLIN: 028 (NR) (Rep)
WLN: PNM (A) (Rep)
MOIM: 028 (Rep)

Given the tendency of music to have more than its share of generic titles, which makes it difficult to distinguish among similar items, catalogers seize upon any hint of bibliographic uniqueness to identify better a score or recording. The publisher number, in its various forms, is among the more useful aids in identifying editions, establishing dates, and tracing bibliographic histories.

As the repository of the publisher's number in coded form, the 028 field finds itself trying to satisfy two sometimes contradictory roles: that of the indexable access point and that of the note and/or added entry generator. Further complications arise from the lack of standardization in any of the various music publisher numbers. They can be of any length and in any alphanumeric configuration.

Because the problem of note generation from the 028 field can be circumvented by the explicit input of a 500 note, the indexing function of the 028 field tends to take precedence. When no notes are to be generated from the 028 fields, their order in the record is immaterial. In RLIN and WLN, any 028 field with a printing second indicator will generate a note; however in OCLC, only a first 028 field with a printing second indicator will generate a note. Both the indexing and note-generation capabilities of local systems also need to be kept in mind. Consideration of these quirks is necessary in order for notes to print in the proper order (for scores, notes for plate numbers should follow notes for other publisher's numbers). If trying to sort out system capabilities and the number of saved keystrokes becomes too confusing, it is probably best to input explicitly all the music publisher number 500 notes as they should appear. The priority for the 028 field must be proper indexing; note generation is a bonus that should be used only when its results are clear and descriptively correct.

Indicators

First indicator: Type of publisher number

The value of the first indicator identifies the type of music publisher number found in the field.

Sound recordings

OCLC & RLIN	WLN	
0	I	**Issue number**

Sometimes called a label number, this is the supposedly unique serial designation given by the manufacturer to a sound recording or set of recordings. It usually appears on the recording label and/or on the container.

1	M	**Matrix number**

Used to identify a sound recording in the absence of an issue or label number, the matrix number appears etched into an analog disc, usually somewhere between the innermost grooves and the label. Matrix numbers most often are found on recordings that are privately produced or on small record labels. In the WLN system only, first indicator "M" generates the display constant "Matrix no.:" when the second indicator is set to generate a note.

Scores

2	P	**Plate number**

As a means of identification, many music publishers assign plate numbers to their publications as part of the preparations for printing. The plate number must appear at the bottom of each page of music (and sometimes on the title page, as well). Initials, abbreviations, or words identifying the publisher also might appear in conjunction with the plate number. This first indicator generates the display constant "Pl. no.:" when the second indicator is set to generate a note.

3	T	**Other publisher number**

An identifying number that appears only on the title page, cover, and/or the first page of music (or on the first page of each signature, rather than on each page of music) is regarded as a publisher number. This first indicator value generates the display constant "Publisher's no.:" when the second indicator is set to generate a note.

Second indicator: Note/added entry controller

The generation of a note and/or an added entry from the 028 field is determined by the value of the second indicator. In *AACR 2R* records, when the 028 field cannot generate an intelligible note, one must be input explicitly as a 500 field and the 028 second indicator set to a nonprinting value.

OCLC & RLIN	*WLN*	
0	N	**No note, no added entry**

Neither a note nor an added entry is generated. Usually an explicit 500 note will need to be input to reflect the information found in coded form in the 028 field.

1	A	**Note, added entry required**

Both a note and an added entry are generated. Depending on the first indicator, a display constant might preface the note.

2	R	**Note, no added entry**

A note is generated, but not an added entry. Depending on the first indicator, a display constant might preface the note.

3	E	**No note, added entry required**

An added entry is generated, but not a note.

Circumstances that might necessitate the use of nonprinting 028 fields and the explicit input of 500 fields include:

- Variant forms of a publisher's number appear on the container, label, accompanying material, etc., of a sound recording or in different places on a score.

```
028 00   Cla D 907 ‡b Claves
028 00   D 907 ‡b Claves
500      Claves: Cla D 907 (on container: D 907).

028 30   17 527 ‡b Universal Edition
028 30   ue 17 527 ‡b Universal Edition
500      Publisher's no.: Universal Edition Nr. 17
         527 (cover: ue 17 527).
```

- A score is a reprint or a sound recording is a reissue, and information about the publisher's numbers or plate numbers of the original versions is noted.

```
028 20   4801 ‡b Breitkopf & H¨artel
500      Reissued from Breitkopf & H¨artel plates.  Pl.
         no.: 4801.

028 22   2532 037 ‡b Deutsche Grammophon
028 00   2741 005 ‡b Deutsche Grammophon
500      Previously released as 2741 005.
```

•   Note is made of the fact that a sound recording has been issued in multiple physical versions.

```
028 02   ASD 3906 ‡b His Master's Voice
028 00   065-03 825 ‡b His Master's Voice
500      Issued also as cassette: 065-03 825.
```

•   Because of the construction of the publisher number, the form for correct indexing and the form for proper transcription in a note differ.

```
028 30   8579 ‡b H. Litolff's Verlag/C.F. Peters
500      Publisher's no.: Edition Peters Nr. 8579.
```

Subfields

‡a   Publisher number

The number portion of the publisher number is transcribed here as it appears on the item. (However, remember to transliterate characters not in the roman alphabet; for instance, Cyrillic characters in the matrix or music publisher numbers of Melodiíá recordings are sometimes mistaken for their roman look-alikes.) Include any numeric characters, words, abbreviations, or alphabetic devices that indicate numbering, but *exclude* abbreviations for the terms "number," "catalog number," and the like, regardless of the language, unless they are embedded in the publisher number.

    Publisher's number as it appears on item: Cat. no. 07 0137 07
    ("Cat. no." is not an integral part of the publisher's number)
```
028 32   07 0137 07 ‡b Novello
```

    Publisher's number as it appears on item: E.C.S. no. 264
    ("no." is embedded within the publisher's number and so is an integral part of it)
```
028 32   E.C.S. no. 264 ‡b E.C. Schirmer
```

The terms "plate number," "publisher's number," and their abbreviations *should not* be input in subfield ‡a. Likewise, any numbers, usually following a hyphen or other punctuation, corresponding to the page number of a score or the side number of a recording, are not considered part of the publisher number.

‡b   Source

For sound recordings, the name of the record label appears in subfield ‡b. For scores, the name of the publisher goes in subfield ‡b for plate numbers; for publisher numbers, the publisher's name, the designation of the publisher, or other word or phrase that appears with the number is recorded in subfield ‡b.

Multiple Publisher Numbers and Multiple 028 Fields

More than one music publisher number might be associated with an item being cataloged. A multipart set likely will have multiple numbers, usually a separate number for each individual part and often an overall number for the entire set as well. However, even a monographic item can have numerous numbers attached to it. A single score, for example, might have not just one plate number and/or just one publisher's number, but might have more than one of either or both.

Different systems have different capabilities for both note generation and indexing. The USMARC format, RLIN, and WLN require that each number to be indexed be put in a separate 028 field; if a single note condensing consecutive or multiple numbers is desired, it must be input explicitly. WLN stipulates that if more than 15 fields would result, only the first and last numbers should be input. In addition, it should be noted that the WLN print program does not reverse the order of the subfields in any note or added entry generated from a PNM field. Hence, the number (from subfield ‡a) will precede the source (from subfield ‡b) in notes and added entries in WLN.

OCLC is able to accommodate and index multiple numbers in the same 028 field, although it is permissible to enter each number in a separate field. The capabilities of individual local systems also will influence the choice of using single or multiple 028 fields.

Nonconsecutive numbers

RLIN and WLN require that each number be entered in its own 028 field, with a 500 field being explicitly input; in OCLC, this approach is optional.

In RLIN, separate 028s and an explicitly input 500 field:

```
028 00   SMLP 4024‡bMelbourne
028 00   SMLP 4027‡bMelbourne
500      Melbourne: SMLP 4024, SMLP 4027.
```

In WLN, separate PNMs and an explicitly input NOG field:

```
PNMIN‡ab      ‡SMLP 4024‡Melbourne
PNMIN‡ab      ‡SMLP 4027‡Melbourne
NOG‡a         ‡Melbourne: SMLP 4024, SMLP 4027.
```

In OCLC, a single 028 field may be used, with each number being separated by a comma-space.

In OCLC, this 028 field:

```
028 02   SMLP 4024, SMLP 4027 ‡b Melbourne
```

indexes both numbers and generates this note:

```
500      Melbourne: SMLP 4024, SMLP 4027.
```

In OCLC and RLIN, separate 028s and one explicitly input 500 field:

```
028 32   29628 ‡b Edition Wilhelm Hansen
028 30   4382 ‡b Wilhelm Hansen edition
500      Publisher's no.: Wilhelm Hansen edition, no. 4382.
```

index both numbers and generate this note:

```
500      Publisher's no.: 29628.
```

In WLN, separate PNMs:

```
PNMTR‡ab      ‡29628‡Edition Wilhelm Hansen
PNMTR‡ab      ‡4382‡Wilhelm Hansen edition
```

index both numbers and generate two notes:

```
NOG‡a         ‡Publisher's no.: 29628 Edition Wilhelm Hansen.
NOG‡a         ‡Publisher's no.: 4382 Wilhelm Hansen edition.
```

Consecutive numbers

In RLIN and WLN, consecutive numbers must be input in separate non-printing 028/PNM fields with an explicitly input 500/NOG field; this is optional in OCLC.

In OCLC, a single 028 field can be used for a range of consecutive arabic numbers (but not roman numerals), with a double hyphen separating the first and last of the sequence. Fields that contain both a set number and individual numbers for items in the set (as described in LCRI 6.7B19) also are permissible and fully indexed in OCLC. When it encounters a double hyphen, the OCLC system checks that the number to the right is higher than the number to the left and that any alphabetic prefixes are identical. When parentheses are found, it checks that they are correct and consistent and indexes the numbers within them apart from those outside.

In RLIN, separate 028s and an explicitly input 500 field:

```
028 00   BG 4004‡bBourg Records
028 00   BG 4005‡bBourg Records
500      Bourg Records: BG 4004--BG 4005.
```

In WLN, separate PNMs and an explicitly input NOG field:

```
PNMIN‡ab      ‡BG 4004‡Bourg Records
PNMIN‡ab      ‡BG 4005‡Bourg Records
NOG‡a         ‡Bourg Records: BG 4004--BG 4005.
```

In OCLC, this 028 field:

```
028 02   BG 4004--BG 4005 ‡b Bourg Records
```

indexes both numbers and generates this note:

```
500      Bourg Records: BG 4004--BG 4005.
```

In RLIN, separate 028s and an explicitly input 500 field:

```
028 00   RLS 739‡bEMI His Master's Voice
028 00   HLM 7168‡bEMI His Master's Voice
028 00   HLM 7169‡bEMI His Master's Voice
028 00   HLM 7170‡bEMI His Master's Voice
028 00   HLM 7171‡bEMI His Master's Voice
500      EMI His Master's Voice: RLS 739 (HLM 7168--HLM
         7171).
```

In WLN, separate PNMs and an explicitly input NOG field:

```
PNMIN‡ab      ‡RLS 739‡EMI His Master's Voice
PNMIN‡ab      ‡HLM 7168‡EMI His Master's Voice
PNMIN‡ab      ‡HLM 7169‡EMI His Master's Voice
PNMIN‡ab      ‡HLM 7170‡EMI His Master's Voice
PNMIN‡ab      ‡HLM 7171‡EMI His Master's Voice
NOG‡a         ‡EMI His Master's Voice: RLS 739 (HLM 7168--HLM
              7171).
```

In OCLC, this 028 field:

```
028 02   RLS 739 (HLM 7168--HLM 7171) ‡b EMI His Master's
         Voice
```

indexes all five numbers and generates this note:

```
500      EMI His Master's Voice: RLS 739 (HLM 7168--HLM
         7171).
```

Consecutive numbers separated by increments other than one (that is, ranges of numbers in which a digit other than the final one changes) always must be input in separate non-printing 028 fields in order to index correctly in the OCLC system. An explicit 500 field also must be input.

In RLIN and OCLC, separate 028s and an explicitly input 500 field:

```
028 00   411 459-1 ‡b Philips
028 00   411 460-1 ‡b Philips
028 00   411 461-1 ‡b Philips
028 00   411 462-1 ‡b Philips
500      Philips: 411 459-1 (411 460-1--411 462-1).
```

In WLN, separate PNMs and an explicitly input NOG field:

```
PNMIN‡ab      411 459-1‡Philips
PNMIN‡ab      411 460-1‡Philips
PNMIN‡ab      411 461-1‡Philips
PNMIN‡ab      411 462-1‡Philips
NOG‡a         Philips: 411 459-1 (411 460-1--411 462-1).
```

Truncated set numbers

According to Music Cataloging Decision 6.7B19 (*Music Cataloging Bulletin* 19:11 (November 1988) p. 2), when multipart items contain a publisher's number that represents the numbers of the individual items in truncated form, it is not to be transcribed as it appears. Hence, such truncated set numbers should not be put into 028 fields nor be transcribed in a 500 field.

In addition to individual numbers on labels, container has: "1102/3".

In OCLC, this 028 field:

```
028 02   1102--1103 ‡b IPAM Records
```

indexes both numbers and generates this note:

```
500      IPAM Records: 1102--1003.
```

In RLIN, separate 028s and an explicitly input 500 field:

```
028 00 1102‡bIPAM Records
028 00 1103‡bIPAM Records
500    IPAM Records: 1102--1103.
```

In WLN, separate PNMs and an explicitly input NOG field:

```
PNMIN‡ab      ‡1102‡IPAM Records
PNMIN‡ab      ‡1103‡IPAM Records
NOG‡a         ‡IPAM Records: 1102-1103.
```

Do not transcribe "1102/3" into 028/PNM or 500/NOG fields in any of the systems.

In addition to individual numbers on labels, container has: "SM 92814/15".

In OCLC, this 028 field:

```
028 02   SM 92814--SM 92815 ‡b Da Camera Magna
```

indexes both numbers and generates this note:

```
500      Da Camera Magna: SM 92814--SM 92815.
```

In RLIN, separate 028s and an explicitly input 500 field:

```
028 00   SM 92814‡bDa Camera Magna
028 00   SM 92815‡bDa Camera Magna
500      Da Camera Magna: SM 92814--SM 92815.
```

In WLN, separate PNMs and an explicitly input NOG field:

```
PNMIN‡ab      ‡SM 92814‡Da Camera Magna
PNMIN‡ab      ‡SM 92815‡Da Camera Magna
NOG‡a         ‡Da Camera Magna: SM 92814--SM 92815.
```

Do not transcribe "SM 92814/15" into 028/PNM or 500/NOG fields in any of the systems.

Matrix Numbers

The input of matrix numbers does not differ greatly from the input of other music publisher numbers. Follow the same multiple publisher number guidelines for multiple matrix numbers. In OCLC and RLIN, when a printing 028 field contains matrix numbers, include the designation "(matrix)" after each number; when the second indicator is set not to generate a printed note, the inclusion of the "(matrix)" designation is optional. Because in WLN the first indicator "M" generates the display constant "Matrix no.:" when the second indicator is set to generate a note, no further action is necessary.

In OCLC, this 028 field:

```
028 12   M40-42491 (matrix)--M40-42492 (matrix) ‡b Melodiˊiˋa
```

indexes both matrix numbers and generates this note:

```
500      Melodiˊiˋa: M40-42491 (matrix)--M40-42492 (matrix).
```

In RLIN, separate 028s and an explicitly input 500 field:

```
028 10   M40-42491‡bMelodiˊiˋa
028 10   M40-42492‡bMelodiˊiˋa
500      Melodiˊiˋa: M40-42491 (matrix)--M40-42492 (matrix).
```

In WLN, separate PNMs and an explicitly input NOG field:

```
PNMMN‡ab      ‡M40-42491‡Melodiˊiˋa
PNMMN‡ab      ‡M40-42492‡Melodiˊiˋa
NOG‡a         ‡Matrix no.: M40-42491--M40-42492 Melodiˊiˋa.
```

In RLIN and OCLC, separate 028s and an explicitly input 500 field:

```
028 10   808-54-A ǂb L. Franklin
028 10   808-54-B ǂb L. Franklin
500      L. Franklin: 808-54-A (matrix)--808-54-B (matrix).
```

In WLN, separate PNMs and an explicitly input NOG field:

```
PNMMNǂab     ǂ808-54-AǂL. Franklin
PNMMNǂab     ǂ808-54-BǂL. Franklin
NOGǂa        ǂMatrix no.: 808-54-A--808-54-B L. Franklin.
```

In RLIN and OCLC, separate 028s and an explicitly input 500 field:

```
028 10   S10-08811(a) ǂb Melodi῀i῀a
028 10   33S-0995(a) ǂb Melodi῀i῀a
028 00   33 S 10-08811-S 0995(a) ǂb Melodi῀i῀a
500      Melodi῀i῀a: S10-08811(a) (matrix), 33S-0995(a)
         (matrix) (on container: 33 S 10-08811-S 0995(a)).
```

In WLN, separate PNMs and an explicitly input NOG field:

```
PNMMNǂab     ǂS10-08811(a)ǂMelodi῀i῀a
PNMMNǂab     ǂ33S-0995(a)ǂMelodi῀i῀a
PNMINǂab     ǂ33 S 10-08811-S 0995(a)Melodi῀i῀a
NOGǂa        ǂMatrix no.: S10-08811(a), 33S-0995(a)
             Melodi῀i῀a (on container: 33 S10-08811-S
             0995(a)).
```

In addition to individual numbers on labels, container has: "S10-16753-4".

In OCLC, this 028 field:

```
028 12   S10-16753 (matrix)--S10-16754 (matrix) ǂb
         Melodi῀i῀a
```

indexes both numbers and generates this note:

```
500      Melodi῀i῀a: S10-16753 (matrix)--S10-16754
         (matrix).
```

In RLIN, separate 028s and an explicitly input 500 field:

```
028 10   S10-16753ǂbMelodi῀i῀a
028 10   S10-16754ǂbMelodi῀i῀a
500      Melodi῀i῀a: S10-16753 (matrix)--S10-16754
         (matrix).
```

In WLN, separate PNMs and an explicitly input NOG field:

```
PNMMN‡ab      ‡S10-16753‡Melodiˊiˋa
PNMMN‡ab      ‡S10-16754‡Melodiˊiˋa
NOG‡a         ‡Matrix no.: S10-16753--S10-16754
              Melodiˊiˋa.
```

Do not transcribe "S10-16753-4" into 028/PNM or 500/NOG field in either system.

Examples — Scores — OCLC

```
028 32   E.P. 13119 ‡b Edition Peters
028 30   5550 ‡b Edition Peters
500      Publisher's no.: Edition Peters Nr. 5550.


028 20   271 ‡b Hoffmeister et Kˮuhnel
500      Reissued from Hoffmeister et Kˮuhnel plates of the 1st ed.
         Pl. no.: 271.


028 22   D.d.T.I.B.N.F.IV ‡b Breitkopf & Hˮartel


028 30   12 0575 07 ‡b Novello
028 30   12 0575 07 01 ‡b Novello
500      Publisher's no.: 12 0575 07 (score), 12 0575 07 01 (parts).


028 30   8441 ‡b Edition Peters
500      "Included in Edition Peters as no. 8441."


028 32   10832-B ‡b Excelsior Music Pub. Co.
028 20   10832-BS ‡b Excelsior Music Pub. Co.
028 20   10832-BA ‡b Excelsior Music Pub. Co.
028 20   10832-BB ‡b Excelsior Music Pub. Co.
500      Pl. no.: 10832-BS (parts: 10832-BA; 10832-BB).


028 30   JWC 55672 A ‡b Chester Music
028 30   55672 A ‡b Chester Music
500      Publisher's no.: JWC 55672 A (on p. 4 of cover: 55672 A).


028 22   G. 5965 Z. ‡b Edizioni G. Zambon


028 22   E.P. 13208 ‡b Edition Peters
028 30   5597 ‡b Edition Peters
500      Publisher's no.: Edition Peters Nr. 5597.


028 22   47633 ‡b G. Schirmer
028 30   Ed. 3367 ‡b G. Schirmer
500      Publisher's no.: Ed. 3367.


028 22   T & J 8001 ‡b Tischer & Jagenberg


028 22   4046 ‡b M.P. Belaieff
028 30   Bel. Nr. 495 ‡b M.P. Belaieff
500      Publisher's no.: Bel. Nr. 495.
```

```
028 22   B. Two Pa. 68 ‡b Boosey & Hawkes


028 20   UE 17191 ‡b Universal Edition
028 20   UE 17191a ‡b Universal Edition
028 20   UE 17191b ‡b Universal Edition
028 20   UE 17191c ‡b Universal Edition
028 30   17191 ‡b Universal Edition
028 30   17191a ‡b Universal Edition
028 30   17191b ‡b Universal Edition
028 30   17191c ‡b Universal Edition
500      Publisher's no.: Universal Edition 17191 (score), 17191a--
         17191c (parts).
500      Pl. no.: UE 17191 (score), 17191a--17191c (parts).


028 32   BP 2021--BP 2022 ‡b Amadeus
```

Examples — Scores — RLIN

```
028 32   E.P. 13119‡bEdition Peters
028 30   5550‡bEdition Peters
500      Publisher's no.: Edition Peters Nr. 5550.


028 20   271‡bHoffmeister et Kühnel
500      Reissued from Hoffmeister et Kühnel plates of the 1st ed.
         Pl. no.: 271.


028 22   D.d.T.I.B.N.F.IV‡bBreitkopf & Härtel


028 30   12 0575 07‡bNovello
028 30   12 0575 07 01‡bNovello
500      Publisher's no.: 12 0575 07 (score), 12 0575 07 01 (parts).


028 30   8441‡bEdition Peters
500      "Included in Edition Peters as no. 8441."


028 32   10832-B‡bExcelsior Music Pub. Co.
028 20   10832-BS‡bExcelsior Music Pub. Co.
028 20   10832-BA‡bExcelsior Music Pub. Co.
028 20   10832-BB‡bExcelsior Music Pub. Co.
500      Pl. no.: 10832-BS (parts: 10832-BA; 10832-BB).


028 30   JWC 55672 A‡bChester Music
028 30   55672 A‡bChester Music
500      Publisher's no.: JWC 55672 A (on p. 4 of cover: 55672 A).


028 22   G. 5965 Z.‡bEdizioni G. Zambon


028 22   E.P. 13208‡bEdition Peters
028 30   5597‡bEdition Peters
500      Publisher's no.: Edition Peters Nr. 5597.


028 22   47633‡bG. Schirmer
028 32   Ed. 3367‡bG. Schirmer
```

```
028 22   T & J 8001‡bTischer & Jagenberg

028 22   4046‡bM.P. Belaieff
028 32   Bel. Nr. 495‡bM.P. Belaieff

028 22   B. Two Pa. 68‡bBoosey & Hawkes

028 22   UE 17191‡bUniversal Edition
028 20   UE 17191a‡bUniversal Edition
028 20   UE 17191b‡bUniversal Edition
028 20   UE 17191c‡bUniversal Edition
028 30   17191‡bUniversal Edition
028 30   17191a‡bUniversal Edition
028 30   17191b‡bUniversal Edition
028 30   17191c‡bUniversal Edition
500      Publisher's no.: Universal Edition 17191 (score), 17191a--
         17191c (parts).
500      Pl. no.: UE 17191 (score), 17191a--17191c (parts).

028 30   BP 2021‡bAmadeus
028 30   BP 2022‡bAmadeus
500      Publisher's no.: BP 2021--BP 2022.
```

Examples — Scores — WLN

```
PNMTR‡ab    ‡E.P. 13119‡Edition Peters
PNMTN‡ab    ‡5550‡Edition Peters
NOG‡a       ‡Publisher's no.: Edition Peters Nr. 5550.

PNMPN‡ab    ‡271‡Hoffmeister et K¨uhnel
NOG‡a       ‡Reissued from Hoffmeister et K¨uhnel plates of the 1st
            ed. Pl. no.: 271.

PNMPR‡ab    ‡D.d.T.I.B.N.F.IV‡Breitkopf & H¨artel

PNMTN‡ab    ‡12 0575 07‡Novello
PNMTN‡ab    ‡12 0575 07 01‡Novello
NOG‡a       ‡Publisher's no.: 12 0575 07 (score), 12 057 07 01
            (parts).

PNMTN‡ab    ‡8441‡Edition Peters
NOG‡a       ‡"Included in Edition Peters as no. 8441."

PNMTR‡ab    ‡10832-B‡Excelsior Music Pub. Co.
PNMPN‡ab    ‡10832-BS‡Excelsior Music Pub. Co.
PNMPN‡ab    ‡10832-BA‡Excelsior Music Pub. Co.
PNMPN‡ab    ‡10832-BB‡Excelsior Music Pub. Co.
NOG‡a       ‡Pl. no.: 10832-BS (parts: 10832-BA; 10832-BB).

PNMTN‡ab    ‡JWC 55672 A‡Chester Music
PNMTN‡ab    ‡55672 A‡Chester Music
NOG‡a       ‡Publisher's no.: JWC 55672 A (on p. 4 of cover: 55672
            A).
```

```
PNMPR‡ab        ‡G. 5965 Z.‡Edizioni G. Zambon

PNMPR‡ab        ‡E.P. 13208‡Edition Peters
PNMTN‡ab        ‡5597‡Edition Peters
NOG‡a           ‡Publisher's no.: Edition Peters Nr. 5597.

PNMPR‡ab        ‡47633‡G. Schirmer
PNMTR‡ab        ‡Ed. 3367‡G. Schirmer

PNMPR‡ab        ‡T & J 8001‡Tischer & Jagenberg

PNMPR‡ab        ‡4046‡M.P. Belaieff
PNMTR‡ab        ‡Bel. Nr. 495‡M.P. Belaieff

PNMPR‡ab        ‡B. Two Pa. 68‡Boosey & Hawkes

PNMPN‡ab        ‡UE 17191‡Universal Edition
PNMPN‡ab        ‡UE 17191a‡Universal Edition
PNMPN‡ab        ‡UE 17191b‡Universal Edition
PNMPN‡ab        ‡UE 17191c‡Universal Edition
PNMTN‡ab        ‡17191‡Universal Edition
PNMTN‡ab        ‡17191a‡Universal Edition
PNMTN‡ab        ‡17191b‡Universal Edition
PNMTN‡ab        ‡17191c‡Universal Edition
NOG‡a           ‡Publisher's no.: Universal Edition 17191 (score),
                17191a--17191c (parts).
NOG‡a           ‡Pl. no.: UE 17191 (score), 17191a--17191c (parts).

PNMTN‡ab        ‡BP 2021‡Amadeus
PNMTN‡ab        ‡BP 2022‡Amadeus
NOG‡a           ‡Publisher's no.: BP 2021--BP 2022.
```

Examples — Sound Recordings — OCLC

```
028 00   KZ 1068a ‡b Pacifica Radio Archive
028 00   KZ 1068b ‡b Pacifica Radio Archive
500      Pacifica Radio Archive: KZ 1068a--KZ 1068b.


028 02   01-A-XI ‡b Etnos


028 00   MDP I ‡b California Continuing Education of the Bar
028 00   MDP II ‡b California Continuing Education of the Bar
028 00   MDP III ‡b California Continuing Education of the Bar
028 00   MDP IV ‡b California Continuing Education of the Bar
500      California Continuing Education of the Bar: MDP I--MDP IV.


028 00   A 29 ‡b Nose & Toes
028 00   B 29 ‡b Nose & Toes
028 00   C 29 ‡b Nose & Toes
500      Nose & Toes: A 29--C 29.


028 02   MHS 4373 ‡b Musical Heritage Society
028 00   71179 ‡b Erato
500      "Licensed from Erato 71179 [1980]."
```

```
028 02   MFCD 802 ‡b Mobile Fidelity Sound Lab
028 00   QTV-S 34595 ‡b Turnabout
500      Reissue: Turnabout QTV-S 34595 (analog disc).


028 00   FSM 53 416 aud ‡b Audite
028 00   FSM 53 417 aud ‡b Audite
500      Audite: FSM 53 416 aud--FSM 53 417 aud.


028 10   S10-05435—S10-05436 ‡b Melodi⌣i⌣a
028 00   33 S 10-05435-6 ‡b Melodi⌣i⌣a
500      Melodi⌣i⌣a: S10-05435 (matrix)--S10-05436 (matrix) (on
         container: 33 S 10-05435-6).


028 02   SST-0120, SST-0122 ‡b Sound-Star-Ton


028 02   6514 221 ‡b Philips
028 00   7337 221 ‡b Philips
500      Issued also on cassette: 7337 221.


028 02   4 (RPL 2410--RPL 2412) ‡b Replica


028 00   27 836 XCK ‡b Eurodisc
028 00   27 834 XK ‡b Eurodisc
028 00   27 835 XK ‡b Eurodisc
500      Eurodisc: 27 836 XCK (27 834 XK--27 835 XK).


028 02   1416 2781--1416 2783 ‡b Supraphon
```

Examples — Sound Recordings — RLIN

```
028 00 KZ 1068a‡bPacifica Radio Archive
028 00 KZ 1068b‡bPacifica Radio Archive
500    Pacifica Radio Archive: KZ 1068a--KZ 1068b.


028 02 01-A-XI‡bEtnos


028 00 MDP I‡bCalifornia Continuing Education of the Bar
028 00 MDP II‡bCalifornia Continuing Education of the Bar
028 00 MDP III‡bCalifornia Continuing Education of the Bar
028 00 MDP IV‡bCalifornia Continuing Education of the Bar
500    California Continuing Education of the Bar: MDP I--MDP IV.


028 00 A 29‡bNose & Toes
028 00 B 29‡bNose & Toes
028 00 C 29‡bNose & Toes
500    Nose & Toes: A 29--C 29.


028 02 MHS 4373‡bMusical Heritage Society
028 00 71179‡bErato
500    "Licensed from Erato 71179 [1980]."


028 02 MFCD 802‡bMobile Fidelity Sound Lab
028 00 QTV-S 34595‡bTurnabout
500    Reissue: Turnabout QTV-S 34595 (analog disc).
```

```
028 00 FSM 53 416 aud‡bAudite
028 00 FSM 53 417 aud‡bAudite
500    Audite: FSM 53 416 aud--FSM 53 417 aud.


028 10 S10-05435‡bMelodiˊiˋa
028 10 S10-05436‡bMelodiˊiˋa
028 00 33 S 10-05435-6‡bMelodiˊiˋa
500    Melodiˊiˋa: S10-05435 (matrix)--S10-05436 (matrix) (on
       container: 33 S 10-05435-6).


028 00 SST-0120‡bSound-Star-Ton
028 00 SST-0122‡bSound-Star-Ton
500    Sound-Star-Ton: SST-0120, SST-0122.


028 02 6514 221‡bPhilips
028 00 7337 221‡bPhilips
500    Issued also on cassette: 7337 221.


028 00 4‡bReplica
028 00 RPL 2410‡bReplica
028 00 RPL 2411‡bReplica
028 00 RPL 2412‡bReplica
500    Replica: 4 (RPL 2410--RPL 2412).


028 00 27 836 XCK‡bEurodisc
028 00 27 834 XK‡bEurodisc
028 00 27 835 XK‡bEurodisc
500    Eurodisc: 27 836 XCK (27 834 XK--27 835 XK).


028 00 1416 2781‡bSupraphon
028 00 1416 2782‡bSupraphon
028 00 1416 2783‡bSupraphon
500    Supraphon: 1416 2781--1416 2783.
```

Examples — Sound Recordings — WLN

```
PNMIN‡ab      ‡KZ 1068a‡Pacifica Radio Archive
PNMIN‡ab      ‡KZ 1068b‡Pacifica Radio Archive
NOG‡a         ‡Pacifica Radio Archive: KZ 1068a--KZ 1068b.


PNMIR‡ab      ‡01-A-XI‡Etnos


PNMIN‡ab      ‡MDP I‡California Continuing Education of the Bar
PNMIN‡ab      ‡MDP II‡California Continuing Education of the Bar
PNMIN‡ab      ‡MDP III‡California Continuing Education of the Bar
PNMIN‡ab      ‡MDP IV‡California Continuing Education of the Bar
NOG‡a         ‡California Continuing Education of the Bar: MDP I--MDP
              IV.


PNMIN‡ab      ‡A 29‡Nose & Toes
PNMIN‡ab      ‡B 29‡Nose & Toes
PNMIN‡ab      ‡C 29‡Nose & Toes
NOG‡a         ‡Nose & Toes: A 29--C 29.
```

```
PNMIR‡ab        ‡MHS 4373‡Musical Heritage Society
PNMIN‡ab        ‡71179‡Erato
NOG‡a           ‡"Licensed from Erato 71179 [1980]."

PNMIR‡ab        ‡MFCD 802‡Mobile Fidelity Sound Lab
PNMIN‡ab        ‡QTV-S 34595‡Turnabout
NOG‡a           ‡Reissue: Turnabout QTV-S 34595 (analog disc).

PNMIN‡ab        ‡FSM 53 416 aud‡Audite
PNMIN‡ab        ‡FSM 53 417 aud‡Audite
NOG‡a           ‡Audite: FSM 53 416 aud--FSM 53 417 aud.

PNMMN‡ab        ‡S10-05435‡Melodi⌢i⌣a
PNMMN‡ab        ‡S10-05436‡Melodi⌢i⌣a
PNMMN‡ab        ‡33 S 10-05435-6‡Melodi⌢i⌣a
NOG‡a           ‡aMatrix no.: S10-05435--S10--05436 Melodi⌢i⌣a (on
                container: 33 S 10-05435-6).

PNMIN‡ab        ‡SST-0120‡Sound-Star-Ton
PNMIN‡ab        ‡SST-0122‡Sound-Star-Ton
NOG‡a           ‡Sound-Star-Ton: SST-0120, SST-0122.

PNMIR‡ab        ‡6514 221‡Philips
PNMIN‡ab        ‡7337 221‡Philips
NOG‡a           ‡Issued also on cassette: 7337 221.

PNMIN‡ab        ‡4‡Replica
PNMIN‡ab        ‡RPL 2410‡Replica
PNMIN‡ab        ‡RPL 2411‡Replica
PNMIN‡ab        ‡RPL 2412‡Replica
NOG‡a           ‡Replica: 4 (RPL 2410--RPL 2412).

PNMIN‡ab        ‡27 836 XCK‡Eurodisc
PNMIN‡ab        ‡27 834 XK‡Eurodisc
PNMIN‡ab        ‡27 835 XK‡Eurodisc
NOG‡a           ‡Eurodisc: 27 836 XCK (27 834 XK--27 835 XK).

PNMIN‡ab        ‡1416 2781‡Supraphon
PNMIN‡ab        ‡1416 2782‡Supraphon
PNMIN‡ab        ‡1416 2783‡Supraphon
NOG‡a           ‡Supraphon: 1416 2781--1416 2783.
```

033 Date and Place of Capture/Finding

UFBD: 033 (A/A) (Rep)
OCLC: 033 (O/O) (Rep)
RLIN: 033 (NR) (Rep)
WLN: CAP (NR) (Rep)
MOIM: 033 (Rep)

For sound recordings, information on the date(s) and place(s) that the sound initially was captured (recording session, concert, lecture, conference, etc.) is coded in the 033 field. The same information should appear elsewhere in the record in natural language form, usually in a 518 note, but sometimes in the title, other title information, or other notes.

How the dates and places of a recording are presented in the 518 and other areas helps determine whether a single 033 field or multiple 033 fields are created. Use a single 033 field when:

- There is a single work

```
033 0    19770124 ‡b 4144 ‡c S44
518      Address recorded on Jan. 24, 1977, at the thirteenth Nobel
         Conference held at Gustavus Adolphus College.
```

- There are multiple works, but the date and place of each work is not specifically identified

```
033 2    197906-- ‡a 198010-- ‡b 6954 ‡c S7
518      Recorded between June 1979 and Oct. 1980, principally in
         Stockholm.
```

```
033 1    19790817 ‡a 19790823 ‡a 19790917 ‡a 19790923 ‡b 3804 ‡c N4
518      Recorded Aug. 17 and 23, and Sept. 17 and 23, 1979, at
         Soundmixers, New York City.
```

- There is an approximate date or a range of dates

```
033 1    1945---- ‡a 19461014
518      Recorded early 1945 (1st-5th, 8th-10th, 12th, 14th, 16th
         works) and Oct. 14, 1946 (6th-7th, 11th, 13th, 15th
         works).
```

```
033 2    19801211 ‡a 19801219 ‡b 6694 ‡c L5
518      Recorded Dec. 11-19, 1980, in the Igreja de Nossa Senhora
         das Merc´es, Lisbon.
```

- A single place of recording is implied, but not stated explicitly

```
033      ‡b 6524 ‡c W3
518      Recorded by Polskie Nagrania, Warsaw, Poland.
```

```
033      ‡b 6004 ‡c A5
511 0    Feike Asma playing the organ in the Old Church in
         Amsterdam.
```

Use multiple 033 fields when:

- There is more than one major work and different dates and/or places are specified for each

```
033        ǂb 4034 ǂc D2
033        ǂb 3804 ǂc S9
033        ǂb 4144 ǂc S4
033        ǂb 3824 ǂc P6
518        The 1st work recorded in Caruth Auditorium, Southern
           Methodist University; the 2nd work recorded at Crouse
           College, Syracuse University; the 3rd work recorded at
           St. Catherine's College, St. Paul; the 4th work recorded
           in Carnegie Music Hall, Pittsburgh.
```

```
033 0      198111-- ǂb 5834 ǂc P3
033 0      198010-- ǂb 5834 ǂc P3
518        The 1st work recorded Nov. 1981 in 'Eglise Notre-Dame du
           Liban, Paris; the 2nd in Oct. 1981 in Studio 103, Radio
           France, Paris.
```

- When the relationships of dates and places are too complex to convey in a single 033 field

```
033        ǂb 5834 ǂc S9
033 0      1982---- ǂb 6044 ǂc L8
518        Recorded on the Silbermann organ in Saint Pierre-le-Jeune,
           Strassburg (v. 1), and on the Metzler organ in the
           Jesuitenkirche, Lucerne during the summer of 1982 (v. 3).
```

Indicators

The *first indicator* is coded according to the type of date information found in the subfield ǂa.

OCLC & RLIN	WLN	
[blank]	**[blank]**	**No date information**

When there is no information concerning the date of the recording, that is, when there is no subfield ǂa, the first indicator is blank

0	**S**	**Single date**

Any single date, whether year-month-day, year-month, or year alone receives the first indicator "0" (zero) or "s"

1	**M**	**Multiple single dates**

More than one single date is assigned first indicator "1" or "M"; consider two consecutive dates as multiple single dates

2	**R**	**Range of dates**

When the recording dates cover a span of more than two consecutive days and the individual dates are either unknown or too numerous to specify, use code "2" or "R" for the first indicator

The *second indicator* is blank.

Subfields

‡a   **Date of capture/finding**

The actual or approximate date(s) of a recording, when known, are coded in subfield ‡a, in the eight-character format YYYYMMDD (year, month, day). Any part of the date not known is represented by substituting hyphens for the unknown digits; if no date is known, do not use subfield ‡a. For multiple single dates and dates in a range, separate subfields ‡a are used.

```
033  1    19380704 ‡a 19110504 ‡a 1932----
518       The 1st-2nd selections recorded at a testimonial dinner
          in honor of Cohan's 60th birthday, July 4, 1938; the
          4th-7th are studio recordings from May 4, 1911; the
          motion picture excerpts are from 1932.
```

```
033  2    1950---- ‡a 1955----
518       Recorded in the early 1950's.
```

```
033  0    197511-- ‡b 5754 ‡c L7
518       Recorded Nov. 1975, St. George the Martyr, Holborn,
          London.
```

‡b   **Geographic classification area code**

The place of recording, either specified or implied, is represented in subfield ‡b by the four-to-six-digit numeric code derived from the latest edition of the *Library of Congress Classification—Class G* (Geography), by omitting the initial letter "G" from the appropriate class number found in the range G3190-G9980. When the place is unknown, omit subfield ‡b; if more than one place is associated with the recording, subfield ‡b may be repeated.

```
033  2    1972---- ‡a 1977---- ‡b 8710
245 00    Anthologie de la musique des pygm´ees Aka ‡h [sound
          recording] : ‡b Empire centrafricain.
500       Field recordings, notes, and photos. by Simha Arom.
518       Recorded 1972-1977.
```

```
033       ‡b 5750
518       Recorded in England.
```

```
033  2    19490117 ‡a 19540302 ‡b 4364 ‡c L8 ‡b 4364 ‡c S5
518       Recorded between Jan. 17, 1949, and Mar. 2, 1954,
          principally in Los Angeles or San Francisco.
```

‡c   **Geographic classification subarea code**

Alphanumeric Cutter numbers for a geographic region, political subdivision, or natural feature that is part of the geographic area coded in subfield ‡b are contained in subfield ‡c. These codes are derived from the latest edition of the *Library of Congress Classification—Class G* (Geography) and the expanded Cutter number lists for place names; those for the United States also are published in *Geographic Cutters*. Each code is in a separate subfield ‡c; if more than one place is associated with the recording, subfield ‡c may be repeated, but each subfield ‡c must directly follow its associated subfield ‡b. Omit the decimal point preceding the Cutter number.

```
033       ‡b 4164 ‡c S4
518       Recorded in Powell Symphony Hall, St. Louis.
```

```
033 2    1919----  ‡a 1931----  ‡b 6299 ‡c B3 ‡b 5754 ‡c H3 ‡b
         5754 ‡c L7 ‡b 5834 ‡c P3
518      Recorded 1919-1931, Berlin; Hayes, Middlesex; London;
         and Paris.


033 0    1980----  ‡b 6563 ‡c C9
518      Recorded in 1980 at the Iglesia de San Miguel, Cuenca,
         during the XIX Semana de Música Religiosa.
```

Following the guidelines in the *Library of Congress Classification—Class G*, regions (in this context, colleges and universities are considered regions, for example) and political subdivisions within larger jurisdictions may also be specified. These further subdivisions are placed after a colon (:) and the number "2", following the Cutter number in subfield ‡c.

```
033 2    1981----  ‡a 1983----  ‡b 4364 ‡c S4:2S5
518      Recorded in the music building on the campus of San
         Diego State University, San Diego, Calif., between
         1981 and 1983.
```

Examples

```
033      ‡b 4334 ‡c T4:2A7
518      Recorded in the Grammage Center for the Performing Arts,
         Arizona State University, Tempe, Ariz.


033      ‡b 4034 ‡c A9 ‡b 4104 ‡c C6
518      Recorded at Cedar Creek Recording, Austin, Tex., and
         Streeterville Recording Studios, Chicago.


033 0    19750725 ‡b 8090
518      Recorded July 25, 1975, at Notoyuden, Java.


033 0    19500523
518      "Recorded live" May 23, 1950.


033 0    1979----  ‡b 6954 ‡c S7
518      Recorded in Studio 2, Radiohuset, Stockholm, at various times
         during 1979.


033 1    19800922 ‡a 19810504 ‡b 4034 ‡c D2
518      Recorded Sept. 22, 1980, and May 4, 1981, Cliff Temple
         Baptist Church, Dallas.


033 2    197401--  ‡a 197404--  ‡b 8310
518      Recorded in the Sudan, Jan.-Apr. 1974.


033 1    19810406 ‡a 19810407 ‡b 6514 ‡c P7
033 0    19810905 ‡b 6514 ‡c P7
518      Recorded Apr. 6-7, 1981 (1st-2nd works) and Sept. 5, 1981
         (3rd work) in the Supraphon studio at the House of Artists,
         Prague.
```

```
033  2    19481018 ‡a 19481108 ‡b 3804 ‡c N4
033  0    19481229 ‡b 3814 ‡c C32
518       Recorded between Oct. 18 and Nov. 8, 1948, at the Hotel New
          Yorker, New York City, and Dec. 29, 1948, at the Meadowbrook,
          Cedar Grove, N.J.


033  0    19500120 ‡b 6299 ‡c B3
033  0    19570719 ‡b 6299 ‡c C6
518       "Recorded live" Jan. 20, 1950, Berlin (op. 90) and July 19,
          1957, Cologne (op. 107).


033  1    19750817 ‡a 19771022 ‡b 8964 ‡c A2
033  1    19840805 ‡a 19840806 ‡b 8964 ‡c A2
518       Recorded Aug. 17, 1975, Oct. 22, 1977, and Aug. 5-6, 1984, in
          Adelaide, S. Aust.
```

041   Language Code

UFBD: 041 (NRep) (A/O)
OCLC: 041 (NRep) (R/O)
RLIN: 041 (NRep) (NR)
WLN: LAN (NRep) (A)
MOIM: 041 (NRep)

When the single code in the Language fixed field element is insufficient to convey all the information concerning the language content of a score or sound recording, the 041 field offers further detail in coded form. Use the 041 field when an item:

- is multilingual
- is a translation or contains a translation
- has accompanying material such as summaries, performance instructions, librettos, prefaces, etc.

Languages are represented by three-character lowercase alphabetic codes as found in the *USMARC Code List for Languages;* spaces do not separate multiple codes in the same subfield.

Indicators

The *first indicator* specifies whether or not the main content of the item itself is or includes a translation.

OCLC & RLIN	WLN	
0	**[blank]**	**Item is not a translation or does not include a translation**

Disregard program notes, commentary, prefaces, etc., regardless of their extent, when considering the presence of a translation. For example, a recording in the original language accompanied by a libretto that includes a translation is not considered a translation.

1	**X**	**Item is or includes a translation**

Ordinarily, accompanying material is disregarded when determining whether an item is a translation. However, if printed music includes a translation of a vocal text printed as separate text, consider the item to include a translation and code the 041 first indicator as "1" or "x". The work in the original language need not have been published for a translation to be coded as such. Texts that have been adapted extensively as well as translated are not considered translations.

The *second indicator* is blank.

Subfields

‡a   **Language code of text/soundtrack or separate title**

The language(s) of the text of printed or manuscript music are coded in subfield ‡a. The first language must correspond to the language code in the fixed field unless it contains blanks ("ƀƀƀ") or "N/A". When multiple languages are involved, record the codes in the order of their predominance in the item, or if that cannot be determined, alphabetically. When more than six languages are involved, record only the language of the title (or the first title when there is more than one) and the code "mul" (for multiple languages). When a translation is present, code subfield ‡a for all languages represented in the item, translation(s) and original(s). The code(s) for any original languages or intermediate translations also are recorded in subfield ‡h. Subfield ‡a is *not* used for sound recordings; instead use subfield ‡d for the sung or spoken text of a recording.

```
Language fixed field: eng
041 1    eng ‡h lat
500      English words, in part translated from Latin.
```

Language fixed field: dut
```
041 0    dutengger
500      Dutch (1st-2nd songs), English (3rd, 5th songs), and
         German (4th song) words.
```

Language fixed field: esk
```
041 0    esk ǂg eng
500      Eskimo words, accompanying material in English.
```

Language fixed field: eng
```
041 0    engmul
500      Words in English and other languages.
```
         [Total number of languages exceeds six]

ǂb   **Language code of summary or abstract/overprinted title or subtitle**

When the language(s) of summaries differ from that of the main text, subfield ǂb contains the code(s) for the summary language(s) in alphabetical order. For sound recordings, use subfield ǂb when accompanying material includes:

- summaries of nonmusical contents
- summaries (not translations) of the texts of songs or other vocal works

For sound recordings, subfield ǂb should follow a subfield ǂd or a subfield ǂh associated with a subfield ǂd.

Language fixed field: ger
```
041 0    ger ǂb eng ǂg eng
```
         [German opera with introduction and synopsis in English]

Language fixed field: fre
```
041 0    ǂd fre ǂb freengger ǂg freengger
500      Program notes ... and synopsis in French, English, and
         German laid in container.
```
         [Opera sung in French]

ǂd   **Language code of sung or spoken text**

Codes for the sung or spoken content of a sound recording are recorded in subfield ǂd. The first language in subfield ǂd must correspond to the language code in the fixed field unless it contains blanks ("ƀƀƀ") or "N/A". Subfield ǂd is *not* used for scores; instead use subfield ǂa for the textual language(s) of printed and manuscript music.

Language fixed field: ger
```
041 0    ǂd gerrus
500      Sung in German (Strauss) and Russian (Tcha¨ikowsky).
```

Language fixed field: cze
```
041 1    ǂd cze ǂh freitarus
500      Opera excerpts sung in Czech.
```
         [Originally in French, Italian, and Russian]

Language fixed field: ita

041 0	‡d ita ‡e itaengfreger ‡h ita ‡g engfreger
500	Program notes ... in English, French, and German, and texts with English, French, and German translations ... laid in container.

[Recording of Italian madrigals]

Language fixed field: run

041 0	‡d run ‡g engfre
500	Sung in Kirundi.
500	Program notes in English and French on container.

‡e   Language code of librettos

The language(s) of the vocal/textual content of the score or sound recording printed as text, either as part of the item or as accompanying material, are coded in subfield ‡e. Despite its name, this subfield is not limited to librettos, but also includes song texts, narrations, scripts, etc., not covered in subfield ‡g.

Language fixed field: ita

041 0	‡d ita ‡e itaengfreger ‡h ita
500	Texts with English, French, and German translations.

[Italian madrigals]

Language fixed field: fre

041 0	frespa ‡e engfrespa ‡h frespa ‡g eng
500	Commentary (includes "Sources and sigla" and French and Spanish texts with English translations) ...

Language fixed field: ita

041 0	‡d ita ‡e ita ‡g engita ‡h ita
500	Program notes in Italian ... with English translation, and libretto in Italian ...

[Recording of an opera in Italian]

‡g   Language code of accompanying material other than librettos

Codes for the languages of program notes, performance instructions, prefaces, commentaries, etc., are entered in subfield ‡g. Summaries are coded in subfield ‡b; librettos and other text transcriptions are coded in subfield ‡e.

Language fixed field: ♭♭♭ (RLIN & WLN); N/A (OCLC)

041 0	‡g engfre
500	Program notes in English and French ...

[Instrumental work]

Language fixed field: ssa

041 0	‡d ssa ‡e ssaengger ‡h ssa ‡g engger
500	Program notes ... in English and German, texts in Mangbetu with translations, and bibliography ...

Language fixed field: raj

041 0	‡d raj ‡g engfre ‡h fre
500	Traditional songs and instrumental music.
500	Program notes in English and French on container.

[Songs sung in Rajasthani]

‡h   **Language code of original and/or intermediate translations of text**

When a sound recording, manuscript, or printed score or any accompanying material for any of these items is or includes a translation, subfield ‡h contains the code(s) for the original language(s). Subfield ‡h may be repeated in score and sound recording records immediately after any associated subfields ‡a, ‡d, ‡e, or ‡g. Note that if any subfield ‡h relates to a subfield ‡a (for scores) or ‡d (for sound recordings), the first indicator should be "1" (OCLC & RLIN) or "X" (WLN); if subfields ‡h relate only to subfields ‡e or ‡g, the first indicator should be "0" (OCLC & RLIN) or "blank" (WLN). Subfield ‡h may repeat codes entered in its related subfield ‡a, ‡d, ‡e, or ‡g. Because a subfield ‡h has meaning only in relation to the preceding subfield, it never appears alone. When an item is known to be or contain a translation but the original language is not known, subfield ‡h contains the code "und." If an intermediate translation is involved, enter the intermediate language(s) before the original language(s) in the subfield ‡h.

Language fixed field: ita
```
041 1    ‡d ita ‡h fre ‡e ita ‡h fre
```
> *[Recording in Italian of an opera originally in French, accompanied by an Italian translation of the libretto]*

Language fixed field: ger
```
041 1    gerfre ‡h fre ‡e gerfre ‡h fre
500      The players recite texts in German and French from
         Rimbaud's Illuminations.
500      Words printed as texts on p. 2.
```

Language fixed field: lat
```
041 0    lat ‡e lateng ‡h lat
500      Latin words, also printed as text with English
         translations.
```

Language fixed field: ⱫⱫⱫ (RLIN & WLN); N/A (OCLC)
```
041 0    ‡g eng ‡h spa
```
> *[Program notes in English translated from the Spanish]*

Language fixed field: eng
```
041 1    eng ‡h und
```
> *[Text is known to be an English translation, but the original language cannot be determined]*

Examples

Language fixed field: mul
```
041 1    mul ‡e eng ‡h mul
500      Includes original texts and English translations of
         paraphrases of each song.
```

Language fixed field: ara
```
041 0    ara ‡e ara ‡g ger
```
> *[Arabic songs; words printed as text with commentary in German]*

Language fixed field: eng
```
041 1    engrus ‡h rus ‡g eng
245      ... with English and Russian text ...
500      English translations by Robert Hess.
500      Foreword in English.
```

Language fixed field: ita
```
041 1    itaeng ǂh ita ǂb eng
245      ... vocal score (Italian and English) ...
500      Synopsis on 3rd prelim. p.
```
[Italian opera]

Language fixed field: ger
```
041 0    gerlateng ǂe gerlateng
500      Principally German words, with some in Latin or English, from
         the Bible and other sources.
500      Words printed as text ...
```

Language fixed field: ita
```
041 0    ǂd ita ǂe itaengfreger ǂh ita ǂg gerengfreita ǂh ger
500      Program notes in German ... with English, French, and Italian
         translations, and Italian words of the vocal works with
         English, French, and German translations.
```
[Vocal works sung in Italian]

Language fixed field: ♭♭♭ (RLIN); N/A (OCLC)
```
041 0    ǂg spa ǂb engfre
500      Each container includes a booklet with notes in Spanish on
         the instruments, bibliographies, and summaries in English and
         French ...
```
[Recordings of instrumental folk music from Argentina]

Language fixed field: crp
```
041 0    ǂd crpfre ǂe crpfre ǂh crpfre ǂg fre
500      Sung in Creole and French.
500      Words of the vocal music, with French translations,
         transcriptions of the music, and ethnographic information ...
         bound in container.
```

Language fixed field: alb
```
041 0    ǂd albgreroascrtur ǂe albmul ǂh albgreroascrtur ǂg engger
500      Program notes ... in English and German, texts in Greek,
         Albanian, Serbo-Croatian, Turkish, and Aromanian with English
         and German translations, and bibliography ... inserted in
         container.
```

Language fixed field: fre
```
041 0    ǂd fregeritarusund
500      Principally songs.
```
[Sung in French, German, Italian, and Russian; includes a wordless vocalise]

Language fixed field: swe
```
041 1    ǂd swe ǂh rusger ǂe swe ǂh rusger ǂg engswe ǂh swe
500      Songs, sung in Swedish.
500      Program notes in English and Swedish ... and texts in
         Swedish, bound and inserted in container.
```
[Songs originally in Russian and German]

045   Time Period of Content

UFBD: 045 (O/O) (NRep)
OCLC: 045 (O/O) (NRep)
RLIN: 045 (NR) (NRep)
WLN: CRO (NR) (NRep)
MOIM: 045 (NRep)

Field 045 contains a formatted date and/or a code representing the year (exact, approximate, or a range) or the period during which a work was composed. This allows a chronological approach to stylistic periods of composition. When exact dates of composition cannot be determined, an approximate date or range of dates may be used; such dates may be based on the composer's dates or an estimate of her or his productive years. Catalogers need not feel obligated to search beyond the item in hand to determine such information. The date(s) and time period recorded here should not be confused with the date of publication (recorded in field 260 subfield ‡c and the fixed field element for dates) or any sound recording capture date (field 033).

Indicators

The *first indicator* is coded for the presence or absence of subfield ‡b or ‡c and, given the presence of either one, the kind of time period it represents.

OCLC & RLIN	*WLN*	
[blank]	[blank]	**Subfield ‡b and ‡c not present**

Neither subfield ‡b nor ‡c is present; instead, only a subfield ‡a containing a time period code is present

0	S	**Single date/time**

Either subfield ‡b or ‡c is present and contains a single date

1	M	**Multiple single dates/times**

Multiple subfields ‡b and/or ‡c are present, each containing a known individual date

2	R	**Range of dates/times**

Two subfields ‡b and/or ‡c are present, representing a range of dates

The *second indicator* is blank.

Subfields

‡a   **Time period code**

A four-character alphanumeric code is devised to represent the period of composition: the first two characters for the earliest period, the last two for the latest. If a single two-character code suffices to cover the entire period, repeat the code to create a full four-character code. For B.C. dates, the lowercase alphabetic character represents the millennium and the digit represents the century; when the century is unknown, substitute a hyphen for the digit. For A.D. dates, the lowercase alphabetic character represents the century and the digit represents the decade; when the decade is unknown, substitute a hyphen for the digit. If more than one four-character code applies, each one is input in a separate, repeatable subfield ‡a.

B.C. Time Period Code Table

Code	Time period	Code	Time period
a0	before 2999	c5	1499-1400
b0	2999-2900	c6	1399-1300
b1	2899-2800	c7	1299-1200
b2	2799-2700	c8	1199-1100
b3	2699-2600	c9	1099-1000
b4	2599-2500	d0	999-900
b5	2499-2400	d1	899-800
b6	2399-2300	d2	799-700
b7	2299-2200	d3	699-600
b8	2199-2100	d4	599-500
b9	2099-2000	d5	499-400
c0	1999-1900	d6	399-300
c1	1899-1800	d7	299-200
c2	1799-1700	d8	199-100
c3	1699-1600	d9	99-1
c4	1599-1500		

A.D. Time Period Code Table
(Add 0, 1, 2, ... 9 to each letter for the decade)

Code	Time period	Code	Time period
e	1-99	p	1100-1199
f	100-199	q	1200-1299
g	200-299	r	1300-1399
h	300-399	s	1400-1499
i	400-499	t	1500-1599
j	500-599	u	1600-1699
k	600-699	v	1700-1799
l	700-799	w	1800-1899
m	800-899	x	1900-1999
n	900-999	y	2000-2099
o	1000-1099		

The convention for expressing a century A.D. is to repeat the alphabetic code and hyphen (for instance, 20th century "x-x-") rather than coding for the first and last decades of the century (x0x9).

```
045      v-v-
245 00   Musiche organistiche del Settecento italiano / ‡c a
         cura di Ennio Cominetti.
650  0   Music ‡z Italy ‡y 18th century.

045      s-s-
245 00   Fifteenth-century liturgical music.

045      x4x5
```
[A collection of works composed during the 1940s and 1950s]

```
045      x8x8
```
[A collection of works composed during the 1980s]

```
045       t-t-  ‡a w-w-
650   0   Music ‡z Netherlands ‡y 16th century.
650   0   Music ‡z Netherlands ‡y 19th century.
```

Lacking more specific information about the date of a particular work, a cataloger may estimate the active compositional years of a composer (commonly by adding 20 years to the birth date).

```
045       w7x4
100 10    Smyth, Ethel, ‡d 1858-1944.
```

For music materials, the Library of Congress does not use subfield ‡a.

‡b   Formatted 9999 B.C. through A.D. time period

A specific time period formatted as YYYYMMDDHH and prefaced with an indication of the era is input in subfield ‡b. If subfield ‡b is used, the era and year (that is, the first five characters) must be present; month, day, and hour are optional. If the first five characters cannot be determined, use only the subfield ‡a time period code.

- Era is expressed as a single alphabetic code: "c" for B.C., "d" for A.D.
- Year is four digits, right justified with leading zeroes where needed (0000-9999)
- Month is two digits, right justified with leading zero where needed (01-12)
- Day is two digits, right justified with leading zero where needed (01-31)
- Hour is two digits, right justified with zero where needed, using the 24-hour clock (00-23)

When more than one formatted date is needed to express the appropriate multiple dates (first indicator "1" or "M") or range of dates (first indicator "2" or "R"), each is recorded in a separate subfield ‡b.

```
045 0    ‡b d1983
245 00   Fantasy for harpsichord (1983) / ‡c Ellen Taaffe
         Zwilich.
```

```
045 1    ‡b d1924 ‡b d1943 ‡b d1923 ‡b d1958
245 10   Franz¨osische Fl¨otenmusik des 20. Jahrhunderts ‡h
         [sound recording].
```

```
045 2    ‡b d1700 ‡b d1750
245 00   Oboe sonatas between 1700-1550 ‡h [sound recording].
```

```
045 0    ‡b d1953062917
```
         [Manuscript is dated "5 P.M., June 29, 1953."]

‡c   Formatted pre-9999 B.C. time period

Any formatted time period predating 9999 B.C. is input in subfield ‡c. As many numeric characters as are necessary to represent the year may be input. Subfield ‡c may be repeated. Because little music survives from before 9999 B.C., it is unlikely that this subfield will ever be used in a music-related record.

```
045 2    ‡c 60000000 ‡c 40000000
650   0  Geology, Stratigraphic ‡y Eocene.
```
         [The Eocene epoch is thought to have lasted from about 60 million to about 40 million B.C.]

Examples

```
045      t-t-
650   0  Chansons, Polyphonic ǂy 16th century.


045      w9x7
100  10  Daniels, Mabel W. ǂq (Mabel Wheeler), ǂd 1878-1971.


045      j0s5
245  00  Medieval polyphonic sequences : ǂb an anthology / ǂc
         [compiled] by Bryan Gillingham.


045      x7x8
245  10  Mental sailing ǂh [sound recording] / ǂc Beverly De Fries
         D'Albert.
              [Electronic works from the 1970s and 1980s]


045  0   ǂb d1747
500      Facsim. of the original 1747 ed. supervised by the composer,
         in 3 fascicles (the trio sonata in part format).


045  0   ǂb d198304
245  10  Cityscape #1 : ǂb for two performers / ǂc Netty Simons.
              [Holograph score is dated "April 1983" at end]


045  0   ǂb d19720918
245  10  Pastorale d'hiver : ǂb für fünf Instrumentalisten, 1972 /
         ǂc Robert Suter.


045  0   ǂb d1500
245  10  Occelino ǂh [sound recording] : ǂb Popular music in Italy,
         c1500.


045  1   ǂb d1975 ǂb d1982
245  00  String quartet (1975) / ǂc Sheila Silver. Voices : for string
         quartet (1982) / John Anthony Lennon ǂh [sound recording].


045  1   ǂb d1968 ǂb d1969 ǂb d1973
245  00  Sinfonie Nr. 1 : ǂb Fogli ; Sinfonie Nr. 2 : Ricordanze ;
         Sinfonie Nr. 3 : Menschen-Los ǂh [sound recording] / ǂc
         Wilhelm Killmeyer.
              [Program notes list respective dates of composition]


045  1   ǂb d1926 ǂb d1983
245  10  Rudepoema / ǂc Heitor Villa-Lobos. Under neonlight II : für
         Klavier / Detlev Müuller-Siemens ǂh [sound recording].
              [Program notes list respective dates of composition]


045  1   ǂb d1760 ǂb d1772
245  00  Three concerti ǂh [sound recording] / ǂc Carl Philipp Emanuel
         Bach, Johann Christian Bach.
```

```
045 2    ‡b d1784 ‡b d1786
245 10   Zw¨olf Lieder auf ihrer Reise in Musik gesetzt : ‡b 1784-86 /
         ‡c Maria Theresia von Paradis ; edited by Hidemi Matsushita.


045 2    ‡b d1944 ‡b d1973
505 0    Fanfare to precede the National Anthem in G : (1960) -- The
         right of the line : (1965) -- Fanfare for the Princess Anne :
         (1973) -- High sheriff's fanfare : (1963) -- A salute to
         painting : (1953) -- Research fanfare : (1973) -- Peace
         fanfare for children : (1944) -- Let the people sing :
         (1960).


045 2    ‡b d1442 ‡b d1556
505 0    At the court of Alfonso I and Ferdinand I (1442-1494) ...
         The age of Charles V (1516-1556) ...


045 2    ‡b d1780 ‡b d1820
245 00   Russische Klaviermusik, 1780-1820 / ‡c herausgegeben von
         Alexej Lubimov.
```

047   Form of Composition

UFBD: 047 (O/O) (NRep)
OCLC: 047 (R/O) (NRep)
RLIN: 047 (NR) (NRep)
WLN: FCC (NR) (NRep)
MOIM: 047 (NRep)

When the Form of Composition fixed field contains the code "mu" for multiple forms, the codes for the specific forms and genres are recorded in order of importance in field 047, each in a separate subfield ‡a.

Codes are selected based on the titles and subtitles of the works themselves, on uniform titles, on subject headings, and on contents and other notes in the bibliographic record. The chosen code should apply to an individual work as a whole (that is, code a concerto as "co" and disregard the facts that the first movement might be in sonata form and the finale a rondo; code a suite as "su" and not for its constituent movements).

Use this field *only* when more than one specific code applies to a record. Never list any of the nonspecific codes ("mu" for multiple forms, "nn" for not applicable, "uu" for unknown, and "zz" for other forms of composition) in the 047 field. The list of codes and their definitions appear in the Form of Composition fixed field section (pp. 12-18).

Examples

Subject headings:

```
650  0  Violin and piano music, Arranged.
650  0  Sonatas (Violin and piano)
650  0  Variations (Violin and piano), Arranged.
```

Form of Composition fixed field: mu
```
047     sn ‡a vr
```

Title:

```
245 10  Night music for John Lennon : ‡b (prelude, fugue,
        and chorale) : for large or small orchestra and
        brass quintet concertante / ‡c Lukas Foss.
```

Form of Composition fixed field: mu
```
047     pr ‡a fg ‡a ch
```

Contents:

```
505 0   Rondino, op. 32 / Vieuxtemps. Mazurkas, op. 19 /
        Wieniawski. Finale from E minor concerto /
        Mendelssohn (Eug`ene Ysa¨ye, violin) -- Ave Maria
        / Schubert (Mischa Elman, violin) --
        Zigeunerweisen ; Tarantella ; Zapateado /
        Sarasate (Pablo de Sarasate, violin) -- Minuet in
        G / Beethoven (Maud Powell, violin) -- Hungarian
        dance : no. 1 / Brahms. Prelude in G minor / Bach
        (Joseph Joachim, violin).
```

Form of Composition fixed field: mu
```
047     rd ‡a mz ‡a co ‡a df ‡a mi ‡a pr
```

Note:

```
500     Ragtime music, in part with vocals, composed
        between 1903 and 1920; various arrangers.
```

Subject headings:

```
650  0  Ragtime music.
650  0  Popular music ‡y 1901-1910.
650  0  Popular music ‡y 1911-1920.
```

Form of Composition fixed field: mu
```
047     rg ‡a pp
```

048   Number of Instruments or Voices Code

UFBD: 048 (O/O) (Rep)
OCLC: 048 (O/O) (Rep)
RLIN: 048 (NR) (Rep)
WLN: IVC (NR) (Rep)
MOIM: 048 (Rep)

Information on the medium of performance for a musical composition can appear in numerous places in a bibliographic record: the title, the uniform title, a medium of performance note, a note on the performer(s), or a subject heading. The 048 field provides the same information on medium in coded form, using a two-character alphabetic code. When known, the number of parts is specified by a two-digit number immediately following the voice or instrument code. Within the field, the codes may be recorded in score order (preferably) or any other logical order (the order in which they appear in the title or subtitle, any notes, or subject headings, for example), with any soloists listed first, where possible. The field may be repeated when there are multiple compositions with differing performance forces or when a single composition offers alternative media.

When the performance medium of a work is not stated explicitly and cannot be inferred, it is best not to record a field 048, as subject headings and form of composition codes usually afford as much information and better access. Operas, musical comedies, folk songs, hymns, school songbooks, many popular music recordings, and collections for miscellaneous vocal and/or instrumental forces are among those types for which the medium often is not stated, making a field 048 inappropriate, or is too complex to make a field 048 practical.

It generally is acknowledged that the existing list of codes is limited and heavily weighted toward traditional Western instruments and ensembles. Proposals to broaden the list to include more non-Western, premodern, and ethnic instruments have proven to be cumbersome. In other words, it will not always be possible or desirable to formulate a field 048 for each composition being cataloged. In any case, the USMARC format stipulates that no more than five 048 fields should be input in a record. The "unspecified" codes are used only when a composition itself does not indicate the specific vocal and/or instrumental forces; when those forces have been specified in the work but cannot be determined, use the "unknown" codes. (One curious exception, judging by Library of Congress practice, is the accordion and its family, which always seem to be coded as "unspecified.") The lists of instruments included in the "ethnic" and "other" codes are meant to be suggestive and are by no means exhaustive.

Instruments or Voices Codes

Brass

ba	Horn
bb	Trumpet
bc	Cornet
bd	Trombone
be	Tuba
bf	Baritone
bn	Brass, Unspecified
bu	Brass, Unknown
by	Brass, Ethnic (includes lur, Russian horn, shofar, etc.)
bz	Brass, Other (includes alpenhorn, bugle, cornett, euphonium, fluegelhorn, ophicleide, sackbut, etc.)

Choruses

ca	Mixed
cb	Women's
cc	Men's
cd	Children's
cn	Choruses, Unspecified
cu	Choruses, Unknown
cy	Choruses, Ethnic

Electronic

ea	**Synthesizer**
eb	**Tape**
ec	**Computer**
ed	**Ondes Martinot**
en	**Electronic, Unspecified**
eu	**Electronic, Unknown**
ez	**Electronic, Other** (includes Theremin, Trautonium, etc.)

Keyboard

ka	**Piano**
kb	**Organ**
kc	**Harpsichord**
kd	**Clavichord**
ke	**Continuo**
kf	**Celeste**
kn	**Keyboard, Unspecified**
ku	**Keyboard, Unknown**
ky	**Keyboard, Ethnic**
kz	**Keyboard, Other** (includes harmonium, etc.)

Larger Ensemble

oa	**Full orchestra**
ob	**Chamber orchestra**
oc	**String orchestra**
od	**Band**
oe	**Dance orchestra**
of	**Brass band** (brass with some doubling, with or without percussion)
on	**Larger ensemble, Unspecified**
ou	**Larger ensemble, Unknown**
oy	**Larger ensemble, Ethnic** (includes gamelan, klezmer, etc.)
oz	**Larger ensemble, Other** (includes concertina ensembles, etc.)

Percussion

pa	**Timpani**
pb	**Xylophone**
pc	**Marimba**
pd	**Drum**
pn	**Percussion, Unspecified**
pu	**Percussion, Unknown**
py	**Percussion, Ethnic** (includes mridangam, tabla, etc.)
pz	**Percussion, Other** (includes Jew's harp, vibraphone, etc.)

Strings, Bowed

sa	**Violin**
sb	**Viola**
sc	**Violoncello**
sd	**Double bass**
se	**Viol**
sf	**Viola d'amore**
sg	**Viola da gamba**
sn	**Strings, Bowed, Unspecified**
su	**Strings, Bowed, Unknown**
sy	**Strings, Bowed, Ethnic** (includes hardanger fiddle, hu ch'in, etc.)
sz	**Strings, Bowed, Other** (includes arpeggione, baryton, keyed fiddle, etc.)

Strings, Plucked

ta	**Harp**
tb	**Guitar**
tc	**Lute**
td	**Mandolin**
tn	**Strings, Plucked, Unspecified**
tu	**Strings, Plucked, Unknown**
ty	**Strings, Plucked, Ethnic** (includes balalaika, bouzouki, cheng, dulcimer, koto, vina, yüeh ch'in, etc.)
tz	**Strings, Plucked, Other** (includes banjo, cimbalom, mandola, tambura, theorbo, etc.)

Voices

va	**Soprano**
vb	**Mezzo soprano**
vc	**Alto**
vd	**Tenor**
ve	**Baritone**
vf	**Bass**
vg	**Counter tenor**
vh	**High voice**
vi	**Medium voice**
vj	**Low voice**
vn	**Voices, Unspecified** (includes narrator, speaker, etc.)
vu	**Voices, Unknown**
vy	**Voices, Ethnic**

Woodwinds

wa	**Flute**
wb	**Oboe**
wc	**Clarinet**
wd	**Bassoon**
we	**Piccolo**
wf	**English horn**
wg	**Bass clarinet**
wh	**Recorder**
wi	**Saxophone**
wn	**Woodwinds, Unspecified**
wu	**Woodwinds, Unknown**
wy	**Woodwinds, Ethnic** (includes bagpipes, pipe, ti tzu, etc.)
wz	**Woodwinds, Other** (includes basset horn, crumhorn, flageolet, kazoo, oboe d'amore, shawm, etc.)

Unspecified

zn	**Unspecified instruments** (including accordion, bandonion, etc.)
zu	**Unknown**

A few special cases need further clarification:

- For large ensembles, the numbers following the code are used when more than one such ensemble is called for.

```
048      oa02 ǂa ec
245 10   Evocation d'Ockghem : ǂb f¨ur zwei Orchestergruppen und
         computererzeugtes Zuspielband (1977/8) = for two
         orchestra groups and tape, produced by computer / ǂc
         Irmfried Radauer.
```

- For choruses, the numbers following the code indicate the number of parts into which the chorus is divided; code multiple choruses in separate subfields.

```
048        ǂb vb01 ǂa cb03 ǂa wz01 ǂa wa01 ǂa sa02 ǂa sb01 ǂa sc01
245 10     Psalm of these days I : ǂb mezzo-soprano solo, women's
           chorus, kazoo, flute, and string quartet / ǂc Edwin
           London.
500        Chorus: SMzA.
```

```
048        ǂb ve01 ǂa cd ǂa ca ǂa oa
245 14     Une cantate de No¨el : ǂb for baritone, children's and
           mixed choruses, organ, and orchestra / ǂc Arthur
           Honegger.
```

- Code arrangements for the medium of the work in hand, not for the original forces.

```
048        ǂb bd01 ǂa ka01
245 00     Concerto for tenor trombone and orchestra / ǂc Carlos
           Ch´avez ; reduction for trombone and piano.
```

- Although practice has varied over the years, and instances should be judged individually, LC now is trying to be consistent in considering a voice (or solo voices) with piano (or other solo instrument; piano, 4 hands; or multiple keyboards) accompaniment *regardless of whether it has been reduced from larger forces*, as equals, each coded in subfield ǂa.

```
048        va01 ǂa ka01
048        vb01 ǂa ka01
245 10     Rainer Maria Rilke Lieder ǂh [sound recording] / ǂc Inger
           Wikstr¨om.
650  0     Songs (High voice) with piano.
650  0     Songs (Medium voice) with piano.
```

```
048        vi01 ǂa ka01
245 10     Kindertotenlieder : ǂb f¨ur eine Singstimme mit Klavier /
           ǂc Gustav Mahler.
500        For medium voice and piano; acc. originally for orchestra.
650  0     Songs (Medium voice) with orchestra ǂx Vocal scores with
           piano.
```

```
048        va01 ǂa vc01 ǂa vd01 ǂa vf01 ǂa ka01 ǂa ka01
500        For vocal quartet (SATB) and 2 pianos.
```

For solo voice(s) with two or more instruments (except for multiple keyboards, which are covered in the previous example), code the voice(s) as subfield ǂb.

```
048        ǂb vd01 ǂa wa01 ǂa ka01
500        For tenor, flute, and piano.
```

```
048        ǂb va01 ǂb vd01 ǂb vf01 ǂa wb01 ǂa pz01 ǂa ty01
500        Vocal trios with instrumental ensemble.
```

• Code an unaccompanied solo instrument or voice as a performer (subfield ‡a) rather than as a soloist (subfield ‡b).

```
048        sa01
245 10     Ambitus sonore : ‡b pour violon seul / ‡c Alina
           Piechowska.
650  0     Violin music.
```

• If a single performer plays more than one instrument in a work, code for the principal instrument, if it can be determined; otherwise, code for the first named instrument.

```
048        ‡b vc01 ‡b ve01 ‡a wa02 ‡a wb01 ‡a wf01 ‡a wc01 ‡a wd02 ‡a
           ba02 ‡a pz02 ‡a sa02 ‡a sc02
500        For solo voices (ABar), 2 flutes (1 player doubles on
           piccolo, the other on alto flute), oboe, English horn,
           clarinet, bassoon, contrabassoon, 2 horns, percussion (2
           players), 2 violins, and 2 violoncellos.
```

• For keyboards, code each instrument separately and use the number to indicate the performers on each instrument.

```
048        ka03
048        ka02
245 14     Der Eid des Hippokrates : ‡b f¨ur Klavier zu drei H¨anden
           / ‡c Mauricio Kagel.
500        For 3 pianists, 1 hand each; may also be performed by 2
           pianists.
650  0     Piano music (3 hands) ‡x Scores.

048        kc01 ‡a kc01
245 00     Zwei Duette f¨ur zwei Cembali / ‡c Christoph Schaffrath ;
           herausgegeben von Hugo Ruf.
650  0     Harpsichord music (Harpsichords (2)) ‡x Scores.

048        ka01 ‡a ka01
048        ka02
048        ka01 ‡a ka02
500        The 1st and 5th works are ballets arr. for 2 pianos, 4
           hands; the 2nd work for piano, 4 hands; the 4th work for
           2 pianos, 5 hands.
```

• Code percussion for the number of performers rather than the number of instruments; for all other instruments and voices, code for the number of parts, not for the number of performers.

```
048        pb01
048        pz02
048        pb01 ‡a pz01
505 0      Circulus 1 : Solo f¨ur Xylophon -- Circulus 2 : Solo f¨ur
           Xylophon und Vibraphon -- Circulus 3 : Duo f¨ur Vibraphon
           und Marimbaphon -- Circulus 4 : Duo f¨ur Xylophon und
           Marimbaphon.
```

- For narrated works and monologues with music, code the narrator or speaker as unspecified voice (vn).

```
048       ca04 ‡a vn01 ‡a ta01 ‡a sa02 ‡a sb01 ‡a sc01
048       ca04 ‡a vn01 ‡a ka01 ‡a sa02 ‡a sb01 ‡a sc01
245 10    For a small planet : ‡b for mixed choir, string quartet,
          harp/piano, and recitation, op. 100 / ‡c Knut Nystedt.
```

- Because continuo can comprise one or two or more instruments, omit the number of parts constituting the continuo unless it is specifically noted.

```
048       sa02 ‡a ke
048       wb02 ‡a ke
048       wa02 ‡a ke
245 00    Sonata no. 1 in G for 2 violins (oboes/flutes) and basso
          continuo / ‡c Elisabeth Jacquet de La Guerre ; edited by
          R.P. Block.
500       For 2 violins, 2 oboes, or flutes and continuo; figured
          bass realized for keyboard instrument.
```

Indicators

Both indicators are blank.

Subfields

‡a **Performer or ensemble**

Codes for ensembles, members of ensembles, and unaccompanied soloists are entered as subfields ‡a. The subfield is repeatable, with each individual code in a separate subfield ‡a.

```
048       pz01 ‡a ka01
500       For percussion (1 player) and piano.

048       sa01
245 10    Threnody : ‡b for solo violin / ‡c David Sheinfeld.

048       oa
245 10    Grisaille : ‡b for orchestra / ‡c Barbara Kolb.

048       wa01 ‡a wc01 ‡a ba01 ‡a tb01 ‡a pz01 ‡a ka01 ‡a kb01
500       For flute, clarinet, horn, guitar, percussion, piano,
          and electric organ.
```

‡b **Soloist**

Codes for accompanied soloists are entered in subfields ‡b. The subfield is repeatable.

```
048       ‡b pz01 ‡b tz01 ‡a oc
100 10    Albrechtsberger, Johann Georg, ‡d 1736-1809.
240 10    Concertos, ‡m Jew's harp, mandola, string orchestra, ‡r
          E major

048       ‡b va01 ‡b vc02 ‡b vd01 ‡b vf01 ‡a ca04 ‡a oc ‡a ke
500       For soloists (SAATB) and chorus (SATB) with strings and
          continuo.
```

```
048        ‡b ty01 ‡a ka01
048        ‡b ty01 ‡a oa
650    0   Variations (Balalaika with orchestra) ‡x Solo with
           piano.
650    0   Concertos (Balalaika)


048        ‡b vn01 ‡a cn ‡a ka01
500        For narrator, chorus (principally unison) with
           incidental soloists, and stage band; acc. arr. for
           piano.
```

Examples

```
048        wa01 ‡a sa01 ‡a ke
048        zn
500        Principally for unspecified instruments.
500        Contains 2 ricercars (3- and 6-voice), a trio sonata for
           flute, violin, and continuo, and various canons, including a
           canonic fugue.


048        of
048        ‡b bd01 ‡a of
650    0   Brass band music.
650    0   Concertos (Trombone with brass band), Arranged.


048        ez01
245   10   Music for carillon : ‡b no. 4 for a 2-octave electronic
           instrument with accompaniment / ‡c John Cage.


048        cn ‡a cn ‡a cn ‡a cn ‡a cn ‡a oa
500        For 5 choruses of equal voices and orchestra.


048        ‡b bb03 ‡a oc
048        sa02 ‡a sb01 ‡a ke
048        ‡b wh01 ‡b wa01 ‡a oc
048        oc
048        ‡b wa01 ‡b wz01 ‡b sf01 ‡a oc
650    0   Concertos (Trumpets (3) with string orchestra)
650    0   Quartets (Violins (2), viola, continuo)
650    0   Concertos (Flute and recorder with string orchestra)
650    0   Concertos (String orchestra)
650    0   Concertos (Flute, oboe d'amore, viola d'amore with string
           orchestra)


048        pa01 ‡a pd03 ‡a pz06
500        For snare drum, tenor drum, cymbals, bass drum, timpani,
           tambourine, cowbell, triangle, wood block, and temple blocks.
                 [Each is played by an individual percussionist]


048        wa01 ‡a pz01 ‡a sa02 ‡a sb01 ‡a sc01
245   00   Pastoral for flute, bell, string quartet, and tom-tom / ‡c B.
           Arkhimandritov.
500        "The bell (campanello manuale) is played by a flutist"-- P.
           3.
```

```
048        zn05
048        va02 ‡a vc01 ‡a vd01 ‡a vf01
245 10     Intradas and Lieder : ‡b from Venuskr¨antzlein (1609) : for 5
           instruments (voices) / ‡c Johann Hermann Schein.
500        For cantus, quinta vox, altus, tenor, and bassus.


048        wz01 ‡a ke
650  0     Sonatas (Flageolet and continuo)


048        pz01
500        For 1 performer playing multiple percussion instruments.


048        ‡b vn01 ‡a zn01 ‡a sa01 ‡a tb01
511  0     Octa Clark, vocals and accordion ; Hector Duhon, fiddle ;
           Michael Doucet, guitar.


048        pc ‡a wn ‡a bn ‡a pn
511  0     Performed by the ensemble Marimba Quich´e (marimbas, winds
           and drums) ; C´esar Garc´ia, artistic director.


048        wi01 ‡a ka01 ‡a sd01 ‡a pd01 ‡a tb01
511  0     Mary Fettig, alto saxophone or flute ; Marian McPartland,
           piano ; Ray Brown, bass ; Jeff Hamilton, drums ; Peter
           Sprague, guitar.


048        ‡b vn01 ‡a oe
511  0     Ella Fitzgerald, vocals ; with orchestra ; arr. and conducted
           by Nelson Riddle.


048        pn03
500        For percussion trio and conductor.


048        cb03 ‡a ka01
500        For women's voices (SSA with divisi) and piano.


048        ka01
245 00     Intermezzo & Capriccio f¨ur die linke Hand allein, Klavier /
           ‡c Josef Dichler.
650  0     Piano music (1 hand)


048        ka02
245 10     Musiche originali per pianoforte a quattro mani ‡h [sound
           recording].
650  0     Piano music (4 hands)


048        ka01 ‡a ka01
245 10     Three polyphonic masterpieces for two pianos ‡h [sound
           recording].
```

```
048      ǂb ka01 ǂb ka01 ǂb ka01 ǂb ka01 ǂa oc
048      ǂb ka01 ǂb ka01 ǂa oc
048      ǂb ka01 ǂb ka01 ǂb ka01 ǂa oc
245 00   Konzerte f¨ur 2, 3 & 4 Klaviere ǂh [sound recording] / ǂc
         J.S. Bach.
650  0   Concertos (Pianos (4) with string orchestra)
650  0   Concertos (Pianos (2) with string orchestra)
650  0   Concertos (Pianos (3) with string orchestra)
```

Variable Fields

100 Main Entry — Personal Name

UFBD: 100 (A/A) (NRep)
OCLC: 100 (R/R) (NRep)
RLIN: 100 (NR) (NRep)
WLN: MEP (A) (NRep)
MOIM: 100 (NRep)

600 Subject Added Entry — Personal Name

UFBD: 600 (A/O) (Rep)
OCLC: 600 (R/O) (Rep)
RLIN: 600 (NR) (Rep)
WLN: SUP (A) (Rep)
MOIM: 600 (Rep)

700 Added Entry — Personal Name

UFBD: 700 (A/O) (Rep)
OCLC: 700 (R/R) (Rep)
RLIN: 700 (NR) (Rep)
WLN: AEP (A) (Rep)
MOIM: 700 (Rep)

Personal names take numerous forms including initials, identifying words, numerals, or phrases, forenames alone, surnames alone, and multiple surnames, as well as the more common surname-comma-forename pattern. All of the following types of personal names can appear as main entries (100), subjects (600), or added entries (700), except as noted.

- The names of persons who actually or probably lived and are, or were, capable of authorship. The criterion of "capability of authorship" is especially crucial in the coding of subject headings. Most biblical characters, except for "God," the "Devil," angels and archangels, and gods such as "Baal," are considered so capable, and therefore are coded as 600s. "God," the "Devil," etc., as well as fictional characters (Superman, Mighty Mouse, etc.) are considered incapable of authorship and are coded as 650s.

- The names of families and clans. *AACR 2R* does not allow these types of names as main or added entries, but they may be used as subject entries.

- Headings for anonymous classics based on the lives of persons.

- Phrases that characterize or identify an author and that have the structure of forenames or surnames.

Indicators

First Indicator
The first indicator is defined the same for each of the personal name fields. In the 100, 600, and 700 fields, it describes the form of the name and was intended to aid in machine filing.

OCLC & RLIN	*WLN*	
0	F	Forename
1	S	Single surname
2	M	Multiple surname
3	N	Family name [In *AACR 2R* cataloging, this value is used in field 600 only]

Treated as *forenames* are

Names entered in direct (natural language) order

```
100 00   Gace Brul´e, ǂd fl. 1200.
100 00   Tiny Tim.
100 00   Sun Ra.
```

Names that have the structure of a forename or are ambiguous as to their being forenames or surnames

```
100 00   Walther, ǂc von der Vogelweide, ǂd 12th cent.
100 00   Fabian, ǂd 1943-
100 00   Cher, ǂd 1946-
```

Words, phrases, initials, or numerals that have the form of forenames (direct order)

```
100 00   Celebrated composer in London.
100 00   Anonymous ǂb II, ǂd 13th cent.
100 00   B. M.
600 00   H. D. ǂq (Hilda Doolittle), ǂd 1886-1961 ǂx
         Musical settings.
```

The most common *single surnames* follow the usual surname-comma-forename pattern.

```
100 10   Musgrave, Thea.
100 10   Parry, C. Hubert H. ǂq (Charles Hubert Hastings),
         ǂd 1848-1918.
```

Also included are:

Names that have the inverted order structure of surnames

```
100 10   Chou, Wˆen-chung, ǂd 1923-
100 10   Tseng, Hsing-k'uei, ǂd 1946-
```

Names known to be surnames, even if they lack forenames

```
100 10   Davide, ǂc da Bergamo, padre, ǂd 1791-1863.
100 10   Mills, ǂd 1952-
100 10   Hartway.
```

Surnames with multiple entry elements that include prefixes, such as articles, prepositions, or combinations of the two (this includes single-letter prefixes followed by an apostrophe and single words followed by an apostrophe); a list of these prefixes appears as the LC Guidelines to the "X00 Personal Names—General Information" section of *UFBD*

```
100 10   Dello Joio, Norman, ǂd 1913-
100 10   'O Domhnaill, M´iche´al.
100 10   Dall'Abaco, Evaristo Felice, ǂd 1674-1742.
100 10   Te Kanawa, Kiri.
100 10   Van der Slice, John.
100 10   D'India, Sigismondo, ǂd ca. 1580-1629.
600 10   De la Mare, Walter, ǂd 1873-1956 ǂx Musical
         settings.
```

Not to be confused with the preceding category are *multiple* or *compound surnames*. These surnames consist of two or more words or proper names (not prefixes only, although the names often are joined by prepositions or conjunctions), either with or without a hyphen, and receive the first indicator value "2" or "M".

```
100 20   Ĺopez Cobos, Jeśus.
100 20   Saint-Evremond, ǂd 1613-1703.
100 20   Jacquet de La Guerre, Elisabeth-Claude, ǂd
         ca. 1664-1729.
100 20   De la Motte-Haber, Helga, ǂd 1938-
100 20   Vaughan Williams, Ralph, ǂd 1872-1958.
100 20   Villa-Lobos, Heitor.
100 20   Pi de la Serra, Francesc, ǂd 1942-
100 20   Mart́in y Soler, Vicente, ǂd 1754-1806.
```

First indicator value "3" or "N" will not be used often in *AACR 2R* records, as *names of families* cannot be main or added entries, but only subject entries. Names of families include surnames followed by the word "family" and the names of noble families consisting of such terms as "House of," "Dynasty," "Dukes of," "Earls of," and "Counts of."

```
600 30   Bach family.
600 30   Medici, House of.
600 30   Henneberg, Counts of.
600 30   Atholl, Dukes of.
600 30   ́Sunga dynasty, ǂd ca. 185 B.C.-ca. 73
         B.C.
```

Second Indicator

The second indicator differs according to the field. In the 100 Main Entry Field, the second indicator specifies whether the main entry is also the subject. Value "1" or "X" is used rarely, as the practice of omitting the subject heading because it duplicates the main entry no longer is followed.

OCLC & RLIN	WLN	
0	[blank]	**Main entry/subject relationship irrelevant**
1	X	**Main entry is subject**

In the 600 Subject Added Entry Field, the second indicator identifies the subject heading list or authority file used to establish the heading.

OCLC & RLIN	WLN	
0	L	**Library of Congress Subject Headings (LCSH)/LC Authority files**
1	C	**Children's subject heading (LC Annotated Card Program)**
2	M	**National Library of Medicine subject authority file (Medical Subject Headings (MeSH))**
3	A	**National Agricultural Library subject authority file**
4	V	**Source not specified**
5	E	**Canadian subject heading/National Library of Canada authority file English headings**
6	F	**Répertoire des vedettes-matières/National Library of Canada authority file French headings**
7	S	**Source specified in subfield ǂ2**

In the 700 Added Entry Field, the second indicator specifies the type of added entry to aid in machine filing arrangements.

OCLC & RLIN	WLN	
0	A	**Alternative entry**
1	S	**Secondary entry**
2	N	**Analytical entry**

In practice over the years, coding of this second indicator in the 700 field has been erratic and arbitrary, due in part to changes in the definitions. Present usage is outlined in the following discussion.

Alternative entry

Use an alternative entry when the added entry could be subfiled by title or when the added entry is likely to be thought of as an author of the work. In general, it is used for most name-only added entries.

Secondary entry

Use a secondary entry when the added entry could be subfiled by the main entry and for all added entries not covered by Alternative or Analytical. Nonanalytical title and name-title entries (that is, headings for works not contained in the item represented by the bibliographic record) are Secondary entries. The USMARC Format, RLIN, and WLN also advise its use for added entries for illustrators, translators, arrangers, and editors, when the main entry is a personal name.

Analytical entry

Use an analytical entry when the item contains the work represented by the name-title added entry, for example, individual works found on a sound recording or in a score.

Subfields

For the sake of consistency (and the sanity of MARC format users), subfields valid for use in the personal name fields generally have been given the same definition across all of those similar fields, although the use of some subfields in certain fields is highly unlikely. In the 100 field, those subfields most likely to be used are ǂa, ǂb, ǂc, ǂd, ǂe, ǂq, and ǂ4.

ǂa   Personal name

All surnames and forenames and all initials, letters, or numerals that take the place of such names are entered in subfield ǂa.

```
100 10   Schafer, R. Murray.
100 10   Fitzgerald, Ella.
```

ǂb   Numeration

A Roman numeral alone or a Roman numeral with an additional name (forename, family, dynasty, etc.) that follows the numeral without intervening punctuation is entered here. The most common use of this subfield is for Roman numerals associated with royal names. It should be used only in forename (first indicator "0" or "F") headings.

```
100 00   John ǂb IV, ǂc King of Portugal, ǂd 1604-1656.
100 00   John ǂb VI Cantacuzenus, ǂc Emperor of the East,
         ǂd 1292-1383.
```

‡c   **Titles and other words associated with a name**

- Titles designating nobility, office, or rank
- Terms of address (Mrs., Mr., and the like)
- Initials signifying academic degrees or membership in an organization
- Roman numerals associated with parts of the name other than the entry element
- Other words or phrases associated with a name

Although *AACR 2R* (22.12B, 22.15B, etc.) places some titles and terms between the surname and forename, they should be input following the name subfield.

```
100 10    Sargent, Malcolm, ‡c Sir, ‡d 1895-1967.
100 00    Taj Mahal ‡c (Musician)
100 10    Beach, H. H. A., ‡c Mrs., ‡d 1867-1944.
100 00    Vladimir, ‡c Saint, Grand Duke of Kiev, ‡d ca.
          956-1015.
100 00    Eustachio, ‡c Romano, ‡d 16th cent.
100 10    Goodman, Andrew, ‡c LL. B.
100 10    Smith, Jennifer, ‡c soprano.
700 10    Lomax, John, ‡c III.
```

‡d   **Dates associated with a name**

All dates of birth, death, or flourishing go in subfield ‡d.

- Dates of birth alone (such as "b. 1771" or open dates such as "1953-")
- Dates of death alone ("d. 1643")
- Dates of birth and death ("1756-1791")
- Dates of flourishing ("fl. 1672-1699")
- Dates of activity ("12th cent.")

Remember that *AACR 2R* rule interpretation 22.17 stipulates that "B.C." is placed at the end of a date or span of dates before the common or Christian era. "A.D." is used only when dates span both eras and is placed after the appropriate date.

```
100 00    Jacques, ‡c de Li`ege, ‡d ca. 1260-ca. 1330.
100 10    Bernhardt, Robert, ‡d b. 1859.
100 00    Ugolino, ‡c de Orvieto, ‡d 15th cent.
600 00    Ovid, ‡d 43 B.C.-17 or 18 A.D. ‡x Musical
          settings.
```

‡e   **Relator term**

A term or phrase that characterizes the relationship between the name and the work. This rarely will be used in an *AACR 2R* record, although similar information in coded form may appear in a subfield ‡4 (for which, see below).

```
100 10    Hofmann, Charles, ‡d 1914- ‡e ed.
              [pre-AACR 2]
```

‡q   **Fuller form of name**

        Used to
- Expand any parts of the name represented by initials
- Supply any forename or surname either not used or not represented by an initial

These fuller forms of the name are enclosed in parentheses.

```
100 20   S´ainz de la Maza, R. ‡q (Regino), ‡d 1897-
100 10   Butler, Patricia ‡q (Patricia J.)
100 10   Chalaev, Sh. ‡q (Shirvani)
700 10   La Motte, ‡c M. de ‡q (Antoine Houdar), ‡d 1672-
         1731.
100 20   Fuller-Maitland, J. A. ‡q (John Alexander), ‡d
         1856-1936.
```

‡4   **Relator code**

        The Library of Congress maintains an ever-expanding list of three-character alphabetic codes that identify the relationship between the name and the work. Although subfields ‡e and ‡4 perform the same function in explicit (printing) and coded (nonprinting) form, respectively, they will be used only rarely in the same field. When multiple relator codes apply to a single name entry, each code should be entered in a separate subfield ‡4. This subfield is placed after the entire name portion of the heading and before any title portion.

```
700 20   Garc´ia Ascensio, Enrique, ‡d 1937- ‡4 cnd
700 10   Bernstein, Leonard, ‡d 1918- ‡4 cnd ‡4 itr
700 00   Lady. ‡4 lbt
```

In addition to these preceding subfields, it would not be unusual to find subfields ‡k, ‡t, ‡x, or ‡z in a 600 field.

‡k   **Form subheading**

        A standardized phrase added to a heading in order to collect records for certain types of materials.

```
600 10   Stein, Gertrude, ‡d 1874-1946, ‡k in fiction,
         drama, poetry, etc.
```

‡t   **Title of a work**

        The title of a work or a genre of works in a name/title heading in a 600 or 700 field. Other subfields associated with a uniform title (which are explained in the 240 field) may follow the subfield ‡t.

```
600 10   Chopin, Fr´ed´eric, ‡d 1810-1849. ‡t Etudes, ‡m
         piano.
600 10   Smith, Patti. ‡t Land.
600 10   Me˘ison, Rikhard A. E. ‡q (Rikhard Andri˘i
         Edvard). ‡t Tri⁀i⁀umf Khresta.
```

‡x   **General subdivision**

        Subject heading subdivisions other than those considered chronological or geographical.

```
600 10   Cummings, E. E. ‡q (Edward Estlin), ‡d 1894-1962
         ‡x Musical settings.
```

```
600 20   Coulombe Saint-Marcoux, Micheline, +d 1938- +x
         Manuscripts +x Facsimiles.
```

+z   Geographic subdivision

Subject heading subdivision for a place name.

```
600 10   Wagner, Richard, +d 1813-1883 +x Performances +z
         Germany (West) +z Bayreuth.
600 10   Beethoven, Ludwig van, +d 1770-1827 +x Homes and
         haunts +z Austria +z Vienna.
```

Any 700 field that happens to be an analytical added entry also should have a subfield +f.

+f   Date of a work

The publication date of the edition of the work in hand is entered in subfield +f. This should not be confused with any other dates associated with a personal name or a title. According to *AACR 2R* 21.30M and its rule interpretation, all analytical added entries (entries that provide access to a work contained within the item being cataloged) require the addition of the publication date. LCRI 21.30M (*Cataloging Service Bulletin* 20 (spring 1983), p. 12-14) explains how to choose the date to use in subfield +f; in virtually every case, Date 1 from the fixed field will be the date of choice.

```
700 02   Atli Heimir Sveinsson. +t Aria, +m soprano,
         instrumental ensemble. +f 1980.
700 12   Talma, Louise, +d 1906- +t Diadem. +f 1984.
700 22   Garrido-Lecca, Celso. +t Symphonies, +n no. 1. +f
         1961.
```

Aside from most of the preceding subfields, 700 fields and occasional 600 fields may contain many of the title-related subfields (see the section on field 240).

Examples

```
100 00   Prince.
100 00   Sting +c (Musician)
100 00   Muddy Waters, +d 1915-
100 00   E., +c Episcopus, +d 11th cent.
100 00   Frederick +b II, +c King of Prussia, +d 1712-1786.
100 00   _Surayy¯a Maq.s¯ud.
100 00   ´Askell M´asson, +d 1953-
100 00   Little Richard.
100 00   Dion, +d 1939-
100 00   Longhair, +c Professor, +d 1918-1980.

100 10   Eno.
100 10   Murray, Marcia +q (Marcia D.)
100 10   Rozelli, +c sigr., +d fl. 1740-1770.
100 10   Seeger, Ruth Crawford, +d 1901-1953.
100 10   Charles, Daniel, +c maˆitre-assistant.
100 10   Mengoli, A. +q (Annibale), +d b. 1851.
100 10   Delusse, +c Monsieur +q (Charles), +d b. ca. 1720.
100 10   La Rue, Pierre de, +d d. 1518.
100 10   Destouches, +c M. +q (Andr´e Cardinal), +d 1672-1749.
100 10   Del Tredici, David.
```

```
100 20   Lucha-Burns, Carol.
100 20   Uribe Holguín, Guillermo, ‡d 1880-1971.
100 20   Eckhardt-Gramatté, S. C. ‡q (Sophie-Carmen), ‡d 1899-1974.
100 20   Saraeva-Bondar', A. M. ‡q (Avgusta Mikhaĭlovna)
100 20   Saint-Georges, Joseph Boulogne, ‡c chevalier de, ‡d d. 1799.
100 20   Saint-Germain, ‡c comte de, ‡d d. 1784 ‡c (Spirit)
100 20   Caix d'Hervelois, Louis de, ‡d ca. 1670-ca. 1760.
100 20   Fatḥ Allāh, Lindā.
100 20   Gil García, Bonifacio.
100 20   Lamote de Grignon, Ricardo, ‡d 1899-1962.


600 00   Anne Boleyn, ‡c Queen, consort of Henry VIII, King of England, ‡d
         1507-1536 ‡x Drama.
600 00   Alfonso ‡b X, ‡c King of Castile and Leon, ‡d 1221-1284. ‡t
         Cantigas de Santa María.
600 00   Marie de l'Incarnation, ‡c mère, ‡d 1599-1672 ‡x Songs and music.

600 10   Ono, Yōko ‡x Iconography.
600 10   Bach, Johann Sebastian, ‡d 1685-1750. ‡t Cantatas ‡x Indexes.
600 10   Schoenberg, Arnold, ‡d 1874-1951 ‡x Anniversaries, etc., 1974.
600 10   Rebeyrol, Pierre, ‡d 1798-1850 ‡x Thematic catalogs.

600 20   García Lorca, Federico, ‡d 1898-1936 ‡x Musical settings.
600 20   Figuš-Bystrý, Viliam, ‡d 1875-1937 ‡x Bibliography.
600 30   Mendelssohn family.


700 00   John, ‡c Dr., ‡d 1941- ‡4 itr ‡4 voc
700 00   'Agústa 'Agústsdóttir. ‡4 voc
700 00   Midori, ‡d 1971- ‡4 itr
700 02   Leadbelly, ‡d 1885?-1949. ‡4 cmp ‡t Songs. ‡k Selections. ‡f 1988.

700 10   Beecham, Thomas, ‡c Sir, ‡d 1879-1961. ‡4 cnd
700 11   Gilbert, W. S. ‡q (William Schwenck), ‡d 1836-1911. ‡4 lbt ‡t
         Mikado. ‡s Libretto.

700 20   Bishop-Kovacevich, Stephen, ‡d 1941- ‡4 itr
700 21   Lloyd Webber, Julian, ‡d 1951- ‡4 arr
```

CORPORATE NAME HEADINGS

110	**Main Entry — Corporate Name**	UFBD: 110 (A/A) (NRep)
		OCLC: 110 (R/R) (NRep)
		RLIN: 110 (NR) (NRep)
		WLN: MEC (A) (NRep)
		MOIM: 110 (NRep)
610	**Subject Added Entry — Corporate Name**	UFBD: 610 (A/O) (Rep)
		OCLC: 610 (R/O) (Rep)
		RLIN: 610 (NR) (Rep)
		WLN: SUC (A) (Rep)
		MOIM: 610 (Rep)
710	**Added Entry — Corporate Name**	UFBD: 710 (A/O) (Rep)
		OCLC: 710 (R/R) (Rep)
		RLIN: 710 (NR) (Rep)
		WLN: AEC (A) (Rep)
		MOIM: 710 (Rep)

Corporate names are borne by any organization or group of individuals that acts or might act as an entity. Among the typical sorts of corporate bodies are institutions, associations, societies, governments, foundations, musical ensembles, local churches, business firms, and, of course, libraries. Such corporate names are coded as 110 or 710 fields if they are entered

- under their own names
- under the names of political jurisdictions
- as political jurisdictions standing alone

Geographic names as subject headings pose special problems. Religious jurisdictions, for example, always are coded as 610 fields. However, political jurisdictions are coded as 610 fields *except* when they

- stand alone, that is, without a subordinate body (subfield ǂb), form subheading (subfield ǂk), or title (subfield ǂt), or
- are followed directly by a subject heading subdivision (subfield ǂx)

More details about the disposition of geographic subject headings can be gleaned from the section concerning them.

Named conferences or meetings (including music festivals) entered directly under their own names are coded 111, 611, or 711. However, those meetings, conferences, and festivals entered indirectly, either under the name of a corporate body or under the name of a political jurisdiction, are coded 110, 610, or 710.

```
710 20   International Music Council. ǂb World Music Conference
         ǂd (1983 : ǂc Stockholm, Sweden)
```

Among the special types of corporate names that might be encountered in music-related records are:

Names of musical ensembles:

```
710 20   X (Musical group)
710 20   Beatles.
710 20   Musica Nova (Musical group : Sweden)
710 20   Philharmonia Orchestra (London, England)
710 20   Ensemble vocal "Da Camera".
```

Names of libraries, museums, archives, and other institutions serving as manuscript repositories:

```
710 20   Steierm¨arkisches Landesarchiv. ǂk Manuscript. ǂn
         Hs. 1869.
710 20   Mus´ee Cond´e. ǂb Biblioth`eque. ǂk Manuscript.
         ǂn 564. ǂk Selections.
710 20   British Library. ǂk Manuscript. ǂn Royal Appendix
         74-76.
```

Names of churches, cathedrals, parishes, mosques, temples, abbeys, monasteries, priories, missions, and denominations, and their subordinate bodies:

```
710 20   Ged¨achtnis-Kirche (Stuttgart, Germany). ǂb
         Figuralchor.
710 20   Cath´edrale de Strasbourg. ǂb Maˆitrise.
710 20   Spanish and Portuguese Jews' Congregation
         (London, England). ǂb Choir.
710 20   York Minster. ǂb Choir.
710 20   S. Agostino (Monastery : Cremona, Italy). ǂb
         Biblioteca.
710 20   Saint-Benoˆit d'Encalcat (Abbey : Dourgne,
         France)
710 20   S¨uleymaniye Camii (Istanbul, Turkey)
610 20   Catholic Church.
610 20   Orthodox Eastern Church.
```

Names of television and radio broadcast organizations:

```
710 20   Punch (Television station : Bogot´a, Colombia)
710 20   KANU (Radio station : Lawrence, Kan.)
710 20   Voz Dominicana (Radio/television station : Santo
         Domingo, Dominican Republic)
```

Names of studies, funds, projects, and programs:

```
710 20   New Music Concerts.
710 20   Martha Baird Rockefeller Aid to Music Program.
710 20   Funda¸c˜o Calouste Gulbenkian.
710 20   Traditional Ethnic Music and the Elderly
         (Project)
710 20   University of California, Los Angeles. ǂb Program
         in Ethnomusicology.
```

Names of vessels:

```
610 20   Clearwater (Sloop)
610 20   Edmund Fitzgerald (Ship)
610 20   Challenger (Spacecraft)
```

In corporate headings, close up spaces between initials, but leave a space between initials and parts of the name that are not initials.

```
110 20   Ensemble polyphonique de l'O.R.T.F.
110 20   N.C.R.V. Vocaalensemble.
110 20   Federal Music Project (N.J.)
110 20   J. & W. Chester (Firm)
```

Indicators

First Indicator

The first indicator is defined in the same way for each of the corporate name fields. In the 110, 610, and 710 fields, it describes the form of the entry element of the name and was intended to help in machine filing.

OCLC & RLIN	WLN	
0	S	**Inverted name**
1	P	**Jurisdiction name**
2	N	**Name in direct order**

Extremely rare in *AACR 2R* is the *inverted* name corporate name, actually a corporate name beginning with a personal name in inverted order. The forename often is enclosed in parentheses and might be represented by initials or abbreviations.

```
710 00   Peters (C.F.) Corporation.    [pre-AACR 2]
710 00   Simrock, N., firm, Berlin.    [pre-AACR 2]
710 00   Fischer (Carl) Inc., New York.    [pre-AACR 2]
```

More common is the *jurisdiction name*, the name of a place alone or a place plus name. When a political or religious jurisdiction is used alone or as the entry element for a government agency (named in subfield ǂb), a form subheading (in subfield ǂk), or a title (in subfield ǂt), use first indicator value "1" or "P".

```
110 10   Basel (Switzerland : Ecclesiastical principality)
110 10   Cremona (Italy). ǂb Biblioteca governativa e
         biblioteca civica.
110 10   France. ǂb Biblioth`eque nationale. ǂk Manuscript. ǂn
         Fran¸cais 25425.
610 10   United States. ǂt Declaration of Independence.
```

Most common of all is the corporate *name in direct order*. When place names are integral parts of corporate names (that is, they are not set off from the remainder of the heading by a full stop), they also are considered to be in direct order. Corporate names established in direct order are assigned first indicator value "2" or "N".

```
110 20   Indiana University, Bloomington. ǂb School of Music. ǂb
         Early Music Institute.
110 20   Little Joe, Johnny, y Familia (Musical group)
110 20   G. Schirmer, Inc.
110 20   Radion kamarikuoro (Finland)
110 20   New York Pro Musica Antiqua. ǂb Primavera Singers.
110 20   Dˇekansk´y kostel sv. Ign´ace v Bˇreznici.
```

Second Indicator

The second indicator for the corporate name fields is assigned following the same criteria found in the corresponding personal name fields: 100 for 110, 600 for 610, and 700 for 710 (see pp. 113-14).

Subfields

For the most part, subfields valid for use in the corporate name fields have been defined similarly across all related fields and will be applied in much the same way. However, some subfields more are likely to be used in some fields than in others.

In the 110 field, the most common subfields used are ‡a, ‡b, ‡c, ‡d, ‡k, ‡n, and ‡4.

‡a Corporate name or jurisdiction name as entry element

The name of the highest hierarchical unit of the corporate entity, which may be either the entry element of the corporate name or a geographical name, is entered in subfield ‡a. Parenthetical data that *do not* pertain to conferences or meetings are not separately subfielded. Neither are places, dates, and numbers set off from a corporate name by a comma.

```
110 20   U2 (Musical group)
110 20   Live Aid (Fund raising enterprise)
110 20   New Orleans Rhythm Kings (1922-1925)
110 20   Da Camera (Musical group : ˚Arhus, Denmark)
110 20   Musica Antiqua (Musical group : 1962- )
110 20   "Muzyka" (Firm)
110 20   Choeur d'enfants du Festival international d'art
         lyrique (Aix-en-Provence, France)
110 20   5UV (Radio station : Adelaide, S. Aust.)
```

‡b Subordinate unit

Each subordinate body in a corporate hierarchy is identified in a separate subfield ‡b. Corporate names entered under a political jurisdiction also are assigned subfield ‡b. Parenthetical data unrelated to conferences or meetings *are not* separately subfielded. Neither are places, dates, and numbers set off from a corporate name by a comma.

```
110 10   France. ‡b Biblioth`eque nationale. ‡b
         D´epartement de la phonoth`eque nationale et de
         l'audiovisuel. ‡b Service du d´ep^ot l´egal.
110 20   Istituto musicale "A. Corelli" (Cesena, Italy).
         ‡b Biblioteca musicale.
610 10   United States. ‡b Army. ‡b Court-martial (French
         : 1878)
110 20   Opera Rom^an˘a (Bucharest). ‡b Orchestra.
610 10   Great Britain. ‡b Army. ‡b Border Regiment. ‡b
         Battalion, 9th. ‡b B Company.
```

Two subfields (‡c and ‡d) are used exclusively in connection with the names of conferences, meetings, festivals, and similar events that are entered subordinately under a sponsoring organization represented by a corporate name or a political jurisdiction.

‡c Location of meeting

Use this subfield *only* when the place name identifies where a conference, meeting, or festival took place (as stipulated in *AACR 2R* 24.7B4 and 24.8B), not for any other geographic name in a corporate heading. Although multiple places might be named, include all of them in a single subfield ‡c.

‡d **Date of meeting or treaty signing**

Use this subfield *only* when the date identifies when a conference, meeting, or festival took place (as stipulated in *AACR 2R* 24.7B3 and 24.8B), not for any other dates in a corporate heading. Subfield ‡d may be repeated.

```
110 20   Deutsche Gesellschaft f¨ur Volkskunde. ‡b
         Kommission f¨ur Lied-, Tanz- und Musikforschung.
         ‡b Arbeitstagung ‡d (1980 : ‡c Aichwald,
         Germany)
110 20   American Musicological Society. ‡b Meeting ‡n
         (44th : ‡d 1978 : ‡c Minneapolis, Minn.)
```

‡k **Form subheading**

Certain standard phrases added to corporate headings in order to gather together records for particular types of materials are entered in subfield ‡k. In music records, the most common form subheadings are "Selections" and "Manuscript".

```
110 20   New York Public Library. ‡b Music Division. ‡k
         Manuscript. ‡n Drexel 5612. ‡k Selections.
```

‡n **Number of part/section/meeting**

Use this subfield to identify the serial number of a conference, meeting, or festival; the repository designation of a manuscript; or (rarely under a corporate heading) the serial, opus, or thematic index number of a musical work. Remember that a number that is an integral part of a corporate name is not separately subfielded.

```
110 20   International Folk Music Council. ‡b United
         Kingdom National Committee. ‡b Conference ‡n
         (6th : ‡d 1980 : ‡c Newnham College)
110 20   Institut f¨ur Neue Musik und Musikerziehung
         Darmstadt. ‡b Hauptarbeitstagung ‡n (37th : ‡d
         1983)
110 20   Biblioteca del Monumento nazionale di
         Montecassino. ‡k Manuscript. ‡n Cod. Casin. 334.
         ‡n p. 1-72.
110 10   Cambrai (France). ‡b Biblioth`eque municipale. ‡k
         Manuscript. ‡n 1328.
110 20   8 Bayreuther Festspiel-Hornisten.
110 20   Heeresmusikkorps 5 der Bundeswehr.
```

‡4 **Relator code**

Identifies, in coded form, the relationship between the corporate name and the work, that is, the function the corporate entity has performed. This subfield works much as it does in the Personal Name fields.

```
710 20   Library of Congress. ‡b Elizabeth Sprague
         Coolidge Foundation. ‡4 fnd
710 20   King Crimson (Musical group) ‡4 prf
710 20   Dimensi´on Coste˜na (Musical group) ‡4 prf
```

In addition to the preceding subfields, other subfields might be found in 610 and 710 fields. Most of these will be title-related and are detailed in the section on uniform titles, field 240. The three subfields that follow (‡t, ‡l, and ‡f), along with the previously-described subfields ‡k and ‡n, are among the more common.

‡t   Title of a work

In a corporate name/title heading, subfield ‡t contains the title. This will not occur in 110 fields in *AACR 2R* records, but is common in 610 and 710 fields. Parenthetical qualifiers to the title proper are not subfielded separately.

‡l   Language of a work

The language of the text of a work is entered in subfield ‡l. Multiple languages are put in the same subfield ‡l, since it is not repeatable.

‡f   Date of a work

The publication date of the edition of the work in hand is entered in subfield ‡f. This should not be confused with any other dates associated with a corporate heading or a title. According to *AACR 2R* 21.30M and its rule interpretation, all analytical added entries (entries that provide access to a work contained within the item being cataloged) require the addition of the publication date. LCRI21.30M (*Cataloging Service Bulletin* 20 (spring 1983), p. 12-14) explains the choice of date for subfield ‡f; in virtually every case, the date of choice is Date 1 from the fixed field.

```
710 12   Cyprus (Archdiocese). ‡t Anastasimatarion.
710 22   Rolling Stones. ‡t Sucking in the seventies. ‡f
         1981.
710 22   Catholic Church. ‡t Gradual (Salisbury : Ms.
         British Library. Additional 12194)
710 22   Catholic Church. ‡t Ordo Missae (Pre-Vatican II).
         ‡l French & Latin. ‡k Selections.
710 22   Orthodox Eastern Church. ‡t Liturgy of St. John
         Chrysostom.  ‡l Polyglot.
710 22   Catholic Church. ‡t Mass, 33rd Sunday of ordinary
         time (Chant). ‡f 1979.
710 22   ROVA Saxophone Quartet. ‡t Trobar clus, ‡n no. 3.
         ‡f 1979.
```

Aside from many of the previously-described subfields, ‡x and ‡z might be found in 610 fields.

‡x   General subdivision

Subject heading subdivisions other than those considered chronological or geographic.

```
610 20   B. Schott's S¨ohne (Mainz, Rhineland-Palatinate,
         Germany) ‡x Catalogs.
610 20   Frente Sandinista de Liberaci´on Nacional ‡x
         Songs and music.
610 20   Cath´edrale Saint-Pierre (Beauvais, Oise, France)
         ‡x Organs.
610 10   United States. ‡b Navy ‡x Songs and music.
```

‡z   Geographic subdivision

Subject heading subdivision for a place name.

```
610 20   Moravian Church ‡z United States ‡x Hymns.
610 20   Catholic Church ‡z France ‡x Liturgy.
```

Examples

```
110 10   Great Britain. ‡b Working Party on Music.
110 10   Germany. ‡b Heer. ‡b Armee, 12.
```

```
110 10   Salzburg (Ecclesiastical principality)
110 10   United States. ǂb Navy. ǂb Fleet, 7th.


710 10   France. ǂb Biblioth`eque nationale. ǂk Manuscript. ǂn
         R´eserve Vmd. ms. 18.


110 20   Staatsbibliothek Bamberg. ǂk Manuscript. ǂn Msc. lit. 6.
110 20   Ensemble "Pro Musica Sacra Nova."
110 20   Studiengruppe zur Erforschung und Edition Historischer
         Volksmusikquellen (International Folk Music Council). ǂb
         Tagung ǂn (7th : ǂd 1982 : ǂv Limassol, Cyprus)
110 20   Meet the Composer, Inc.
110 20   Corpus Troporum (Project : Stockholm, Sweden)


610 20   Apollo 15 (Spacecraft) ǂx Songs and music.
610 20   St. Petri und Pauli (Church : Cappel, Germany) ǂx Organ.
610 20   Catholic Church ǂz Ireland ǂx Hymns.


710 20   St. George's Chapel (Windsor Castle). ǂb Choristers.
710 20   ELMERATTO (Group : France)
710 20   Coop. la musica.
710 20   Kongelige Kapel (Denmark). ǂb Blæserkvintet. ǂ4 prf
710 20   Library of Congress. ǂb McKim Fund. ǂ4 fnd
710 20   Superstation WTBS (Television station : Atlanta, Ga.)
710 20   Y.EN.E.D. (Radio station : Athens, Greece)
710 20   Capella Savaria (Hungary)
710 20   Orthodox Eastern Church. ǂt Akathistos hymnos. ǂl Spanish &
         Greek.
710 20   Louisville Orchestra. ǂb New Music Project. ǂ4 fnd
710 20   Pearls Before Swine (Musical group). ǂt One nation
         underground. ǂf 1980.
710 20   Koppelkvartetten. ǂ4 prf
710 20   St. Ludwig (Church : Munich, Germany). ǂb Chor. ǂ4 prf
710 20   Projeto Mem´oria Musical Brasileira.
710 20   Gesellschaft f¨ur Musikforschung (1868-1906)
710 20   Gesellschaft f¨ur Musikforschung (1946- )
710 20   Filharm´oniai T´arsas´ag (Budapest, Hungary) ǂ4 prf
710 20   International Council for Traditional Music. ǂb Conference ǂn
         (27th : ǂd 1983 : ǂc New York, N.Y.)
710 20   Staatsbibliothek Preussischer Kulturbesitz. ǂk Manuscript. ǂn
         Mus. ms. 28.
710 20   Kleine Kreis Freising (Musical group : Germany) ǂ4 prf
710 20   Schools Council (Great Britain). ǂb Project for Music in the
         Secondary School Curriculum.
```

Meeting Name Headings

111	**Main Entry — Meeting Name**	UFBD: 111 (A/A) (NRep)
		OCLC: 111 (R/R) (NRep)
		RLIN: 111 (NR) (NRep)
		WLN: MEM (A) (NRep)
		MOIM: 111 (NRep)
611	**Subject Added Entry — Meeting Name**	UFBD: 611 (A/O) (Rep)
		OCLC: 611 (R/O) (Rep)
		RLIN: 611 (NR) (Rep)
		WLN: SUM (A) (Rep)
		MOIM: 611 (Rep)
711	**Added Entry — Meeting Name**	UFBD: 711 (A/O) (Rep)
		OCLC: 711 (R/R) (Rep)
		RLIN: 711 (NR) (Rep)
		WLN: AEM (A) (Rep)
		MOIM: 711 (Rep)

Conferences, meetings, colloquia, exhibitions and shows, scientific expeditions, expositions, fairs, seminars, symposia, workshops, formally organized music and other festivals, athletic contests and games, marathons and races, congresses, gatherings, councils, round tables, sessions, and talks entered under their own names are considered meeting names. What qualifies as a "meeting" is any gathering of individuals or representatives of various bodies in order to act on or discuss subjects of common interest. Logically, these are a subspecies of Corporate Names, but bibliographically, they are treated separately in order to afford greater control over their notoriously unruly publications.

Any named meeting in *AACR 2R* form entered under a corporate name or a political jurisdiction is recorded in one of the Corporate Name (X10) fields. Likewise, any truly corporate name that includes such words as "conference," "congress," "council," or "round table," but intends to convey the idea of an ongoing organization rather than a meeting of individuals (e.g. Music Educators National Conference), is entered in the Corporate Name fields.

Indicators

The *first indicator* is defined in the same way for each of the meeting name fields, identifying the form of the entry element of the meeting name.

OCLC & RLIN	WLN	
0	S	**Inverted name**
1	P	**Jurisdiction name**
2	N	**Name in direct order**

A meeting name beginning with an *inverted personal name* (first indicator "0" or "S") rarely, if ever, will be found in an *AACR 2R* record. When a meeting name begins with a personal surname alone or a personal surname in direct order, or has a personal name in a position other than the entry element, the first indicator should be "2" or "N".

```
111 00  Busoni (F.) International Piano Competition.  [pre-AACR 2]
```

When a *political jurisdiction* followed by a period is the element under which a meeting name is entered, the first indicator is "1". This will rarely occur in *AACR 2R* records. Meeting names with a jurisdiction as an integral part of the name or as a place-name qualifier have the first indicator "2".

```
111 10  Florence. ‡q Maggio musicale fiorentino.  [pre-AACR 2]
```

126

Most *AACR 2R* meeting names will be entered in direct order and will have the first indicator value "2". Meeting names that begin with personal names, geographic names, acronyms, or initials also are assigned this value.

```
111 20   Newport Music Festival.
111 20   Boston Early Music Festival & Exhibition.
111 20   Gustav Mahler Kolloquium ǂd (1979 : ǂc Vienna, Austria)
111 20   Wagner-Symposium ǂd (1983 : ǂc Munich, Germany)
111 20   Kuopio Tanssi ja Soi ǂd (1984)
111 20   Unesco-IMC Symposium on Music and Modern Media ǂd (1983
           : ǂc Stockholm, Sweden)
111 20   ASEAN Festival of Performing Arts ǂn (3rd : ǂd 1983 :
           ǂc Bangkok, Thailand)
```

The *second indicator* differs according to the field and corresponds to the descriptions outlined in the personal name section: 111 to 100, 611 to 600, and 711 to 700, respectively (see pp. 113-14).

Subfields

Subfields valid for use in the meeting name fields have generally been defined similarly across all similar fields, although some subfields are more likely to be used than others. In 111, 611, and 711 fields, subfields ǂa, ǂc, ǂd, ǂe, and ǂn are the ones most likely to be used.

ǂa   Meeting name or jurisdiction name as entry element

The meeting name along with any parenthetical qualifier added, in accordance with *AACR 2R* 24.4B, to clarify its corporate nature, is entered in subfield ǂa. Parenthetical qualifiers signifying number, date, or place *are* separately subfielded unless they are intended merely to distinguish between like-named meetings.

```
611 20   Presidential Symposium (Consortium for
           International Development) ǂn (2nd : ǂd 1985 :
           ǂc University of Wyoming-National Park Service
           Research Center) ǂx Songs and music.
111 20   CityFolk (Festival) ǂd (1981 : ǂc Portland, Or.)
111 20   H¨andel-Festspiele.
111 20   Convegno internazionale di studio "Parole e
           musica, l'esperienza wagneriana nella cultura
           fra Romanticismo e Decadentismo" ǂd (1983 : ǂc
           Venice, Italy)
111 20   Alabama Project: Music, Society, and Education in
           America.
```

ǂc   Location of meeting

The name of the place or institution where a meeting was held is coded as subfield ǂc. Adjacent multiple places are put in the same subfield ǂc. Parenthetical geographic name qualifiers occasionally used to differentiate among identically named meetings are not subfielded separately.

```
111 20   Concorso polifonico internazionale "Guido
           d'Arezzo" ǂn (32nd : ǂd 1984 : ǂc Arezzo, Italy,
           etc.)
111 20   Internationale Musikalische Festwochen ǂc
           (Lucerne, Switzerland)
111 20   Convegno internazionale sull'opera di Giacomo
           Puccini ǂn (1st : ǂd 1983 : ǂc Torre del Lago
           Puccini (Italy))
```

```
111 20   Beethoven-Woche ǂd (1977 : ǂc Musik-Akademie der
           Stadt Basel)
111 20   Conference on the Musical Theatre in America ǂd
           (1981 : ǂc C.W. Post Center)
111 20   Sympozjum Przedstawicieli Bibliotek i O´srodk´ow
           Dokumentacji Muzycznej Kraj´ow Socjalistycznych
           ǂn (2nd : ǂd 1976 : ǂc Katowice, Poland, and
           Krak´ow, Poland)
611 20   Governor's Conference on Libraries (Idaho) ǂx
           Songs and music.
611 20   Governor's Conference on Libraries (New York) ǂx
           Songs and music.
711 20   Festival de Cultura (Guatemala)
```

ǂd   **Date of meeting**

The date or dates of a meeting or event, whether day, month, and/or year, are entered in subfield ǂd. In those rare cases where an open or inclusive date is added to a meeting name as a parenthetical qualifier to distinguish it from another identically named meeting, the date is not separately subfielded.

```
611 20   International Symposium on Quality Control
           (1967- ) ǂx Songs and music.
611 20   International Symposium on Quality Control
           (1974- ) ǂx Songs and music.
111 20   Exposici´on Itinerante del Libro y del Fonograma
           ǂd (1980?)
111 20   Kolloquium "Johann Sebastian Bach und die
           Aufkl¨arung" ǂd (1979 : ǂc Leipzig, Germany?)
111 20   M´usica en Compostela ǂn (4th : ǂd 1961 : ǂc
           Santiago de Compostela, Spain)
111 20   Colloquia Musicologica ǂd (1972-1973 : ǂc Brno,
           Czechoslovakia)
```

ǂe   **Subordinate unit**

Subordinate entities are entered under meeting names in subfield ǂe. With music-related headings, these most likely are to be performing ensembles entered under the names of music festivals.

```
111 20   English Bach Festival. ǂe Percussion Ensemble.
111 20   Mostly Mozart Festival. ǂe Orchestra.
```

ǂn   **Number of part/section/meeting**

The sequential number of a meeting, be it an alphabetic or numeric designation, is entered in subfield ǂn. This subfield may also be used, though rarely in meeting name headings, for numbered sections or parts of a work or for a serial, opus, or thematic index number.

```
111 20   Schubertiade ǂn (2nd : ǂd 1977 ǂc Hohenems,
           Austria)
111 20   Festival international de Lyon ǂn (36th : ǂd
           1981)
```

Numbers and dates that are inherent parts of a meeting name are not subfielded separately.

```
111 20   MusicArmenia '78 ǂc (London, England)
```

128

```
111 20   Salzburger Sympozion "Die Rezeption des
         Mittelalters in Literatur, Bildender Kunst und
         Musik des 19. und 20. Jahrhunderts".
111 20   Horizonte '82 ǂc (Berlin, Germany)
```

Occasionally, other subfields might be used in meeting name headings. Those associated with titles (subfields ǂt, ǂl, ǂk, and ǂf) are employed in 611 and 711 fields much as they are in the respective personal name and corporate name fields. The Relator Code (subfield ǂ4) works as it does in personal and corporate names, as well.

ǂt   Title of a work

A uniform title or other title associated with a meeting name in a 611 or 711 field is placed in subfield ǂt. Parenthetical qualifiers to the title are not subfielded separately.

```
711 20   Vatican Council ǂn (2nd : ǂd 1962-1965). ǂt
         Constitutio pastoralis de ecclesia in mundo
         huius temporis.
```

ǂl   Language of a work

The language of the text of a work is entered in subfield ǂl. Multiple languages are placed in the same subfield ǂl, as it is not repeatable.

```
711 20   Congreso Internacional "Espa~na en la M´usica de
         Occidente" ǂd (1985 : ǂc Salamanca, Spain). ǂt
         Proceedings. ǂl English & Spanish.
```

ǂk   Form subheading

Certain standard phrases used with the title of a work in order to gather together records for particular types of materials are put in subfield ǂk. Most commonly found in meeting name headings will be the term "Selections".

```
711 20   International Joseph Haydn Congress ǂd (1982 : ǂc
         Hofburg, Vienna, Austria). ǂt Proceedings. ǂk
         Selections.
```

ǂf   Date of a work

The publication date of the edition of the work in hand is entered in subfield ǂf. *Do not* confuse this publication date with any other dates associated with a meeting name or its title. According to *AACR 2R* 21.30M and its rule interpretation, all analytical added entries (entries that provide access to a work contained within the item being cataloged) require the addition of the publication date. LCRI 21.30M (*Cataloging Service Bulletin* 20 (spring 1983), p. 12-14) explains how to choose the date to use in subfield ǂf; in virtually every case, Date 1 from the fixed field will be the date of choice.

```
711 20   International Music and Technology Conference ǂd
         (1981 : ǂc University of Melbourne). ǂt
         Proceedings. ǂf 1981.
```

‡4   **Relator code**

Identifies, in coded form, the relationship between the meeting name and the work. In pointing out the function that the entity has performed, subfield ‡4 works much as it does in the personal name and corporate name fields.

```
711 20   Bayreuther Festspiele. ‡e Orchester. ‡4 prf
711 20   Woche f"ur Elektronische Musik ‡n (1st : ‡d 1975
         : ‡c Basel, Switzerland) ‡4 fnd
```

In meeting name subject headings (field 611), the subfield ‡x also might be found. Other types of subject subdivisions (geographic or chronological) are rather unlikely.

‡x   **General subdivision**

When a topical or form subject subdivision (i.e., one neither geographic nor chronological in nature) is added to a meeting name, use subfield ‡x.

```
611 20   Marlboro Music School and Festival ‡x Fiction.
611 20   Festival de jazz de Paris ‡n (4th : ‡d 1984) ‡x
         Discography.
611 20   Schweizerisches Drehorgel-Festival ‡n (1st : ‡d
         1979 ‡c Arosa, Switzerland) ‡x Programs.
```

Examples

```
111 20   Paolo Borciani International String Quartet Competition ‡n
         (1st : ‡d 1987 : ‡c Teatro municipale Romolo Valli, Reggio
         Emilia, Italy)
111 20   Festival d'Aix-en-Provence. ‡e Ensemble baroque. ‡4 prf
111 20   Internationale Woche f"ur Experimentelle Musik ‡d (1968 : ‡c
         Berlin, Germany)
111 20   Festival "Musica e filologia" ‡d (1982 : ‡c Verona, Italy)
611 20   Bachtage Berlin ‡x Bibliography.
111 20   Asian Traditional Performing Arts ‡n (2nd : ‡d 1978)
711 22   Saint Thyagaraja Music Festival. ‡t Proceedings. ‡l Tamil &
         English. ‡k Selections. ‡f 1981.
711 20   Dain¸u ˇsvent·e ‡d (1985 : ‡c Vilnius, Lithuania). ‡e
         Organizacinis komitetas.
711 20   Bachfest-Symposium ‡d (1978 : ‡c Philipps-Universit"at
         Marburg). ‡t Proceedings. ‡f 1980.
611 20   Festival traditioneller Musik ‡d (1981 : ‡c Berlin, Germany,
         etc.) ‡x Discography.
111 22   Windspread Conference on Music in General Studies ‡d (1981)
111 20   Convegno nazionale Il comporre musicale nello spazio
         educativo e nella dimensione artistica ‡d (1981 : ‡c
         Florence, Italy, and Fiesole, Italy)
711 20   Stour Music Festival. ‡e Orchestra. ‡4 prf
611 20   ISCM World Music Days ‡x Fiction.
111 20   Zambia Church Music Workshop ‡d (1975 : ‡c Mindolo Ecumenical
         Foundation)
111 20   Jornada de M´usica Cubana Contempor´anea ‡n (4th : ‡d 1981)
111 20   Schumannfest ‡n (2nd : ‡d 1985 : ‡c D"usseldorf, Germany)
```

130	**Main Entry — Uniform Title**	UFBD:	130 (A/A) (NRep)
		OCLC:	130 (R/R) (NRep)
		RLIN:	130 (NR) (NRep)
		WLN:	MEU (A) (NRep)
		MOIM:	130 (NRep)
240	**Uniform Title**	UFBD:	240 (A/A) (NRep)
		OCLC:	240 (R/O) (NRep)
		RLIN:	240 (NR) (NRep)
		WLN:	UTI (A) (NRep)
		MOIM:	240 (NRep)
630	**Subject Added Entry — Uniform Title**	UFBD:	630 (A/O) (Rep)
		OCLC:	630 (R/O) (Rep)
		RLIN:	630 (NR) (Rep)
		WLN:	SUU (A) (Rep)
		MOIM:	630 (Rep)
730	**Added Entry — Uniform Title**	UFBD:	730 (A/O) (Rep)
		OCLC:	730 (R/R) (Rep)
		RLIN:	730 (NR) (Rep)
		WLN:	AEU (A) (Rep)
		MOIM:	730 (Rep)

When a work has appeared under various titles, a uniform title is devised to gather together the bibliographic records for the given work under a single conventionalized title. Uniform titles are used:

- when the work has appeared under varying titles proper (including editions and translations) and the title proper of the work in hand differs from the uniform title
- to gather together different physical manifestations of a work (full score, study score, vocal score, etc.)
- to distinguish different works with similar titles or the same title
- when statements of responsibility, introductory words, or other aspects of the wording of the title proper obscure the title
- to gather together items that contain similar types of works under a collective uniform title

Field 130 is used for main entry uniform titles. Field 240 is used for uniform titles associated with a personal (100), corporate (110), or meeting (111) name main entry. Field 630 is used for uniform title subject headings that are not entered under name headings. Field 730 is used for uniform title added entries that are not entered under name headings.

In scores and sound recordings, uniform titles are most likely to represent musical works, particularly in 240 fields. But these are by no means the only uniform titles that might be found in 130, 630, and 730 fields. Among other kinds of uniform titles that might be found are:

Names of composite manuscripts and groups of manuscripts (except those entered under the name of the library or repository)

```
130 00   Ebermannst¨adter Liederhandschrift.
130 00   Beatus de Saint-Sever (Manuscript)
130 00   Schedelsches Liederbuch.
```

Names of radio and television programs and motion pictures

```
730 01  American bandstand (Television program)
730 01  New letters on the air (Radio program)
730 01  Passion de Jeanne d'Arc (Motion picture)
```

Names of journals, newspapers, etc.

```
730 01  Keyboard (Cupertino, Calif.)
730 01  Columbus dispatch.
```

Titles of anonymous works

```
130 00  Beowulf.
130 00  Narbonnais (Chanson de geste)
130 00  Chaconne von Vitali.
```

Titles of sacred scriptures

```
130 00  Book of Mormon. ǂn Book 1-6. ǂk Selections.
130 00  Koran. ǂp Juz´ al-Mulk.
130 00  Bible. ǂl English. ǂs New American Standard.
130 00  Brahmanas.
```

Names of treaties, agreements, concordats, etc.

```
630 00  Treaty of Brest-Litovsk ǂd (1918 Feb. 9)
630 00  Convention on the Elimination of All Forms of
        Discrimination against Women ǂd (1980)
```

Titles of computer programs and software

```
630 00  Print shop companion (Computer program)
630 00  WordPerfect (Computer program)
```

Indicators

The *first indicator* in the 130, 630, and 730 fields and the *second indicator* in the 240 field specify the number of characters to be disregarded for purposes of filing and sorting at the beginning of a uniform title. Only definite and indefinite articles are ignored in filing; diacritics, punctuation, and special characters that begin a uniform title are not counted as nonfiling characters. In *AACR 2R* practice, all initial articles are omitted from uniform titles, so their occurrence will be rare.

For any title that does not begin with an article, code for "0" nonfiling characters; ignore all punctuation, spaces, diacritics, and special characters. Where an initial article is retained but is not to be ignored (most commonly found in place names such as "Los Angeles"), also use "0". For titles that begin with an article that is to be ignored in filing, count the number of characters in the article, plus punctuation, diacritics, special characters, and spaces preceding the first significant word; code for the appropriate number (1-9) of nonfiling characters present.

```
130 00   "Willehalm"-Handschrift K.
```

```
100 10   Gershwin, George, ǂd 1898-1937.
240 10   "I got rhythm" variations
```

```
100 10   Thomson, Virgil, ǂd 1896-
240 10   ´Etudes, ǂm piano, ǂn 1st set. ǂp Parallel chords
```

```
100 10   Stockhausen, Karlheinz, ǂd 1928-
240 10   "Atmen gibt das Leben-- "


100 10   Musgrave, Thea.
240 14   The voice of Ariadne          [pre-AACR 2 form]


100 10   McCabe, John, ǂd 1939-
240 13   Le poisson magique            [pre-AACR 2 form]


130 40   Die Colmarer Liederhandschrift.   [pre-AACR 2 form]


730 00   La Crosse courier.


100 10   Kokkonen, Joonas.
240 10   "--durch einen Spiegel-- "


100 10   Debussy, Claude, ǂd 1862-1918.
240 12   L'isle joyeuse                [pre-AACR 2 form]
```

The *second indicator* for the 130, 630, and 730 Uniform Title fields is assigned following the same criteria found in the corresponding personal name fields: 100 for 130, 600 for 630, and 700 for 730.

The *first indicator* in the 240 field governs the printing of uniform titles on catalog cards.

OCLC & RLIN	WLN	
0	N	**Not printed on card**
		Uniform title does not print on card
1	A	**Printed on card**
		Uniform title prints on card

Subfields

For the most part, uniform title subfields are defined and applied similarly over 130, 630, 730, and 240 fields. In addition, all of these subfield definitions except subfield ǂa also apply to the title portions of 600, 610, 611, 700, 710, and 711 fields. In these fields, the uniform title retains the same form except that what is subfield ǂa in the 240 field is now translated into subfield ǂt, the first title subfield following the name portion of the heading.

ǂa   **Uniform title** (*130, 240, 630, 730*)
ǂt   **Title of a work** (*600, 610, 611, 700, 710, 711*)

Subfield ǂa in uniform title fields and subfield ǂt in name heading fields each contain the basic title element of the uniform title plus most parenthetical information added to the title to distinguish it from other similar titles. One major exception is the separate subfielding of the date of treaty signing in a treaty uniform title (see subfield ǂd). In music uniform titles, parenthetical information generally is not subfielded separately except for dates used as numbers. This applies regardless of where in the uniform title such parenthetical information appears. Among the types of parenthetical and other information not separately subfielded are:

- Descriptive words or phrases or other identifying information (including parenthetical dates to distinguish between identical uniform titles for non-musical works)

```
130 00   Orgel (Amersfoort, Netherlands)
630 00   Star-spangled banner (Song)
730 01   Star is born (Motion picture : 1954)
130 00   ´Olafs saga helga (Oldest version)
```

```
100 10   Handel, George Frideric, ‡d 1685-1759.
240 10   Overtures (Muzio Scevola)


100 10   Milhaud, Darius, ‡d 1892-1974.
240 10   Songes (2-piano work)


700 12   Howells, Herbert, ‡d 1892- ‡t Magnificat and Nunc
         dimittis (St. Augustine's, Birmingham). ‡l
         English. ‡f 1989.


100 10   Chopin, Fr´ed´eric, ‡d 1810-1849.
240 10   Instrumental music. ‡k Selections (Sketches)


700 12   Grieg, Edvard, ‡d 1843-1907. ‡t Peer Gynt. ‡p
         Forspil (Bruderovet. Ingrids klage). ‡f 1979.
```

- Titles of adaptations that follow in parentheses the title of the original work

```
100 10   Offenbach, Jacques, ‡d 1819-1880.
240 10   Mr Choufleuri restera chez lui le-- (Salon
         Blumenkohl)


100 10   Verdi, Giuseppe, ‡d 1813-1901.
240 10   Stiffelio (Guglielmo Wellingrode)


100 10   Herbert, Victor, ‡d 1859-1924.
240 10   Babes in toyland (Toyland tintype)


700 12   Sullivan, Arthur, ‡c Sir, ‡d 1842-1900. ‡t
         Pirates of Penzance (Tailors of Poznance). ‡k
         Selections. ‡f 1980.
```

- Such phrases as "4 hands" that form part of collective uniform titles

```
100 10   Mozart, Wolfgang Amadeus, ‡d 1756-1791.
240 10   Piano music, 4 hands. ‡k Selections
```

- Parenthetical numbers added to distinguish between identical uniform titles or parts having identical titles (under 25.32A2)

```
130 00   Psalter (Codex Vindobonensis 1861)


100 10   Handel, George Frideric, ‡d 1685-1759.
240 10   Concerti grossi, ‡n op. 3. ‡n No. 4 (1st ed.)


700 12   Ferrabosco, Alfonso, ‡d ca. 1575-1628. ‡t Almans,
         ‡m viols (5) (Eg. MS 2485). ‡f 1987.


700 12   Telemann, Georg Philipp, ‡d 1681-1767. ‡t Trio
         sonatas, ‡m recorder, violin, continuo, ‡r A
         minor (Darmstadt 1042/29). ‡f 1985.


100 10   Mil´an, Luis, ‡d 16th cent.
240 10   Maestro. ‡p Pavana (No. 23)
```

‡d   **Date of treaty signing**

The signing date of a treaty or other intergovernmental agreement is put in subfield ‡d. It may be repeated. Do not confuse this subfield with that for the publication date of a work (subfield ‡f) or the date of a musical work used as a number (subfield ‡n).

```
130 00   Convention for the Protection of Cultural Property in
         the Event of Armed Conflict ‡d (1950). ‡l German.
130 00   General Agreement on Tariffs and Trade ‡d (1947). ‡k
         Protocols, etc., ‡d 1963 July 1. ‡l Spanish.
```

‡f   **Date of a work**

The publication date of the edition of the work in hand is entered in subfield ‡f. Do not confuse this with any other date used in uniform titles.

```
130 00   Bible. ‡l Armenian. ‡s Zohrab. ‡f 1805.


700 12   Hensel, Fanny Mendelssohn, ‡d 1805-1847. ‡t Piano
         music. ‡k Selections. ‡f 1984.


700 12   Stravinsky, Igor, ‡d 1882-1971. ‡t Zhar-pti⁀t⁀sa. ‡p
         Suite ‡n (1919). ‡f 1985.
```

‡h   **Medium**

The General Material Designation (GMD), which describes the medium of the material in hand, is placed in subfield ‡h. In *AACR 2R* records, the Library of Congress uses GMDs only in field 245.

```
730 01   Sid and Nancy (Motion picture). ‡h [Sound recording].
         ‡f 1987.


700 12   Morrison, Toni. ‡t Tar baby. ‡k Selections. ‡h [Sound
         recording]. ‡f 1983.
```

‡k   **Form subheading**

Certain standard phrases used with the title of a work in order to gather together records for particular types of materials are called form subheadings and are placed in subfield ‡k. Most commonly found in uniform title headings are "Selections," "Manuscript," and "Protocols, etc."

```
130 00   Bay Psalm book. ‡k Selections.
130 00   Convention for the Protection of Human Rights and
         Fundamental Freedoms ‡d (1950). ‡k Protocols, etc.
130 00   Bible. ‡p N.T. ‡p Gospels. ‡l English. ‡s Pepys
         Library. ‡k Manuscript. ‡n 2498. ‡f 1987.

100 10   Henze, Hans Werner, ‡d 1926-
240 10   Orpheus. ‡p Persephone and Hades. ‡k Selections; ‡o
         arr.


700 12   Kolb, Barbara. ‡t Songs. ‡k Selections. ‡f 1984.
```

‡l   **Language of work**

The language or languages of the text of the work or a term representing the language(s) appears in subfield ‡l. If multiple languages are represented, all go in a single subfield ‡l that may not be repeated.

```
130 00   Koran. ‡l Serbo-Croatian (Roman) & Arabic.
130 00   Berkeley manuscript. ‡l English & Latin.
130 00   Conflict of Adam and Eve with Satan (Arabic version).
         ‡l Italian & Arabic.
130 00   Avesta. ‡p Yasna. ‡p Gathas. ‡l Polyglot.

100 20   Rimsky-Korsakov, Nikolay, ‡d 1844-1908.
240 10   Sadko (Opera). ‡s Vocal score. ‡l English & Russian.

700 12   Moore, Mary Carr, ‡d 1873-1957. ‡t Legende proven‿cale.
         ‡p Etoile du soir; ‡o arr. ‡l English. ‡f 1985.
```

‡m   **Medium of performance for music**

Subfield ‡m contains the entire statement of the medium of performance, as well as any designations of accompaniment (including continuo) or the indication "unacc." Phrases such as "4 hands" are part of the medium statement *except* when they follow a collective uniform title such as "Piano music," in which case they are not subfielded separately. However, consider as a medium statement qualifiers such as "pianos (2)" that follow a collective uniform title. Subfield ‡m may be repeated when the medium statements are separated by other subfields.

```
100 10   Poulenc, Francis, ‡d 1899-1963.
240 10   Piano music, ‡m pianos (2)

700 12   Beethoven, Ludwig van, ‡d 1770-1827. ‡t Lied mit
         Ver¨anderungen, ‡m piano, 4 hands, ‡n WoO 74, ‡r D
         major. ‡f 1989.

100 10   Cooke, Arnold.
240 10   Suites, ‡m recorders (4), ‡n no. 2

700 12   Graupner, Christoph, ‡d 1683-1760. ‡t Trios, ‡m
         bassoon, chalumeau, continuo, ‡r C major. ‡f 1983.

100 10   Levy, Sarah, ‡d 1908-
240 10   Songs, ‡m unacc. ‡k Selections

100 10   Beethoven, Ludwig van, ‡d 1770-1827.
240 10   Lieder, ‡m piano trio acc.

100 10   Schubert, Franz, ‡d 1797-1828.
240 10   Quintets, ‡m piano, violin, viola, violoncello, double
         bass, ‡n D. 667, ‡r A major

100 10   Gastoldi, Giovanni Giacomo, ‡d fl. 1582-1609.
240 10   Balletti, ‡m voices (5). ‡k Selections

100 10   Arne, Thomas Augustine, ‡d 1710-1778.
240 10   Concertos, ‡m keyboard instrument, orchestra. ‡n No. 3.
         ‡p Con spirito, ‡m keyboard instrument
```

- Should the medium of performance be an integral part of the uniform title, it is not separately subfielded.

```
100 10   Cage, John.
240 10   Solo with obbligato accompaniment. ‡p Short inventions

700 12   Erb, Donald, ‡d 1927- ‡t Saint Valentine's Day brass
         quintet. ‡f 1986.

100 10   Kievman, Carson.
240 10   Temporary piano

700 12   Vis´ee, Robert de. ‡t Pi`eces de theorbe et de luth. ‡p
         Suite, ‡n no. 3; ‡o arr. ‡f 1985.
```

- When the statement of medium is the initial element of the uniform title, as it is in many collective uniform titles, record it in subfield ‡a in the 240, 630, or 730 field or in subfield ‡t in the 600, 610, 611, 700, 710, or 711 field.

```
100 10   Beethoven, Ludwig van, ‡d 1770-1827.
240 10   String quartet music. ‡k Selections

700 12   Gotkovsky, Ida. ‡t Trombone, piano music. ‡k
         Selections. ‡f 1984.
```

‡n **Number of part/section of a work**

Any indication of numbering or sequencing for an entire work or a part or section of a work belongs in subfield ‡n. Opus numbers, serial numbers, thematic index numbers, dates used as numbers (i.e., dates added to uniform titles according to 25.30E1), or any combination are considered to be numbering. Consider the following designations (and their abbreviations and translations) to represent numbering when accompanied by any indication of sequencing, whether alphabetical, numerical, or spelled out: book, collection, livre, part, series, Theil, volume, etc. If multiple statements of numbering are separated by a period, each should be in a separate subfield ‡n; if separated by commas, they belong in the same subfield ‡n.

```
130 00   Notenb¨uchlein f¨ur Anna Magdalena Bach ‡n (1725). ‡k
         Selections.
130 00   Chansons nouvelles, ‡n 22e livre.

100 20   Peterson-Berger, Wilhelm, ‡d 1867-1942.
240 10   Svensk lyrik, ‡n serie 2. ‡p L¨angtan heter min
         arvedel.

700 12   Reger, Max, ‡d 1873-1916. ‡t Aus meinem Tagebuch. ‡n
         Bd. 3. ‡n 4. ‡p Humoreske. ‡f 1986.

100 10   Kunad, Rainer, ‡d 1936-
240 10   Concertos, ‡m organ, string orchestra, ‡n conatum 50

100 10   Keller, Gottfried, ‡d d. 1704.
240 10   Sonatas ‡n (1700). ‡n No. 1
```

```
700 12   Britten, Benjamin, ǂd 1913-1976. ǂt Folk song
         arrangements ǂn (1943-1961), v. 1. ǂp Oliver Cromwell.
         ǂf 1979.


700 12   Porter, Cole, ǂd 1891-1964. ǂt Let's face it. ǂn Act 1.
         ǂn Scene 1. ǂf 1982.


100 10   Beethoven, Ludwig van, ǂd 1770-1827.
240 10   Quartets, ǂm strings, ǂn no. 8, op. 59, no. 2, ǂr E
         minor


100 10   Buxtehude, Dietrich, ǂd 1637-1707.
240 10   Sonatas, ǂm violins (2), viola da gamba, continuo, ǂn
         BuxWV 266, ǂr C major
```

- The abbreviation for the term "opus posthumous" is considered numerical, whether or not it actually is accompanied by a numeral, so it is recorded in subfield ǂn.

```
100 10   Webern, Anton, ǂd 1883-1945.
240 10   St¨ucke, ǂm piano, ǂn op. posth.


100 10   Hummel, Johann Nepomuk, ǂd 1778-1837.
240 10   Preludes and fugues, ǂm organ, ǂn op. posth. 7, no. 1,
         ǂr A♭ major.
```

- Number designations that are actually the inverted form of a named part, and named parts that contain chapter and/or verse numbers remain part of subfield ǂp and are not separated out into a subfield ǂn.

```
130 00   Book of Mormon. ǂp Nephi, 1st.
130 00   Bible. ǂp N.T. ǂp Corinthians, 1st, XIII, 1-8, 13.
130 00   Bible. ǂp O.T. ǂp Apocrypha. ǂp Ecclesiasticus XLIV-L.
```

- Numbers that are integral parts of titles are not subfielded separately.

```
130 00   Twelve new songs.


100 10   Anderson, Beth, ǂd 1950-
240 10   8th ancestor


700 12   Sch¨affer, Bogusław. ǂt Berlin 80, ǂn no. 2. ǂf 1985.


700 12   Brown, Earle. ǂt Folio. ǂp December 1952. ǂf 1986.


100 10   Rossini, Gioacchino, ǂd 1792-1868.
240 10   Maometto II. ǂl English & Italian


100 10   Dillon, James.
240 10   East 11th St NY 10003


700 12   Faur´e, Gabriel, ǂd 1845-1924. ǂt Flˆute concours 1898.
         ǂf 1980.
```

```
100 10   Lasso, Orlando di, ǂd 1532-1594.
240 10   Responsoria pro Triduo sacro in nocturno II et III. ǂp
         Feria V in Coena Domini ad Matutinum


100 10   Schumann, Clara, ǂd 1819-1896.
240 10   Cadencias para el Concierto en re menor K.V. 466 de
         Mozart
```

ǂo   Arranged statement for music

The abbreviation "arr." is placed in subfield ǂo, indicating that a work is an arrangement.

```
100 10   Paganini, Nicol`o, ǂd 1782-1840.
240 10   Palpiti; ǂo arr.


700 12   Uhl, Alfred, ǂd 1909- ǂt Wer einsam ist, der hat es
         gut. ǂl English & German. ǂk Selections; ǂo arr. ǂf
         1987.


100 10   Diemer, Emma Lou.
240 10   Concerto, ǂm flute, orchestra; ǂo arr.


700 12   Reutter, Hermann, ǂd 1900- ǂt Passion in 9 Inventionen;
         ǂo arr. ǂf 1986.
```

ǂp   Name of part/section of a work

The name of any section or part of a work, which might follow any other portion of a uniform title, goes in subfield ǂp. This includes the overall title of the work (subfield ǂa or ǂt), a number (subfield ǂn), a medium statement (subfield ǂm), or even the name of another part or section (subfield ǂp). If a part or section is both numbered and named, the number goes in subfield ǂn, the name in subfield ǂp.

```
130 00   Piae cantiones. ǂp Verbum caro factum est.
130 00   Kanjur (Bonpo version). ǂp Mdo. ǂp Gzer mig.


100 10   Leonarda, Isabella, ǂd 1620-1704.
240 10   Messe e motetti, ǂn op. 18. ǂp Messa, ǂn no. 1


100 10   Ives, Charles, ǂd 1874-1954.
240 10   Set of 3 short pieces. ǂp Scherzo


700 12   Brahms, Johannes, ǂd 1833-1897. ǂt Quartets, ǂm mixed
         solo voices, piano, ǂn op. 112. ǂp Zigeunerlieder. ǂp
         Rote Rosenknospen. ǂf 1980.


700 12   Hays, Doris. ǂt Beyond violence. ǂp Celebration of no.
         ǂf 1984.


100 10   Speer, Daniel, ǂd 1636-1707.
240 10   Musicalisch-t¨urckischer Eulen-Spiegel. ǂn 29. ǂp
         Sonata `a 5


100 20   Caix d'Hervelois, Louis de, ǂd ca. 1670-ca. 1760.
240 10   Pi`eces, ǂm flute, continuo ǂn (1731). ǂp Suite, ǂn no.
         3
```

‡r   Key for music

The statement of the key of the work is input in subfield ‡r.

```
100 10   Tartini, Giuseppe, ‡d 1692-1770.
240 10   Sonatas, ‡m violin, continuo, ‡n B. g 10, ‡r G minor

700 12   Hindemith, Paul, ‡d 1895-1963. ‡t Sonatas, ‡m violin,
         piano, ‡n op. 11, no. 2, ‡r D. ‡f 1979.
```

‡s   Version

Nonparenthetical information concerning the version or edition of a work or collection is recorded in subfield ‡s. In music records, this usually is a subheading such as "Vocal score", "Chorus score", "Libretto", "Text", or "Texts". Version data enclosed in parentheses are not subfielded separately.

```
130 00   Han chawidanwˇon ˇui unmyˇong. ‡s Chorus score.

130 00   Bible. ‡p N.T. ‡l Korean. ‡s Ross version. ‡f 1887.

130 00   Bible. ‡p O.T. ‡p Ezekiel I-XX. ‡l English. ‡s
         Greenberg. ‡f 1982.

130 00   Herzog Ernst (Version B). ‡l English.

130 00   Apocalypse of Esdras (Medieval version).

700 12   Carr, Peter. ‡t Songs, ‡m string quartet acc. ‡s Vocal
         score. ‡f 1983.

100 10   Charpentier, Marc Antoine, ‡d 1634-1704.
240 10   David et Jonathas. ‡s Chorus score

700 12   Swados, Elizabeth. ‡t Doonesbury. ‡s Libretto. ‡f 1985.

100 10   Parra, Violeta, ‡d 1917-1967.
240 10   Songs. ‡s Texts. ‡k Selections

100 10   Mussorgsky, Modest Petrovich, ‡d 1839-1881.
240 10   ⌐T⌐Sar´ Saul (2nd version)
```

In addition to the preceding subfields, the following three subfields might be found in subject uniform title fields (630). Remember that titles used in phrase subject headings ("Bible stories," "Koran and science") are input as topical subject added entries in field 650.

‡x   General subdivision

Any general topical or form subject subdivision, neither geographical nor chronological in nature, added to a uniform title is recorded in subfield ‡x.

```
630 00   Bible. ‡p O.T. ‡x Accents and accentuations.
630 00   Vedas ‡x Recitation.
630 00   Sindbad the sailor ‡x Juvenile sound recordings.
630 00   Charlemagne (Play) ‡x Versification.
630 00   Twelve days of Christmas (English folk song) ‡x
         Anecdotes, facetiae, satire, etc.
```

‡y **Chronological subdivision**

Any subject subdivision representing a period of time is input as subfield ‡y.

630 00   Bible ‡x Criticism, interpretation, etc. ‡x History ‡y Middle Ages, 600-1500.
630 00   Arabian nights ‡x History ‡y 20th century.

‡z **Geographic subdivision**

Any subject heading subdivision for a place name goes in subfield ‡z.

630 00   Koran ‡x Publication and distribution ‡z Saudi Arabia.
630 00   Aranyakas ‡x Study ‡z India ‡z Varanasi.

Examples

130 00   Renaut de Montauban (Chanson de geste). ‡l German.
130 00   Armorer. ‡k Selections.
130 00   Bible. ‡l Latin. ‡s Bodleian Library. ‡k Manuscript. ‡n Auct. E. Infra 1 & 2.
130 00   Sonata, ‡m violins (4), continuo, ‡r D major
           [an anonymous work, ca. 1690]
130 00   Canti C. ‡k Selections.
130 00   Nunc dimittis (Parr`oquia de Sant Pere de Canet de Mar, Spain)
130 00   Ars moriendi (Version beginning: Quamvis secundum philosophum tertio Ethicorum)
130 00   Alman, ‡m harpsichord (Fitzwilliam virginal book, 14)
130 00   Division flute. ‡n Part 1.
130 00   Recueil de pi`eces choisies pour de clavessin, 1702.

630 00   Treaty of Utrecht ‡d (1713)
630 00   English lute-songs ‡x Indexes.
630 00   Lamentations of Jeremiah (Music)
630 00   Ten commandments ‡x False witness.

730 01   Grand ole opry (Radio program)
730 02   Batalla (5o tono). ‡f 1977.
730 01   Frog he would a-wooing go (Folk song)
730 01   Lost horizon (Motion picture : 1937)
730 01   Music in time (Television program)
730 02   Queene of Bohemia's dumpe. ‡f 1983.
730 01   Three little kittens.
730 02   Villancicos de diversos autores. ‡k Selections. ‡f 1983.
730 02   Messe de Toulouse. ‡l Latin. ‡f 1981.

100 10   Talma, Louise, ‡d 1906-
240 10   Have you heard? Do you know?

100 10   Jacobi, Carl, ‡d 1791-1852.
240 10   Introduktion, Thema und Variationen, ‡m bassoon, orchestra, ‡n op. 10, ‡r B♭ major

100 10   Bernstein, Leonard, ‡d 1918-
240 10   Dybbuk. ‡n 12

```
110 20   Catholic Church.
240 10   Mass, 23rd Sunday of ordinary time (Chant)


100 10   Boccherini, Luigi, ‡d 1743-1805.
240 10   Sonatas, ‡m violoncello, continuo, ‡r A major


100 10   Vanhal, Johann Baptist, ‡d 1739-1813.
240 10   Symphonies, ‡m string orchestra, ‡r C major ‡n (1980)


100 10   Schubert, Franz, ‡d 1797-1828.
240 10   Sonatas, ‡m piano, 4 hands, ‡n D. 812, ‡r C major; ‡o arr.


100 20   Eckhardt-Gramatt´e, S. C. ‡q (Sophie-Carmen), ‡d 1899-1974.
240 10   Symphonies, ‡n no. 1, ‡r C


100 10   Offenbach, Jacques, ‡d 1819-1880.
240 10   Operas. ‡k Selections; ‡o arr.


100 10   Reid, John, ‡d 1721-1807.
240 10   Solos, ‡m flute, continuo, ‡n 2nd set. ‡n No. 2


100 10   Charpentier, Marc Antoine, ‡d 1634-1704.
240 10   Messe de minuit. ‡p Kyrie. ‡p Kyrie (Joseph est bien mari´e)


100 10   Tailleferre, Germaine, ‡d 1892-
240 10   Partitas, ‡m piano. ‡p Perpetuum mobile


100 10   Sor, Fernando, ‡d 1778-1839.
240 10   Guitar music, ‡m guitars (2). ‡k Selections; ‡o arr.


100 10   Vivaldi, Antonio, ‡d 1678-1741.
240 10   Concertos, ‡n op. 7. ‡n Book 2. ‡n No. 2


100 10   Monteverdi, Claudio, ‡d 1567-1643.
240 10   Vespro della Beata Vergine. ‡p Magnificat, ‡m voices (7),
         instrumental ensemble


100 10   Stockhausen, Karlheinz, ‡d 1928-
240 10   Licht. ‡p Donnerstag. ‡p Michaels Heimkehr. ‡p Festival. ‡p
         Knabenduett


100 10   Hindemith, Paul, ‡d 1895-1963.
240 10   1922


100 10   Strauss, Richard, ‡d 1864-1949.
240 10   Rosenkavalier (Silent film music)


700 12   Brahms, Johannes, ‡d 1833-1897. ‡t St¨ucke, ‡m piano, ‡n op.
         18. ‡p Intermezzo, ‡r A major. ‡f 1987.


700 12   Richter, Marga. ‡t Ricercare, ‡m trumpets (2), trombones (2).
         ‡f 1987.
```

700 12   Purcell, Henry, ǂd 1659-1695. ǂt March and canzona, ǂm trumpets (4), ǂn Z. 860, ǂr F minor. ǂp March. ǂf 1982.

700 12   Geminiani, Francesco, ǂd 1687-1762. ǂt Sonatas, ǂm flute, continuo, ǂr G major ǂn (1720, no. 1). ǂf 1985.

700 12   Chaminade, C'ecile, ǂd 1857-1944. ǂt Concertino, ǂm flute, piano, ǂn op. 107; ǂo arr. ǂf 1980.

700 12   Jan'aˇcek, Leoˇs, ǂd 1854-1928. ǂt Sinfonietta. ǂp Allegretto (1st movement). ǂf 1987.

700 12   Spohr, Louis, ǂd 1784-1859. ǂt Mass, ǂn op. 54, ǂr C major. ǂf 1980.

700 12   Bach, Johann Sebastian, ǂd 1685-1750. ǂt Wachet auf, ruft uns die Stimme (Cantata). ǂp Zion h¨ort die W¨achter singen; ǂo arr. ǂf 1986.

700 12   Dring, Madeleine. ǂt Three piece suite. ǂf 1984.

700 12   Bozay, Attila. ǂt Darabok, ǂm piano, ǂn op. 30b/1. ǂf 1985.

700 12   Hauer, Josef, Matthias, ǂd 1883-1959. ǂt Zw¨olftonspiel, ǂm piano, 4 hands ǂn (1955 Oct.). ǂf 1987.

700 12   Gershwin, George, ǂd 1898-1937. ǂt Porgy and Bess. ǂk Selections; ǂo arr. ǂf 1981.

700 12   Chopin, Fr'ed'eric, ǂd 1810-1849. ǂt Etudes, ǂm piano, op. 25. ǂn No. 1. ǂf 1976.

700 12   Biber, Heinrich Ignaz Franz, ǂd 1644-1704. ǂt Sonatas, ǂm violin, continuo (Bayerische Staatsbibliothek: Mus. Ms. 4123). ǂp Passacaglia, ǂm violin. ǂf 1985.

700 12   Sikora, El˙zbieta, ǂd 1943- ǂt Ariadna. ǂs Libretto. ǂl English & Polish. ǂf 1985.

700 12   Locke, Matthew, ǂd 1621 or 2-1677. ǂt Violins (2), continuo music. ǂk Selections. ǂf 1981.

700 12   Tull, Fisher. ǂt Profiles. ǂn 1. ǂp Very fast. ǂf 1987.

700 12   Chenoweth, Gerald, ǂd 1943- ǂt For viola solo. ǂf 1984.

700 12   Matteis, Nicola, ǂd fl. 1672-1699. ǂt Airs, ǂn 4th part. ǂp Arie `e passaggi ad immatione della trombetta; ǂo arr. ǂf 1983.

700 22   Jacquet de La Guerre, Elisabeth-Claude, ǂd ca. 1664-1729. ǂt Trio sonatas. ǂn No. 1. ǂf 1985.

700 12   Goltermann, Georg, ‡d 1824-1898. ‡t Concertos, ‡m
             violoncello, orchestra, ‡n no. 1, op. 14, ‡r A minor; ‡o arr.
             ‡f 1985.

700 12   Sch¨utz, Heinrich, ‡d 1585-1672. ‡t Memorial, 1651. ‡f 1986.

700 12   Brahms, Johannes, ‡d 1833-1897. ‡t Choralvorspiele, ‡n op.
             22. ‡p Herzlich thut mich verlangen (Nr. 9). ‡f 1981.

700 12   Jan´a˘cek, Leo˘s, ‡d 1854-1928. ‡t Sonata 1.X.1905. ‡f 1982.

650	**Subject Added Entry — Topical Term**	UFBD: 650 (A/O) (Rep) OCLC: 650 (R/O) (Rep) RLIN: 650 (NR) (Rep) WLN: SUT (A) (Rep) MOIM: 650 (Rep)
651	**Subject Added Entry — Geographic Name**	UFBD: 651 (A/O) (Rep) OCLC: 651 (R/O) (Rep) RLIN: 651 (NR) (Rep) WLN: SUG (A) (Rep) MOIM: 651 (Rep)

Field 650 contains topical subject headings that do not fit into the categories covered by other 6XX fields (600 for personal names, 610 for corporate names, 611 for meeting names, 630 for uniform titles, and 651 for geographic names). These topical headings are derived from such lists and thesauri as the *Library of Congress Subject Headings* (LCSH) and *Medical Subject Headings* (MeSH). Topical subjects more or less likely to be found in music-related records include:

- General concepts, items, and things

  ```
  650  0  Peace ‡x Songs and music.
  650  0  Insects ‡x Songs and music.
  650  0  Nursery schools ‡x Music.
  650  0  Varnish and varnishing.
  ```

- Chemical compounds and systematic names of families, genera, and species in botany and zoology

  ```
  650  0  Dichlorophenoxyacetic acid.
  650  0  Mustelidae.
  650  0  Iris pseudacorus.
  650  0  Streptococcus faecalis.
  ```

- Events and holidays

  ```
  650  0  Saint Cecilia's Day ‡x Songs and music.
  650  0  Erie, Lake, Battle of, 1813.
  650  0  Ramadan.
  650  0  Tu bi-Shevat.
  ```

- Names of objects or classes of objects

  ```
  650  0  Studebaker automobile.
  650  0  Tooth paste pot lids.
  650  0  Jukunoid languages.
  650  0  ROBOTRON 4201 (Computer)
  ```

- Deities, mythological figures, fictional characters, and others incapable of authorship

  ```
  650  0  Pied Piper of Hamelin (Legendary character)
  650  0  Theseus (Greek mythology)
  ```

```
650   0   Holmes, Sherlock (Fictitious character)
650   0   Susanoo no Mikoto (Shinto deity)
650   0   Mickey Mouse (Cartoon character)
```

Phrase subject headings that begin with titles, geographic names, or corporate body names also are coded as 650 fields.

```
650   0   Koran as literature.
650   0   Arabian Peninsula in the Bible.
650   0   Catholic Church and humanism.
```

In addition, the unique position of music in the field of human endeavor dictates other types of subject access, such as:

- Medium of performance

```
650   0   Electronic music.
650   0   Jazz vocals.
650   0   Guitar and harpsichord music ǂx Scores and parts.
650   0   Oud with string orchestra.
650   0   Serpent music.
```

- Musical form, genre, or type of composition

```
650   0   Quodlibets (Music)
650   0   Doo-wop (Music)
650   0   Operas.
650   0   Chants (Byzantine)
650   0   Country music.
```

- Combinations of form and medium

```
650   0   Variations (Organ, 4 hands)
650   0   Octets (Harp, violins (2), violas (2), violoncellos
            (2), double bass)
650   0   Concertos (Keyed fiddle)
650   0   Rondos (Oboe and piano)
650   0   Songs (Medium voice) with lute.
```

- Musical topics

```
650   0   Funeral music.
650   0   Humorous songs.
650   0   Holy-Week music.
650   0   Erotic songs.
650   0   Revolutionary ballads and songs.
```

- Ethnic or national groups

```
650   0   Tamils ǂz Malaysia ǂx Music.
650   0   Bara (Malagasy people) ǂx Music.
650   0   Indians of North America ǂz Great Plains ǂx Music.
650   0   Jews ǂx Music.
650   0   Mexican Americans ǂz Texas ǂx Music.
```

- Headings that bring out the language of the musical text

```
650  0  Ballads, Estonian.
650  0  Lullabies, Urdu.
650  0  Folk-songs, Arabic ‡z Bahrain.
650  0  Hymns, Norwegian.
650  0  Songs, Cajun French ‡z Louisiana.
```

- Musical instruments

```
650  0  Chitarrone ‡x Chord diagrams.
650  0  Violoncello ‡x Orchestra studies.
650  0  Gender (Musical instrument) ‡x Methods.
650  0  Racket (Musical instrument) ‡x Studies and exercises.
650  0  Ophicleide ‡x Instruction and study.
```

Geographic names alone or followed by subject subdivisions are coded in field 651. However, when a geographic name is followed by:

- the name of a subordinate body (subfield ‡b)
- a form subheading (subfield ‡k), or
- a title (subfield ‡t)

it is coded in a 610 field. Ecclesiastical entities and religious jurisdictions (dioceses, archdioceses, ecclesiastical principalities, etc.) also are coded as 610 fields.

Most other types of geographical subject headings are coded as 651 fields, including:

- Political jurisdictions (alone or with subject subdivisions), such as countries, states, provinces, cities, towns, etc.

```
651  0  Kiev (Ukraine)
651  0  New York (N.Y.) ‡x History ‡y 1775-1865.
651  0  Rhode Island.
651  0  Burkina Faso.
```

- Natural features, such as rivers, lakes, bays, mountains, deserts, plains, valleys, capes, volcanoes, islands, ocean currents, etc.

```
651  0  Yellow River (China)
651  0  Erie, Lake.
651  0  Scotland Bay (Trinidad)
651  0  Matterhorn (Switzerland and Italy)
651  0  Sonoran Desert.
651  0  Hiep Duc Valley (Vietnam)
651  0  Beaufort, Cape (Alaska)
651  0  Saint Helens, Mount (Wash.)
651  0  Pulltrouser Swamp (Belize)
651  0  Jars, Plain of (Laos)
651  0  Goodenough Island (Papua New Guinea)
651  0  Gulf Stream.
```

- Geographic regions, such as continents, land masses, etc.

  ```
  651  0  Africa ǂx Languages.
  651  0  New England.
  651  0  Benelux countries.
  651  0  Developing countries.
  ```

- Celestial bodies and groupings, such as planets, stars, comets, galaxies, sites on celestial bodies, etc.

  ```
  651  0  Mars (Planet)
  651  0  Nova Cygni 1975.
  651  0  Polestar.
  651  0  Phobos.
  651  0  Virgo Cluster.
  651  0  Milky Way
  651  0  Kohoutek comet.
  651  0  Tranquility Base (Moon)
  651  0  Orion (Constellation)
  ```

- Archaeological sites, caves, ancient cities, etc.

  ```
  651  0  Diana's Vow Rock Shelter (Zimbabwe)
  651  0  Rollright Stones Site (England)
  651  0  Asine (Argolis, Greece : Ancient city)
  651  0  Lascaux Cave (France)
  651  0  Edwin Harness Mound (Ohio)
  651  0  Stonehenge (England)
  ```

- Metropolitan areas, such as city quarters, streets, parkways, roads, squares, etc.

  ```
  651  0  Left Bank (Paris, France)
  651  0  Bond Street (London, England)
  651  0  Spout Run Parkway (Arlington, Va.)
  651  0  Great Ocean Road (Vic.)
  651  0  Plaza Lavalle (Buenos Aires, Argentina)
  ```

- Highways, trails, waterways, bridges, tunnels, etc.

  ```
  651  0  Trans-Canada Highway.
  651  0  Garden State Parkway (N.J.)
  651  0  Continental Divide Trail.
  651  0  Gulf Intracoastal Waterway.
  651  0  Magellan, Strait of (Chile and Argentina)
  651  0  Benjamin Franklin Bridge (Philadelphia, Pa.)
  651  0  Hawks Nest Tunnel (W. Va.)
  ```

- Parks, forts, reservoirs, canals, forests, wildlife sanctuaries, recreation areas, etc., that are incapable of authorship

  ```
  651  0  Rock Creek Park (Washington, D.C.)
  651  0  Fort Sainte-Marie among the Hurons (Ont.)
  651  0  Dismal Swamp Canal (N.C. and Va.)
  651  0  Pampas (Argentina)
  ```

```
651  0  Gardiken Reservoir (Sweden)
651  0  Epping Forest (England)
651  0  Manas Game Sanctuary (Bhutan)
651  0  Superstition Wilderness (Ariz.)
651  0  Delaware Water Gap National Recreation Area (N.J. and
           N.Y.)
651  0  Gulf Islands National Seashore (Fla. and Miss.)
651  0  Whitefish Lake Indian Reservation No. 6 (Ont.)
```

Considerable confusion exists over how to code many types of headings, at least in part because the Library of Congress often changes its practices. However, the documentation of each of the bibliographic networks includes some version of LC's "Alphabetical List of Ambiguous Headings." Updated versions of the list appear occasionally in the *Cataloging Service Bulletin*. The basic list appears as Appendix E of the *USMARC Format for Bibliographic Data* and as Section Z11 of the *Descriptive Cataloging Manual*. When in doubt about coding a particular heading as a 600, 610, 611, 630, 650, or 651, consult any of these sources.

Indicators

For both the 650 and 651 fields, the *first indicator* is blank.

In both fields, the *second indicator* specifies the subject heading list or authority file used to establish the heading.

OCLC & RLIN	WLN	
0	**L**	**Library of Congress Subject Headings (LCSH)**
1	**C**	**LC subject headings for children's literature (LC Annotated Card program)**
2	**M**	**Medical Subject Headings (MeSH)**
3	**A**	**National Agricultural Library subject authority file**
4	**V**	**Source not specified**
5	**E**	**Canadian Subject Heading (National Library of Canada authority file English headings)**
6	**F**	**Répertoire des vedettes-matières (National Library of Canada authority file French headings)**
7	**S**	**Source specified in subfield ǂ2.**

Subfields

ǂa   **Topical term or geographic name used as entry element** *(650)*
ǂa   **Geographic name** *(651)*

In the 650 field, any topical subject term or any geographic name used as the entry element for a topical subject term is coded as subfield ǂa. In the 651 field, any geographic name used as the entry element is coded as subfield ǂa. In the case of each field, parenthetical qualifying information is not separately subfielded. Subfield ǂa may not be repeated.

```
650  0  Trombone music.
650  0  Sonatas (Saxophone and piano)
650  0  Totopotomoy Creek (Va.), Battle of, 1864.
651  0  Mason and Dixon's Line.
651  0  Trans-Alaska Pipeline (Alaska)
```

ǂx   **General subdivision**

Any nonchronological or nongeographic subject subdivision (including certain numerical designations and corporate entities) added to a main subject heading is coded as subfield ǂx. Parenthetical information is not separately subfielded. This subfield may be repeated.

```
650  0  Music ǂx Manuscripts ǂx Facsimiles.
650  0  Concertos (Guitar) ǂx Solo with piano.
```

```
650  0  Psalms (Music) ǂx 129th Psalm.
650  0  Suites (Piano with chamber orchestra) ǂx 2-piano
           scores.
650  0  Operas ǂx Scores and parts (solo)
650  0  Hearing impaired children ǂx Education ǂx Music.
650  0  Church music ǂx Episcopal Church.
651  0  China ǂx History ǂy Long March, 1934-1935 ǂx
           Songs and music.
651  0  Puerto Rico ǂx History ǂx Autonomy and
           independence movements ǂx Songs and music.
```

Subdivisions of the type "Early works to 1800," for works written or published on a topic before the given date, are considered general rather than chronological.

```
650  0  Organ ǂx Methods ǂx Early works to 1800.
```

ǂy   **Chronological subdivision**

Any subdivision that represents a chronological or historical period (dates, a phrase denoting a period, or a combination of the two) is entered in subfield ǂy. When a period is represented by a word, phrase, or name followed by a comma and dates (for instance, "Insurrection, 1919"), treat the entire phrase and dates as a single subfield ǂy. This subfield may be repeated.

```
650  0  Lieder, Polyphonic ǂy 16th century.
650  0  Depressions ǂy 1929 ǂz United States ǂx Songs and
           music.
650  0  Church music ǂx Catholic Church ǂy 500-1400.
650  0  Popular music ǂy To 1901.
650  0  Paleontology ǂy Tertiary.
651  0  Spain ǂx History ǂy Civil War, 1936-1939 ǂx Songs
           and music.
651  0  Soviet Union ǂx History ǂy Revolution, 1917-1921
           ǂx Songs and music.
651  0  Great Britain ǂx History ǂy Elizabeth II, 1952-
           ǂx Songs and music.
```

Some subdivisions that appear to be chronological but that actually do not subdivide a heading into a specific period should be treated as general subdivisions (subfield ǂx). These tend not to follow the subdivision "History."

```
650  0  Dakota Indians ǂx Treaties, 1805.
650  0  Esopus Indians ǂx Wars, 1655-1660.
651  0  United States ǂx Census, 1st, 1790.
651  0  Fort Oswego (Oswego, N.Y.) ǂx Capture, 1756.
```

ǂz   **Geographic subdivision**

Any geographic subdivision of a subject is entered in subfield ǂz. This subfield may be repeated.

```
650  0  Folk-songs, Spanish ǂz Spain ǂz Galicia (Region)
650  0  Folk music ǂz Germany ǂx Instrumental settings.
650  0  Music ǂz Great Britain ǂy 20th century.
650  0  Gays ǂz United States ǂx Songs and music.
650  0  Workers' compensation ǂx Law and legislation ǂz
           California.
```

```
650  0   Feminism ǂz Developing countries.
650  0   Retail trade ǂz European Economic Community
         countries.
651  0   United States ǂx Boundaries ǂz Mexico.
651  0   Japan ǂx Foreign relations ǂz Korea (South)
651  0   Middle East ǂx Study and teaching ǂz United
         States.
```

However, treat the subdivision "States" as a general subdivision, coding it as a subfield ǂx.

```
650  0   Budget ǂz United States ǂx States.
```

Examples

```
650  0   Sacred vocal music ǂy 18th century ǂx Scores.
650  0   Stabat Mater dolorosa (Music)
650  0   War-songs ǂz Spain.
650  0   Piano ǂx Studies and exercises (Jazz)
650  0   Statue of Liberty (New York, N.Y.) ǂx Songs and music.
650  0   Folk-songs, Portuguese ǂz Portugal ǂz Miranda do Douro ǂx
         Texts.
650  0   Motion picture music ǂx Excerpts ǂx Vocal scores with piano.
650  0   Sextets (Piano (4 hands), bugle, clarinet, percussion,
         violin)
650  0   Kotoko (African people) ǂx Music.
650  0   Music ǂx Manuscripts ǂz Germany (West) ǂz Wolfenb¨uttel.
650  0   Operas, Chinese ǂz China ǂz Honan Province ǂx Vocal scores
         without accompaniment.
650  0   Palestinian Arabs ǂz Israel ǂx Music.
650  0   Guitar, unspecified instruments (2) with orchestra.
650  0   Uranium mines and mining ǂx Environmental aspects ǂz Scotland
         ǂz Orkney ǂx Songs and music.
650  0   Chamber music ǂy 16th century.
650  0   Stations of the Cross ǂx Songs and music.
650  0   Popular instrumental music ǂy 1981-
650  0   Sacred vocal music ǂz Germany (West) ǂz Mannheim ǂy 18th
         century ǂx Thematic catalogs.
650  0   Songs ǂz Africa ǂx Instrumental settings.
650  0   World War, 1939-1945 ǂx Songs and music.
650  0   Music ǂz Germany ǂz Potsdam ǂy 18th century.
650  0   Todd, Sweeney (Fictitious character)
650  0   Carnival ǂz Brazil ǂz Rio de Janeiro.
650  0   Bluegrass music ǂy To 1951.
650  0   Marches (Band), Arranged ǂx Scores and parts.
650  0   Choruses, Sacred (Women's voices) with orchestra ǂx Vocal
         scores with piano (4 hands)

651  0   Humber, River (England) ǂx Songs and music.
651  0   Roanoke Island (N.C.) ǂx History ǂx Drama.
651  0   Crab Nebula.
651  0   EPCOT (Fla.) ǂx Songs and music.
651  0   Korean Demilitarized Zone (Korea)
651  0   Dachau (Germany : Concentration camp)
651  0   Confederate Cemetery (Chattanooga, Tenn.)
```

```
651  0  I.C.I.P.E. Farm (Kenya)
651  0  La Guardia Airport (N.Y.)
651  0  Yellow River (China) ǂx Songs and music.
651  0  Fra Mauro Crater (Moon)
```

245   Title Statement

UFBD: 245 (M/M) (NRep)
OCLC: 245 (M/M) (NRep)
RLIN: 245 (R) (NRep)
WLN: TIL (M) (NRep)
MOIM: 245 (NRep)

The title statement comprises the title proper (short title, alternative title, and any name and/or numerical designation of a part or section), the remainder of the title and other title information (subtitles, parallel titles, etc.), and any general material designation (GMD). The statement of responsibility, which also encompasses the transcription of the remainder of the title page (or its substitute chief source of information) up to any musical presentation statement (see field 254), edition statement (see field 250), or imprint (see field 260), completes the title statement area.

Because the formulation of the entire title statement according to *AACR 2R* tends to be intricate, it is advisable to use the ISBD punctuation that *AACR 2R* requires as a guide to subfielding. These marks of ISBD punctuation and their uses include:

=	**Equal sign**	**Parallel title**

```
245 00   Kwartet smyczkowy = ǂb String quartet / ǂc Eugeniusz
         Knapik.
```

:	**Colon**	**Other title information**

```
245 10   Suite of wildflowers : ǂb op. 1 / ǂc words and music by
         Sharon Davis.
```

;	**Semicolon**	**Titles for separate works by same author**

```
245 00   String quartet no. 1 ; Piano trio ; Piano sonata ;
         String quartet no. 2 ǂh [sound recording] / ǂc Israel
         Kremen.
```

.	**Period**	**Dependent title (part or number)**

```
245 10   Julie. ǂp Ouverture / ǂc Gaspare Spontini ; revisione
         di Lorenzo Tozzi.
245 00   Tristan und Isolde ; Lohengrin. ǂn Act 3 ǂh [sound
         recording] / ǂc Richard Wagner.
```

/	**Slash**	**Statement of responsibility**

```
245 10   Dwa oberki / ǂc Bacewicz.
```

;	**Semicolon**	**Subsequent statements of responsibility**

```
245 00   Seven suites / ǂc Jeremiah Clarke ; newly transcribed
         and edited from Choice lessons for the harpsichord or
         spinett (1711) and the manuscript sources by John
         Harley.
```

.	Period	Titles for works by different authors

```
245 10   Parts apart / ǂc Karl Aage Rasmussen. Chamber music II
         / Ole Buck. Drei-klang / Ivar Frounberg. Decet 1982 /
         Lars Hegaard ǂh [sound recording].
```

Indicators

The *first indicator* controls the generation of a title added entry.

OCLC & RLIN	WLN	
0	N	**No title added entry**

No title added entry is generated from the 245 field, either because no such title added entry is desired or because the title is traced differently from the way it appears in the 245 field; this value always is used when there is no 1XX field in the record

| 1 | A | **Title added entry** |

A title added entry is generated; on catalog cards, the added entry tracing "Title" is displayed

The *second indicator* specifies the number of characters to be disregarded at the beginning of a title for purposes of filing and sorting. Only definite and indefinite articles are ignored in filing; diacritics, punctuation, and special characters that begin a title are not counted as nonfiling characters unless they are part of an article or between the article and the first actual filing character. (Remember that in OCLC, RLIN, and WLN, a diacritic is input and displays online in the space directly before the character it modifies. Its possible value as a nonfiling character must be taken into consideration. However, the situation *might* differ in certain local systems that display a diacritic in the same space as the character it modifies.) Where the intent is not to ignore an initial article (for example, when a title begins with proper name such as "Los Alamos" or "La Montaine"), use second indicator "0". For titles that begin with an article that is to be ignored, count the number of characters in the article, plus punctuation, diacritics, special characters, and spaces preceding the first significant word; code for the appropriate number (1-9) of nonfiling characters present.

```
245 00   Los Angeles, music from the 60's & beyond ǂh [sound
         recording]
245 04   Las Canciones folkl´oricas de la Argentina ǂh [sound
         recording] : ǂb antolog´ia.
245 10   "--such words as it were vain to close-- " : ǂb for piano /
         ǂc J.K. Randall. "--my chart shines high where the blue
         milks upset-- " / B. Boretz.
245 10   Time lag zero : ǂb for voice and viola (or v'cello), 1982 /
         ǂc James Dillon.
245 16   --the serpent-snapping eye : ǂb trumpet, percussion, piano,
         and 4-channel computer synthesized sound / ǂc Roger
         Reynolds.
245 14   The resounding lyre : ǂb for high voice and seven instruments
         / ǂc Miriam Gideon.
245 15   Eine Nacht in Venedig ǂh [sound recording] : ǂb
         Gesamtaufnahme / ǂc Johann Strauss, Sohn ; bearb., Erich W.
         Korngold ; Text, F. Zell und Richard Gen´ee ; rev., Ernst
         Marischka.
245 15   Die ¨agyptische Helena ǂh [sound recording] : ǂb Oper in zwei
         Augz¨ugen / ǂc Richard Strauss ; [Text] von Hugo von
         Hofmannsthal.
245 10   ´El´egie sur des motifs du Prince Louis Ferdinand de Prusse :
         ǂb f¨ur Klavier = for piano solo / ǂc Franz Liszt ;
         herausgegeben von Imre Sulyok, Imre Mezo ; Fingersatz
         revidiert von Korn´el Zempl´eni.
```

Subfields

‡a **Title**

The title proper and any alternative titles (joined by the term "or" or its equivalent in other languages) are recorded in subfield ‡a. Since *AACR 2R* records are formulated according to the principles of ISBD, subfield ‡a embraces all the information up to and including the first mark of ISBD punctuation: an equal sign (=), colon (:), or slash (/), or the GMD. Subfield ‡a may not be repeated.

```
245 13   Il principio, or, A regular introduction to
         playing the harpsichord : ‡b a facsimile of the
         original edition of 1760 / ‡c James Nares ; with
         introductory notes by Robin Langley.
245 10   Old American songs : ‡b set 1 ; Old American
         songs : set 2 ; 12 poems of Emily Dickinson ‡h
         [sound recording] / ‡c Aaron Copland.
245 00   Sinfonie Nr. 3 c-Moll op. 78 = ‡b Symphony in C
         minor ; Ouvert"ure zu Jessonda = Overture to
         Jessonda ‡h [sound recording] / ‡c Louis Spohr.
245 00   Songs of Nigeria / ‡c [compiled by] Elsa
         Toffolon.
245 10   Look for the silver lining ‡h [sound recording] /
         ‡c Alberta Hunter.
245 13   La Cecchina, ossia, La buona figliuola / ‡c
         Niccol`o Piccinni ; introduction by Eric Weimer.
```

If an item lacks a collective title, all the titles proper up to the first intervening other title information, statement of responsibility, or GMD are placed in subfield ‡a.

```
245 10   Album lyrique ; and, Derni`eres pens´ees / ‡c
         Maria Malibran ; new introduction by Charlotte
         Greenspan.
245 00   Thirty pieces for five orchestras ; Music for
         piano nos. 4-19, 21-84 ‡h [sound recording] / ‡c
         John Cage.
245 00   Sonate en fa majeur K. 547a ; 6 variations en fa
         majeur K. 398 : ‡b Salve tu, Domine ; Sonate en
         la majeur K. 331 ‡h [sound recording] / ‡c
         Wolfgang Amadeus Mozart.
245 00   Misa ; y, Motetes ‡h [sound recording] / ‡c Juan
         Antonio Garc´ia de Carrasquedo.
245 00   Romance, opus 11, no. 1 ; Romance, opus 11, no. 2
         ; Romance, opus 11, no. 3 ; Romance, op. 21, no.
         1, in a Moll / ‡c Clara Schumann.
         Davidsb"undlert"anze : opus 6 / Robert Schumann
         ‡h [sound recording].
245 00   Gavotta ; Mazurka ; Serenata ; Pas-de-quatre / ‡c
         Misael Domingues.
```

‡b   Remainder of title

Parallel titles and other title information (all the data between the first mark of ISBD punctuation and the GMD or up to and including the slash (/) that introduces the statement of responsibility) are recorded in subfield ‡b. This subfield may not be repeated.

```
245 10   Thirteen ways of looking at a blackbird : ‡b
         tenor or soprano voice, and oboe or flute or
         violin, and piano / ‡c Louise Talma.
245 10   Nice work if you can get it ‡h [sound recording]
         : ‡b Ella Fitzgerald & Andre Previn do Gershwin.
245 10   Harmonica : ‡b Musik f"ur grosses Orchester mit
         Tuba-Solo = Music for full orchestra with tuba-
         solo / ‡c Helmut Lachenmann.
245 10   Early keyboard fingerings : ‡b an anthology =
         Klaviermusik alter Meister mit originalen
         Fingers"atzen / ‡c selected by Mark Lindley and
         Maria Boxall.
245 10   Orpheus : ‡b complete ballet music ; Pulcinella :
         suite from the ballet ‡h [sound recording] / ‡c
         Igor Stravinsky.
```

‡c   Remainder of title page transcription/statement of responsibility

All data following the first slash (/), except for any GMD, are recorded in subfield ‡c. This includes the statement of responsibility and any subsequent title page or title page substitute transcription. Among the information that belongs in field 245 subfield ‡c are any statements of musical format that *imply* intellectual responsibility, even if none is explicitly stated (for example, "Vocal score" implies responsibility for the keyboard reduction, even if no one actually is credited with the intellectual work). For musical presentation statements that imply no intellectual responsibility (for instance, "Set of parts," "In full score") see field 254. Subfield ‡c may not be repeated, so statements of responsibility that follow any second or subsequent slash (/) are not separately subfielded. If no statement of responsibility is recorded, subfield ‡c is omitted.

```
245 00   Piano concerto / ‡c John Harbison ; two-piano
         score.
245 10   A-ronne / ‡c Berio. Heath ; Old North / Billings.
         Hymns and variations / Cage ‡h [sound
         recording].
245 10   Beauty and the beast, really / ‡c piano score.
245 00   Konzert C-Dur f"ur Cello und Orchester op. 20 =
         ‡b Cello concerto in C / ‡c Eug`ene d'Albert.
         Konzert a-Moll f"ur Cello und Orchester op. 33 =
         Cello concerto in A minor / Robert Volkmann ‡h
         [sound recording].
245 10   Messe de Nostre Dame / ‡c Machaut. With
         plainchant High Mass for the Feast of the
         Nativity of Our Lady ‡h [sound recording].
245 10   Cree songs to the newborn : ‡b soprano and
         chamber ensemble / ‡c from Swampy Cree stories
         gathered and translated by Howard Norman ;
         [music by] Laura Clayton.
245 10   Mlada : ‡b an opera ballet in four acts / ‡c
         Nicolai Rimsky-Korsakov ; vocal score ; with
         Russian text.
245 00   Masses ‡h [sound recording] / ‡c by Tallis &
         Sheppard.
```

‡h Medium

The general material designation (GMD), which describes the medium of the material in hand, is placed in subfield ‡h, enclosed in square brackets. Field 245 is the only field in which the Library of Congress uses the GMD in *AACR 2R* records. For sound recordings, the GMD "sound recording" must be used; for scores, the GMD "microform" should be used when appropriate. Placement of the GMD is determined by the cataloging rules, specifically 1.1C2.

```
245 10   Scoop ‡h [sound recording] / ‡c all songs written
         by Pete Townshend.
245 10   Sonata concertante : ‡b for cello & piano ; Four
         epiphanies ; for unaccompanied viola, 1976 / ‡c
         Ruth Schonthal. Sonata for viola & piano ;
         String quartet no. 1 / Nancy Van de Vate ‡h
         [sound recording].
245 10   Water music ‡h [sound recording] = ‡b Wassermusik
         / ‡c Handel.
245 10   Harmonia sacra, or, Divine hymns and dialogues ‡h
         [microform] : ‡b with a thorow-bass for the
         theorbo-lute, bass-viol, harpsichord, or organ /
         ‡c composed by the best masters of the last and
         present age ; the words by several learned and
         pious persons.
245 14   The first lady of the guitar, Liona Boyd, plays
         music by Alb´eniz, Barrios, Sor, Satie, Debussy,
         T´arrega, Payet, Barnes ‡h [sound recording].
245 00   Nahua songs ; The piper at the gates of dawn / ‡c
         Walter Winslow. Panta rhei / Ursula Mamlok. Duo
         / Louis Karchin ‡h [sound recording].
245 00   Toccata ; Appello ; Soundings ‡h [sound
         recording] / ‡c Barbara Kolb.
```

‡n Number of part/section of a work

Any indication of sequencing for a part or section of a larger work is input as subfield ‡n. That sequencing may be spelled out (for instance, "Part two"), numerical ("Supplement 3"), or alphabetical ("Section C"). In musical titles, serial numbers, opus numbers, and thematic index numbers ordinarily *do not* go in subfield ‡n.

```
245 00   32 St¨ucke f¨ur die Fl¨otenuhr, Hob. XIX, 1-32 ‡h
         [sound recording] / ‡c Joseph Haydn.
245 15   Eine Alpensinfonie ‡h [sound recording] : ‡b op.
         64 / ‡c Richard Strauss.
245 00   Sonata for violin and piano no. 2 / ‡c B. Warren.
```

Subfield ‡n may be repeated, but only immediately following a subfield ‡a or ‡p or another subfield ‡n. No subfield ‡n may follow a subfield ‡b, ‡c, or ‡h, so any indication of sequencing for a part or section of a work included in a subfield ‡b or ‡c is not separately subfielded.

```
245 00   Movements for trumpet and various instruments. ‡n
         VII, Trumpet and violoncello / ‡c John Lessard.
245 00   Troisi`eme livre de pi`eces de clavecin. ‡n
         Quatorzi`eme & dix-neuvi`eme ordres ‡h [sound
         recording] / ‡c Fran¸cois Couperin.
245 13   La Walkiria. ‡n Atto primo. ‡n Scena III ‡h
         [sound recording] / ‡c Richard Wagner.
```

‡p   **Name of part/section of a work**
       The name of a part or section of a larger work is input in subfield ‡p. Subfield ‡p may be repeated, but only immediately following a subfield ‡a or ‡n or another subfield ‡p. No subfield ‡p may follow a subfield ‡b, ‡c, or ‡h, so any name for a part or section of a work included in a subfield ‡b or ‡c is not separately subfielded.

```
245 10   Tabulat´urny zborn´ik Samuela Marckfelnera. ‡p
         V´yber = ‡b Tabulaturbuch des Samuel
         Marckfelner. Auswahl / ‡c [editor, Franti˅sek
         Mat´u˅s].

245 00   Konzert a-Moll, BWV 1044, f¨ur Cembalo, Violine,
         Fl¨ote und Streicher ; Konzert c-Moll, BWV 1062,
         f¨ur 2 Cembali und Streicher ; Kantate BWV 29.
         ‡p Sinfonia ‡h [sound recording] / ‡c Johann
         Sebastian Bach.

245 10   Cantica sacra. ‡p Three Latin anthems for three
         voices / ‡c Richard Dering ; edited by Richard
         Lyne.

245 04   The works of Giuseppe Verdi. ‡n Series I, ‡p
         Operas = ‡b Le opere di Giuseppe Verdi. Sezione
         I, Opere teatrali / ‡c editorial board, Phillip
         Gossett, coordinating editor ... [et al.].
```

Examples

```
245 14   The early years. ‡p Supplement ‡h [sound recording].

245 04   The Grand Duke ; Ivanhoe ; The Yeomen of the Guard. ‡p 3 lost
         songs ; The rose of Persia ; Songs ‡h [sound recording] / ‡c
         Sullivan.

245 00   [Catholic choral music].

245 10   Alternative instrumental music ‡h [sound recording] = ‡b
         Alternative Instrumentalmusik.

245 14   Der Ring des Nibelungen. ‡p G¨otterd¨ammerung / ‡c Richard
         Wagner ; dieser Opernf¨uhrer wurde verfasst und herausgegeben
         von Kurt Pahlen unter Mitarbeit von Rosmarie K¨onig.

245 10   Tabulatura nova. ‡n 3e partie ‡h [sound recording] / ‡c
         Samuel Scheidt.

245 10   Modern real estate transactions. ‡n Part 3, ‡p Defaults,
         workouts, and bankruptcy in real estate ‡h [sound recording]
         : ‡b ALI-ABA course of study.

245 00   Office de Quasimodo ; Fioretti. ‡n No. 3 ; Petite rapsodie
         improvis´ee ; Pastorale ; Office de l'Epiphanie ‡h [sound
         recording] / ‡c Charles Tournemire.

245 10   [Andante e polacca, D major].
```

245 00   Konzert c-Moll, BWV 1060, f¨ur Violine, Oboe, Streicher und Continuo ; Oratorium Festo Paschali : ‡b BWV 249. Adagio : 2. Teil der Sinfonia / ‡c Johann Sebastian Bach. Concerto g-Moll, RV 576, per oboe principale, violino principale ed orchestra : per S.A.R. di Sassonia ; Concerto D-Dur, RV 582, per violino e due cori : per la S.S.ma Assontione de Maria Vergine / Antonio Vivaldi ‡h [sound recording].

245 10   Porgy and Bess. ‡p Symphonic suite ‡h [sound recording] / ‡c George Gershwin ; arr. Robert Farnon.

245 10   G. Faur´e par John Clegg ‡h [sound recording].

245 04   The Sacred harp, or, Eclectic harmony : ‡b a new collection of church music : consisting of psalm and hymn tunes, anthems, sentences, and chants, old, new, and original : including many new and beautiful subjects from the most eminent composers / ‡c arranged and harmonized expressly for this work by Lowell Mason and by Timothy B. Mason.

245 14   The New King James Version. ‡p New Testament ‡h [sound recording].

245 10   Sonaria / ‡c by Elizabeth Vercoe ; [edited by Joan Esch].

245 10   Around the world. ‡p Melodrama, Robber in Fogg's flat / ‡c Cole Porter.

Perhaps it only seems that the concept of "edition" is more troublesome for musical items than it is for other materials, but not everything that at first glance appears to be an edition statement should be coded as one. The presence of terms such as "edition" or "version" sometimes indicates an edition statement, but they can be misleading. Some form of numbering often appears in conjunction with edition statements, but not always. When deciding if a particular statement qualifies, keep in mind that true edition statements refer in some way to the production history of the particular physical manifestation of the item.

Based on this criterion, do not code as field 250:

- Musical Presentation Statements, which refer merely to the format ("Score," "Parts," "Study score") in which the music appears and imply no intellectual responsibility; these are coded as Field 254
- Statements that incorporate the name of the person responsible for such elements of musical interpretation as bowing, fingering, phrasing, and so on ("Busoni edition," "Moyse edition"), unless they are part of a statement relating to the particular physical manifestation; these statements may be part of the statement of responsibility in field 245 subfield ǂc
- Statements that consist of or incorporate the name of the publisher or a subsidiary, and which often (but not always) are accompanied by a publisher's number ("Edition Peters," "Edizioni G. Zambon," "English Woodwind Edition," "Universal Orgel Edition"). *Unless* they are part of a statement relating to the particular physical manifestation (such as, "Kunzelmann Octavo Ed."), these statements may be entered appropriately as the name portion of the publisher's number (028 ǂb and 500), a series (4XX), or the publisher statement in field 260 subfield ǂb
- Statements of the arrangement or version of the music that either state explicitly or imply intellectual responsibility ("vocal score," "edition for two pianos"); these constitute part of the statement of responsibility in field 245 subfield ǂc.

To the final type there is one exception: Statements of voice range not grammatically linked to the title, to other title information, or to the statement of responsibility are coded as edition statements, regardless of the presence of the word "edition" or its equivalent (for example, "Medium voice," "Low-medium voice ed.").

Indicators
Both indicators are blank.

Subfields

ǂa   **Edition statement**
Numbers, words, phrases, and abbreviations that describe the edition and distinguish it from other editions are input in subfield ǂa. When the edition statement is in more than one language, only the edition statement in the first language is placed in subfield ǂa. All data up to and including the first equal sign (=) or slash (/) of ISBD punctuation are recorded in subfield ǂa. The subfield is not repeatable.

ǂb   **Remainder of edition statement**
Statements of personal or corporate responsibility relating to the edition, parallel edition statements, and any data that appear following the first equal sign (=) or slash (/) of ISBD punctuation are recorded in subfield ǂb. The subfield is not repeatable.

Examples

250	Urtext der Neuen Bach-Ausg. = ‡b Urtext of the New Bach ed. / herausgegeben von Hans Eppstein.
250	A critical rev. ed. / ‡b by Mina F. Miller.
250	A facsim. ed. from the composer's autograph ms. in the Music Division of the New York Public Library / ‡b introduction by Walter Frisch.
250	Acc. ed. / ‡b edited by Margaret Daly.
250	Instrumental ed.
250	Medium-high voice ed.
250	R´e´ed.
250	Rev. ed., greatly enl., with the addition of many new tunes.
250	Wyd. 2., zmienione.
250	Originalausg., 1. Aufl.
250	Kunzelmann Octavo Ed.
250	Neue Ausg. in modernen Schl¨usseln.
250	Low voice.
250	Facsim. ed. / ‡b with introductory notes and a realisation of the ground basses by Margaret Gilmore.
250	Corr. reprint.
250	2. nach der Quellen revidierte Aufl. der Ausg. von F.X. Haberl und A. Sandberger / ‡b Editionsleitung, Musikhistorische Kommission der Bayerischen Akademie der Wissenschaften.
250	Urtext-Ausg.
250	Ausg. in 4 Heften / ‡b [herausgegeben von] Michael Radulescu.
250	2nd rev. ed., 1st pbk. ed.
250	Carl Fischer facsimile ed.
250	2nd American ed.
250	Redak´t˘si´i´a 1963 goda.
250	Erstdruck.
250	2 dopl., kritick´e a dokumentovan´e vyd.
250	Faksimile-Lichtdruck des Autographs / ‡b mit einem Vorwort herausgegeben von Alfred D¨urr.
250	2. ´ed., enti`erement ref. `a l'aide d'une documentation nouv. (extraite des Archives Dallery, Daublaine-Callinet, Suret, Cavaill´e-Coll).
250	Neue Ausg. nach den Quellen / ‡b von Manfred Grabs.
250	Faksimile nach dem Partiturautograph der S¨achsischen Landesbibliothek Dresden / ‡b mit einem Kommentar von Eberhard Steindorf.

The musical presentation statement is a term or phrase found in the chief source of information of a score or music manuscript that describes the physical format of the music (that is, score, parts, study score, etc.), distinguishing it from other possible presentations of the same work. The 254 field is not used for sound recordings.

Statements that indicate any type of arrangement or "edition" of a musical work, that is, any alteration for which an author, composer, arranger, etc., may be responsible, either through an explicit statement of responsibility or through implication (for instance, vocal score, 2-piano edition), should not be considered musical presentation statements. Statements of this type generally are coded as part of the statement of responsibility in field 245 subfield ǂc. In ambiguous cases, code such statements in the 245 subfield ǂc.

Indicators

Both indicators are blank.

Subfields

ǂa   **Musical presentation area**

The entire musical presentation statement is input in subfield ǂa, which is not repeatable. Where there are parallel musical presentation statements in more than one language separated by equal signs, all are input in the same subfield ǂa.

Examples

```
254       Composer's facsimile study score.
254       Studienpartitur = Study score.
254       Score and parts.
254       Miniature score.
254       Piano-conductor.
254       Orchestra score & analysis.
254       Set of 2 performance scores.
254       In full score.
254       Score in concert [i.e. at concert pitch].
254       Partition d'orchestre.
254       Stimmen = Parts.
254       Partitur und Solostimmen.
254       Partition, r´eproduction du manuscrit de l'auteur.
254       Conductor's score.
254       Full orchestral score.
254       Performing score.
254       Partitura = Partition = Score.
254       Full score.
254       Set of parts.
254       Symphonic set with full score.
```

260 Publication, Distribution, Etc. (Imprint)

UFBD: 260 (A/A) (NRep)
OCLC: 260 (R/R) (NRep)
RLIN: 260 (NR) (NRep)
WLN: IMP (A) (NRep)
MOIM: 260 (NRep)

Information relating to the places of; people or corporate bodies responsible for; and dates of publication, printing, distribution, issue, release, or manufacture of an item is contained in the 260 field. For unpublished items the date might be the only element in this field or the field might be omitted all together. ISBD punctuation may be used as a guide to subfielding the 260 field.

Indicators

The first indicator specifies the presence of a publisher, distributor, etc., in the imprint.

OCLC & RLIN	WLN	
0	**[blank]**	**Publisher, distributor, etc. is present**

The name of the publisher, a noun representing the publisher (for instance "The Conservatory"), or the abbreviation "s.n." (when the publisher's name is unknown) is present in the imprint; use this value whenever a subfield ǂb is present.

1	**X**	**Publisher, distributor, etc. is not present**

Neither the name of the publisher nor a substitute is present in the imprint; use this value whenever there is no subfield ǂb.

The *second indicator* is blank.

Subfields

ǂa **Place of publication, distribution, etc.**

The place of publication plus any additions to that place, such as an address or a bracketed clarification or correction, is coded as subfield ǂa. The abbreviation "s.l.", indicating place unknown, also may appear in subfield ǂa. Use a separate subfield ǂa for each separate place; subfield ǂa is repeatable, either consecutively or with intervening subfields ǂb. All data up to and including the next mark of ISBD punctuation (a colon (:) when a subfield ǂb follows; a semicolon (;) when another subfield ǂa follows; a comma (,) when followed by a subfield ǂc, which not likely in *AACR 2R* records) are contained in subfield ǂa.

```
260 0    New York City (437 5th Ave., New York 10016) : ǂb
         International Music, ǂc c1985.
260 0    Eitwanda [i.e. Etiwanda], CA : ǂb Living History
         Productions, ǂc p1982.
260 0    Calgary, Alta., Canada : ǂb Sefel Records ; ǂa N.Y.
         [i.e. New York] : ǂb Distributed by Qualiton Imports,
         ǂc [1985?]
260 0    Bielefeld : ǂb MD+G ; ǂa [S.l.] : ǂb Im Vertrieb von
         EMI-Electrola, ǂc [1984?]
260 0    Copenhagen ; ǂa New York : ǂb W. Hansen ; ǂa [United
         States] : ǂb Distribution, Magnamusic-Baton, ǂc c1982.
```

ǂb **Name of publisher, distributor, etc.**

The publisher's name plus any qualifications, corrections, or clarifications are input in subfield ǂb. The abbreviation "s.n.", indicating that the publisher is unknown, may appear in subfield ǂb. Separate responsible entities are entered in separate subfields ǂb; the subfield is repeatable, either consecutively or with intervening subfields ǂa. Always preceded by a colon (:), subfield ǂb contains all the data up to and including the next mark of ISBD punctuation (a comma (,) when followed by subfield ǂc; a colon (:) when followed by another subfield ǂb; a semicolon (;) when followed by a subfield ǂa).

```
260 0   New York, N.Y. : ǂb Gryphon : ǂb Distributed by
        Audiofidelity Enterprises, ǂc p1980.
260 0   Leipzig : ǂb Edition Peters ; ǂa Frankfurt ; ǂa
        New York : ǂb C.F. Peters [distributor], ǂc
        c1984.
260 0   [United States : ǂb s.n.], ǂc c1984.
```

ǂc   Date of publication, distribution, etc.

The date of publication, its substitute (according to *AACR 2R* 1.4F6), or its approximation, is recorded as subfield ǂc. Subfield ǂc is not repeatable; adjacent multiple dates, such as publication and copyright dates, are input in the same subfield ǂc. However, if there is both a publication date and a parenthetical manufacture date, the date of manufacture is coded as subfield ǂg. Clarifications of or corrections to a date are placed in the same subfield ǂc. All data following the comma that precedes it are included in subfield ǂc, up to and including the mark of terminal punctuation (a period (.), a hyphen (-) for open dates, a closing bracket ( ]), or a closing parenthesis ( )) that ends the subfield); if another subfield follows, there might be no mark of terminal punctuation.

```
260 0   M"unchen : ǂb Eurodisc, ǂc [between 1978 and
        1985]
260 1   ǂc [17—?]
260 0   Boulder, Colo. : ǂb Convex Industries, ǂc 1981
        printing.
260 0   Frankfurt am Main : ǂb Fischer Taschenbuch
        Verlag, ǂc c1979 ǂg (1980 printing)
260 0   London : ǂb Jasmine, ǂc [between 1980 and 1985],
        p1968.
260 0   T¯oky¯o : ǂb Aoki S¯uzand¯o, ǂc Meiji 37 [1904]
260 0   Ocean, N.J. : ǂb Musical Heritage Society, ǂc
        [1985], p1981.
```

ǂe   Place of manufacture

The place of manufacture and any additions to that place name are coded as subfield ǂe. The abbreviation "s.l." also might appear in the subfield ǂe when the place of manufacture is not known. This subfield will follow any subfield ǂa, ǂb, or ǂc, and its data (along with any accompanying subfield ǂf and ǂg) will be enclosed in parentheses. Subfield ǂe contains all the data from the opening parenthesis up to and including the next mark of ISBD punctuation, in most cases a colon (:).

```
260 0   [S.l. : ǂb s.n., ǂc 1978] ǂe ([S.l.] : ǂf
        Brasilgr´afica)
260 0   [S.l. : ǂb s.n., ǂc 1983] ǂe (Valencia
        [Venezuela] : ǂf Reproven)
```

ǂf   Manufacturer

The manufacturer's name plus any qualifications, corrections, or clarifications are input in subfield ǂf. The abbreviation "s.n." may appear in subfield ǂb when the manufacturer is not known. Always preceded by a colon (:), subfield ǂf contains all the data up to and including the next mark of ISBD punctuation (a comma (,) when followed by subfield ǂg; a closing parenthesis when subfield ǂf ends the field).

```
260 0   [United States] : ǂb Reader's Digest, ǂc [1983],
        p1982 ǂe (New York, N.Y. : ǂf RCA)
260 0   [Brazil : ǂb s.n., ǂc 1985] ǂe (Rio de Janeiro :
        ǂf Polygram do Brasil)
```

‡g   **Date of manufacture**

The date of manufacture is coded as subfield ‡g (except in cases where it has been used instead of the publication date, as stipulated in *AACR 2R* 1.4F6, when it is coded as subfield ‡c). All data following the comma that precedes it are included in subfield ‡g.

```
260 0    Milwaukee, WI : ‡b H. Leonard Pub. Corp., ‡c
         c1983 ‡g (1985 printing)
260 0    Paris : ‡b Seghers, ‡c c1968 ‡g (1981 printing)
```

Examples

```
260 0    London : ‡b ASV ; ‡a [S.l.] : ‡b Allegro Imports
         [distributor], ‡c p1977.
260 0    London : ‡b Anglo-Soviet Music Press ; ‡a Hamburg : ‡b H.
         Sikorski ; ‡a New York : ‡b Sole selling agent for U.S.A., G.
         Schirmer, ‡c c1983.
260 0    Montreal : ‡b Justin Time : ‡b Marketed in Canada by
         Distribution Fusion III, ‡c p1984.
260 0    Silver Spring, MD : ‡b L. Pomerantz, ‡c p1983 ‡e ([United
         States] : ‡f Audio Engineering Association)
260 0    Tokorozawa : ‡b D¯o Hensanshitsu, ‡c Sh¯owa 58 [1983]
260 1    ‡c 1845 July 26.
260 0    Melville, N.Y. (25 Deshon Drive, Melville 11747) : ‡b H.W.
         Gray Publications, ‡c c1983.
260 0    C´aceres : ‡b Instituci´on Cultural "El Brocense", ‡c 1980 ‡g
         (1983 printing)
```

300   Physical Description

UFBD: 300 (M/M) (Rep)
OCLC: 300 (M/M) (NRep)
RLIN: 300 (NR) (Rep)
WLN: COL (A) (Rep)
MOIM: 300 (NRep)

The physical description of the score or recording—the extent of the item, physical details such as illustrations, dimensions, and accompanying material—is contained in the 300 field.

Indicators
Both indicators are blank.

Subfields
Scores

‡a   **Extent**
Subfield ‡a contains the specific material designation (from *AACR 2R* rule 5.5B1) if appropriate, and the extent of the item and/or number of physical units. If more than one type of score and/or part is to be listed, they are separated by a space-plus sign-space (+) in the same subfield ‡a. If other subfields intervene, subfield ‡a may be repeated.

‡b   **Other physical details**
Subfield ‡b contains illustrative matter; the subfield may not be repeated, so multiple illustration statements appear in the same subfield ‡b. It is separated from subfield‡ a by a space-colon-space (:).

‡c   **Dimensions**
Subfield ‡c contains the physical dimensions of an item. When different dimensions correspond to different physical units, the repeatable ‡c follows its own repeatable ‡a. Each ‡c is separated from the preceding subfield by a space-semicolon-space (;).

‡e   **Accompanying material**
In cases where there is accompanying material being recorded in the physical description field, such as a sound recording accompanying a score, that material and its physical description are recorded in a single subfield ‡e. If the physical details are included, they are not separately subfielded. Subfield ‡e is preceded by a space-plus sign-space (+).

Examples — Scores

```
300      1 miniature score (44 p.) : ‡b ports. ; ‡c 18 cm.
300      1 score (v, 13 p.) + 2 parts ; ‡c 30 cm.
300      1 score (47 p.) + 1 part (12 p.) ; ‡c 31 cm.
300      1 score (25 p.) + 1 piano conductor part (10 p.) + 12 parts ;
         ‡c 33 cm.
300      1 score (64 p.) ; ‡c 23 x 31 cm. + ‡a 1 part (16 p.) ; ‡c 27
         cm.
300      1 score (52 p.) : ‡b facsims. + ‡a 1 part (7 p.) ; ‡c 30 cm.
300      3 v. of music ; ‡c 27 cm.
300      1 score (ix, 29 p.) ; ‡c 30 cm. + ‡e 1 sound cassette (12
         min. : analog, stereo.)
300      122 p. of music : ‡b ill. ; ‡c 25 x 35 cm.
300      1 score (xiv, 35 p.) : ‡c 31 cm. + ‡e 1 sound tape reel (23
         min. : analog, 7 1/2 ips, stereo. ; 7 in., 1/2 in. tape) + 14
         slides (col.)
300      4 parts ; ‡c 30 cm.
```

166

Sound Recordings
‡a   Extent

The number of physical units, the specific material designation, and (when appropriate according to *AACR 2R* rule 6.5B2, its rule interpretation, and Music Cataloging Decisions) the playing time of a sound recording are placed in subfield ‡a.

‡b   Other physical details

After a space-semicolon-space (;), subfield ‡b records the following elements, as appropriate, in this order:

* Type of recording

    For discs and tapes, the playback method is designated as "analog" or "digital". It is important to remember here that the physical description field is describing the playback method, the format of the item in hand. Any traditional vinyl, plastic, or shellac disc that plays at such speeds as 33 1/3, 45, or 78 rpm, and is read by a needle or stylus, receives the designation "analog" in the 300 subfield ‡b. "Digital" refers to the newer laser-read technology of the compact digital disc or CD, which is usually 4 3/4 in. in diameter. When the playback method (in the 300 field) differs from the original recording method (how the sound was first captured on a recording medium), a 500 note may be added. This information may appear on the CD liner notes in narrative form, but in many cases it shows up as a three-letter code somewhere on the packaging.

DDD   Indicates that digital technology was used in the original recording session, in subsequent mixing and editing, and in the mastering.

ADD   Indicates that analog technology was used in the original recording session, but digital technology was used in subsequent mixing and editing, and in the mastering.

AAD   Indicates that analog technology was used in the original recording session and in subsequent mixing and editing, but digital technology was used in the mastering.

To make the distinction clear in a catalog record, a compact disc originally recorded by analog methods (both ADD and AAD) would have "digital" in the 300 field, together with a 500 note either reading "Analog recording" or containing an appropriate quotation from the item itself. Conversely, an "LP" disc recorded using digital methods would have "analog" in the 300 field, together with a 500 note reading "Digital recording" or containing an appropriate quotation from the item itself. Add a "Compact disc" note to records for items in that medium to further distinguish them from older technologies. But as CDs move rapidly to predominance in the recording industry, this probably will grow superfluous sooner than we might expect.

A CD made from an analog original:

```
300        1 sound disc (67 min.) : ‡b digital, stereo. ; ‡c
           4 3/4 in.
500        Compact disc.
500        Analog recording.
```

An LP made from a digital original:

```
300        1 sound disc (45 min.) : ‡b analog, 33 1/3 rpm,
           stereo. ; ‡c 12 in.
500        Digital recording.
```

For sound track film, the recording method ("optical" or "magnetic") or the name of a specific recording system ("Phillips-Miller") is identified.

- Playing Speed
  For analog discs, in revolutions per minute (rpm).

  For digital discs, in meters per second (m. per sec.) only if it differs from the standard 1.4 m. per sec. (in which case no speed is recorded—this is the most common circumstance for digital discs).

  For tapes, in inches per second (ips). However, when a medium such as the cassette has a standard speed (most cassettes are 1 7/8 ips), that speed is not recorded.

  For sound track films, in frames per second (fps).

- Groove Characteristics
  For analog discs, indicate this only when it is not standard for the particular type or speed of the recording (for instance, 33 1/3 rpm analog discs are assumed to be "microgroove").

- Track Configuration
  For sound track films, indicate edge track, center track, etc.

- Number of Tracks
  For tapes, indicate the number of tracks unless standard for that medium (4 tracks for cassettes, 8 tracks for cartridges).

- Number of Sound Channels
  For all types of recordings, indicate monophonic (mono.), stereophonic (stereo.), or quadraphonic (quad.); if the item does not explicitly state one of these options, do not record any term.

- Recording and Reproduction Characteristics
  For all types of recordings, add this optional designation only when the information is necessary to select special playback equipment in order to get the full effect of the audio (for example, QS, SQ, and CD-4 encoding for quadraphonic recordings, which require special equipment for quadraphonic reproduction, even if they can be listened to normally in stereo; "Dolby processed" for tapes).

‡c **Dimensions**
Following a space-semicolon-space (;), subfield ‡c contains the dimensions of the sound recording.

- For a disc, record the diameter in inches (in.).

- For tape cassettes, record the dimensions and tape width only if other than standard (3 7/8 × 2 1/2 in. cassette, 1/8 in. tape).

- For cartridges, record the dimensions only if other than the standard (5 1/4 × 7 7/8 in. cartridge, 1/4 in. tape).

- For tape reels, record the reel diameter in inches but include the width only if not the 1/4 in. standard.

- For sound track film, record the width in millimeters (mm.).

Place a space on either side of the "×" between different dimensions; the tape carrier measurements are separated from the tape width by a comma-space, but these are contained within the same subfield ǂc.

ǂe   **Accompanying material**

Any accompanying material deemed important enough to be included in the 300 field, along with its physical description, if needed, is placed in subfield ǂe, after a space-plus sign-space (+) and requires no further subfielding.

Examples — Sound Recordings

300	1 sound disc (39 min.) : ǂb analog, 33 1/3 rpm, mono. ; ǂc 12 in.
300	1 sound disc : ǂb analog, 33 1/3 rpm, quad., QS ; ǂc 12 in.
300	1 sound disc (4 min., 17 sec.) : ǂb analog, 78 rpm ; ǂc 12 in.
300	1 sound disc (69 min.) : ǂb digital, stereo. ; ǂc 4 3/4 in. + ǂe 1 pamphlet (8 p. : ill. ; 12 cm.)
300	2 sound cassettes : ǂb analog, stereo., Dolby processed.
300	3 sound cassettes (118 min.) : ǂb analog, stereo. + ǂe 1 vocal score (157 p. ; 18 cm.)
300	1 sound cassette (49 min.) : ǂb analog, 3 3/4 ips, mono. ; ǂc 7 1/4 x 3 1/2 in., 1/4 in. tape.
300	1 sound tape reel (12 min.) : ǂb analog, 7 1/2 ips, stereo. ; ǂc 7 in., 1/2 in. tape.
300	1 sound tape reel (55 min.) : ǂb analog, 1 7/8 ips, mono. ; ǂc 5 in., 1/2 in. tape + ǂe 1 text.
300	1 sound track film reel (12 min.) : ǂb optical, 25 fps, edge track ; ǂc 16 mm.

306   Duration

UFBD: 306 (A/O) (NRep)
OCLC: 306 (O/O) (NRep)
RLIN: 306 (NR) (NRep)
WLN: DSR (NR) (NRep)
MOIM: 306 (NRep)

The duration of a sound recording or of an item of manuscript or printed music is recorded in coded form in the 306 field. In natural language form, the duration also appears in 500 or 505 fields or, for sound recordings, in the 300 field. Either the duration of the whole or the durations of the parts may be recorded, depending upon which is thought to be more useful.

Indicators

Both indicators are blank.

Subfields

    ‡a   **Duration**

Each duration is recorded in a separate subfield ‡a, in six-character form representing hours, minutes, and seconds: HHMMSS. All six characters always must be present. When the duration is less than one hour, the first two characters are zeroes; when less than one minute, the first four characters are zeroes. Although subfield ‡a may be repeated, if more than six durations are present in a 500 or 505 note, field 306 usually is omitted. Disregard any indication of approximate times by treating such times as though they were exact. Represent a duration of exactly one hour as 006000, of exactly one minute as 000060.

Examples

```
500        Duration: ca. 22:00.
306        002200


300        1 sound disc (69 min.) : ‡b digital, stereo. ; ‡c 4 3/4 in.
306        010900


500        Durations: 8:10 ; 10:17 ; 11:52 ; 9:50.
306        000810 ‡a 001017 ‡a 001152 ‡a 000950


300        2 sound discs (71 min.) : ‡b analog, 33 1/3 rpm, stereo. ; ‡c
           12 in.
306        011100


505 0      Interplay / Barbara Pentland (with the Purcell String
           Quartet) (14:27) -- Acco-music / Ernst Krenek (6:10) --
           Dinosaurus / Arne Nordheim (9:40) -- La testa d'Adriane / R.
           Murray Schafer (with Mary Morrison, soprano) (13:47).
306        001427 ‡a 000610 ‡a 000940 ‡a 001347


500        Durations: 1:29:14 ; :53 ; 14:06.
306        012914 ‡a 000053 ‡a 001406


300        1 sound cassette (47 min.) : ‡b analog, mono.
505 0      Interview (23:29) -- Selected poems (23:07).
306        002329 ‡a 002307
```

440	Series Statement/Added Entry — Title	UFBD:	440 (A/A) (Rep)
		OCLC:	440 (R/O) (Rep)
		RLIN:	440 (NR) (Rep)
		WLN:	SET (A) (Rep)
		MOIM:	440 (Rep)
490	Series Statement	UFBD:	490 (A/A) (Rep)
		OCLC:	490 (R/O) (Rep)
		RLIN:	490 (NR) (Rep)
		WLN:	SER (A) (Rep)
		MOIM:	490 (Rep)
800	Series Added Entry — Personal Name	UFBD:	800 (A/O) (Rep)
		OCLC:	800 (O/O) (Rep)
		RLIN:	800 (NR) (Rep)
		WLN:	SAP (A) (Rep)
		MOIM:	800 (Rep)
810	Series Added Entry — Corporate Name	UFBD:	810 (A/O) (Rep)
		OCLC:	810 (O/O) (Rep)
		RLIN:	810 (NR) (Rep)
		WLN:	SAC (A) (Rep)
		MOIM:	810 (Rep)
811	Series Added Entry — Meeting Name	UFBD:	811 (A/O) (Rep)
		OCLC:	811 (O/O) (Rep)
		RLIN:	811 (NR) (Rep)
		WLN:	SAM (A) (Rep)
		MOIM:	811 (Rep)
830	Series Added Entry — Uniform Title	UFBD:	830 (A/O) (Rep)
		OCLC:	830 (O/O) (Rep)
		RLIN:	830 (NR) (Rep)
		WLN:	SAU (A) (Rep)
		MOIM:	830 (Rep)

Series statements based on information on the cataloged item itself are coded in one of the 4XX fields: 440 when the series is traced in exactly the same form as it appears on the item (save for an initial article and/or an ISSN); 490 when the series is not traced at all or is traced in a form different from that appearing on the item (according to *AACR 2R* rule 21.30L, related rules, and their rule interpretations). These differences may include:

- the addition of parenthetical qualifiers or other information (parenthetical information rarely is subfielded separately)

```
490 1   Document series
830 0   Document series (Finlandia Records)
```

- the elimination of certain information

```
490 1   Walter Beeler memorial commission series / Ithaca
        College
830 0   Walter Beeler memorial commission series.
```

- different wording or some other reformulation of the series information

```
490 1   Chormusik im Kirchenjahr / Heinrich Sch"utz ; ‡v 1
800 1   Sch"utz, Heinrich, ‡d 1585-1672. ‡t Choral music. ‡k
        Selections (Chormusik im Kirchenjahr) ; ‡v 1.
```

- the differentiation of series and subseries

```
490 1   Great virtuosi of the golden age ; ‡v v. 3. ‡a Violin
830 0   Great virtuosi of the golden age ; ‡v v. 3.
830 0   Great virtuosi of the golden age. ‡p Violin.
```

Fields 400, 410, and 411, although they are still valid, are not used for records cataloged according to *AACR 2R*, and so are not addressed here. The parentheses that surround 4XX fields (according to *AACR 2R* rule 1.6A1) are not input in machine-readable records because they are system-generated display constants in OCLC, RLIN, and WLN.

The 8XX fields contain series added entries that have been reformulated somehow to conform to *AACR 2R* practices: 800 for personal name/title series, 810 for corporate name/title series, 811 for meeting name/title series (which are found infrequently, and hence few examples have been included), and 830 for series uniform titles. These 8XX fields serve as series added entries corresponding to 490 fields with a first indicator of "1".

Indicators

440   The *first indicator* is blank in OCLC and RLIN. In WLN it is input as a hyphen.

The *second indicator* specifies the number of characters to be disregarded for purposes of filing and sorting at the beginning of a series statement. Only definite and indefinite articles are ignored in filing; diacritics, punctuation, and special characters that begin a series statement are not counted as nonfiling characters. For further guidelines see the discussion on nonfiling indicators in the section on Uniform Titles (pp. 132-33).

490   The *first indicator* specifies whether the series is traced.

OCLC & RLIN	*WLN*	
0	**U**	**Series not traced**

There is no corresponding series added entry among the 8XX fields.

1	**D**	**Series traced differently**

There is a corresponding 8XX field, the form of which differs from that found in the 490 field.

The *second indicator* is blank in OCLC, RLIN, and WLN.

800   The *first indicator* values correspond to those found in the 100, 600, and 700 fields. Please see pp. 111-13 for details.

The *second indicator* is blank in OCLC, RLIN, and WLN.

810   The *first indicator* values correspond to those found in the 110, 610, and 710 fields. Please see p. 121 for details.

The *second indicator* is blank in OCLC, RLIN, and WLN.

811   The *first indicator* values correspond to those found in the 111, 611, and 711 fields. Please see pp. 126-27 for details.

The *second indicator* is blank in OCLC, RLIN, and WLN.

830   The *first indicator* is blank in OCLC, RLIN, and WLN.

The *second indicator* specifies the number of characters to be disregarded for purposes of filing and sorting at the beginning of a series uniform title. Only definite and indefinite articles are ignored in filing; diacritics, punctuation, and special characters that begin a series statement are not counted as nonfiling characters. Because initial articles routinely are dropped from uniform titles that are reformulated under *AACR 2R*, it is unlikely that any values other than "0" will be used in the 830 field in *AACR 2R* records. For further guidelines see the discussion on nonfiling indicators in the section on Uniform Titles (p. 132-33).

Subfields

Except for the use of subfield ǂv, subfielding practice for the 800 field is identical to that for the 100, 600, and 700 fields; for the 810 field, to that for the 110, 610, and 710 fields; for the 811 field, to that for the 111, 611, and 711 fields; and for the 830 field, to that for the 130, 240, 630, and 730 fields. Please see pp. 114-16, 122-24, 127-30, and 133-40 for details.

Quite different are the subfielding practices for fields 440 and 490. In field 440, only subfields ǂa, ǂn, ǂp, ǂv, and ǂx are used. The 490 field is even simpler, with only subfields ǂa, ǂv, and ǂx being valid.

ǂa   **Title** *(440)*
ǂa   **Series statement** *(490)*

In the 440 field, subfield ǂa contains the title portion of the series in the exact form in which it is traced, excluding the ISSN, any volume numbering, and any part or section name and/or numbering. Subfield ǂa *may not* be repeated in the 440 field.

```
440   0   Orgelmusik der Romantik von 1900-1950 ; ǂv Heft 1

440   4   Das Orgelportrait

440   0   Edition Bach Leipzig

440   0   Skrifter fr°an Musikvetenskapliga institutionen,
          G¨oteborg, ǂx 0348-0879 ; ǂv 4

440   0   Monuments of music and music literature in
          facsimile. ǂn First series, ǂp Music ; ǂv 23
```

In the 490 field, subfield ǂa contains the title plus any statement(s) of responsibility, other title information, part or section name and/or numbering, and dates and other numbering that are inherent parts of the title. Subfield ǂa *may* be repeated in the 490 field when a subseries title is separated from the main series title by subfielded numbering (subfield ǂv) or the ISSN (subfield ǂx), or when a parallel title is present.

```
490 1   Tampereen yliopiston Kansanperinteen laitoksen
        moniste, ‡x 0359-1395 ; ‡v 9, 1984 = ‡a Report /
        University of Tampere, Institute for Folk
        Tradition ; ‡v 9, 1984
830 0   Tampereen yliopiston Kansanperinteen laitoksen
        moniste ; ‡v 9.


490 1   Musical instruments in the Dayton C. Miller flute
        collection at the Library of Congress : a
        catalog ; ‡v v. 1
810 2   Library of Congress. ‡t Musical instruments in
        the Dayton C. Miller flute collection at the
        Library of Congress ; ‡v v. 1.


490 1   The works of Giuseppe Verdi. Series I, Operas ;
        ‡v v. 5 = ‡a Le opere di Giuseppe Verdi. Sezione
        I, Opere teatrali
800 1   Verdi, Giuseppe, ‡d 1813-1901. ‡t Works. ‡f 1983
        ; ‡v ser. 1, v. 5.


490 0   Vanguard audiophile series


490 1   S¨amtliche Werke = ‡a Complete works / Franz
        Berwald ; ‡v Bd. 10
800 1   Berwald, Franz, ‡d 1796-1868. ‡t Works. ‡f 1966 ;
        ‡v Bd. 10.


490 0   Philharmonia Partituren = ‡a Philharmonia scores


490 1   Band 49 der Orpheus-Schriftenreihe zu Grundfragen
        der Musik
830 0   Orpheus-Schriftenreihe zu Grundfragen der Musik ;
        ‡v Bd. 49.
```

In addition to those subfields, the subfield ‡v may be found in fields 800, 810, 811, 830, 440, and 490.

‡v   **Volume number/sequential designation**
    The volume number or other numerical and/or alphabetical designation of sequence within the series is recorded in subfield ‡v. Dates used as sequence numbers also are coded as subfield ‡v; dates and other numerical designations that are integral parts of the series name are not subfielded separately. Numbering may be inclusive (for example, "v. 27-29"), intermittent ("v. 3, 8, 11"), or singular ("v. 1").

```
440 0   Programmhefte der Bayreuther Festspiele, ‡x 0408-
        7283 ; ‡v 1987, 1


440 0   Symphony, 1720-1840. ‡n Series D ; ‡v v. 6


440 0   Red Seal .5 series


440 0   12 Jahre neu Bayreuth (1951-1962)


490 1   Early English church music ; ‡v 20, 25, 30
830 0   Early English church music ; ‡v 20, etc.
```

```
440   0   Camera flauto Amadeus ; ǂv Nr. 4-5
```

When series numbering is integrated grammatically with the series name, it is recorded as such in a 490 field, but the numbering is not separately subfielded. In the corresponding series added entry (8XX), where the numbering is transposed to the correct *AACR 2R* position (see *AACR 2R* RI 1.6G), it is placed in subfield ǂv.

```
490   1   110. Ver¨offentlichung der Gesellschaft der
          Orgelfreunde
830   0   Ver¨offentlichung der Gesellschaft der
          Orgelfreunde ; ǂv 110.


490   1   The Fifteenth Chester book of motets
830   0   Chester book of motets ; ǂv 15th.
```

Subfield ǂx is valid in the 440 and 490 fields but *not valid* in the 8XX fields. The ISSN should *never* be input in a series added entry field.

ǂx   International Standard Serial Number
When the ISSN for a series title is present on an item, it is recorded in subfield ǂx. The designation "ISSN" is not input, because it is a display constant for OCLC, RLIN, and WLN.

```
440   0   Recent researches in the music of the Middle Ages
          and early Renaissance, ǂx 0362-3572 ; ǂv 15
```

Two additional subfields that relate to parts or sections of the series title, subfields ǂn and ǂp, are valid in the 440 field as well as the 8XX fields.

ǂn   Number of part/section of a work
Any numeric, alphabetic, or spelled-out indication of sequencing for a part or section of the series title is coded as subfield ǂn. The occasional opus, serial, or thematic index numbers in music series titles also are entered in subfield ǂn. This subfield is repeatable.

```
490   1   Works for violin unaccompanied / J.S. Bach
800   1   Bach, Johann Sebastian, ǂd 1685-1750. ǂt Sonaten
          und Partiten, ǂm violin, ǂn BWV 1001-1006
          (Temerson).


490   1   Corpus cantilenarum medii aevii. Premi`ere
          s´erie, Les chansonniers des troubadours et des
          trouv`eres ; ǂv no. 2
830   0   Corpus cantilenarum medii aevii. ǂn Premi`ere
          s´erie, ǂp Chansonniers des troubadours et des
          trouv`eres ; ǂv no. 2.


440   0   Fontes musicae Bibliothecae Regiae Belgicae. ǂn
          Series II, ǂp Impressa ; ǂv 1


440   0   Stuttgarter Bach-Ausgaben. ǂn Serie H, ǂp
          Sch¨uler Bachs. ǂn 3. Gruppe, ǂp Kammermusik


440   0   50 interpretazioni liriche indimenticabili. ǂn 3a
          serie ; ǂv 6
```

```
440  0  English school of lutenist song writers. ‡n Sec-
         ond series ; ‡v 1
```

‡p   Name of part/section of a work

The name designation of a part or section of a series title is coded as subfield ‡p. This subfield is repeatable.

```
440  0  Erbe deutscher Musik. ‡n Erste Reihe, ‡p
         Reichsdenkmale. ‡p Abteilung Orgel/Klavier/Laute
         ; ‡v 1. Bd

440  0  Musica viva. ‡n Serie 4, ‡p Pie´s´n solowa i
         ch´oralna. ‡n A, ‡p Pie´s´n solowa z fortepianem

440  0  Encyclop´edie sonore. ‡p S´erie artistique

490  1  Musica da camera. Supplement ; ‡v S 9
830  0  Musica da camera (Oxford University Press). ‡p
         Supplement ; ‡v S 9.

490  1  Polyphonic music of the fourteenth century ; ‡v
         v. 18-19. ‡a French secular music
830  0  Polyphonic music of the fourteenth century ; ‡v
         v. 18-19.
830  0  Polyphonic music of the fourteenth century. ‡p
         French secular music.
```

Examples

```
440  0  Chamber music from Georgian England. ‡p Trio sonatas ; ‡v CM
         1

440  0  Stuttgarter Bach-Ausgaben. ‡n Serie C, ‡p Supplement, ‡p
         Durch Johann Sebastian Bach ¨uberlieferte Werke

440  4  The HMV treasury

440  0  Organum. ‡n 4. Reihe, ‡p Orgelmusik ; ‡v Nr. 11

440  0  Thesaurus musicus. ‡p Nova series. ‡n S´erie A, ‡p Manuscrits
         ; ‡v 3

440  0  Museum collection Berlin (West) ; ‡v 9

440  0  Editio '80

440  0  Musica antiqua Bohemica. ‡n Seria II ; ‡v 7

440  0  Great performer's edition

440  0  Kirchenmusik der Mannheimer Schule ; ‡v 2. Auswahl

440  0  Collegium musicum (Yale University) ‡x 0147-0108 ; ‡v 2nd
         ser., v. 11
```

440 0   Anthologie Ostdeutscher Musik. ‡p Bereich Schlesien

440   4   The English poets from Chaucer to Yeats

490 0   PRT collector

490 0   B¨arenreiter Studienpartituren = ‡a B¨arenreiter study scores ; ‡v 252

490 0   Hi-fi scores

490 0   Schirmer's library of musical classics ; ‡v 1934

490 0   Anthologie classique

490 0   Kunzelmann general music series ; ‡v GM 291

490 1   London Lassus series ; ‡v no. 5
800 1   Lasso, Orlando di, ‡d 1532-1594. ‡t Vocal music. ‡k Selections (London Lassus series) ; ‡v no. 5.

490 1   Int´egrale des quatuors / Beethoven ; ‡v 5
800 1   Beethoven, Ludwig van, ‡d 1770-1827. ‡t String quartet music (Calliope (Firm)) ; ‡v 5.

490 1   Sousa American bicentennial collection ; ‡v v. 1
800 1   Sousa, John Philip, ‡d 1854-1932. ‡t Marches, ‡m band. ‡k Selections (Sousa American bicentennial collection) ; ‡v v. 1.

490 1   Sobranie sochineni˘i v gramzapisi / Aram Khachatur´i⁀an = ‡a Collected works on records / Aram Khachaturian
800 1   Khachatur´i⁀an, Aram Il'ich, ‡d 1903-1978. ‡t Works. ‡f 1982. ‡s Melodi´i⁀a.

490 1   Furtw¨angler edition
800 1   Furtw¨angler, Wilhelm, ‡d 1886-1954. ‡4 cnd ‡t Furtw¨angler edition (Compact disc)

490 1   The works of Giuseppe Verdi
800 1   Verdi, Giuseppe, ‡d 1813-1901. ‡t Works. ‡f 1985. ‡s University of Chicago Press (Works of Giuseppe Verdi)

490 1   Satsangs of Swami Amar Jyoti
800 0   Amar Jyoti, ‡c Swami. ‡t Satsangs of Swami Amar Jyoti.

490 1   Marimba Nacional de Concierto ; ‡v v. 3
810 2   Marimba Nacional de Concierto. ‡4 prf ‡t Marimba Nacional de Concierto (Series) ; ‡v v. 3.

490 1   Early American vocal music ; ‡v v. 2
810 2   Western Wind (Vocal group) ‡4 prf ‡t Early American vocal music ; ‡v v. 2.

```
490 1    Historic recordings ; ǂv v. 6
810 2    New York Philharmonic. ǂ4 prf ǂt Historic recordings ; ǂv v.
         6.


490 1    Akten des XXV. Internationalen Kongresses für
         Kunstgeschichte ; ǂv Bd. 1
811 2    International Congress of the History of Art ǂn (25th : ǂd
         1983 : ǂc Vienna, Austria). ǂt Akten des XXV. Internationalen
         Kongresses für Kunstgeschichte ; ǂv Bd. 1.


490 1    Mapa Mundi : Renaissance performing scores. Series A, Spanish
         church music ; ǂv no. 49
830 0    Mapa Mundi (Series). ǂn Series A, ǂp Spanish church music ;
         ǂv no. 49.


490 1    Supplementary publication / Viola da Gamba Society of Great
         Britain ; ǂv no. 148
830 0    Supplementary publication (Viola da Gamba Society (Great
         Britain)) ; ǂv no. 148.


490 1    Historical performances ; ǂv 21
830 0    Historical performances (CLS) ; ǂv 21.


490 1    Denkmäler deutscher Tonkunst. 1. Folge ; ǂv Bd. 1
830 0    Denkmäler deutscher Tonkunst. ǂn 1. Folge (1957) ; ǂv Bd. 1.


490 1    Aurex Jazz Festival '80
830 0    Aurex Jazz Festival '80 (Series)


490 1    Original music for the recorder = ǂa Originalmusik für
         Blockflöte ; ǂv OFB 1018
830 0    Originalmusik für Blockflöte ; ǂv OFB 1018.


490 1    I Gioielli della lirica ; ǂv 22 = ǂa Masterpieces of the
         opera ; ǂv 22
830 0    Gioielli della lirica ; ǂv 22.


490 1    Musica antiqua Bohemica
830 0    Musica antiqua Bohemica (Sound recording)


490 1    English lute songs ; ǂv no. 1
830 0    English lute songs (Menston, West Yorkshire) ; ǂv no. 1.


490 1    Das Erbe deutscher Musik ; ǂv Bd. 89. ǂa Elfter Band der
         Abteilung Oper und Sologesang
830 0    Erbe deutscher Musik ; ǂv Bd. 89.
830 0    Erbe deutscher Musik. ǂp Abteilung Oper und Sologesang ; ǂv
         11. Band.
```

Notes

500   **General Note**

UFBD: 500 (O/O) (Rep)
OCLC: 500 (O/O) (Rep)
RLIN: 500 (NR) (Rep)
WLN: NOG (NR) (Rep)
MOIM: 500 (Rep)

501   **With Note**

UFBD: 501 (O/O) (Rep)
OCLC: 501 (R/R) (Rep)
RLIN: 501 (NR) (Rep)
WLN: NOW (A) (Rep)
MOIM: 501 (Rep)

503   **Bibliographic History Note**

UFBD: 503 (O/O) (Rep)
OCLC: 503 (O/O) (Rep)
RLIN: 503 (NR) (Rep)
WLN: NOH (NR) (Rep)
MOIM: [not present]

504   **Bibliography Note**

UFBD: 504 (O/O) (Rep)
OCLC: 504 (R/O) (Rep)
RLIN: 504 (NR) (Rep)
WLN: NOB (NR) (Rep)
MOIM: 504 (Rep)

505   **Formatted Contents Note**

UFBD: 505 (O/O) (NRep)
OCLC: 505 (R/O) (Rep)
RLIN: 505 (NR) (Rep)
WLN: NOC (NR) (NRep)
MOIM: 505 (NRep)

511   **Participant or Performer Note**

UFBD: 511 (A/A) (Rep)
OCLC: 511 (R/O) (Rep)
RLIN: 511 (NR) (Rep)
WLN: NOR (NR) (Rep)
MOIM: 511 (Rep)

518   **Date and Place of Capture/Finding Note**

UFBD: 518 (O/O) (Rep)
OCLC: 518 (R/O) (NRep)
RLIN: 518 (NR) (Rep)
WLN: CAN (NR) (Rep)
MOIM: 518 (NRep)

520   **Summary, Abstract, Annotation, Scope, etc. Note**

UFBD: 520 (O/O) (Rep)
OCLC: 520 (O/O) (Rep)
RLIN: 520 (NR) (Rep)
WLN: NOA (NR) (Rep)
MOIM: 520 (Rep)

533 **Reproduction Note**	**UFBD:** 533 (A/A) (Rep)
	OCLC: 533 (R/R) (Rep)
	RLIN: 533 (NR) (Rep)
	WLN: NOX (A) (Rep)
	MOIM: [not present]
534 **Original Version Note**	**UFBD:** 534 (A/O) Rep)
	OCLC: 534 (Do not use)
	RLIN: 534 (NR) (Rep)
	WLN: NIR (NR) (Rep)
	MOIM: [not present]

Fields 5XX carry the various notes called for in *AACR 2R*. Justifying, qualifying, or amplifying data found elsewhere in the record, each note occupies its own variable field. Whereas most notes tend to be of the general variety and are tagged as 500 fields, some specialized fields have been devised to accommodate particular kinds of information. When machine access to the information in a note is necessary or when a distinctive word or phrase prefaces the note, a specialized field often is defined.

In a few cases, information coded elsewhere in a record can generate a note. For example, the Publisher Number for Music (028) can be coded to print a note automatically; when a note on the music publishers' number must be input explicitly, it goes in a general 500 note field.

Punctuation within a note varies. When data in a note correspond to data found in the title and statement of responsibility, edition, music presentation, publication date, physical description, or series area, use in the note the prescribed punctuation appropriate to that area. Of course, quotations are transcribed as they appear and are enclosed in quotation marks, followed by a reference to the source.

Order of Notes

Notes are entered in a MARC record in the order prescribed by *AACR 2R* and its rule interpretations, although, of course, not every bibliographic record will require every type of note. The numerical value of a note field has nothing to do with the order of input. In the following lists, the field numbers are suggestive of the most common cases; for certain types of note, the Library of Congress tends to prefer a general note (500) over a more specific tag, although some libraries might make different choices. In many cases, different information elements can be combined in a single note (for instance, statements of responsibility, performance media, and durations combined with a contents note).

Not every variety of note listed here receives full explanation in the text that follows. Those omitted tend to be rare in score and sound recording records and/or are applied the same in these records as they are in records for books and other formats.

For scores, the order of notes is:

- Form of composition and medium of performance (500)
- Language(s) of the text (500)
- Source of title proper (500)
- Variations in title (500)
- Parallel titles and other title information (500)
- Statements of responsibility (500)
- Edition and history (500, 503, 533, 534)
- Notation (500)
- Publication, distribution, etc. (500, 533)
- Duration of performance and physical description (500, 533)
- Accompanying material (500, 504)
- Series (500)
- Dissertation note (500, 502)
- Audience (500)
- Contents (formatted in 505; unformatted in 500)
- Publishers' numbers (500)
- Plate numbers (500)

- Copy being described and library's holdings (59X)
- "With" notes (501)

For sound recordings, notes are input in this order:

- Publishers' numbers (500)
- Nature or artistic form and medium of performance (500)
- Language(s) of sung or spoken content (500)
- Source of title proper (500)
- Variations in title (500)
- Parallel titles and other title information (500)
- Statements of responsibility (500, 511)
- Edition and history (500, 503, 518)
- Publication, distribution, etc. (500)
- Physical description (500)
- Accompanying material (500, 504)
- Series (500)
- Dissertation note (500, 502)
- Audience (500)
- Other formats available (500)
- Summary (520)
- Contents (formatted in 505; unformatted in 500)
- Copy being described and library's holdings (59X)
- "With" notes (501)

500   General Note

By far the most common variety of note is the general note, any note for which a specific note field has not been defined. Most unformatted notes that state or elaborate upon the form and medium of the work, the title, statement of responsibility, imprint, physical description, duration, program notes and other accompanying material, language of text and/or translations, audience, series, and publishers' or plate numbers are input as 500 fields. Informal contents notes are input as 500 notes. This field is also used to repeat, as an explicit note, information that might be found elsewhere in the record but in a form that cannot generate a coherent note.

Both *indicators* are blank. The entire text of the note is contained in a single subfield ǂa.

500	Eds. recorded: Stockholm : W. Hansen (1st work); Stockholm : C. Gehrmans musikf¨orlag (2nd work).
500	Cover title: Beitr¨age zur Musikgeschichte des Paderborner Raumes.
500	Distributor from label on container.
500	Graphic notation, continuous over p. [2]-[3].
500	"Digitally remastered analog recordings."
500	Viola part edited by Joseph Vieland; violoncello parts edited by Nathan Stutch.
500	Compact disc.
500	Parallel title on container: "Breathing gives life-- ."
500	Number notation.
500	Issued also as cassette.
500	Contains over 50 fragments of vocal and instrumental music in a continuous (unbanded) recording; program notes on container.
500	"About grade four level"--Verso t.p.
500	Originally presented as the author's thesis (doctoral) --Johann Wolfgang Goethe-Universit¨at in Frankfurt am Main, 1982.

```
500        Reprint of the ed. published by Yale University Press,
           New Haven, which was issued in Music theory
           translation series.         [pre-AACR 2]
500        Performance attributed on labels to the Vienna
           Philharmonic Orchestra.
```

Particular varieties of general notes peculiar to scores and sound recordings include:

- Form of composition and medium of performance

```
500        For string quartet.
500        Folk songs; unacc.
500        Improvised dialogue songs, traditional in Northeastern
           Brazil.
500        Principally songs and opera excerpts with piano acc.
500        For 2 sopranos, 2 altos, 2 typewriters (2 typists), 2
           telephones (1 operator), tape, and percussion (3
           players).
500        "Ragtime cakewalks & stomps from 1898-1923"--Container.
500        For narrator, chorus (unison or mixed), and chamber
           orchestra, with optional pantomime action and visuals;
           acc. arr. for piano.
500        The 1st work for harpsichord; the 2nd work originally
           for violin and piano/harpsichord.
500        Fantasias on zarzuela melodies.
500        Flute is played with left hand; piano is played with
           right hand.
```

- Language of sung or spoken text

```
500        Italian words, also printed as texts, p. 219-223.
500        Sung in Kirundi.
500        Latin words.
500        The players recite texts in German and French from
           Rimbaud's Illuminations.
500        Translated from the German.
500        Text in Czech and German.
500        Recited in English; the music originally composed for a
           German translation of the poem.
```

- Duration

```
500        Durations: 27:08; 29:25.
500        Durations on container.
```

- Program notes and accompanying material

```
500        Text in English (4 p. : ports.) inserted in container.
500        Program notes by Hans Florey on container, with English
           translation and texts (8 p. : ill. ; 30 cm.) inserted.
500        Texts on sleeve.
500        Libretto by Hugo von Hofmannsthal, with English
           translation by Alfred Kalisch, and commentary (128 p.
           : ill. ; 22 cm.) inserted in container.
```

```
500      Program notes in German by Knut Franke on container.
```

• Publisher's numbers and plate numbers

```
500      Publisher's no.: Edition Peters Nr. 9443.
500      On container: Deutsche Grammophon 2864 029. On discs:
         2862 150-2862 153.
500      Deutsche Grammophon: 413 455-1 (413 456-1-413 458-1).
500      Reissue of: Supraphon 1 10 1127 (p1972).
500      Also issued as compact disc (CD-285).
500      "Licensed from Arion 34583."
```

501 *With Note*

Although catalogers employ this option much less often under *AACR 2R* than under previous rules, the use of "with" notes to link more than one bibliographic work contained in the same physical item is still legitimate (cf. *AACR 2R* rules 5.7B21, 6.1G1, 6.1G4, and 6.7B21). The note describes distinct works that are issued together at the time of publication or release, *not* separate works bound together or somehow combined by the cataloging institution. Sound recordings containing the works of different composers and lacking a collective title are sometimes treated in this manner. The field includes an explicitly input introductory word or phrase such as "With" or "Issued with".

Both *indicators* are blank. The entire text of the 501 field is contained in a single subfield ‡a. Where appropriate, use the prescribed punctuation that would be used in the title and statement of responsibility area.

```
501      With: Metamorfose / Wilfried Westerlinck -- Capriccio /
         Rafa¨el d'Haene -- Orkeststudie / Peter Bruyland.
501      With: Chromatic fantasy ; and, Three place settings /
         Barbara Kolb.
501      Bound with the composer's The consolation of music.
```

503 *Bibliographic History Note*

The item being cataloged is related to other works—predecessors, successors, sequels, abridgements, dramatizations, etc.—as well as to other editions of the same work, through the Bibliographic History Note, entered in field 503. The Library of Congress uses the 500 field for such notes rather than the 503. WLN does not use the 503 field, preferring to follow LC practice. OCLC also prefers the use of 500 instead of 503, but allows either. RLIN places no restrictions on the use of field 503.

Both *indicators* are blank. The entire contents of the 503 field is placed in a single subfield ‡a.

```
503      Edited from: XII solos for a violin or flute. London :
         Sold by Iohn Barrett and Wm. Smith, 1724.
503      Incorporated by the composer into his Requiem polskie
         (1983).
503      Separate ed. taken from Ferenc Liszt, new edition of
         the complete works, ser. 1, v. 9.
503      Based on Shakespeare's King John.
503      From incidental music for the play by Maurice
         Maeterlinck.
503      Based on themes taken from Goehr's Psalm 4, op. 38a.
503      Offprint from Acta musicologica, v. 49, fasc. 1.
```

504 *Bibliography Note*

When the cataloging for an item or its accompanying material contains a note for a bibliography, discography, filmography, or other list of bibliographic references, that note is entered as a 504 field. Bibliography notes that also mention the presence of an index still use the 504 note, but when other contents are mentioned and the bibliography is not substantive enough to warrant its own note, use field 500.

Both *indicators* are blank. The entire contents of the 504 field is placed in a single subfield ‡a. The 504 is a species of unformatted contents note.

```
504      Filmography: p. 299-304.
504      Includes bibliographical references.
504      Bibliography: p. xxv-xxvi.
504      Includes bibliographies, a discography, and index.
504      "Discography and anecdota": p. 134-144.
504      "Quellenverzeichnis": p. 221-222.
504      Checklist of songs: p. [217]-228.
504      "Recommended recordings": p. 203-226.
504      "The published works of Stephen Foster": p. 403-412.
504      "List of sources" and index to discs ([2] p.) inserted
         in container.
```

505   *Formatted Contents Note*

Formatted contents notes list titles of separate works or parts of a single work, prefaced by the word "Contents" or the phrase "Partial contents". Informal (unformatted) contents notes are entered as general 500 notes or as other types of 5XX notes, depending upon the type of contents described in the note. Statements of responsibility, indications of sequence such as volume numbers, and, occasionally, certain elements of physical description (durations, pagination, etc.) may be incorporated into the formal contents note.

A single subfield ‡a contains the entire text of the 505 note. When appropriate, use the prescribed punctuation used in the title and statement of responsibility area.

- Individual titles with or without a statement of responsibility are separated by a space-dash-space

```
505 \0   Don't let the deal go down -- Twin fiddle rag -- Say
         ole man -- That's a plenty -- Billy in the lowground
         -- Silver Lake blues -- Sop'n the gravy -- Pole cat
         hornpipe -- Honey boy -- Jessie polka -- Dusty Miller
         -- Sally Goodin -- La golendrina [i.e., golondrina] --
         Tom & Jerry.
505 0    Deviation (43:23) -- Reverie (1:27) -- Nuns for Nixon
         (4:06) -- Malone / Kenny Malone (1:08) -- Moontides
         (5:31) -- Ambrose (6:26) -- OMAC / Mark O'Connor (:33)
         -- Jalmon with salmon / Fleck ... [et al.] (2:17) --
         Mbanza (1:18) -- Places (7:11).
```

- Titles that share the same statement of responsibility are separated by a space-semicolon-space

```
505 0    Sonata in D minor for cello & piano / Claude Debussy --
         Romance op. 69 ; Papillon op. 77 ; Elegy op. 24 /
         Gabriel Faur´e -- Sonata in A for cello & piano /
         C´esar Franck.
```

- For multipart works and multivolume items, separate the larger designation (collective title, act of an opera, volume, etc.) from the individual titles with a period-space; volumes are separated with a space-dash-space

```
505 0    Partita no. 4 in D major, BWV 828 / Johann Sebastian
         Bach (30:04) -- Suite no. 5 in E major / George
         Frideric Handel (12:31) -- Three sonatas. E minor, K.
         233 (5:18) ; B minor, K. 27 (4:10) ; F minor, K. 239
         (3:29) / Domenico Scarlatti.
```

```
505 0   Muzio Scevola.  Overture (3:30) -- Rodrigo.  Overture
        (19:00) -- Il pastor fido.  Overture (18:00) -- Silla.
        Overture (5:24).
505 0   Vol. 1. No. 1-5 -- v. 2. No. 6-9.
```

Indicators

The *first indicator* serves the double purpose of designating the type of contents note (the completeness of the contents) and generating the requisite display constant. None of the display constants should be input explicitly into the 505 field.

OCLC & RLIN	*WLN*	
0	**C**	**Complete contents**
1	**I**	**Incomplete contents**
2	**P**	**Partial contents**

Value "0 "or "C" designates a contents note that represents the entire contents of an item; it generates the "Contents:" display constant.

```
505 0   Drei Pr"aludien und Fugen op 37 / Felix Mendelssohn-
        Bartholdy -- Sonate : "Der 94. Psalm" / Julius Reubke.
505 0   Introduction -- Myrtho -- Interlude 1 -- Delfica --
        Interlude 2 -- Lanassa.
505 0   Brass-quartet nr. 4, A flat-major op. 37 for cornet,
        trumpet, tenorhorn (barytone), and tuba (21:00) --
        Brass-quartet nr. 1 F-major op. 20 for cornet,
        trumpet, tenorhorn (barytone), and tuba (20:00).
505 0   Akt 1.  Einleitung ; Schaukle, Liebchen, schaukle ;
        Einer wird kommen ; Wolgalied ; Finale -- Akt 2.
        Herz, warum schl"agst du so bang? ; Was mir einst an
        dir gefiel ; Bleib' bei mir ; Das Leben ruft! ; Ob
        dort wohl viele sch"one Damen sind? ; Finale -- Akt 3.
        Kosende Wellen ; Finale.
505 0   Dreams = R^eves ; Sketches, op. 4 = Esquisses ;
        Sketches, op. 5 = Esquisses / Bed˘rich Smetana --
        Fantasia in F minor, op. 49 ; Scherzo in B flat minor,
        op. 31 / Fr'ed'eric Chopin -- Carnaval : op. 9 /
        Robert Schumann.
505 0   In E minor, RV 277 : (Il favorito) (14:00) -- In E-flat
        major, RV 253 : La tempesta di mare (9:00) -- In A
        major, RV 353 (11:00) -- In E major, RV 271 :
        L'amoroso (12:00).
```

Value "1" or "I" designates a contents note that is incomplete because not all parts of a multipart item are available for examination; the display constant "Contents:" (OCLC, RLIN, WLN) or "Incomplete contents:" (USMARC) is generated. Where missing parts might be added between existing data at some later time, place three blank spaces.

```
505 1   Vol. 1.  La veille (11:05) ; Le balcon (11:08) ; Les
        filles du roi d'Espagne (11:08) ; Trois chants d'amour
        (14:00) ; Violin sonata (21:45) ; String quartet
        (25:55) (2 discs)    -- v. 3. Cello sonata no. 1
        (20:55) ; Pr'elude des origines (9:40) ; Trois
        salutations `a Notre Dame (13:17) ; String trio
        (18:57) ; On ne passe pas (1:52) ; The soldier (3:10)
```

(continued on next page)

```
                    ; Cello sonata no. 2 (24:12) ; Symphony no. 6 : Les
                    minutes heureuses (25:40) (2 discs).
        505 1       Vol. 1.  The Mannheim sonatas.
```

Value "2" or "P" designates a contents note that lists only selected parts of a work, even though the complete item is available for examination. The display constant "Partial contents:" is generated.

```
        505 2       Trois complexes.  Sisyphe ; Sisyphe heureux.
        505 2       Il figliuol prodigo -- Assalone punito -- Il lutto
                    dell'universo -- L'eternit`a sogetta al tempo -- La
                    vita nella morte -- La fede sacrilega -- David.
```

The *second indicator* is blank.

511   *Participant or Performer Note*

For sound recordings, the 511 field contains the note made according to *AACR 2R* rule 6.7B6 that names participants, performers, players, narrators, and presenters; the field is not used in score records. Any personal or corporate name that appears in this field can be entered formally in a 700 or 710 field. The medium of performance often is incorporated into a 511 note. Subfield ǂa contains the entire text of the note.

Indicators

The *first indicator* characterizes the nature of the names that appear in the note and determines the display constant that may introduce those names.

OCLC & RLIN	WLN	Display Constant
0	**G**	[No display constant generated]
1	**C**	**Cast:**
2	**P**	**Presenter:**
3	**N**	**Narrator:**

For musical sound recordings, first indicator "0" or "G" will be used almost exclusively, generating no display constant. It also is used whenever the 511 note is general in nature, making none of the other display constant options appropriate.

```
        511 0       Ilona Telm´anyi, violin or viola ; Annette Schiøler
                    Telm´anyi, piano ; unidentified string orchestra, Emil
                    Telm´anyi, conductor (4th work).
        511 0       Instrumentalists, singers, and chorus of the Royal
                    Palace of Yogyakarta, Java.
        511 0       Sung by Temo accompanying himself on the tembur.
        511 0       Anthony Braxton, sopranino or alto saxophone, clarinet
                    or contrabass clarinet, flute or alto flute ; Kenny
                    Wheeler, trumpet, flugelhorn ; Dave Holland, bass ;
                    Barry Altschul, drums.
        511 0       Lysenko Quartet.
```

The display constant "Cast:", generated by the first indicator "1" or "C" will be used mostly for nonmusical sound recordings when members of the cast (and often, the roles played) are listed.

```
        511 1       Prunella Scales (Helena), Ian McKellen (Lysander),
                    Miles Malleson (Quince), and the Marlowe Dramatic
                    Society.
        511 1       Irene Worth, George Voskovec.
```

```
511 1    Arletty (Madame Jourdain), Sophie Desmarets (Nicole),
         Fran¸coise Dorl´eac (Lucile), Maria Mauban
         (Dorim`ene), Jacques Fabbri (M. Jourdain).
511 1    Michael Redgrave, Michael Hordern, Donald Pleasence,
         Lynn Redgrave.
```

The display constant "Presenter:", generated by the first indicator "2" or "P", is rather ambiguous in its application. It probably will be used rarely for musical sound recordings, but occasionally for spoken word recordings. In U.S. usage, a "presenter" usually has something to do with production, financing, or distribution of an item. In British usage, a "presenter" is a newscaster.

```
511 2    Dick Clark.
511 2    National Public Radio.
511 2    Alistair Cooke.
511 2    Bill of Rights Radio Education Project.
```

The display constant "Narrator:", generated by first indicator "3" or "N", will be used mostly in spoken word sound recording records, but probably also will appear occasionally in records for musical recordings of narrated works.

```
511 3    Walter Cronkite.
511 3    Henry Fonda.
511 3    Gert Westphal.
511 3    Robert J. Lurtsema.
```

Remember that, because first indicator value "1" or "C", "2" or "P", or "3" or "N" generates the appropriate display constant, the introductory terms "Cast:", "Presenter:", or "Narrator:" are not explicitly input.

The *second indicator* is blank.

518   *Date and Place of Capture/Finding Note*

The note formulated according to *AACR 2R* 6.7B7 indicating the date and/or place a recording was made, plus any other details of a recorded event, is entered as a 518 field. Subfield ǂa contains the entire text of the 518 note. Both indicators are blank. Each 518 note should have a corresponding 033 field, which carries the same information in coded form.

```
518      Recorded at the House of the Association of the Bar of
         the City of New York on May 15, 1978.
033 0    19780515 ǂb 3804 ǂc N4

518      Originally recorded 1934-1935.
033 2    1934---- ǂa 1935----

518      Recorded at St. Timothy's Anglican Church, Edmonton.
033      ǂb 3504 ǂc E3

518      Recorded during trips to New England and the Mid-West
         between 1976 and 1978.
033 2    1976---- ǂa 1978----

518      Recorded Dec. 1983 to Mar. 1984 in the homes of the
         fiddlers.
033 2    198312-- ǂa 198403-- ǂb 4080
```

```
518        Recorded at Cedar Creek Recording, Austin, Tex., and
           Streeterville Recording Studios, Chicago.
033        ǂb 4034 ǂc A9 ǂb 4104 ǂc C6

518        Recorded July 22-26, 1982, at the 8th Festival della
           Valle d'Itria, Martina Franca, Italy.
033  2     19820722 ǂa 19820726 ǂb 6710

518        Recorded live Aug. 20 and Sept. 9, 1980, Kunsthaus
           Luzern.
033  1     19800820 ǂa 19800909 ǂb 6044 ǂc L8
```

520   Summary, Abstract, Annotation, Scope, Etc., Note

Although predominantly musical sound recordings rarely will contain one, the 520 field contains a brief, objective summary of the content of a nonmusical sound recording (*AACR 2R* 6.7B17). Occasional scores and musical recordings, usually juvenile materials, might contain such a summary note. When the word "Summary:" introduces the note, use the blank first indicator; do not explicitly input the word "Summary".

The entire text of the summary note is contained in subfield ǂa.

Indicators

The *first indicator* controls the generation of a display constant preceding the text of the note.

OCLC & RLIN	*WLN*	*Display Constant*
[blank]	**[blank]**	**Summary:**
0	**S**	**Subject:**
8	**N**	[No display constant generated]

The *second indicator* is blank.

```
520        Friends, relatives, and admirers talk about the life of
           Charles Ives, the American composer, who started out
           in Danbury, Conn.
520        Presents bird calls of many types of birds found in
           North America, such as the brown thrasher, Baltimore
           oriole, scarlet tanager, screech owl, robin, winter
           wren, common loon, and many more.  Also includes sound
           of timber wolves, chipmunks, and various types of
           frogs and squirrels.
520        An illustrated collection of sixty easy-to-play,
           humorous songs including camp songs, parodies, Bible
           songs, and silly ditties.
520        Presents a number of actors reading dramatizations of
           selected folktales by Hungarian author Gyula Illy´es.
```

533   Reproduction Note

The Library of Congress bases the cataloging of microreproductions and certain types of macroreproductions on the bibliographic description of the original materials, then describes the reproduction itself in a note. (For a full statement on the policy, see LC's rule interpretation on *AACR 2R* chapter 11). OCLC, RLIN, and WLN all have chosen to follow LC's retention of *AACR 1* practices regarding reproductions. Description of the reproduction is recorded in the 533 field.

Be sure to code the Form of Item fixed field (008/23 in UFBD, "Repr" in OCLC, "REP" in RLIN, and "REPRO" in WLN) for the appropriate type of reproduction. If a microreproduction is involved, remember that a 007 field for microforms is necessary. This field is appropriate for scores but *not* for sound recordings.

Indicators

　　Both *indicators* are blank.

Subfields

‡a　**Type of reproduction**

　　The introductory word or phrase that identifies the kind of reproduction goes in subfield ‡a. It may not be repeated.

　　533　　Microfilm. ‡b London : ‡c Royal College of Music, ‡d 1987. ‡e 1 microfilm reel ; 35 mm.

‡b　**Place of reproduction**

　　The place where the reproduction was made is recorded in subfield ‡b. If more than one place is transcribed, put each in a separate subfield ‡b.

　　533　　Microfilm. ‡b [Milano : ‡c Conservatorio de Musica G. Verdi, Biblioteca, ‡d 1984]. ‡e 1 microfilm reel : negative ; 35 mm.

‡c　**Agency responsible for reproduction**

　　The party responsible for the reproduction is recorded in subfield ‡c. The subfield should be repeated for multiple responsible parties.

　　533　　Microfilm. ‡b Bologna : ‡c Civico museo bibliografico musicale ; ‡c A. Bonavera, ‡d [1984?]. ‡e 1 microfilm reel : negative ; 35 mm.

‡d　**Date of reproduction**

　　The date of the reproduction goes in subfield ‡d. It may not be repeated.

　　533　　Microfilm. ‡b Stockholm : ‡c Kungliga Musikaliska Akademiens Bibliotek, ‡d 1984. ‡e 1 microfilm reel : negative ; 35 mm.

‡e　**Physical description of reproduction**

　　Any information concerning the physical description of the reproduction is placed in subfield ‡e. This includes the extent of the item or number of pieces, the designation of negative polarity or other details of physical description such as illustrations, and the dimensions. Within the physical description itself, punctuation should follow that prescribed by *AACR 2R* for the physical description area. The subfield may not be repeated.

　　533　　Microfilm. ‡b London : ‡c British Library, ‡d [1986?]. ‡e 1 microfilm reel : negative ; 35 mm. Library copy wanting string parts.

　　533　　Microfilm. ‡b Berlin : ‡c Westdeutsche Bibliothek, Sammlungen der ehem. Preuss. Staatsbibliothek, ‡d [1982]. ‡e 1 microfilm reel ; 35 mm. Low reduction. Violin 2 part filmed out of sequence; 2 pages found at end of ms.

```
533        Microfilm. +b [Urbana, Ill.] : +c Photographic
           Services, U of I Library, +d 1974. +e 1
           microfilm reel ; 35 mm.  Film of conductor's
           copy owned by John Garvey; with annotations,
           corrections, and paste-over alterations made by
           Partch for the 1962 performance.
```

+f   **Series statement of reproduction**
      The series in which a reproduction has been published is recorded in subfield +f. Multiple series go in separate subfields +f. The text of the subfield always is enclosed in parentheses.

```
533        Microfiche. +b M¨unchen : +c K.G. Saur, +d 1983.
           +e 1 microfiche. +f (Oettingen-Wallerstein´sche
           Musiksammlung ; 1408)
```

```
533        Microfiche. +b New York : +c University Music
           Editions, +d 1969. +e 108 microfiches ; 11 x 15
           cm., in binder. +f (Microfiche reprint series)
```

```
533        Microopaque. +b New York : +c Readex Microprint,
           +d 1967. +e 1 microopaque ; 23 x 15 cm. +f
           (English and American drama of the nineteenth
           century. English)
```

534   Original Version Note
      AACR 2R rule 1.11A stipulates that reproductions be described in the body of a bibliographic description and that data relating to the original item that differ from those of the reproduction be described in a note. This formally structured note is entered in the 534 field. The Library of Congress, OCLC, and WLN each has chosen to continue applying *AACR 1* in cataloging microform reproductions and on-demand photoreproductions. Hence, LC rarely uses the 534 field (preferring the 500 field for such notes that they do include), and WLN and OCLC users are cautioned not to use it unless and until LC policy changes. RLIN users, however, are free to use field 534. In any case, its use would be inappropriate for sound recordings, although it could be used for scores.

Indicators
      Both *indicators* are blank.
Subfields
  +p   **Introductory phrase**
        Every formatted Original Version Note requires a phrase that introduces the citation of the original, so every 534 note requires a subfield +p as the first subfield.

```
534        +p Photoreproduction of: +c Leipzig : Vogelin,
           1598.
534        +p Reprint in a reduced format of the full score
           originally published: +c Vienna : Universal
           Edition, 1920. +n With corrections.
```

  +a   **Main entry of original**
        When the main entry of the reproduction differs from that of the original publication, the main entry of the original is entered in the subfield +a.

```
534        +p Reprinted from: +a Phal`ese, Pierre. +t Liber
           musicus. +c Leuven, 1571.
```

‡b Edition statement of original

The edition statement of the original publication appears in subfield ‡b.

```
534        ‡p Reprint. Originally published: ‡b 2nd ed. ‡c
           1927. ‡n With new introd.
```

‡c Publication, distribution, etc., of original

Any place, name, or date information pertaining to the publication, distribution, release, issue, or manufacture of the original is entered in subfield ‡c.

```
534        ‡p Originally published: ‡t Sing a song of
           England. ‡c London : Phoenix House, 1954.
```

‡e Physical description, etc., of original

Details of the original's physical description appear in subfield ‡e.

```
534        ‡p Reprint. Originally published: ‡c Leipzig :
           C.F. Peters, 1870. ‡e 3 v. ; 28 cm.
```

‡f Series statement of the original

The series statement of the original publication appears in subfield ‡f. Subseries are not subfielded separately; however, the subfield may be repeated when more than one series is cited. An ISSN that is part of a series statement is not separately subfielded.

```
534        ‡p Reprint. Originally published: ‡c Wien :
           Artaria, 1901. ‡f (Denkm¨aler der Tonkunst in
           ¨Osterreich ; v. 17).
534        ‡p Reprint. Originally published: ‡c Seattle,
           Wash. : Asian Music Publications, c1977. ‡f
           (Asian music publications. Series D, Monographs
           ; no. 4). ‡n With new introd.
534        ‡p Originally issued in series: ‡f Denkm¨aler
           norddeutscher Musik, 0418-6400.
534        ‡p Reprint. Originally published: ‡c Frankfurt/M
           : Ullstein, c1984. ‡f (Idole ; 2) ‡f (Popul¨are
           Kultur) ‡f (Ullstein Sachbuch)
```

‡k Key title of original

Any key title (the unique name given to a serial by the International Serials Data System) associated with the original item is coded as subfield ‡k. This subfield is repeatable and will not be used in *AACR 2R* records.

```
534        ‡p Reprinted from: ‡k Acta musicologica, ‡m vol.
           49, fasc. 1, ‡x 0001-6241.        [pre-AACR 2]
```

‡l Location of original

The location of the original item is put in subfield ‡l.

```
534        ‡p Reproduction of: ‡t Mottetti a voce sola. ‡c
           Roma : Per il Successor al Mascardi, 1676. ‡n
           Microfilm of the copy in the ‡l Civico Museo
           Bibliografico Musicale, Bologna.
```

‡m   **Material specific details**

Data specific to the type of material, such as frequency or date/chronological designations, appear in subfield ‡m.

```
534        ‡p Originally published in: ‡t New music. ‡m Vol.
           4, no. 2, ‡x 0706-7984.
```

‡n   **Note about the original**

Notes concerning the original publication are coded as subfield ‡n. This subfield may be repeated when multiple notes are cited.

```
534        ‡p Reprint. Originally published: ‡b 2nd ed. ‡c
           London : Oxford University Press, 1951, c1948.
           ‡n With new introd.
```

‡t   **Title statement of original**

The title proper of the original item is placed in subfield ‡t.

```
534        ‡p Reprint. Originally published: ‡t Cantates
           fran‚coises, livre 3. ‡c Paris : Ballard, 1711.
```

‡x   **International Standard Serial Number**

ISSNs linked to the original serial publication go in subfield ‡x, which is repeatable. ISSNs that are part of a *series* statement are not separately subfielded.

```
534        ‡p Originally published in: ‡k Keyboard classics
           & virtuoso. ‡m Vol. 2, no. 1, ‡x 0744-3218.
```

‡z   **International Standard Book Number**

Any ISBN associated with the original item is coded as subfield ‡z, which may be repeated.

```
534        ‡p Vol. 1 originally published: ‡c Boston :
           Crescendo Pub. Co., 1973. ‡n With corrections
           and new pref. ‡z ISBN 0-87597-079-6.
```

APPENDICES

APPENDIX A
LIST OF OBSOLETE AND PRE-*AACR* 2 FIELDS

Although retrospective practices generally are not addressed in this book, a list of the major music-related fields and fixed field elements that are either obsolete (that is, deleted from the USMARC format) or reserved for pre-*AACR* 2 retrospective use only, follows. Note that a field's status in USMARC might not exactly reflect its treatment in each individual bibliographic system.

Existence of Parts Fixed Field

UFBD: 008/21 [Obsolete]
OCLC: Prts [Do not use]
RLIN: PTS
WLN: PARTS
MOIM: Box 04 (PARTS)

This fixed field element was made *obsolete* in the USMARC format in 1988.

262   Imprint Statement for Sound Recordings (Pre-*AACR* 2)

UFBD: 262
OCLC: 262
RLIN: 262
WLN: PRS
MOIM: [not present]

In 1980, the USMARC format restricted use of this field to sound recordings cataloged according to pre-*AACR* 2 rules.

305   Physical Description for Sound Recordings (Pre-*AACR* 2)

UFBD: 305
OCLC: 305
RLIN: 305
WLN: PHR
MOIM: [not present]

In 1980, the USMARC format restricted use of this field to sound recordings cataloged according to pre-*AACR* 2 rules.

705   Added Entry — Personal Name (Performer)

UFBD: 705 [Obsolete]
OCLC: 705 [Do not use]
RLIN: [not present]
WLN: [not present]
MOIM: [not present]

In 1980, the USMARC format made this field *obsolete*.

715   Added Entry — Corporate Name (Performing Group)

UFBD: 715 [Obsolete]
OCLC: 715 [Do not use]
RLIN: [not present]
WLN: [not present]
MOIM: [not present]

In 1980, the USMARC format made this field *obsolete*.

APPENDIX B
OCLC, RLIN, AND WLN FORMAT DIFFERENCES

Most users of the MARC formats, including OCLC, RLIN, and WLN, have adapted, changed, and added to the basic USMARC formats to make each manifestation of the formats somewhat different, if recognizably similar. In most cases throughout this volume, examples have been presented only in the OCLC format, mainly because it is the most widely used and is readily adaptable by users of the other MARC-based systems. However, the guidelines presented in this manual apply equally to MARC format records as adapted by the other bibliographic utilities. Here are presentations of the music format workforms and the mostly cosmetic differences among the OCLC-, RLIN-, and WLN-MARC formats.

OCLC

OCLC has divided the USMARC Music Format into two formats, one for scores (printed and manuscript music), the other for sound recordings. Except for the Type of Material code ("c" for printed music and "d" for manuscript music; "i" for nonmusical sound recordings and "j" for musical sound recordings) and a few minor variations in defaults, fields, and subfields displayed, the workforms are very similar.

OCLC Score format workform

```
Type: c Bib lvl: m Lang:  N/A Source:  | Accomp mat:
Repr:    Enc lvl: | Ctry: xx  Dat tp:  | MEBE: 1
         Mod rec:   Comp:       Format:   Prts:
Desc: | Int lvl:   LTxt:  n   Dates: ||||,
 1 010
 2 040      ǂc XXX
 3 028 ||   ǂb
 4 041 |    ǂh  ǂb  ǂe
 5 047
 6 048      ǂb
 7 050 |    ǂb
 8 090      ǂb
 9 049      XXXX
10 1|| ||   ǂd
11 240 ||
12 245 ||   ǂb  ǂc
13 250
14 260 |    ǂb  ǂc
15 300      ǂb  ǂc
16 4|| ||   ǂv
17 5|| |
18 6|| ||
19 7|| ||   ǂd
```

OCLC Sound Recording format workform

```
Type: j Bib lvl: m Lang:  N/A Source: | Accomp mat:
Repr:     Enc lvl: | Ctry:  xx Dat tp: | MEBE: 1
          Mod rec:   Comp:       Format: n Prts:
Desc: | Int lvl:    LTxt:       Dates: |||,
  1 010
  2 040         ‡c XXX
  3 007         ‡b  ‡c  ‡d  ‡e  ‡f  ‡g  ‡h  ‡i
  4 028 ||      ‡b
  5 041 |       ‡d  ‡h  ‡e  ‡g
  6 048         ‡b
  7 050 |       ‡b
  8 090         ‡b
  9 049      XXXX
 10 1|| ||     ‡d
 11 240 ||
 12 245 ||     ‡b  ‡c
 13 260 |      ‡b  ‡c
 14 300        ‡b  ‡c  ‡e
 15 306
 16 4|| ||     ‡v
 17 5|| |
 18 6|| ||
 19 7|| ||     ‡d  ‡4
```

The fixed field, the paragraph at the top of each record, comprises elements from the Leader and 008 Field of the USMARC record. OCLC has rearranged these coded elements to display as mnemonic labels followed by the coded information.

Each variable field is introduced by a line number, a blank space, and a three-digit numeric field tag. Following another blank space, there is room for two numeric indicators, followed by two more blank spaces. Where an indicator is undefined, its position remains blank. Within the field itself, the subfield ‡a, when it is the first subfield, is understood and is not explicitly input. Any other subfield appearing first and all subsequent subfields are identified by the subfield delimiter (‡) followed directly by the subfield code, a lowercase letter or a numeral. Before the delimiter and after the code are blank spaces. Delimiter and code together are explicitly input where they belong in the field.

```
29 700 10  Boulez, Pierre, ‡d 1925- ‡4 cnd
```

RLIN

RLIN has divided the USMARC Music Format into two formats, one for scores (printed and manuscript music), the other for sound recordings. The BIBliographic segment display for each is slightly different.

RLIN BIBliographic segment input display for Scores

```
ID:                    RTYP:c    ST:p   FRN:     MS:     EL:     AD:mm-dd-yy
CC:        BLT:        DCF:?  CSC:?  MOD:?  SNR:    ATC:    UD:
CP:        L:          FCP:?? INT:?  MEI:?  AMC:??????
PC:        PD:     /          SCO:?  REP:?
MMD:       OR:    POL:  DM:        RR:        COL:    EML:   GEN:   BSE:
028 __
040 __
041 __
045 __
048 __
1XX __
240 __
245 __
260 __
300 __
    __
    __
    __
    __
    __
    __
```

RLIN BIBliographic segment input display for Sound Recordings

```
ID:                    RTYP:c    ST:p   FRN:     MS:     EL:     AD:mm-dd-yy
CC:        BLT:        DCF:?  CSC:?  MOD:?  SNR:    ATC:    UD:
CP:        L:          FCP:?? INT:?  MEI:?  AMC:??????
PC:        PD:     /          LIT:??
RMD:  OR:  SPD:  SND:  GRV:  DIM:  WID:  TC:  KD:  KM:  KC:  RC:  CAP:
028 __
040 __
045 __
048 __
1XX __
240 __
245 __
260 __
300 __
    __
    __
    __
    __
    __
    __
```

The fixed field, the paragraph at the top of each record, comprises elements from the Leader, 007, and 008 Fields of the USMARC record. RLIN has rearranged these coded elements to display as mnemonic labels followed by the coded information. The first three lines of the score and the sound recording fixed fields are identical; the fourth lines differ slightly. The fifth line of the score fixed field display corresponds to the USMARC 007 field for microform information. The fifth line of the sound recording fixed field display corresponds to the USMARC 007 field for sound recordings.

Each variable field is introduced by a three-digit numeric field tag. Following a blank space, three character positions are reserved for field indicators, the first two for numeric indicators, the third for an alphabetic indicator. Where a numeric indicator is undefined, its position remains blank. In the *RLIN Bibliographic Field Guide*, examples do not show a third indicator and do not leave a space for one. In the place of the third indicator and the following blank space is found each field's first "subfield delimiter pair." This consists of the subfield delimiter (‡) followed directly by the letter, number, or symbol identifying the subfield. There are no spaces on either side of the subfield delimiter pair. The pair is explicitly input at each point in a field where it belongs, except for any initial subfield ‡a, which is understood.

```
700 10 Boulez, Pierre,‡d1925-‡4cnd
```

WLN

WLN has divided the USMARC Music Format into two formats, one for scores (printed and manuscript music), the other for sound recordings. The WLN system offers four different input screens for each: current cataloging, copy cataloging, recon cataloging, and interim record. Except for minor variations, the input screens are similar. For our purposes, the current cataloging input screens are most appropriate.

WLN Score current cataloging input screen

```
REC TYPE   c      BIB LV  m      ENC LV          RID
REPLACE RID
HNW
MSG
ME
UTI
TIL
MPS
EDN
IMP
COL
SE
NO
SU
AE
SA
OTHERS
PNM
GAC                               SBN
LAN                               CAL
DDC                               SCN
IVC
CAS    ‡ac‡XXX‡XXX
   DATE KY            DATE 1           DATE 2
      COMP            SCORE            PARTS           ACC MAT
    ME IN B           CNTRY            REPRO           MOD REC
   INTEL LV           LIT TEXT  n      CAT S   d       CAT FORM   a
```

WLN Sound Recording current cataloging input screen

```
REC TYPE  j      BIB LV  m      ENC LV         RID
REPLACE RID
HNW
MSG
ME
UTI
TIL
IMP
COL
SE
NO
SU
AE
SA
OTHERS
PNM
GAC                                    DFF
LAN                                    CAL
DDC                                    SCN
IVC                                    DSR
CAS    ‡ac‡XXX‡XXX
   DATE KY              DATE 1           DATE 2
      COMP              SCORE  n         PARTS  n         ACC MAT
   ME IN B              CNTRY            REPRO            MOD REC
  INTEL LV              LIT TEXT         CAT S  d         CAT FORM  a
```

Fixed field elements are divided between the top of the display (Type of Record, Bibliographic Level, Encoding Level, and Record ID) and the paragraph at the bottom of each record, which contains elements from the Leader and 008 Fields of the USMARC record. WLN has rearranged these coded elements to display as mnemonic labels followed by the coded information. Except for a few default values, the score and sound recording fixed fields are identical.

Variable fields are marked by alphabetic mnemonics. Space is left for the indicators, which follow directly. After a subfield delimiter (‡) are placed all the subfield codes in the order found in the respective field, including any initial subfield ‡a. Subfield delimiters (‡) alone are placed at their proper points within the field, without spaces on either side of the delimiter.

```
     AEPSA    ‡ad4    ‡Boulez, Pierre,‡1925-‡cnd
```

APPENDIX C
FULL-RECORD EXAMPLES

The field-level examples found throughout this volume should be useful in working with individual fields, but fields reflect their true meaning only within the context of full records. As such, a dozen sample records for scores and another dozen sample records for sound recordings follow. These twenty-four records appear in three parallel sections, the first in OCLC format, the second in RLIN format, and the third in WLN format. Except for the differences dictated by the varying formats and the capabilities of each bibliographic system, the records in the three sections are identical.

Obviously, neither every field nor records for each possible type of score and recording could be included, but a broadly representative sample has been assembled. Among the scores are two manuscript records and a microform record. Compact discs, analog discs, cassette tapes, and reel-to-reel tapes are found among the sound recordings. Each record is based on *AACR 2R* cataloging by the Library of Congress, although every record has been edited for the purposes of this book. The brief comments following each record highlight some of the interesting features, but are by no means comprehensive examinations of cataloging, coding, or tagging practices.

Example 1

```
Type: c Bib lvl: m Lang:  N/A Source:    Accomp mat: hi
Repr:     Enc lvl:    Ctry:  ge Dat tp: r MEBE: 1
          Mod rec:    Comp:  mu Format: z Prts:
Desc: a Int lvl:      LTxt:  n    Dates: 1984,1731
  1 010       87-750963/M
  2 028 32    9314 ‡b Edition Peters
  3 041 0      ‡g engger ‡h ger
  4 045       v2v4
  5 047       su ‡a ov ‡a pr ‡a fg ‡a cl ‡a vr
  6 048       kc01
  7 048       kb01
  8 050 0     M3.1.B2 ‡b K48 1984
  9 100 10    Bach, Johann Sebastian, ‡d 1685-1750.
 10 240 10    Keyboard music. ‡k Selections (Clavier-¨Ubung)
 11 245 10    Clavier-¨Ubung / ‡c Johann Sebastian Bach.
 12 250       Faksimile-Ausg. / ‡b herausgegeben von Christoph Wolff.
 13 260 0     Leipzig : ‡b Edition Peters ; ‡a Frankfurt ; ‡a New York : ‡b
C.F. Peters, ‡c c1984.
 14 300       4 v. of music ; ‡c 26 x 32 cm.
 15 440  0    Musikwissenschaftliche Studienbibliothek Peters
 16 490 0     Peters reprints
 17 500       For harpsichord or organ.
 18 500       Second imprint from label on t.p.
 19 503       Reprint of works originally published 1731-1741.
 20 500       Accompanied by: Johann Sebastian Bachs Klavier¨ubung : Kommentar
zur Faksimile-Ausgabe / Christoph Wolff (32 p. : facsims.) (in English and
German).
 21 505 0     1. Sechs Partiten BWV 825-830 -- 2. Italienisches Konzert : BWV
971 ; Franz¨osische Ouvert¨ure : BWV 831 -- 3. Pr¨aludium und Fuge Es-Dur
BWV 552 ; Orgelchor¨ale BWV 669-689 ; Duette BWV 802-805 -- 4. Goldberg-
Variationen : BWV 988.
 22 650  0    Harpsichord music.
 23 650  0    Organ music.
 24 700 10    Wolff, Christoph.
```

The Type of Date (Dat tp) and Dates fixed fields and the 503 note all indicate that this is a facsimile reprint of a published score. The edition statement includes a statement of responsibility. Note the presence of both traced and untraced series, a multiple imprint, and that accompanying material is described in the last 500 note.

Example 2

```
Type: c Bib lvl: m Lang:   N/A Source:   Accomp mat:
Repr:    Enc lvl:   Ctry:  it Dat tp: c MEBE: 1
         Mod rec:   Comp:  uu Format: a Prts:
Desc: a Int lvl:    LTxt:  n   Dates: 1985,1982
 1 010       88-751200/M
 2 028 22    133507 ǂb Ricordi
 3 041 0     ǂg ita
 4 045 0     ǂb d19811121
 5 048       ǂb wa01 ǂb sa01 ǂa oa
 6 050 0     M1040.B94 ǂb C37 1985
 7 100 10    Bussotti, Sylvano.
 8 240 10    Catalogo `e questo. ǂp Raragramma
 9 245 13    Il catalogo `e questo. ǂn II, ǂp Raragramma / ǂc Sylvano
Bussotti.
10 260 0     Milano : ǂb Ricordi, ǂc 1985, c1982.
11 300       1 score (30 p.) : ǂb 1 col. facsim. ; ǂc 41 cm.
12 490 1     Bussottioperaballet
13 500       For flutes (1 player), violin, and orchestra.
14 500       Reproduced from holograph.
15 505 0     Raragramma -- R. & R. -- Enfant prodige -- Paganini -- Calando
symphony.
16 650  0    Flute and violin with orchestra ǂx Scores.
17 650  0    Music ǂx Manuscripts ǂx Facsimiles.
18 600 10    Bussotti, Sylvano ǂx Manuscripts ǂx Facsimiles.
19 740 01    Raragramma.
20 800 1     Bussotti, Sylvano. ǂt Selections.
```

   In this score for two solo instruments and orchestra, the dates of publication and copyright are both recorded in the 260 subfield ǂc and are reflected in the Type of Date (Dat tp) and Dates fixed field positions. The date in the 045 field derives from the date inscribed at the end of the holograph score. The single player on multiple flutes mentioned in the first 500 note is reflected in the 048 field. Subfields ǂn and ǂp are both found in the 245 field. Note the illustration statement in the 300 subfield ǂb. A series traced in different form is found in the 490 and its corresponding author/title 800 series field. A personal name as subject heading is found in the 600 field.

Example 3

```
Type: c Bib lvl: m Lang:   lat Source:    Accomp mat: i
Repr:     Enc lvl:   Ctry:  sp Dat tp: s MEBE: 0
          Mod rec:   Comp:  uu Format: a Prts:
Desc: a Int lvl:    LTxt:  n   Dates: 1983,
  1 010       86-754683/M/r87
  2 041 0     lat ‡g cateng
  3 048       ca08 ‡a wy02 ‡a bd01 ‡a ke
  4 050 0     M2021 ‡b .N8 1983
  5 130 00    Nunc dimittis (Parr`oquia de Sant Pere de Canet de Mar, Spain)
  6 245 00    Nunc dimittis a 11, s. XVII / ‡c an`onim ; transcripci´o i
estudi, Francesc Bonastre.
  7 260 0     Barcelona : ‡b Institut Universitari de Documentaci´o i
Investigaci´o Musicol`ogica "Josep Ricart i Matas", ‡c 1983.
  8 300       1 score (22 p.) ; ‡c 30 cm.
  9 440  0    Quaderns de m´usica hist`orica catalana ; ‡v 4
 10 500       For chorus (TipleA/TipleT/TipleATB), cobla ensemble (2 xeremias,
trombone), and continuo; bass unrealized.
 11 500       Latin words.
 12 503       Edited from a ms. in the Arxiu Musical de la Parr`oquia de Sant
Pere de Carnet de Mar.
 13 500       Prefatory notes in Catalan and English.
 14 650  0    Choruses, Sacred (Mixed voices) with instrumental ensemble.
 15 650  0    Nunc dimittis (Music)
 16 700 10    Bonastre, Francesc.
```

In this record for an accompanied choral work, the prefatory notes mentioned in the final 500 note show up in the Accompanying Matter (Accomp mat) fixed field element as well as the 041 subfield ‡g. The 048 field corresponds to the first 500 field ("tiple" is a high voice; a cobla ensemble is a Catalan dance band; a xeremia is a Catalan wind instrument). Note the uniform title main entry (130) and the 503 note.

Example 4

```
Type: c Bib lvl: m Lang:   gae Source:   Accomp mat: b
Repr:    Enc lvl: 1 Ctry:  onc Dat tp: r MEBE: 0
         Mod rec:   Comp:  fm  Format: z Prts:
Desc: a Int lvl:    LTxt:  n    Dates: 1979,1964
  1 010       82-771219/M/r85
  2 028 30    NM93-198/1979 ǂb National Museum of Man
  3 041 1     gae ǂe eng ǂh gae
  4 043       n-cn-ns
  5 050 0     M1678 ǂb .G144 1979
  6 245 00    Gaelic songs in Nova Scotia / ǂc [compiled by] Helen Creighton
and Calum MacLeod ; with a new preface by Helen Creighton.
  7 260 0     Ottawa, Canada : ǂb National Museum of Man, National Museums of
Canada, ǂc 1979.
  8 300       xi p., 308 p. of music : ǂb ill. ; ǂc 25 cm.
  9 500       Unacc.
 10 500       Words in Gaelic with English translations.
 11 534       ǂp Reprint. Originally published: ǂc 1964. ǂf (Bulletin /
National Museum of Canada ; no. 196. Anthropological series ; no. 66).
 12 504       Bibliography: p. 298-300.
 13 500       Includes index.
 14 500       Catalogue no.: NM93-198/1979.
 15 650  0 Folk music ǂz Nova Scotia.
 16 650  0 Folk-songs, Gaelic ǂz Nova Scotia.
 17 700 10 Creighton, Helen.
 18 700 10 MacLeod, Calum.
 19 830  0 Bulletin (National Museum of Canada) ; ǂv no. 196.
 20 830  0 Bulletin (National Museum of Canada). ǂp Anthropological series
; ǂv no. 66.
```

The fact that this score is a reprint is noted in the Type of date (Dat tp) and Dates fixed fields, the 534 note, and the two corresponding series uniform title added entries (830). The bibliography is noted in the 504 field and in the Accompanying Matter fixed field (Accomp mat).

Example 5

```
Type: c Bib lvl: m Lang:   gre Source:    Accomp mat:
Repr:     Enc lvl:    Ctry:   gw  Dat tp: s MEBE: 1
          Mod rec:    Comp:   uu  Format: a Prts:
Desc: a Int lvl:      LTxt:   n    Dates: 1986,
 1 010       87-751402/M/r88
 2 028 22  CV 40-482/01 ‡b Carus-Verlag
 3 045 0    ‡b d18250506
 4 048       ca05 ‡a oa
 5 050 0   M2020.M36 ‡b K94 1986
 6 100 20  Mendelssohn-Bartholdy, Felix, ‡d 1809-1847.
 7 240 10  Kyrie, ‡r D minor. ‡l Greek
 8 245 00  Kyrie in d, f¨ur Chor und Orchester / ‡c [Felix Mendelssohn
Bartholdy].
 9 250       Erstausg. / ‡b herausgegeben von R. Larry Todd.
10 254       Partitur.
11 260 0   Stuttgart : ‡b Carus-Verlag, ‡c c1986.
12 300       1 score (32 p.) ; ‡c 30 cm.
13 306       001000
14 490 1   Ausgew¨ahlte Werke vokaler Kirchenmusik / Felix Mendelssohn
Bartholdy
15 500       Chorus: SSATB.
16 500       Duration: 10:00.
17 650   0  Choruses, Sacred (Mixed voices) with orchestra.
18 650   0  Kyrie eleison (Music)
19 700 10  Todd, R. Larry.
20 800 2   Mendelssohn-Bartholdy, Felix, ‡d 1809-1847. ‡t Vocal music. ‡k
Selections (Ausgew¨ahlte Werke vokaler Kirchenmusik)
```

A score with both an edition statement (250) and a musical presentation statement (254), this record has a 490/800 combination as well. The Duration field (306) corresponds to the final 500 note. Mendelssohn-Bartholdy's compound surname requires appropriate first indicators in both the 100 and 800 fields.

Example 6

```
Type: c Bib lvl: m Lang:   ita Source:   Accomp mat:
Repr:     Enc lvl:   Ctry: nyu Dat tp: r MEBE: 1
          Mod rec:   Comp:  op Format: c Prts:
Desc: a Int lvl:    LTxt:  n   Dates: 1985,1839
 1 010      85-750511/M/r86
 2 020      0824065697 : ‡c $75.00
 3 028 22   H. 11231 H. ‡b Garland
 4 045 0    ‡b d1838
 5 050 0    M1503.M553 ‡b E4 1985
 6 100 10   Mercadante, Saverio, ‡d 1795-1870.
 7 240 10   Elena da Feltre. ‡s Vocal score
 8 245 10   Elena da Feltre / ‡c libretto by Salvatore Cammarano ; music by
Saverio Mercadante.
 9 250      A facsim. ed. of the printed piano-vocal score / ‡b with an
introduction by Philip Gossett.
10 260 0    New York : ‡b Garland, ‡c 1985.
11 300      1 vocal score (237, 11 p.) : ‡b facsims. ; ‡c 24 x 32 cm.
12 440 0    Italian opera, 1810-1840 ; ‡v v. 20
13 500      Italian words.
14 534      ‡p Reprint. Originally published: ‡c Milano : Ricordi, 1839.
15 500      "Recito. e cavatina : 'Parmi che alfin dimentica' : aggiunta
all'opera Elena da Feltre": p. 1-11 (2nd group).
16 650 0    Operas ‡x Vocal scores with piano.
17 700 10   Cammarano, Salvatore, ‡d 1801-1852.
```

The Type of Date (Dat tp) and Dates fixed field elements, the edition statement (250), and the 534 note all indicate that this is a facsimile edition of a previously published vocal score. The dates in the series statement (440) are not separately subfielded, because they are considered an integral part of the series title.

Example 7

```
Type: c Bib lvl: m Lang:  N/A Source:   Accomp mat:
Repr:    Enc lvl:    Ctry: nyu Dat tp: s MEBE: 1
         Mod rec:    Comp:  uu  Format: a Prts:
Desc: a Int lvl:    LTxt:  n    Dates: 1985,
 1 010      86-754626/M
 2 045 0    ǂb d1985
 3 048      ec01 ǂa wb01 ǂa sa02 ǂa sb01 ǂa sc01
 4 050 0    M562.K754 ǂb T5 1985
 5 100 10   Kolb, Barbara.
 6 245 10   Time-- and again / ǂc Barbara Kolb.
 7 260 0    New York, NY (24 W. 57th St., New York 10019) : ǂb Boosey &
Hawkes, ǂc c1985.
 8 300      1 score (18 p.) ; ǂc 36 x 45 cm.
 9 500      Caption title.
10 500      For computer, oboe, 2 violins, viola, and violoncello.
11 500      Reproduced from holograph.
12 650   0  Quintets (Oboe, violins (2), viola, violoncello) ǂx Scores.
13 650   0  Computer music.
14 650   0  Music ǂx Manuscripts ǂx Facsimiles.
15 600 10   Kolb, Barbara ǂx Manuscripts ǂx Facsimiles.
```

The title of this score features some out-of-the-ordinary punctuation. The publisher's address appears in the subfield ǂa of the 260 field. Formulation of the 048 field corresponds to the second 500 note.

Example 8

```
Type: c Bib lvl: m Lang:   N/A Source:   Accomp mat:
Repr:     Enc lvl:   Ctry:  mbc Dat tp: c MEBE: 1
          Mod rec:   Comp:  sy  Format: a Prts:
Desc: a Int lvl:     LTxt:  n   Dates: 1980,1970
 1 010       86-753526/M
 2 045 0     ‡b d1970
 3 048       oa
 4 050 0     M3.1.E27 ‡b E8 1980 vol. 2 ‡a M1001
 5 100 20    Eckhardt-Gramatt´e, S. C. ‡q (Sophie-Carmen), ‡d 1899-1974.
 6 240 10    Symphonies, ‡n no. 2
 7 245 00    Symphony II (E. 158) : ‡b Manitoba symphony / ‡c [Eckhardt-
Gramatt´e].
 8 250       Restricted ed. for archival purposes only / ‡b an[n]otations and
corrections by the composer.
 9 254       Orchestra score & analysis.
10 260 0     Winnipeg, Canada : ‡b Estate S.C. Eckhardt-Gramatt´e, ‡c 1980,
c1970.
11 300       1 score (58, 62, 55, 67 p.) : ‡b port. ; ‡c 29 cm.
12 306       003400
13 490 1     Selected works / S.C. Eckhardt-Gramatt´e ; ‡v v. 2
14 500       Duration: 34:00.
15 650  0    Symphonies ‡x Scores.
16 740 01    Manitoba symphony.
17 800 2     Eckhardt-Gramatt´e, S. C. ‡q (Sophie-Carmen), ‡d 1899-1974. ‡t
Selections (Selected works) ; ‡v v. 2.
```

The 250 field in this special edition of a score includes a statement of responsibility without a proper name. A musical presentation statement (254) also is present. Note the 490/800 pair and the multiple surname in the 100 and 800 fields.

Example 9

```
Type: c Bib lvl: m Lang:   spa Source:    Accomp mat: bei
Repr:     Enc lvl:   Ctry:   mx  Dat tp: s MEBE: 0
          Mod rec:   Comp:   mu  Format: a Prts:
Desc: a Int lvl:     LTxt:   n    Dates: 1985,
  1 010      86-192870/M/r872
  2 020      9688890006
  3 043      n-mx---
  4 047      pp ‡a df
  5 048      vn01 ‡a ka01
  6 048      ka01
  7 050 0    M1683.18 ‡b A57 1985
  8 245 00   Antolog´ia folkl´orica y musical de Tabasco / ‡c [compilaci´on]
Francisco J. Santamar´ia ; arreglo y estudio musical de Ger´onimo Baqueiro
F´oster.
  9 250      2a ed.
 10 260 0    Villahermosa : ‡b Gobierno del Estado de Tabasco, ‡c 1985.
 11 300      1 score (600 p.) ; ‡c 21 cm.
 12 440  0   Biblioteca b´asica tabasque˜na ; ‡v 1
 13 490 1    Serie antolog´ias
 14 500      Principally popular songs for voice and piano and dances for
piano.
 15 504      Bibliography: p. 89-91.
 16 500      Includes historical notes and biographies of the composers.
 17 650  0   Popular music ‡z Mexico ‡z Tabasco (State) ‡y 1981-
 18 650  0   Piano music.
 19 650  0   Dance music ‡z Mexico ‡z Tabasco (State)
 20 700 10   Santamar´ia, Francisco Javier, ‡d 1889-
 21 700 20   Baqueiro F´oster, Ger´onimo. ‡4 arr
 22 830  0   Serie antolog´ias (Instituto de Cultura de Tabasco)
```

This score of ethnic popular and dance music has the code "mu" in the Form of Composition fixed field (Comp), meaning that the 047 field must also be present. The Accompanying Matter fixed field (Accomp mat) codes the information in both the 504 and the final 500 note. Two series statements (440 and 490) and one corresponding series uniform title added entry (830) are present. Note the edition statement (250) and the subfield ‡4 for the arranger in the last 700 field.

Example 10

```
Type: d Bib lvl: m Lang:  N/A Source:   Accomp mat:
Repr:     Enc lvl: 1 Ctry:  xx  Dat tp: s MEBE: 1
          Mod rec:   Comp:  pr  Format: z Prts:
Desc: a Int lvl:   LTxt:  n   Dates: 1859,
 1 010      82-770783/M/r85
 2 045 0    ‡b d1859
 3 048      ka01
 4 050 0    ML31 ‡b .S4a No. 11
 5 100 10   Liszt, Franz, ‡d 1811-1886.
 6 245 10   Weinen, Klagen, Sorgen, Zagen : ‡b Praeludium (nach J.S. Bach's
Cantate) / ‡c von F. Liszt.
 7 260 1    ‡c [1859]
 8 300      [4] p. of ms. music ; ‡c 28 x 35 cm.
 9 500      Holograph, in ink.
10 500      For piano.
11 503      Based on a theme from the opening chorus of the cantata.
12 503      Published: Berlin : Schlesinger, 1863.
13 650  0   Piano music.
14 650  0   Music ‡x Manuscripts.
15 600 10   Liszt, Franz, ‡d 1811-1886 ‡x Manuscripts.
16 700 11   Bach, Johann Sebastian, ‡d 1685-1750. ‡t Weinen, Klagen, Sorgen,
Zagen. ‡p Weinen, Klagen, Sorgen, Zagen.
```

In this music manuscript (Type: d), notice the two 503 notes (one explaining the work's derivation, the other its first publication), the 260 with only a date, and the formulation of the 300 field. The author/title added entry for J.S. Bach formalizes the information found in the 245 and the first 503 field.

Example 11

```
Type: d Bib lvl: m Lang:   N/A Source:    Accomp mat:
Repr:     Enc lvl:    Ctry:  dcu Dat tp: s MEBE: 1
         Mod rec:    Comp:  uu  Format: a Prts:
Desc: a Int lvl:     LTxt:  n    Dates: 1976,
  1 010      87-753561/M
  2 045 0     ‡b d19760629
  3 048      wa01 ‡a wb01 ‡a wc01 ‡a ba01 ‡a wd01
  4 050 0    ML30.3c ‡b .J64 no. 1
  5 100 10   Jolas, Betsy.
  6 245 10   O wall : ‡b op´era de poup´ee = a puppet opera : 1976 / ‡c Betsy
Jolas.
  7 260 1     ‡c 1976 June 29.
  8 300      1 ms. score (12 leaves) ; ‡c 44 cm.
  9 306      001500
 10 500      Holograph.
 11 500      For flute, oboe, clarinet, horn, and bassoon.
 12 500      "For the Serge Koussevitzky Music Foundation in the Library of
Congress, and dedicated to the memory of Serge and Natalie Koussevitzky."
 13 500      Duration: ca. 15:00.
 14 500      At end: Paris.
 15 500      In ink; on transparencies.
 16 500      Accompanied by photocopy (39 cm.) and sketches ([2] p. ; 44
cm.).
 17 650  0  Wind quintets (Bassoon, clarinet, flute, horn, oboe) ‡x Scores.
 18 650  0  Musical sketches.
 19 710 20  Library of Congress. ‡b Serge Koussevitzky Music Foundation.
```

In this manuscript score (Type: d), the date in the 260 field is derived from the date on the holograph and is coded in the 045 field. The quoted 500 note justifies the corporate added entry. Accompanying material is described in the final 500 note.

Example 12

```
Type: c Bib lvl: m Lang:  ger Source:   Accomp mat:
Repr: a Enc lvl: 7 Ctry:  dcu Dat tp: r MEBE: 1
        Mod rec:   Comp:  sg Format:   Prts:
Desc: a Int lvl:   LTxt:  n    Dates: 1988,1920
  1 010     88-953290
  2 007     h ǂb d ǂc u ǂd a ǂe f ǂf a— ǂg b ǂh a ǂi c ǂj a
  3 007     h ǂb d ǂc u ǂd b ǂe f ǂf a— ǂg b ǂh a ǂi a ǂj a
  4 041 1   gerfre ǂh fre
  5 048     vu01 ǂa ka01
  6 100 10  Berlioz, Hector, ǂd 1803-1869.
  7 240 10  Songs. ǂk Selections
  8 245 10  Ausgew¨ahlte Lieder ǂh [microform] / ǂc von Hector Berlioz ;
eingeleitet und herausgegeben von Karl Blessinger.
  9 260 0   M¨unchen : ǂb Drei Masken Verlag, ǂc 1920.
 10 300     1 score (xii, 74 p.) : ǂb port. ; ǂc 19 cm.
 11 490 0   Musikalische Stundenb¨ucher
 12 500     For voice and piano.
 13 500     French and German words.
 14 500     Call number of original: M2.M93B45.
 15 500     Master microform held by: DLC.
 16 533     Microfilm. ǂb Washington, D.C. : ǂc Library of Congress
Photoduplication Service, ǂd 1988. ǂe 1 microfilm reel : positive ; 35 mm.
 17 501     With: Quartetto e coro dei maggi / da H. Berlioz.
 18 650  0  Songs with piano accompaniment.
 19 700 10  Blessinger, Karl, ǂd 1888-
```

This microform reproduction of a printed score has two microform 007 fields, the first for the positive item being cataloged, the second for the negative master mentioned in the final 500 field. Note the GMD in the 245 field. The physical description of the positive microfilm appears in the 533 note. Another work filmed with this one is noted in the 501 field.

OCLC FULL RECORD EXAMPLES—SOUND RECORDINGS

Example 13

Compact Disc

```
Type: j Bib lvl: m Lang:  fre Source:   Accomp mat: defi
Repr:    Enc lvl:   Ctry:  fr Dat tp: p MEBE: 1
         Mod rec:   Comp:  mu Format: n Prts:
Desc: a Int lvl:    LTxt:     Dates: 1986,1985
 1 010      89-751546/R
 2 007      s ǂb d ǂd f ǂe s ǂf n ǂg g ǂh n ǂi n ǂj m ǂk m ǂl n ǂm e ǂn e
 3 028 00   ARN 268012--ARN 268013 ǂb Arion
 4 033 0    198503--
 5 041 0    ǂd fre ǂe freengger ǂh fre ǂg freengger ǂh fre
 6 045 1    ǂb d1695 ǂb d1715
 7 047      ct ǂa ts
 8 048      va01 ǂa ke
 9 048      va02 ǂa ke
10 048      sa02 ǂa ke
11 048      va01 ǂa ve01 ǂa ke
12 048      sa01 ǂa kc01
13 100 20   Jacquet de La Guerre, Elisabeth-Claude, ǂd ca. 1664-1729.
14 240 10   Selections
15 245 00   Cantates & pi`eces vari´ees ǂh [sound recording] / ǂc Elisabeth
Jacquet de La Guerre.
16 260 0    [France] : ǂb Arion, ǂc p1986.
17 300      2 sound discs : ǂb digital ; ǂc 4 3/4 in.
18 490 0    Les Joyaux de votre discoth`eque
19 500      Arion: ARN 268012 (ARN 268012--ARN 268013).
20 500      Title on container: Cantates bibliques ; Pi`eces instrumentales.
21 500      Title on spine of container: Cantates bibliques ; Pi`eces
instrumentales et vocale[s].
22 500      The 1st 4 works for soprano and continuo; the 5th for 2 sopranos
and continuo; the 6th for 2 violins and continuo; the 7th and 9th for
soprano, baritone, and continuo; the 8th for violin and harpsichord.
23 511 0    Sophie Boulin, Isabelle Poulenard, sopranos ; Michel Verschaeve,
baritone ; Bernadette Charbonnier, Catherine Giardelli, violins ;
Fran‚coise Bloch, viola da gamba ; Claire Giardelli, violoncello ; Guy
Robert, theorbo ; Brigitte Haudebourg, harpsichord ; Georges Guillard,
organ or harpsichord.
24 518      Recorded in Mar. 1985.
25 500      Compact disc.
26 500      Analog recording.
27 500      Program notes in French by Philippe Beaussant and words of the
vocal works with English and German translations (32 p. : ill.) in
container.
28 505 0    Suzanne -- Judith -- Esther -- Jacob et Rachel -- Jepth´e --
Sonate no 4 `a 2 viol. et violonc. -- Le D´eluge -- Les pi`eces de clavecin
qui peuvent se jouer sur le violon -- Le raccommodement comique de Pierrot
et de Nicole.
29 650  0   Solo cantatas, Sacred (High voice)
```

```
30 650  0  Cantatas, Sacred.
31 650  0  Trio-sonatas (Violins (2), continuo)
32 650  0  Violin and harpsichord music.
33 650  0  Cantatas, Secular.
34 700 10  Boulin, Sophie. ‡4 prf
35 700 10  Poulenard, Isabelle. ‡4 prf
36 700 10  Verschaeve, Michel. ‡4 prf
37 700 10  Charbonnier, Bernadette. ‡4 prf
38 700 10  Giardelli, Catherine. ‡4 prf
39 700 10  Bloch, Fran coise. ‡4 prf
40 700 10  Giardelli, Claire. ‡4 prf
41 700 10  Robert, Guy, ‡d 1943-  ‡4 prf
42 700 10  Haudebourg, Brigitte. ‡4 prf
43 700 10  Guillard, Georges. ‡4 prf
44 700 22  Jacquet de La Guerre, Elisabeth-Claude, ‡d ca. 1664-1729. ‡t
Cantates fran coises sur des sujets tirez de l'Ecriture, ‡n bk. 1. ‡k
Selections. ‡f 1986.
45 700 22  Jacquet de La Guerre, Elisabeth-Claude, ‡d ca. 1664-1729. ‡t
Cantates fran coises sur des sujets tirez de l'Ecriture, ‡n bk. 2. ‡p
Jepht´e. ‡f 1986.
46 700 22  Jacquet de La Guerre, Elisabeth-Claude, ‡d ca. 1664-1729. ‡t
Trio sonatas. ‡n No. 4. ‡f 1986.
47 700 22  Jacquet de La Guerre, Elisabeth-Claude, ‡d ca. 1664-1729. ‡t
Cantates fran coises sur des sujets tirez de l'Ecriture, ‡n bk. 2. ‡p
D´eluge. ‡f 1986.
48 700 22  Jacquet de La Guerre, Elisabeth-Claude, ‡d ca. 1664-1729. ‡t
Pi`eces de clavecin. ‡k Selections. ‡f 1986.
49 700 22  Jacquet de La Guerre, Elisabeth-Claude, ‡d ca. 1664-1729. ‡t
Cantates fran coises ‡n (1715). ‡p Raccommodement comique de Pierrot et de
Nicole. ‡f 1986.
```

This digital compact disc derived from an analog recording. The Form of Composition fixed field (Comp) has a corresponding 047 field. The Type of Date (Dat tp) and Dates in the fixed field reflect the 260 subfield ‡c and the 518 note; the 033 field is derived from the 518 field. The item had no indication of stereo (hence, no mention in the 300 field), but the cataloger surmised that it was stereo and coded the 007 subfield ‡e as such. Note the complex 041 field and its relation to the last 500 note. Multiple musical publisher's numbers are input as a range in a single 028 field but an explicitly input 500 note still is needed. Also note the multiple surname in the main and some of the added entries.

Example 14

Compact disc

```
Type: j Bib lvl: m Lang:  N/A Source:   Accomp mat:
Repr:    Enc lvl:   Ctry:  enk Dat tp: p MEBE: 1
         Mod rec:   Comp:  op  Format: n Prts:
Desc: a Int lvl:    LTxt:       Dates: 1986,1985
 1 010       87-750942/R
 2 007       s ‡b d ‡d f ‡e s ‡f n ‡g g ‡h n ‡i n ‡j m ‡k m ‡l n ‡m e ‡n e
 3 028 02    CHAN 8412 ‡b Chandos
 4 033 1     19850218 ‡a 19850219 ‡b 5754 ‡c L7
 5 045 1     ‡b d1866 ‡b d1941
 6 048       oa
 7 050 1     M1000
 8 100 10    Smetana, Bed⌄rich, ‡d 1824-1884.
 9 240 10    Prodan´a nev⌄esta. ‡k Selections
10 245 14    The bartered bride. ‡p Overture and dances ; From my life : ‡b
string quartet in E minor ‡h [sound recording] / ‡c Bed⌄rich Smetana ;
orchestral version [of 2nd work] by George Szell.
11 260 0     London, England : ‡b Chandos, ‡c p1986.
12 300       1 sound disc : ‡b digital, stereo. ; ‡c 4 3/4 in.
13 306       002423 ‡a 003030
14 511 0     London Symphony Orchestra ; Geoffrey Simon, conductor.
15 518       Recorded Feb. 18-19, 1985, All Saints' Church, Tooting, London.
16 500       Compact disc.
17 500       Durations: 24:23; 30:30.
18 505 2     The bartered bride. Overture (6:32) ; Dance of the villagers
(4:28) ; Polka (4:57) ; Furiant (1:58) ; Fanfare (:41) ; Dance of the
comedians (5:32).
19 650  0    Operas ‡x Excerpts.
20 650  0    Orchestral music, Arranged.
21 700 10    Simon, Geoffrey, ‡d 1946-
22 700 12    Smetana, Bed⌄rich, ‡d 1824-1884. ‡t Quartets, ‡m strings, ‡n no.
1, ‡r E minor; ‡o arr. ‡f 1986.
23 710 20    London Symphony Orchestra.
24 740 01    From my life.
```

The Type of Date (Dat tp) and Dates fixed fields are determined by information in the 260 subfield ‡c and the 518 field in this record for a digital compact disc. The 245 field includes a subfield ‡p and a GMD in subfield ‡h. The 033 field is derived from information in the 518 note. The 505 field first indicator is coded for "Partial contents" and the note is punctuated accordingly.

Example 15

Compact disc

```
Type: j Bib lvl: m Lang:  N/A Source:    Accomp mat:
Repr:    Enc lvl:    Ctry:  fr Dat tp: p MEBE: 0
         Mod rec:    Comp:  sn Format: n Prts:
Desc: a Int lvl:    LTxt:        Dates: 1987,1986
 1 010       88-752942/R
 2 007       s ‡b d ‡d f ‡e s ‡f n ‡g g ‡h n ‡i n ‡j m ‡k m ‡l n ‡m e ‡n e
 3 028 02    HMC 905184 ‡b Harmonia Mundi France
 4 033 0     198612—
 5 045 1      ‡b d1762 ‡b d1939 ‡b d1943
 6 048       ta01
 7 050 1     M116
 8 100 10    Moretti, Isabelle, ‡d 1964-  ‡4 prf
 9 245 10    R´ecital de harpe ‡h [sound recording].
10 260 0     Arles : ‡b Harmonia Mundi France, ‡c p1987.
11 300       1 sound disc : ‡b digital ; ‡c 4 3/4 in.
12 306       001400 ‡a 000700 ‡a 001100 ‡a 001700 ‡a 000900
13 490 1     Cr´eations en val de Charente
14 511 0     Isabelle Moretti, harp.
15 518       Recorded Dec. 1986.
16 500       Compact disc.
17 505 0     Sonate en sol majeur, Wotq 139 / Carl Philipp Emanuel Bach
(14:00) -- Sonate pour harpe / Johann Ladislav Dussek (7:00) -- Sonate f¨ur
Harfe, 1939 / Paul Hindemith (11:00) -- Sonata per arpa, op. 68 / Alfredo
Casella (17:00) -- Sonate pour harpe / Germaine Tailleferre (9:00).
18 650  0    Sonatas (Harp)
19 700 12    Bach, Carl Philipp Emanuel, ‡d 1714-1788. ‡t Solos, ‡m harp, ‡n
H. 563, ‡r G major. ‡f 1987.
20 700 12    Dussek, Johann Ladislaus, ‡d 1760-1812. ‡t Sonatas, ‡m harp, ‡r
C minor. ‡f 1987.
21 700 12    Hindemith, Paul, ‡d 1895-1963. ‡t Sonatas, ‡m harp. ‡f 1987.
22 700 12    Casella, Alfredo, ‡d 1883-1947. ‡t Sonatas, ‡m harp, ‡n op. 68.
‡f 1987.
23 700 12    Tailleferre, Germaine, ‡d 1892-  ‡t Sonatas, ‡m harp. ‡f 1987.
24 830  0    Cr´eations en val de Charente (Series)
```

This digital compact disc had no indication of stereo (hence, no mention in the 300 field), but the cataloger surmised that it was stereo and coded the 007 subfield ‡e as such. The Type of Date (Dat tp) and Dates fixed fields are determined by information in the 260 subfield ‡c and the 518 field. The 033 field is derived from information in the 518 note. Note the subfield ‡4 for performer in the 100 field.

Example 16

Compact disc

```
Type: j Bib lvl: m Lang:   N/A Source:    Accomp mat: i
Repr:    Enc lvl:    Ctry:  wau Dat tp: r MEBE: 0
         Mod rec:    Comp:   mu  Format: n Prts:
Desc: a Int lvl:    LTxt:      Dates: 1986,
 1 010      88-750309/R
 2 007      s ‡b d ‡d f ‡e s ‡f n ‡g g ‡h n ‡i n ‡j m ‡k m ‡l n ‡m e ‡n e
 3 028 02   CD200 ‡b Crystal Records
 4 033 2    1977---- ‡a 1984----
 5 045 0     ‡b d1961
 6 047      df ‡a cz ‡a sn ‡a su
 7 048      bb02 ‡a ba01 ‡a bd01 ‡a be01
 8 050 1    M555
 9 245 00   Brass bonanza ‡h [sound recording].
10 260 0    Sedro Woolley, WA : ‡b Crystal Records, ‡c p1986.
11 300      1 sound disc : ‡b digital ; ‡c 4 3/4 in.
12 500      The 1st work originally for brass ensemble and percussion.
13 511 0    Metropolitan Brass Quintet (1st and 12th works) ; Berlin Brass
Quintet (2nd-4th works) ; Annapolis Brass Quintet (5th-7th works) ; New
York Brass Quintet (8th work) ; Dallas Brass Quintet (9th work) ; Saint
Louis Brass Quintet (10th work) ; I-5 Brass Quintet (11th work).
14 503      Reissued from various Crystal Records albums.
15 503      Eds. recorded: Atlantis Publications (5th-6th works); Bruxelles
: Editions Maurer (8th work); C.F. Peters (9th work); Paterson's
Publications (10th work); Canada : Touch of Brass (11th work); Novello
(12th work).
16 518      Recorded 1977-1984 in various locations.
17 500      Compact disc.
18 500      Analog recording.
19 500      Program notes (4 folded p.) included.
20 505 0    Fanfares for the jubilee of Rimsky-Korsakov / Liadov-Glazunov --
Allemande [i.e. Gaillard] / William Brade -- Canzona per sonare : no. 1 /
Giovanni Gabrieli -- Sonata from Die B¨ankels¨angerlieder : ca. 1648 /
anon. [i.e. Daniel Speer] -- Sonata no. 4 ; Sonata no. 6 / Daniel Speer --
Sonata no. 2 / Johann Kessel -- Par monts et par vaux / Michel Leclerc --
Six dances / Alan Hovhaness -- Quintet / Malcolm Arnold -- The carnival of
Venice / Brent Dutton -- Music hall suite / Joseph Horovitz.
21 650  0   Brass quintets (Horn, trombone, trumpets (2), tuba)
22 650  0   Brass quintets (Horn, trombone, trumpets (2), tuba), Arranged.
23 700 12   Lyadov, Anatoly Konstantinovich, ‡d 1855-1914. ‡t Slavleni´i`a;
‡o arr. ‡f 1986.
24 700 12   Brade, William, ‡d 1560-1630. ‡t Newe ausserlesene Paduanen,
Galliarden, Cantzonen, Allmand und Coranten. ‡p Gaillard. ‡f 1986.
25 700 12   Gabrieli, Giovanni, ‡d 1557-1612. ‡t Spiritata. ‡f 1986.
26 700 12   Speer, Daniel, ‡d 1636-1707. ‡t Musicalisch-t¨urckischer Eulen-
Spiegel. ‡k Selections. ‡f 1986.
27 700 12   Kessel, Johann, ‡d fl. 1657-1672. ‡t Symphonien, Sonaten, ein
Canzon, nebst Allmanden, Couranten, Balletten und Sarabanden. ‡p Sonata, ‡n
no. 2. ‡f 1986.
28 700 12   Leclerc, Michel, ‡d 1914-  ‡t Par monts et par vaux. ‡f 1986.
```

29 700 12 Hovhaness, Alan, ǂd 1911- ǂt Dances, ǂm brasses, ǂn op. 79. ǂf 1986.
30 700 12 Arnold, Malcolm. ǂt Quintets, ǂm trumpets, horn, trombone, tuba. ǂf 1986.
31 700 12 Dutton, Brent, ǂd 1950- ǂt Carnival of Venice. ǂf 1986.
32 700 12 Horovitz, Joseph, ǂd 1926- ǂt Music hall suite. ǂf 1986.
33 710 20 Metropolitan Brass Quintet. ǂ4 prf
34 710 20 Berlin Brass Quintet. ǂ4 prf
35 710 20 Annapolis Brass Quintet. ǂ4 prf
36 710 20 New York Brass Quintet. ǂ4 prf
37 710 20 Dallas Brass Quintet. ǂ4 prf
38 710 20 Saint Louis Brass Quintet. ǂ4 prf
39 710 20 I-5 Brass Quintet. ǂ4 prf

Although this digital compact disc derived from an analog recording had no indication of stereo, and so no mention of it in the 300 field, the cataloger surmised that it was stereo and coded the 007 subfield ǂe as such. The Type of Date (Dat tp) fixed field is coded "r" (for reissue) but the Dates fixed field has only a single date because of the first 503 note, which mentions no original release date. Type of Date code "r" has precedence over "p", for which the recording dates in field 518 would be evidence. The 033 field is derived from information in the 518 note.

Example 17

Analog Disc

```
Type: j Bib lvl: m Lang:  N/A Source:   Accomp mat:
Repr:    Enc lvl:   Ctry:  enk Dat tp: s MEBE: 0
         Mod rec:   Comp:  pp  Format: n Prts:
Desc: a Int lvl:    LTxt:      Dates: 1972,
 1 010      86-750617/R/r87
 2 007      s ǂb d ǂd b ǂe s ǂf m ǂg e ǂh n ǂi n ǂj m ǂk p ǂl l ǂm u ǂn e
 3 028 02   SDL 2232 ǂb Saydisc
 4 043      e-uk-en
 5 050 1    M175 ǂb .B3
 6 245 00   Mechanical music hall ǂh [sound recording].
 7 260 0    Badminton, Glos. : ǂb Saydisc, ǂc [1972?]
 8 300      1 sound disc : ǂb analog, 33 1/3 rpm, stereo. ; ǂc 12 in.
 9 440 0    Golden age of mechanical music ; ǂv v. 10
10 500      "Street, penny & player pianos, musical boxes & other Victorian
automata"--Container.
11 500      Songs identified with various English music hall performers.
12 500      Instruments from the collection of Roy Mickleburgh, Bristol.
13 505 0    Miscellany -- Florrie Ford songs -- Eugene Stratton song --
Miscellany -- Tom Costello songs -- Ellaline Terris song -- Harry Champion
songs -- Miscellany -- Albert Chevalier songs -- Marie Lloyd songs --
Lottie Collins song -- Leo Dryden song -- Miscellany.
14 650 0    Barrel-organ music.
15 650 0    Player-piano music.
16 650 0    Music box music.
17 650 0    Popular instrumental music ǂz England.
18 650 0    Musical revues, comedies, etc. ǂx Excerpts, Arranged.
19 650 0    Musical instruments (Mechanical)
20 700 10   Mickleburgh, Roy.
```

This is a record for an analog disc with title main entry.

Example 18

Analog disc

```
Type: j Bib lvl: m Lang:  N/A Source:   Accomp mat:
Repr:    Enc lvl:   Ctry:  sz  Dat tp: s MEBE: 0
         Mod rec:   Comp:  vr  Format: n Prts:
Desc: a Int lvl:    LTxt:      Dates: 1979,
 1 010      86-753061/R
 2 007      s ‡b d ‡d b ‡e s ‡f m ‡g e ‡h n ‡i n ‡j m ‡k p ‡l l ‡m u ‡n e
 3 028 00   Cla D 907 ‡b Claves
 4 028 00   D 907 ‡b Claves
 5 033 2    19790720 ‡a 19790722 ‡b 6044 ‡c A87
 6 048      zn01
 7 048      kb01 ‡a zn01
 8 050 1    M175 ‡b .B3
 9 245 00   1. Schweizerisches Drehorgel-Festival, Arosa ‡h [sound
recording].
10 260 0    Thun/Schweiz : ‡b Claves, ‡c p1979.
11 300      1 sound disc : ‡b analog, 33 1/3 rpm, stereo. ; ‡c 12 in.
12 500 .    Claves: Cla D 907 (on container: D 907).
13 500      Twenty barrel-organ pieces and "a dialogue between a church
organ and a barrel-organ, played by Hannes Meyer and Heinrich Brechb¨uhl:
Variations on the theme 'God save the king'"--Container.
14 518      Recorded July 20-22, 1979, on the streets and in the squares of
Arosa, Switzerland.
15 650  0   Barrel-organ music.
16 650  0   Variations (Organ)
17 700 10   Meyer, Hannes, ‡d 1939-  ‡4 prf
18 700 10   Brechb¨uhl, H. ‡q (Heinrich) ‡4 prf
19 711 20   Schweizerisches Drehorgel-Festival ‡n (1st : ‡d 1979 : ‡c Arosa,
Switzerland)
20 740 01   Erste Schweizerisches Drehorgel-Festival, Arosa.
```

Because two forms of the music publisher's number are found on this analog disc (see the first 500 field), two 028 fields are needed. Information in the 033 is derived from the 518 field. The 711 field is used for the name of the festival.

Example 19

Analog disc

```
Type: j Bib lvl: m Lang:   eng Source:    Accomp mat: dfhz
Repr:    Enc lvl:    Ctry:   cau Dat tp: s MEBE: 1
         Mod rec:    Comp:   op Format: n Prts:
Desc: a Int lvl:    LTxt:       Dates: 1985,
 1 010      85-754264/R/r872
 2 007      s ‡b d ‡d b ‡e s ‡f m ‡g e ‡h n ‡i n ‡j m ‡k p ‡l l ‡m u ‡n d
 3 024 1    7777339741
 4 028 02   DSC-3974 ‡b Angel
 5 028 00   EX 27 0232 3 ‡b EMI
 6 033       ‡b 5754 ‡c L7
 7 041 1     ‡d eng ‡h ita ‡b eng ‡e eng ‡h ita ‡g engger
 8 050 1    M1500
 9 100 10   Handel, George Frideric, ‡d 1685-1759.
10 240 10   Giulio Cesare. ‡l English
11 245 10   Julius Caesar ‡h [sound recording] / ‡c Handel ; libretto by
Haym ; transl. Trowell.
12 260 0    [Hollywood, Calif.] : ‡b Angel, ‡c p1985.
13 300      3 sound discs : ‡b analog, 33 1/3 rpm, stereo. ; ‡c 12 in.
14 500      EMI: EX 27 0232 3.
15 500      Opera; sung in English.
16 503      "Edition by Noel Davies and Sir Charles Mackerras"--Container.
17 511 0    Valerie Masterson, soprano ; Dame Janet Baker, Sarah Walker,
Della Jones, mezzo-sopranos ; James Bowman, David James, countertenors ;
Christopher Booth-Jones, baritone ; John Tomlinson, bass ; English National
Opera Chorus & Orchestra ; Sir Charles Mackerras, conductor.
18 518      "Recorded at the Abbey Road Studios, London, in association with
the Peter Moores Foundation"--Booklet, p. 1.
19 500      Digital recording.
20 500      Manual sequence.
21 500      Program notes by Brian Trowell in English and German and by Sir
Charles Mackerras in English, synopsis in English and German, biographical
notes on the singers and conductor in English, and English translation of
the Italian libretto (24 p. : ill.) laid in container.
22 650  0   Operas.
23 600 10   Caesar, Julius ‡x Drama.
24 700 10   Haym, Nicola Francesco. ‡4 lbt
25 700 10   Trowell, Brian. ‡4 trl
26 700 10   Davies, Noel.
27 700 10   Mackerras, Charles, ‡c Sir, ‡d 1925-  ‡4 cnd
28 700 10   Masterson, Valerie. ‡4 prf
29 700 10   Baker, Janet. ‡4 prf
30 700 10   Walker, Sarah. ‡4 prf
31 700 10   Jones, Della. ‡4 prf
32 700 10   Bowman, James. ‡4 prf
33 700 10   James, David. ‡4 prf
34 700 20   Booth-Jones, Christopher. ‡4 prf
35 700 10   Tomlinson, John, ‡d 1946 Sept. 22-  ‡4 prf
36 710 20   English National Opera. ‡4 prf
```

The third 500 note and the 007 subfield ǂn indicate that this analog disc was derived from a digital recording. The U.S. Universal Product Code for sound recordings is recorded in the 024 field. The second 028 field's second indicator is set not to print and its contents are explicitly input in the first 500 field, because only the first 028 field will print in OCLC. The 041 field is derived from the information found in the last 500 field.

Example 20

Analog disc

```
Type: j Bib lvl: m Lang:   N/A Source:    Accomp mat: f
Repr:     Enc lvl:    Ctry:   nyu Dat tp: p MEBE: 1
          Mod rec:    Comp:   mu  Format: n Prts:
Desc: a Int lvl:      LTxt:       Dates: 1986,1939
  1 010       88-751052/R
  2 007       s ‡b d ‡d b ‡e m ‡f m ‡g e ‡h n ‡i n ‡j m ‡k p ‡l l ‡m u ‡n e
  3 024 1     7863556581
  4 028 02    5658-1 RB ‡b Bluebird
  5 033 2     19371011 ‡a 19560120 ‡b 3804 ‡c N4
  6 043       n-us---
  7 047       jz ‡a pp
  8 050 1     M1366
  9 100 10    Hawkins, Coleman. ‡4 prf
 10 245 10    Body and soul ‡h [sound recording] / ‡c [performed by] Coleman
Hawkins.
 11 260 0     New York, N.Y. : ‡b Bluebird, ‡c p1986.
 12 300       2 sound discs : ‡b analog, 33 1/3 rpm, mono. ; ‡c 12 in.
 13 511 0     Coleman Hawkins, tenor saxophone, with various jazz ensembles,
big bands, and with strings.
 14 518       Recorded between Oct. 11, 1937, and Jan. 20, 1956, in New York
City.
 15 500       Biographical notes on container.
 16 650  0    Jazz ensembles.
 17 650  0    Big band music.
 18 650  0    Popular music ‡y 1951-1960.
```

The code in the Accompanying Matter fixed field (Accomp mat) reflects the last 500 note in this record for an analog disc. Information in the 033 is derived from the 518 field. The U.S. Universal Product Code for sound recordings is recorded in the 024 field. The gap between the dates of the original recordings and the date of this release is brought out in the Type of date (Dat tp) and Dates fixed fields.

Example 21

Analog disc

```
Type: i Bib lvl: m Lang:  N/A Source:    Accomp mat:
Repr:    Enc lvl:   Ctry:  enk Dat tp: p MEBE: 0
         Mod rec:   Comp:  nn  Format: n Prts:
Desc: a Int lvl:    LTxt:  s    Dates: 1979,1957
  1 010       85-755141/R
  2 007       s ǂb d ǂd b ǂe s ǂf m ǂg e ǂh n ǂi n ǂj m ǂk p ǂl l ǂm u ǂn e
  3 028 02    ATR 7016 ǂb ASV Transacord
  4 028 00    ZC ATR 7016 ǂb ASV Transacord
  5 033 2     1957---- ǂa 1971---- ǂb 5740
  6 033 0     1970---- ǂb 6840
  7 033 0     1978---- ǂb 6890
  8 050 1     TJ608
  9 245 00    Trains in trouble ǂh [sound recording].
 10 260 0     London : ǂb ASV Transacord ; ǂa Mitcham, Surrey : ǂb Distributed
by P.R.T. Records, ǂc p1979.
 11 300       1 sound disc : ǂb analog, 33 1/3 rpm, stereo. ; ǂc 12 in.
 12 440 0     Sounds of the steam age
 13 518       Recorded between 1957 and 1971 in Great Britain, in 1970 in
Yugoslavia, and in 1978 in Austria.
 14 500       Notes on container.
 15 500       Issued also as cassette: ZC ATR 7016.
 16 520       Presents the sounds of steam trains in adverse weather
conditions and with mechanical difficulties as they attempt to pull freight
and passenger trains.
 17 650  0    Locomotive sounds.
 18 650  0    Railroad sounds.
```

In this analog disc of nonmusical sounds (Type: i), the Literary Text for Sound Recordings fixed field (LTxt) is coded for sounds. Multiple 033 fields correspond to the times and places of the recordings detailed in the 518 note. A second, nonprinting 028 field gives access to the item's publisher's number in another recording medium (cassette), cited in the last 500 note. Note both publisher and distributor in the 260 field. The gap between the original recording and the release dates is brought out in the Type of date (Dat tp) and Dates fixed fields.

Example 22

Analog Cassette Tape

```
Type: j Bib lvl: m Lang:  N/A Source:   Accomp mat:
Repr:    Enc lvl:   Ctry:  gt  Dat tp: q MEBE: 1
         Mod rec:   Comp:  pp  Format: n Prts:
Desc: a Int lvl:    LTxt:      Dates: 1980,1986
 1 010      86-754808/R/r87
 2 007      s ǂb s ǂd l ǂe u ǂf n ǂg j ǂh l ǂi c ǂj m ǂk n ǂl n ǂm u ǂn u
 3 028 02   1001 ǂb DYCSA
 4 043      ncgt---
 5 048      oy
 6 050 1    M1685
 7 110 20   Marimba "Ind´igena Pura". ǂ4 prf
 8 245 10   Sones nativos ǂh [sound recording] / ǂc [interpretado por la]
Marimba "Ind´igena Pura".
 9 260 0    Guatemala : ǂb DYCSA, ǂc [198-?]
10 300      1 sound cassette : ǂb analog.
11 500      Popular Guatemalan instrumental music.
12 500      Title on container: La ´unica chimalteca.
13 505 0    El xap -- Sal negra -- Maconaj -- Guarda barranca -- El son de
los bricadores -- Juventino -- San Rafael -- Cuando llora la malin -- Tadeo
Solares -- Frescas ma~nanitas -- Santiago -- El son de Mashico.
14 650  0   Popular instrumental music ǂz Guatemala ǂy 1981-
15 650  0   Marimba music.
16 740 01   ´Unica chimalteca.
```

The Type of Date (Dat tp) code "q" and the two dates in the Dates fixed field are based on the uncertain date in the 260 subfield ǂc (this musical cassette tape was cataloged in 1986). The corporate name main entry (110) is the musical group, with a subfield ǂ4 for performer.

Example 23

Analog cassette tape

```
Type: i Bib lvl: m Lang:   eng Source:   Accomp mat:
Repr:    Enc lvl:   Ctry:  dcu Dat tp: s MEBE: 1
         Mod rec:   Comp:  nn  Format: n Prts:
Desc: a Int lvl:    LTxt:  l    Dates: 1983,
 1 010       88-740281/R
 2 007       s ‡b s ‡d l ‡e u ‡f n ‡g j ‡h l ‡i c ‡j m ‡k n ‡l n ‡m u ‡n u
 3 028 02  NP-830411 ‡b National Public Radio
 4 033       ‡b 3850
 5 050 1   D804.3
 6 100 10  Wiesel, Elie, ‡d 1928-
 7 245 10  Elie Wiesel at the National Press Club ‡h [sound recording].
 8 260 0   Washington, D.C. : ‡b National Public Radio, ‡c p1983.
 9 300       1 sound cassette (1 hr.) : ‡b analog.
10 306       006000
11 500       Publisher's catalog title: Elie Wiesel on remembering.
12 518       Recorded at a National Press Club luncheon held in Washington,
D.C.
13 500       Broadcast Apr. 11, 1983, on National Public Radio.
14 520       Noted author, Holocaust survivor, and chairman of the U.S.
Holocaust Memorial Council Elie Wiesel discusses attempts by journalists in
World War II to tell the world what was happening in Germany and describes
his own mission to ensure that people will never forget the Holocaust.
15 650  0  Holocaust, Jewish (1939-1945) ‡x Censorship.
16 710 20  National Press Club (U.S.)
17 710 20  National Public Radio (U.S.)
18 740 01  Elie Wiesel on remembering.
```

The 033 field codifies the place of capture stated in the 518 field of this record for a spoken word cassette tape. A summary of the lecture appears in the 520 note. The Literary Text for Sound Recordings fixed field (LTxt) is coded for a lecture. Note that the dates in the 650 field are not separately subfielded and that the duration of one hour (300) is coded in the 306 field.

Example 24

Analog Tape Reel

```
Type: i Bib lvl: m Lang:  eng Source:   Accomp mat:
Repr:    Enc lvl:   Ctry:  mou Dat tp: s MEBE: 1
         Mod rec:   Comp:  nn  Format: n Prts:
Desc: a Int lvl:    LTxt:  p    Dates: 1985,
  1 010      85-752880/R
  2 007      s ‡b t ‡d o ‡e m ‡f n ‡g c ‡h m ‡i u ‡j m ‡k n ‡l n ‡m u ‡n e
  3 033       ‡b 3934 ‡c G2
  4 050 1    PS3509 ‡b .B456
  5 100 10   Eberhart, Richard, ‡d 1904-
  6 240 10   Florida poems. ‡k Selections
  7 245 10   Richard Eberhart ‡h [sound recording].
  8 260 0    [Kansas City, Mo. : ‡b New Letters, ‡c 1985]
  9 300      1 sound tape reel (29 min.) : ‡b analog, 7 1/2 ips, mono. ; ‡c 7
in.
 10 306      002900
 11 518      Recorded at WUFT-FM in Gainesville, Fla.
 12 500      Broadcast Jan. 1985 on the radio program New letters on the air.
 13 520      Pulitzer Prize winning poet Richard Eberhart reads from his
collection entitled Florida poems.
 14 730 01   New letters.
 15 730 01   New letters on the air (Radio program)
```

The 033 field codifies information found in the 518 note of this record for a spoken word sound tape reel. Note the two uniform title added entries, one for the journal *New letters*, the other for the related radio program.

RLIN FULL-RECORD EXAMPLES — SCORES

Example 1

```
ID:XXXXXXXXXXXX-X RTYP:c    ST:p  FRN:     MS:c  EL:    AD:01-01-01
CC:9110  BLT:cm    DCF:a  CSC:    MOD:    SNR:  ATC:   UD:01-01-01
CP:ge    L:        FCP:mu INT:    MEI:1  AMC:hi
PC:r     PD:1984/1731    SCO:z  REP:
MMD:     OR:     POL:  DM:     RR:     COL:   EML:  GEN:  BSE:
010       87750963/M
028 32    9314‡bEdition Peters
041 0     ‡gengger‡hger
045       v2v4
047       su‡aov‡apr‡afg‡acl‡avr
048       kc01
048       kb01
050 0     M3.1.B2‡bK48 1984
100 10    Bach, Johann Sebastian,‡d1685-1750.
240 10    Keyboard music.‡kSelections (Clavier-¨Ubung)
245 10    Clavier-¨Ubung /‡cJohann Sebastian Bach.
250       Faksimile-Ausg. /‡bherausgegeben von Christoph Wolff.
260 0     Leipzig :‡bEdition Peters ;‡aFrankfurt ;‡aNew York :‡bC.F.
Peters,‡cc1984.
300       4 v. of music ;‡c26 x 32 cm.
440 0     Musikwissenschaftliche Studienbibliothek Peters
490 0     Peters reprints
500       For harpsichord or organ.
500       Second imprint from label on t.p.
503       Reprint of works originally published 1731-1741.
500       Accompanied by: Johann Sebastian Bachs Klavier¨ubung : Kommentar
zur Faksimile-Ausgabe / Christoph Wolff (32 p. : facsims.) (in English and
German).
505 0     1. Sechs Partiten BWV 825-830 -- 2. Italienisches Konzert : BWV 971
; Franz¨osische Ouvert¨ure : BWV 831 -- 3. Pr¨aludium und Fuge Es-Dur BWV
552 ; Orgelchor¨ale BWV 669-689 ; Duette BWV 802-805 -- 4. Goldberg-
Variationen : BWV 988.
650 0     Harpsichord music.
650 0     Organ music.
700 10    Wolff, Christoph.
```

The Type of Date (PC) and Dates (PD) fixed fields and the 503 note all indicate that this is a facsimile reprint of a published score. The edition statement includes a statement of responsibility. Note the presence of both traced and untraced series, a multiple imprint, and that accompanying material is described in the final 500 note.

Example 2

```
ID:XXXXXXXXXXXX-X RTYP:c   ST:p  FRN:    MS:n   EL:    AD:01-01-01
CC:9110  BLT:cm   DCF:a CSC:   MOD:   SNR:   ATC:   UD:01-01-01
CP:it     L:      FCP:uu INT:   MEI:1  AMC:
PC:c      PD:1985/1982    SCO:a REP:
MMD:      OR:    POL: DM:     RR:      COL:   EML:  GEN:  BSE:
010      88751200/M
028 22   133507‡bRicordi
045 0    ‡bd19811121
048      ‡bwa01‡bsa01‡aoa
050 0    M1040.B94‡bC37 1985
100 10   Bussotti, Sylvano.
240 10   Catalogo `e questo.‡pRaragramma
245 13   Il catalogo `e questo.‡nII,‡pRaragramma /‡cSylvano Bussotti.
260 0    Milano :‡bRicordi,‡c1985, c1982.
300      1 score (30 p.) :‡b1 col. facsim. ;‡c41 cm.
490 1    Bussottioperaballet
500      For flutes (1 player), violin, and orchestra.
500      Reproduced from holograph.
505 0    Raragramma -- R. & R. -- Enfant prodige -- Paganini -- Calando
symphony.
650  0   Flute and violin with orchestra‡xScores.
650  0   Music‡xManuscripts‡xFacsimiles.
600 10   Bussotti, Sylvano‡xManuscripts‡xFacsimiles.
740 01   Raragramma.
800 1    Bussotti, Sylvano.‡tSelections.
```

In this score for two solo instruments and orchestra, the dates of publication and copyright are both recorded in the 260 subfield ‡c and are reflected in the Type of Date (PC) and Dates (PD) fixed field positions. The date in the 045 field derives from the date inscribed at the end of the holograph score. The single player on multiple flutes mentioned in the first 500 note is reflected in the 048 field. Subfields ‡n and ‡p are both found in the 245 field. Notice the illustration statement in the 300 subfield ‡b. A series traced in different form is found in the 490 and its corresponding author/title 800 series field. A personal name as subject heading is found in the 600 field.

Example 3

```
ID:XXXXXXXXXXXX-X RTYP:c    ST:p   FRN:    MS:c   EL:    AD:01-01-01
CC:9110  BLT:cm    DCF:a  CSC:    MOD:    SNR:   ATC:   UD:01-01-01
CP:sp      L:lat   FCP:uu INT:   MEI:0   AMC:i
PC:s      PD:1983/        SCO:a  REP:
MMD:      OR:    POL:  DM:    RR:      COL:   EML:  GEN:  BSE:
010      86754683/M/r87
041  0   lat‡gcateng
048      ca08‡awy02‡abd01‡ake
050  0   M2021‡b.N8 1983
130 00   Nunc dimittis (Parr`oquia de Sant Pere de Canet de Mar, Spain)
245 00   Nunc dimittis a 11, s. XVII /‡can`onim ; transcripci´o i estudi,
Francesc Bonastre.
260  0   Barcelona :‡bInstitut Universitari de Documentaci´o i Investigaci´o
Musicol`ogica "Josep Ricart i Matas",‡c1983.
300      1 score (22 p.) ;‡c30 cm.
440  0   Quaderns de m´usica hist`orica catalana ;‡v4
500      For chorus (TipleA/TipleT/TipleATB), cobla ensemble (2 xeremias,
trombone), and continuo; bass unrealized.
500      Latin words.
503      Edited from a ms. in the Arxiu Musical de la Parr`oquia de Sant
Pere de Carnet de Mar.
500      Prefatory notes in Catalan and English.
650  0   Choruses, Sacred (Mixed voices) with instrumental ensemble.
650  0   Nunc dimittis (Music)
700 10   Bonastre, Francesc.
```

In this record for an accompanied choral work, the prefatory notes mentioned in the final 500 note show up in the Accompanying Matter (AMC) fixed field element as well as the 041 subfield ‡g. The 048 field corresponds to the first 500 field ("tiple" is a high voice; a cobla ensemble is a Catalan dance band; a xeremia is a Catalan wind instrument). Note the uniform title main entry (130) and the 503 note.

Example 4

```
ID:XXXXXXXXXXXX-X RTYP:c   ST:p   FRN:     MS:n   EL:    AD:01-01-01
CC:9120  BLT:cm   DCF:a  CSC:   MOD:   SNR:   ATC:   UD:01-01-01
CP:onc    L:gae   FCP:fm INT:   MEI:0  AMC:b
PC:r      PD:1979/1964    SCO:z  REP:
MMD:     OR:    POL: DM:    RR:       COL:   EML:  GEN:   BSE:
100      82771219/M/r85
028 30   NM93-198/1979‡bNational Museum of Man
041 1    gae‡eeng‡hgae
043      n-cn-ns
050 0    M1678‡b.G144 1979
245 00   Gaelic songs in Nova Scotia /‡c[compiled by] Helen Creighton and
Calum MacLeod ; with a new preface by Helen Creighton.
260 0    Ottawa, Canada :‡bNational Museum of Man, National Museums of
Canada,‡c1979.
300      xi p., 308 p. of music :‡bill. ;‡c25 cm.
500      Unacc.
500      Words in Gaelic with English translations.
534      ‡pReprint. Originally published:‡c1964.‡f(Bulletin / National
Museum of Canada ; no. 196. Anthropological series ; no. 66).
504      Bibliography: p. 298-300.
500      Includes index.
500      Catalogue no.: NM93-198/1979.
650  0   Folk music‡zNova Scotia.
650  0   Folk-songs, Gaelic‡zNova Scotia.
700 10   Creighton, Helen.
700 10   MacLeod, Calum.
830  0   Bulletin (National Museum of Canada) ;‡vno. 196.
830  0   Bulletin (National Museum of Canada).‡pAnthropological series
;‡vno. 66.
```

The fact that this score is a reprint is noted in the Type of Date (PC) and Dates (PD) fixed fields, the 534 note, and the two corresponding series uniform title added entries (830). The bibliography is noted in the 504 field and in the Accompanying Matter fixed field (AMC).

Example 5

```
ID:XXXXXXXXXXXX-X RTYP:c    ST:p   FRN:    MS:c   EL:    AD:01-01-01
CC:9110   BLT:cm    DCF:a  CSC:    MOD:    SNR:   ATC:   UD:01-01-01
CP:gw       L:gre   FCP:uu INT:    MEI:1   AMC:
PC:s        PD:1986/        SCO:a  REP:
MMD:        OR:    POL:  DM:      RR:      COL:   EML:  GEN:  BSE:
010         87751402/M/r88
028 22      CV 40-482/01‡bCarus-Verlag
045 0       ‡bd18250506
048         ca05‡aoa
050 0       M2020.M36‡bK94 1986
100 20      Mendelssohn-Bartholdy, Felix,‡d1809-1847.
240 10      Kyrie,‡rD minor.‡lGreek
245 00      Kyrie in d, f¨ur Chor und Orchester /‡c[Felix Mendelssohn
Bartholdy].
250         Erstausg. /‡bherausgegeben von R. Larry Todd.
254         Partitur.
260 0       Stuttgart :‡bCarus-Verlag,‡cc1986.
300         1 score (32 p.) ;‡c30 cm.
306         001000
490 1       Ausgewahlte Werke vokaler Kirchenmusik / Felix Mendelssohn
Bartholdy
500         Chorus: SSATB.
500         Duration: 10:00.
650  0      Choruses, Sacred (Mixed voices) with orchestra.
650  0      Kyrie eleison (Music)
700 10      Todd, R. Larry.
800 2       Mendelssohn-Bartholdy, Felix,‡d1809-1847.‡tVocal music.‡kSelections
(Ausgew¨ahlte Werke vokaler Kirchenmusik)
```

A score with both an edition statement (250) and a musical presentation statement (254), this record has a 490/800 combination as well. The Duration field (306) corresponds to the final 500 note. Mendelssohn-Bartholdy's compound surname requires appropriate first indicators in both the 100 and 800 fields.

Example 6

```
ID:XXXXXXXXXXXX-X RTYP:c    ST:p   FRN:      MS:c    EL:     AD:01-01-01
CC:9110   BLT:cm    DCF:a   CSC:   MOD:      SNR:    ATC:    UD:01-01-01
CP:nyu     L:ita   FCP:op INT:    MEI:1  AMC:
PC:r      PD:1985/1839    SCO:c  REP:
MMD:      OR:    POL: DM:     RR:      COL:    EML:   GEN:   BSE:
010      85750511/M/r86
020      0824065697 :‡c$75.00
028 22   H. 11231 H.‡bGarland
045 0    ‡bd1838
050 0    M1503.M553‡bE4 1985
100 10   Mercadante, Saverio,‡d1795-1870.
240 10   Elena da Feltre.‡sVocal score
245 10   Elena da Feltre /‡clibretto by Salvatore Cammarano ; music by
Saverio Mercadante.
250      A facsim. ed. of the printed piano-vocal score /‡bwith an
introduction by Philip Gossett.
260 0    New York :‡bGarland,‡c1985.
300      1 vocal score (237, 11 p.) :‡bfacsims. ;‡c24 x 32 cm.
440  0   Italian opera, 1810-1840 ;‡vv. 20
500      Italian words.
534      ‡pReprint. Originally published:‡cMilano : Ricordi, 1839.
500      "Recito. e cavatina : 'Parmi che alfin dimentica' : aggiunta
all'opera Elena da Feltre": p. 1-11 (2nd group).
650  0   Operas‡xVocal scores with piano.
700 10   Cammarano, Salvatore,‡d1801-1852.
```

The Type of Date (PC) and Dates (PD) fixed field elements, the edition statement (250), and the 534 note all indicate that this is a facsimile edition of a previously published vocal score. The dates in the series statement (440) are not separately subfielded, because they are considered an integral part of the series title.

Example 7

```
ID:XXXXXXXXXXXX-X RTYP:c    ST:p   FRN:    MS:n   EL:    AD:01-01-01
CC:9110   BLT:cm    DCF:a  CSC:   MOD:    SNR:   ATC:   UD:01-01-01
CP:nyu    L:        FCP:uu INT:   MEI:1   AMC:
PC:s      PD:1985/         SCO:a  REP:
MMD:      OR:    POL:  DM:     RR:      COL:   EML:  GEN:  BSE:
010       86754626/M
045 0     ‡bd1985
048       ec01‡awb01‡asa02‡asb01‡asc01
050 0     M562.K754‡bT5 1985
100 10    Kolb, Barbara.
245 10    Time-- and again /‡cBarbara Kolb.
260 0     New York, NY (24 W. 57th St., New York 10019) :‡bBoosey &
Hawkes,‡cc1985.
300       1 score (18 p.) ;‡c36 x 45 cm.
500       Caption title.
500       For computer, oboe, 2 violins, viola, and violoncello.
500       Reproduced from holograph.
650  0    Quintets (Oboe, violins (2), viola, violoncello)‡xScores.
650  0    Computer music.
650  0    Music‡xManuscripts‡xFacsimiles.
600 10    Kolb, Barbara‡xManuscripts‡xFacsimiles.
```

The title of this score features some out-of-the-ordinary punctuation. The publisher's address appears in the subfield ‡a of the 260 field. Formulation of the 048 field corresponds to the second 500 note.

Example 8

```
ID:XXXXXXXXXXXX-X RTYP:c   ST:p  FRN:     MS:n   EL:    AD:01-01-01
CC:9110  BLT:cm    DCF:a  CSC:    MOD:    SNR:   ATC:   UD:01-01-01
CP:mbc    L:       FCP:sy INT:    MEI:1  AMC:
PC:c      PD:1980/1970    SCO:a  REP:
MMD:      OR:    POL:  DM:     RR:        COL:   EML:  GEN:   BSE:
010      86753526/M
045 0    ‡bd1970
048      oa
050 0    M3.1.E27‡bE8 1980 vol. 2‡aM1001
100 20   Eckhardt-Gramatt´e, S. C.‡q(Sophie-Carmen),‡d1899-1974.
240 10   Symphonies,‡nno. 2
245 00   Symphony II (E. 158) :‡bManitoba symphony /‡c[Eckhardt-Gramatt´e].
250      Restricted ed. for archival purposes only /‡ban[n]otations and
corrections by the composer.
254      Orchestra score & analysis.
260 0    Winnipeg, Canada :‡bEstate S.C. Eckhardt-Gramatt´e,‡c1980, c1970.
300      1 score (58, 62, 55, 67 p.) :‡bport. ;‡c29 cm.
306      003400
490 1    Selected works / S.C. Eckhardt-Gramatt´e ;‡vv. 2
500      Duration: 34:00.
650  0   Symphonies‡xScores.
740 01   Manitoba symphony.
800 2    Eckhardt-Gramatt´e, S. C.‡q(Sophie-Carmen),‡d1899-1974.‡tSelections
(Selected works) ;‡vv. 2.
```

The 250 field in this special edition of a score includes a statement of responsibility without a proper name. A musical presentation statement (254) also is present. Note the 490/800 pair and the multiple surname in the 100 and 800 fields.

Example 9

```
ID:XXXXXXXXXXXX-X RTYP:c    ST:p   FRN:    MS:c   EL:    AD:01-01-01
CC:9110  BLT:cm    DCF:a  CSC:    MOD:   SNR:   ATC:   UD:01-01-01
CP:mx      L:spa   FCP:mu INT:   MEI:0  AMC:bei
PC:s       PD:1985/        SCO:a  REP:
MMD:       OR:    POL:  DM:     RR:      COL:   EML:  GEN:  BSE:
010        86192870/M/r872
020        9688890006
043        n-mx---
047        pp‡adf
048        vn01‡aka01
048        ka01
050 0      M1683.18‡bA57 1985
245 00     Antolog´ia folkl´orica y musical de Tabasco /‡c[compilaci´on]
Francisco J. Santamar´ia ; arreglo y estudio musical de Ger´onimo Baqueiro
F´oster.
250        2a ed.
260 0      Villahermosa :‡bGobierno del Estado de Tabasco,‡c1985.
300        1 score (600 p.) ;‡c21 cm.
440  0     Biblioteca b´asica tabasque~na ;‡v1
490 1      Serie antolog´ias
500        Principally popular songs for voice and piano and dances for piano.
504        Bibliography: p. 89-91.
500        Includes historical notes and biographies of the composers.
650  0     Popular music‡zMexico‡zTabasco (State)‡y1981-
650  0     Piano music.
650  0     Dance music‡zMexico‡zTabasco (State)
700 10     Santamar´ia, Francisco Javier,‡d1889-
700 20     Baqueiro F´oster, Ger´onimo.‡4arr
830  0     Serie antolog´ias (Instituto de Cultura de Tabasco)
```

This score of ethnic popular and dance music has the code "mu" in the Form of Composition fixed field (FCP), meaning that the 047 field must also be present. The Accompanying Matter fixed field (AMC) codes the information in both the 504 and the final 500 note. Two series statements (440 and 490) and one corresponding series uniform title added entry (830) are present. Note the edition statement (250) and the subfield ‡4 for the arranger in the last 700 field.

Example 10

```
ID:XXXXXXXXXXXX-X RTYP:c   ST:p  FRN:    MS:n   EL:1  AD:01-01-01
CC:9120  BLT:dm     DCF:a CSC:   MOD:   SNR:   ATC:   UD:01-01-01
CP:xx      L:       FCP:pr INT:   MEI:1  AMC:
PC:s      PD:1859/         SCO:z  REP:
MMD:      OR:    POL:  DM:     RR:      COL:   EML:  GEN:   BSE:
010       82770783/M/r85
045 0     ‡bd1859
048       ka01
050 0     ML31‡b.S4a No. 11
100 10    Liszt, Franz,‡d1811-1886.
245 10    Weinen, Klagen, Sorgen, Zagen :‡bPraeludium (nach J.S. Bach's
Cantate) /‡cvon F. Liszt.
260 1     ‡c[1859]
300       [4] p. of ms. music ;‡c28 x 35 cm.
500       Holograph, in ink.
500       For piano.
503       Based on a theme from the opening chorus of the cantata.
503       Published: Berlin : Schlesinger, 1863.
650  0    Piano music.
650  0    Music‡xManuscripts.
600 10    Liszt, Franz,‡d1811-1886‡xManuscripts.
700 11    Bach, Johann Sebastian,‡d1685-1750.‡tWeinen, Klagen, Sorgen,
Zagen.‡pWeinen, Klagen, Sorgen, Zagen.
```

In this music manuscript (BLT first position: d), note the two 503 notes (one explaining the work's derivation, the other its first publication), the 260 with only a date, and the formulation of the 300 field. The author/title added entry for J.S. Bach formalizes the information found in the 245 and the first 503 field.

Example 11

```
ID:XXXXXXXXXXXX-X RTYP:c   ST:p   FRN:     MS:n   EL:    AD:01-01-01
CC:9110   BLT:dm    DCF:a  CSC:   MOD:   SNR:   ATC:   UD:01-01-01
CP:dcu    L:        FCP:uu INT:   MEI:1  AMC:
PC:s      PD:1976/         SCO:a  REP:
MMD:      OR:     POL:  DM:     RR:      COL:   EML:  GEN:  BSE:
010       87753561/M
045 0     ‡bd19760629
048       wa01‡awb01‡awc01‡aba01‡awd01
050 0     ML30.3c‡b.J64 no. 1
100 10    Jolas, Betsy.
245 10    O wall :‡bop´era de poup´ee = a puppet opera : 1976 /‡cBetsy Jolas.
260 1     ‡c1976 June 29.
300       1 ms. score (12 leaves) ;‡c44 cm.
306       001500
500       Holograph.
500       For flute, oboe, clarinet, horn, and bassoon.
500       "For the Serge Koussevitzky Music Foundation in the Library of
Congress, and dedicated to the memory of Serge and Natalie Koussevitzky."
500       Duration: ca. 15:00.
500       At end: Paris.
500       In ink; on transparencies.
500       Accompanied by photocopy (39 cm.) and sketches ([2] p. ; 44 cm.).
650  0    Wind quintets (Bassoon, clarinet, flute, horn, oboe)‡xScores.
650  0    Musical sketches.
710 20    Library of Congress.‡bSerge Koussevitzky Music Foundation.
```

In this manuscript score (BLT first position: d), the date in the 260 field is derived from the date on the holograph and is coded in the 045 field. The quoted 500 note justifies the corporate added entry. Accompanying material is described in the final 500 note.

Example 12

```
ID:XXXXXXXXXXX-X RTYP:c    ST:p    FRN:     MS:n    EL:    AD:01-01-01
CC:9650   BLT:cm     DCF:a CSC:    MOD:    SNR:    ATC:    UD:01-01-01
CP:dcu     L:ger    FCP:sg INT:    MEI:1  AMC:
PC:r       PD:1988/1920    SCO:a  REP:a
MMD:d      OR:?    POL:a DM:f     RR:a-   COL:b  EML:a GEN:c  BSE:a
MMD:d      OR:?    POL:b DM:f     RR:a-   COL:b  EML:a GEN:a  BSE:a
010       88953290
041 1     gerfre‡hfre
048       vu01‡aka01
100 10    Berlioz, Hector,‡d1803-1869.
240 10    Songs.‡kSelections
245 10    Ausgew"ahlte Lieder‡h[microform] /‡cvon Hector Berlioz ;
eingeleitet und herausgegeben von Karl Blessinger.
260 0     M"unchen :‡bDrei Masken Verlag,‡c1920.
300       1 score (xii, 74 p.) :‡bport. ;‡c19 cm.
490 0     Musikalische Stundenb"ucher
500       For voice and piano.
500       French and German words.
500       Call number of original: M2.M93B45.
500       Master microform held by: DLC.
533       Microfilm.‡bWashington, D.C. :‡cLibrary of Congress
Photoduplication Service,‡d1988.‡e1 microfilm reel : positive ; 35 mm.
501       With: Quartetto e coro dei maggi / da H. Berlioz.
650  0    Songs with piano accompaniment.
700 10    Blessinger, Karl,‡d1888-
```

This microform reproduction of a printed score has two microform 007 fields as the final two lines of the fixed field, the first for the positive item being cataloged, the second for the negative master mentioned in the final 500 field. Note the GMD in the 245 field. The physical description of the positive microfilm appears in the 533 note. Another work filmed with this one is noted in the 501 field.

Example 13

Compact disc

```
ID:XXXXXXXXXXXX-X RTYP:c   ST:p   FRN:   MS:n   EL:   AD:01-01-01
CC:9110   BLT:jm   DCF:a CSC:   MOD:   SNR:   ATC:   UD:01-01-01
CP:fr     L:fre    FCP:mu INT:   MEI:1  AMC:defi
PC:p      PD:1986/1985   LIT:
RMD:d OR:? SPD:f SND:s GRV:n DIM:g WID:n TC:n KD:m KM:m KC:n RC:e CAP:e
010       89751546/R
028 00    ARN 268012‡bArion
028 00    ARN 268013‡bArion
033 0     198503—
041 0     ‡dfre‡efreengger‡hfre‡gfreengger‡hfre
045 1     ‡bd1695‡bd1715
047       ct‡ats
048       va01‡ake
048       va02‡ake
048       sa02‡ake
048       va01‡ave01‡ake
048       sa01‡akc01
100 20    Jacquet de La Guerre, Elisabeth-Claude,‡dca. 1664-1729.
240 10    Selections
245 00    Cantates & pi`eces vari´ees‡h[sound recording] /‡cElisabeth Jacquet
de La Guerre.
260 0     [France] :‡bArion,‡cp1986.
300       2 sound discs :‡bdigital ;‡c4 3/4 in.
490 0     Les Joyaux de votre discoth`eque
500       Arion: ARN 268012 (ARN 268012--ARN 268013).
500       Title on container: Cantates bibliques ; Pi`eces instrumentales.
500       Title on spine of container: Cantates bibliques ; Pi`eces
instrumentales et vocale[s].
500       The 1st 4 works for soprano and continuo; the 5th for 2 sopranos
and continuo; the 6th for 2 violins and continuo; the 7th and 9th for
soprano, baritone, and continuo; the 8th for violin and harpsichord.
511 0     Sophie Boulin, Isabelle Poulenard, sopranos ; Michel Verschaeve,
baritone ; Bernadette Charbonnier, Catherine Giardelli, violins ;
Fran̦coise Bloch, viola da gamba ; Claire Giardelli, violoncello ; Guy
Robert, theorbo ; Brigitte Haudebourg, harpsichord ; Georges Guillard,
organ or harpsichord.
518       Recorded in Mar. 1985.
500       Compact disc.
500       Analog recording.
500       Program notes in French by Philippe Beaussant and words of the
vocal works with English and German translations (32 p. : ill.) in
container.
505 0     Suzanne -- Judith -- Esther -- Jacob et Rachel -- Jepth´e -- Sonate
no 4 `a 2 viol. et violonc. -- Le D´eluge -- Les pi`eces de clavecin qui
peuvent se jouer sur le violon -- Le raccommodement comique de Pierrot et
de Nicole.
```

```
650  0   Solo cantatas, Sacred (High voice)
650  0   Cantatas, Sacred.
650  0   Trio-sonatas (Violins (2), continuo)
650  0   Violin and harpsichord music.
650  0   Cantatas, Secular.
700 10   Boulin, Sophie.‡4prf
700 10   Poulenard, Isabelle.‡4prf
700 10   Verschaeve, Michel.‡4prf
700 10   Charbonnier, Bernadette.‡4prf
700 10   Giardelli, Catherine.‡4prf
700 10   Bloch, Fran͵coise.‡4prf
700 10   Giardelli, Claire.‡4prf
700 10   Robert, Guy,‡d1943- ‡4prf
700 10   Haudebourg, Brigitte.‡4prf
700 10   Guillard, Georges.‡4prf
700 22   Jacquet de La Guerre, Elisabeth-Claude,‡dca. 1664-1729.‡tCantates
fran͵coises sur des sujets tirez de l'Ecriture,‡nbk. 1.‡kSelections.‡f1986.
700 22   Jacquet de La Guerre, Elisabeth-Claude,‡dca. 1664-1729.‡tCantates
fran͵coises sur des sujets tirez de l'Ecriture,‡nbk. 2.‡pJepht´e.‡f1986.
700 22   Jacquet de La Guerre, Elisabeth-Claude,‡dca. 1664-1729.‡tTrio
sonatas.‡nNo. 4.‡f1986.
700 22   Jacquet de La Guerre, Elisabeth-Claude,‡dca. 1664-1729.‡tCantates
fran͵coises sur des sujets tirez de l'Ecriture,‡nbk. 2.‡pD´eluge.‡f1986.
700 22   Jacquet de La Guerre, Elisabeth-Claude,‡dca. 1664-1729.‡tPi`eces de
clavecin.‡kSelections.‡f1986.
700 22   Jacquet de La Guerre, Elisabeth-Claude,‡dca. 1664-1729.‡tCantates
fran͵coises‡n(1715).‡pRaccommodement comique de Pierrot et de
Nicole.‡f1986.
```

This digital compact disc derived from an analog recording. The Form of Composition fixed field (FCP) has a corresponding 047 field. The Type of Date (PC) and Dates (PD) in the fixed field reflect the 260 subfield ‡c and the 518 note; the 033 field is derived from the 518 field. The item had no indication of stereo (hence, no mention in the 300 field) but the cataloger surmised that it was stereo and coded the 007 SND element as such. Note the complex 041 field and its relation to the last 500 note. Multiple music publisher's numbers are input in multiple 028 fields and an explicitly input 500 note. Also note the multiple surname in the main and some of the added entries.

Example 14

Compact disc

```
ID:XXXXXXXXXXXX-X RTYP:c    ST:p   FRN:    MS:n   EL:    AD:01-01-01
CC:9110   BLT:jm    DCF:a  CSC:   MOD:   SNR:   ATC:   UD:01-01-01
CP:enk     L:       FCP:op INT:   MEI:1  AMC:
PC:p       PD:1986/1985    LIT:
RMD:d OR:? SPD:f SND:s GRV:n DIM:g WID:n TC:n KD:m KM:m KC:n RC:e CAP:e
010      87750942/R
028 02   CHAN 8412‡bChandos
033 1    19850218‡a19850219‡b5754‡cL7
045 1    ‡bd1866‡bd1941
048      oa
050 1    M1000
100 10   Smetana, Bed⌄rich,‡d1824-1884.
240 10   Prodan´a nev⌄esta.‡kSelections
245 14   The bartered bride.‡pOverture and dances ; From my life :‡bstring
quartet in E minor‡h[sound recording] /‡cBed⌄rich Smetana ; orchestral
version [of 2nd work] by George Szell.
260 0    London, England :‡bChandos,‡cp1986.
300      1 sound disc :‡bdigital, stereo. ;‡c4 3/4 in.
306      002423‡a003030
511 0    London Symphony Orchestra ; Geoffrey Simon, conductor.
518      Recorded Feb. 18-19, 1985, All Saints' Church, Tooting, London.
500      Compact disc.
500      Durations: 24:23: 30:30.
505 2    The bartered bride. Overture (6:32) ; Dance of the villagers (4:28)
; Polka (4:57) ; Furiant (1:58) ; Fanfare (:41) ; Dance of the comedians
(5:32).
650  0   Operas‡xExcerpts.
650  0   Orchestral music, Arranged.
700 10   Simon, Geoffrey,‡d1946-
700 12   Smetana, Bed⌄rich,‡d1824-1884.‡tQuartets,‡mstrings,‡nno. 1,‡rE
minor;‡oarr.‡f1986.
710 20   London Symphony Orchestra.
740 01   From my life.
```

The Type of Date (PC) and Dates (PD) fixed fields are determined by information in the 260 subfield ‡c and the 518 field in this record for a digital compact disc. The 245 field includes a subfield ‡p and a GMD in subfield ‡h. The 033 field is derived from information in the 518 note. The 505 field first indicator is coded for "Partial contents" and the note is punctuated accordingly.

Example 15

Compact disc

```
ID:XXXXXXXXXXXX-X RTYP:c   ST:p  FRN:    MS:n   EL:    AD:01-01-01
CC:9110  BLT:jm    DCF:a  CSC:   MOD:    SNR:   ATC:   UD:01-01-01
CP:fr      L:      FCP:sn INT:   MEI:0   AMC:
PC:p       PD:1987/1986    LIT:
RMD:d OR:? SPD:f SND:s GRV:n DIM:g WID:n TC:n KD:m KM:m KC:n RC:e CAP:e
010       88752942/R
028 02    HMC 905184‡bHarmonia Mundi France
033 0     198612--
045 1     ‡bd1762‡bd1939‡bd1943
048       ta01
050 1     M116
100 10    Moretti, Isabelle,‡d1964- ‡4prf
245 10    R´ecital de harpe‡h[sound recording].
260 0     Arles :‡bHarmonia Mundi France,‡cp1987.
300       1 sound disc :‡bdigital ;‡c4 3/4 in.
306       001400‡a000700‡a001100‡a001700‡a000900
490 1     Cr´eations en val de Charente
511 0     Isabelle Moretti, harp.
518       Recorded Dec. 1986.
500       Compact disc.
505 0     Sonate en sol majeur, Wotq 139 / Carl Philipp Emanuel Bach (14:00)
-- Sonate pour harpe / Johann Ladislav Dussek (7:00) -- Sonate f¨ur Harfe,
1939 / Paul Hindemith (11:00) -- Sonata per arpa, op. 68 / Alfredo Casella
(17:00) -- Sonate pour harpe / Germaine Tailleferre (9:00).
650 0     Sonatas (Harp)
700 12    Bach, Carl Philipp Emanuel,‡d1714-1788.‡tSolos,‡mharp,‡nH. 563,‡rG
major.‡f1987.
700 12    Dussek, Johann Ladislaus,‡d1760-1812.‡tSonatas,‡mharp,‡rC
minor.‡f1987.
700 12    Hindemith, Paul,‡d1895-1963.‡tSonatas,‡mharp.‡f1987.
700 12    Casella, Alfredo,‡d1883-1947.‡tSonatas,‡mharp,‡nop. 68.‡f1987.
700 12    Tailleferre, Germaine,‡d1892- ‡tSonatas,‡mharp.‡f1987.
830 0     Cr´eations en val de Charente (Series)
```

This digital compact disc had no indication of stereo (hence, no mention in the 300 field), but the cataloger surmised that it was stereo and coded the 007 SND element as such. The Type of Date (PC) and Dates (PD) fixed fields are determined by information in the 260 subfield ‡c and the 518 field. The 033 field is derived from information in the 518 note. Note the subfield ‡4 for performer in the 100 field.

Example 16

Compact disc

```
ID:XXXXXXXXXXXX-X RTYP:c   ST:p  FRN:    MS:n  EL:   AD:01-01-01
CC:9110  BLT:jm   DCF:a  CSC:   MOD:   SNR:  ATC:  UD:01-01-01
CP:wau      L:      FCP:mu INT:   MEI:0  AMC:i
PC:r       PD:1986/        LIT:
RMD:d OR:? SPD:f SND:s GRV:n DIM:g WID:n TC:n KD:m KM:m KC:n RC:e CAP:e
010      88750309/R
028 02   CD200‡bCrystal Records
033 2    1977----‡a1984----
045 0    ‡bd1961
047      df‡acz‡asn‡asu
048      bb02‡aba01‡abd01‡abe01
050 1    M555
245 00   Brass bonanza‡h[sound recording].
260 0    Sedro Woolley, WA :‡bCrystal Records,‡cp1986.
300      1 sound disc :‡bdigital ;‡c4 3/4 in.
500      The 1st work originally for brass ensemble and percussion.
511 0    Metropolitan Brass Quintet (1st and 12th works) ; Berlin Brass
Quintet (2nd-4th works) ; Annapolis Brass Quintet (5th-7th works) ; New
York Brass Quintet (8th work) ; Dallas Brass Quintet (9th work) ; Saint
Louis Brass Quintet (10th work) ; I-5 Brass Quintet (11th work).
503      Reissued from various Crystal Records albums.
503      Eds. recorded: Atlantis Publications (5th-6th works); Bruxelles :
Editions Maurer (8th work); C.F. Peters (9th work); Paterson's Publications
(10th work); Canada : Touch of Brass (11th work); Novello (12th work).
518      Recorded 1977-1984 in various locations.
500      Compact disc.
500      Analog recording.
500      Program notes (4 folded p.) included.
505 0    Fanfares for the jubilee of Rimsky-Korsakov / Liadov-Glazunov --
Allemande [i.e., Gaillard] / William Brade -- Canzona per sonare : no. 1 /
Giovanni Gabrieli -- Sonata from Die B¨ankels¨angerlieder : ca. 1648 /
anon. [i.e., Daniel Speer] -- Sonata no. 4 ; Sonata no. 6 / Daniel Speer --
Sonata no. 2 / Johann Kessel -- Par monts et par vaux / Michel Leclerc --
Six dances / Alan Hovhaness -- Quintet / Malcolm Arnold -- The carnival of
Venice / Brent Dutton -- Music hall suite / Joseph Horovitz.
650  0  Brass quintets (Horn, trombone, trumpets (2), tuba)
650   0  Brass quintets (Horn, trombone, trumpets (2), tuba), Arranged.
700 12  Lyadov, Anatoly
Konstantinovich,‡d1855-1914.‡tSlavleni˜i˙a;‡oarr.‡f1986.
700 12  Brade, William,‡d1560-1630.‡tNewe ausserlesene Paduanen,
Galliarden, Cantzonen, Allmand und Coranten.‡pGaillard.‡f1986.
700 12  Gabrieli, Giovanni,‡d1557-1612.‡tSpiritata.‡f1986.
700 12  Speer, Daniel,‡d1636-1707.‡tMusicalisch-t¨urckischer
Eulen-Spiegel.‡kSelections.‡f1986.
700 12  Kessel, Johann,‡dfl. 1657-1672.‡tSymphonien, Sonaten, ein Canzon,
nebst Allmanden, Couranten, Balletten und Sarabanden.‡pSonata,‡nno.
2.‡f1986.
700 12  Leclerc, Michel,‡d1914- ‡tPar monts et par vaux.‡f1986.
700 12  Hovhaness, Alan,‡d1911- ‡tDances,‡mbrasses,‡nop. 79.‡f1986.
```

```
700 12   Arnold, Malcolm.‡tQuintets,‡mtrumpets, horn, trombone, tuba.‡f1986.
700 12   Dutton, Brent,‡d1950- ‡tCarnival of Venice.‡f1986.
700 12   Horovitz, Joseph,‡d1926- ‡tMusic hall suite.‡f1986.
710 20   Metropolitan Brass Quintet.‡4prf
710 20   Berlin Brass Quintet.‡4prf
710 20   Annapolis Brass Quintet.‡4prf
710 20   New York Brass Quintet.‡4prf
710 20   Dallas Brass Quintet.‡4prf
710 20   Saint Louis Brass Quintet.‡4prf
710 20   I-5 Brass Quintet.‡4prf
```

Although this digital compact disc derived from an analog recording had no indication of stereo, and so no mention of it in the 300 field, the cataloger surmised that it was stereo and coded the 007 SND element as such. The Type of Date (PC) fixed field is coded "r" (for reissue) but the Dates (PD) fixed field has only a single date because of the first 503 note, which mentions no original release date. Type of Date code "r" has precedence over "p", for which the recording dates in field 518 would be evidence. The 033 field is derived from information in the 518 note.

Example 17

Analog disc

```
ID:XXXXXXXXXXX-X RTYP:c    ST:p   FRN:    MS:c   EL:    AD:01-01-01
CC:9110   BLT:jm    DCF:a   CSC:   MOD:   SNR:   ATC:   UD:01-01-01
CP:enk    L:        FCP:pp  INT:   MEI:0  AMC:
PC:s      PD:1972/          LIT:
RMD:d OR:? SPD:b SND:s GRV:m DIM:e WID:n TC:n KD:m KM:p KC:1 RC:u CAP:e
010       86750617/R/r87
028 02    SDL 2232‡bSaydisc
043       e-uk-en
050 1     M175‡b.B3
245 00    Mechanical music hall‡h[sound recording].
260 0     Badminton, Glos. :‡bSaydisc,‡c[1972?]
300       1 sound disc :‡banalog, 33 1/3 rpm, stereo. ;‡c12 in.
440  0    Golden age of mechanical music ;‡vv. 10
500       "Street, penny & player pianos, musical boxes & other Victorian
automata"--Container.
500       Songs identified with various English music hall performers.
500       Instruments from the collection of Roy Mickleburgh, Bristol.
505 0     Miscellany -- Florrie Ford songs -- Eugene Stratton song --
Miscellany -- Tom Costello songs -- Ellaline Terris song -- Harry Champion
songs -- Miscellany -- Albert Chevalier songs -- Marie Lloyd songs --
Lottie Collins song -- Leo Dryden song -- Miscellany.
650  0    Barrel-organ music.
650  0    Player-piano music.
650  0    Music box music.
650  0    Popular instrumental music‡zEngland.
650  0    Musical revues, comedies, etc.‡xExcerpts, Arranged.
650  0    Musical instruments (Mechanical)
700 10    Mickleburgh, Roy.
```

This is a record for an analog disc with title main entry.

Example 18

Analog disc

```
ID:XXXXXXXXXXXX-X RTYP:c   ST:p  FRN:    MS:n   EL:    AD:01-01-01
CC:9110  BLT:jm   DCF:a  CSC:   MOD:   SNR:   ATC:   UD:01-01-01
CP:sz     L:      FCP:vr INT:   MEI:0  AMC:
PC:s       PD:1979/        LIT:
RMD:d OR:? SPD:b SND:s GRV:m DIM:e WID:n TC:n KD:m KM:p KC:l RC:u CAP:e
010      86753061/R
028 00   Cla D 907‡bClaves
028 00   D 907‡bClaves
033 2    19790720‡a19790722‡b6044‡cA87
048      zn01
048      kb01‡azn01
050 1    M175‡b.B3
245 00   1. Schweizerisches Drehorgel-Festival, Arosa‡h[sound recording].
260 0    Thun/Schweiz :‡bClaves,‡cp1979.
300      1 sound disc :‡banalog, 33 1/3 rpm, stereo. ;‡c12 in.
500      Claves: Cla D 907 (on container: D 907).
500      Twenty barrel-organ pieces and "a dialogue between a church organ
and a barrel-organ, played by Hannes Meyer and Heinrich Brechb"uhl:
Variations on the theme 'God save the king'"--Container.
518      Recorded July 20-22, 1979, on the streets and in the squares of
Arosa, Switzerland.
650  0   Barrel-organ music.
650  0   Variations (Organ)
700 10   Meyer, Hannes,‡d1939- ‡4prf
700 10   Brechb"uhl, H.‡q(Heinrich)‡4prf
711 20   Schweizerisches Drehorgel-Festival‡n(1st :‡d1979 :‡cArosa,
Switzerland)
740 01   Erste Schweizerisches Drehorgel-Festival, Arosa.
```

Because two forms of the music publisher's number are found on this analog disc (see the first 500 field), two 028 fields are needed. Information in the 033 is derived from the 518 field. The 711 field is used for the name of the festival.

Example 19

Analog disc

```
ID:XXXXXXXXXXX-X RTYP:c    ST:p   FRN:    MS:c   EL:    AD:01-01-01
CC:9110  BLT:jm    DCF:a  CSC:   MOD:   SNR:   ATC:   UD:01-01-01
CP:cau      L:eng   FCP:op INT:   MEI:1  AMC:dfhz
PC:s       PD:1985/        LIT:
RMD:d OR:? SPD:b SND:s GRV:m DIM:e WID:n TC:n KD:m KM:p KC:l RC:u CAP:d
010      85754264/R/r872
024 1    7777339741
028 02   DSC-3974‡bAngel
028 02   EX 27 0232 3‡bEMI
033      ‡b5754‡cL7
041 1    ‡deng‡hita‡beng‡eeng‡hita‡gengger
050 1    M1500
100 10   Handel, George Frideric,‡d1685-1759.
240 10   Giulio Cesare.‡lEnglish
245 10   Julius Caesar‡h[sound recording] /‡cHandel ; libretto by Haym ;
transl. Trowell.
260 0    [Hollywood, Calif.] :‡bAngel,‡cp1985.
300      3 sound discs :‡banalog, 33 1/3 rpm, stereo. ;‡c12 in.
500      Opera; sung in English.
503      "Edition by Noel Davies and Sir Charles Mackerras"--Container.
511 0    Valerie Masterson, soprano ; Dame Janet Baker, Sarah Walker, Della
Jones, mezzo-sopranos ; James Bowman, David James, countertenors ;
Christopher Booth-Jones, baritone ; John Tomlinson, bass ; English National
Opera Chorus & Orchestra ; Sir Charles Mackerras, conductor.
518      "Recorded at the Abbey Road Studios, London, in association with
the Peter Moores Foundation"--Booklet, p. 1.
500      Digital recording.
500      Manual sequence.
500      Program notes by Brian Trowell in English and German and by Sir
Charles Mackerras in English, synopsis in English and German, biographical
notes on the singers and conductor in English, and English translation of
the Italian libretto (24 p. : ill.) laid in container.
650  0   Operas.
600 10   Caesar, Julius‡xDrama.
700 10   Haym, Nicola Francesco.‡4lbt
700 10   Trowell, Brian.‡4trl
700 10   Davies, Noel.
700 10   Mackerras, Charles,‡cSir,‡d1925- ‡4cnd
700 10   Masterson, Valerie.‡4prf
700 10   Baker, Janet.‡4prf
700 10   Walker, Sarah.‡4prf
700 10   Jones, Della.‡4prf
700 10   Bowman, James.‡4prf
700 10   James, David.‡4prf
700 20   Booth-Jones, Christopher.‡4prf
700 10   Tomlinson, John,‡d1946 Sept. 22- ‡4prf
710 20   English National Opera.‡4prf
```

The second 500 note and the 007 CAP element indicate that this analog disc was derived from a digital recording. The U.S. Universal Product Code for sound recordings is recorded in the 024 field. The second indicator of both 028 fields are set to print; both will generate notes in RLIN. The 041 field is derived from the information found in the last 500 field.

Example 20

Analog disc

```
ID:XXXXXXXXXXXX-X RTYP:c    ST:p   FRN:    MS:n   EL:   AD:01-01-01
CC:9110   BLT:jm    DCF:a  CSC:   MOD:   SNR:   ATC:   UD:01-01-01
CP:nyu     L:      FCP:mu INT:   MEI:1  AMC:f
PC:p        PD:1986/1939    LIT:
RMD:d OR:? SPD:b SND:m GRV:m DIM:e WID:n TC:n KD:m KM:p KC:1 RC:u CAP:e
010      88751052/R
024 1    7863556581
028 02   5658-1 RB‡bBluebird
033 2    19371011‡a19560120‡b3804‡cN4
043      n-us---
047      jz‡app
050 1    M1366
100 10   Hawkins, Coleman.‡4prf
245 10   Body and soul‡h[sound recording] /‡c[performed by] Coleman Hawkins.
260 0    New York, N.Y. :‡bBluebird,‡cp1986.
300      2 sound discs :‡banalog, 33 1/3 rpm, mono. ;‡c12 in.
511 0    Coleman Hawkins, tenor saxophone, with various jazz ensembles, big
bands, and with strings.
518      Recorded between Oct. 11, 1937, and Jan. 20, 1956, in New York
City.
500      Biographical notes on container.
650  0   Jazz ensembles.
650  0   Big band music.
650  0   Popular music‡y1951-1960.
```

The code in the Accompanying Matter fixed field (AMC) reflects the last 500 note in this record for an analog disc. Information in the 033 is derived from the 518 field. The U.S. Universal Product Code for sound recordings is recorded in the 024 field. The gap between the dates of the original recordings and the date of this release is brought out in the Type of Date (PC) and Dates (PD) fixed fields.

Example 21

Analog disc

```
ID:XXXXXXXXXXXX-X RTYP:c   ST:p  FRN:    MS:n   EL:    AD:01-01-01
CC:9110  BLT:im   DCF:a  CSC:  MOD:   SNR:   ATC:    UD:01-01-01 CP:enk
L:       FCP:nn INT:   MEI:0  AMC:
PC:p        PD:1979/1957    LIT:s
RMD:d OR:? SPD:b SND:s GRV:m DIM:e WID:n TC:n KD:m KM:p KC:l RC:u CAP:e
010      85755141/R
028 02   ATR 7016‡bASV Transacord
028 00   ZC ATR 7016‡bASV Transacord
033 2    1957----‡a1971----‡b5740
033 0    1970----‡b6840
033 0    1978----‡b6890
050 1    TJ608
245 00   Trains in trouble‡h[sound recording].
260 0    London :‡bASV Transacord ;‡aMitcham, Surrey :‡bDistributed by
P.R.T. Records,‡cp1979.
300      1 sound disc :‡banalog, 33 1/3 rpm, stereo. ;‡c12 in.
440  0   Sounds of the steam age
518      Recorded between 1957 and 1971 in Great Britain, in 1970 in
Yugoslavia, and in 1978 in Austria.
500      Notes on container.
500      Issued also as cassette: ZC ATR 7016.
520      Presents the sounds of steam trains in adverse weather conditions
and with mechanical difficulties as they attempt to pull freight and
passenger trains.
650  0   Locomotive sounds.
650  0   Railroad sounds.
```

In this analog disc of nonmusical sounds (BLT first element: i), the Literary Text for Sound Recordings fixed field (LIT) is coded for sounds. Multiple 033 fields correspond to the times and places of the recordings detailed in the 518 note. A second, nonprinting 028 field gives access to the item's publisher's number in another recording medium (cassette), cited in the last 500 note. Note both publisher and distributor in the 260 field. The gap between the original recording and the release dates is brought out in the Type of Date (PC) and Dates (PD) fixed fields.

Example 22

Analog Cassette Tape

```
ID:XXXXXXXXXXXX-X RTYP:c    ST:p  FRN:    MS:c   EL:    AD:01-01-01
CC:9110  BLT:jm   DCF:a  CSC:   MOD:   SNR:   ATC:   UD:01-01-01 CP:gt
L:       FCP:pp INT:   MEI:1  AMC:
PC:q       PD:1980/1986    LIT:
RMD:s OR:? SPD:l SND:u GRV:n DIM:j WID:l TC:c KD:m KM:n KC:n RC:u CAP:u
010        86754808/R/r87
028 02   1001‡bDYCSA
043        ncgt---
048        oy
050 1    M1685
110 20   Marimba "Ind´igena Pura".‡4prf
245 10   Sones nativos‡h[sound recording] /‡c[interpretado por la] Marimba
"Ind´igena Pura".
260 0    Guatemala :‡bDYCSA,‡c[198-?]
300        1 sound cassette :‡banalog.
500        Popular Guatemalan instrumental music.
500        Title on container: La ´unica chimalteca.
505 0    El xap -- Sal negra -- Maconaj -- Guarda barranca -- El son de los
bricadores -- Juventino -- San Rafael -- Cuando llora la malin -- Tadeo
Solares -- Frescas ma~nanitas -- Santiago -- El son de Mashico.
650  0   Popular instrumental music‡zGuatemala‡y1981-
650  0   Marimba music.
740 01   ´Unica chimalteca.
```

The Type of Date (PC) code "q" and the two dates (PD) in the fixed field are based on the uncertain date in the 260 subfield ‡c (this musical cassette tape was cataloged in 1986). The corporate name main entry (110) is the musical group, with a subfield ‡4 for performer.

Example 23

Analog cassette tape

```
ID:XXXXXXXXXXXX-X RTYP:c   ST:p  FRN:     MS:n    EL:    AD:01-01-01
CC:9110  BLT:im    DCF:a  CSC:   MOD:  SNR:   ATC:    UD:01-01-01 CP:dcu
L:eng    FCP:nn INT:   MEI:1  AMC:
PC:s        PD:1983/        LIT:l
RMD:s OR:? SPD:l SND:u GRV:n DIM:j WID:l TC:c KD:m KM:n KC:n RC:u CAP:u
010      88740281/R
028 02   NP-830411‡bNational Public Radio
033      ‡b3850
050 1    D804.3
100 10   Wiesel, Elie,‡d1928-
245 10   Elie Wiesel at the National Press Club‡h[sound recording].
260 0    Washington, D.C. :‡bNational Public Radio,‡cp1983.
300      1 sound cassette (1 hr.) :‡banalog.
306      006000
500      Publisher's catalog title: Elie Wiesel on remembering.
518      Recorded at a National Press Club luncheon held in Washington, D.C.
500      Broadcast Apr. 11, 1983, on National Public Radio.
520      Noted author, Holocaust survivor, and chairman of the U.S.
Holocaust Memorial Council Elie Wiesel discusses attempts by journalists in
World War II to tell the world what was happening in Germany and describes
his own mission to ensure that people will never forget the Holocaust.
650  0 Holocaust, Jewish (1939-1945)‡xCensorship.
710 20   National Press Club (U.S.)
710 20   National Public Radio (U.S.)
740 01   Elie Wiesel on remembering.
```

    The 033 field codifies the place of capture stated in the 518 field of this record for a spoken word cassette tape. A summary of the lecture appears in the 520 note. The Literary Text for Sound Recordings fixed field (LIT) is coded for a lecture. Note that the dates in the 650 field are not separately subfielded and that the duration of one hour (300) is coded in the 306 field.

Example 24

Analog Tape Reel

```
ID:XXXXXXXXXXXX-X RTYP:c    ST:p  FRN:    MS:n   EL:    AD:01-01-01
CC:9110   BLT:im   DCF:a  CSC:  MOD:   SNR:   ATC:   UD:01-01-01 CP:mou
L:eng    FCP:nn INT:   MEI:1  AMC:
PC:s       PD:1985/        LIT:p
RMD:t OR:? SPD:o SND:m GRV:n DIM:c WID:m TC:u KD:m KM:n KC:n RC:u CAP:e
010       85752880/R
033       ‡b3934‡cG2
050 1     PS3509‡b.B456
100 10    Eberhart, Richard,‡d1904-
240 10    Florida poems.‡kSelections
245 10    Richard Eberhart‡h[sound recording].
260 0     [Kansas City, Mo. :‡bNew Letters,‡c1985]
300       1 sound tape reel (29 min.) :‡banalog, 7 1/2 ips, mono. ;‡c7 in.
306       002900
518       Recorded at WUFT-FM in Gainesville, Fla.
500       Broadcast Jan. 1985 on the radio program New letters on the air.
520       Pulitzer Prize winning poet Richard Eberhart reads from his
collection entitled Florida poems.
730 01    New letters.
730 01    New letters on the air (Radio program)
```

The 033 field codifies information found in the 518 note of this record for a spoken word sound tape reel. Note the two uniform title added entries, one for the journal *New letters*, the other for the related radio program.

Example 1

```
cm        87-750963
     CRD         ‡a          ‡/M
     MEPS        ‡ad         ‡Bach, Johann Sebastian,‡1685-1750.
     UTIA0       ‡ak         ‡Keyboard music.‡Selections (Clavier-"Ubung)
     TILA0       ‡ac         ‡Clavier-"Ubung /‡Johann Sebastian Bach.
     EDN         ‡ab         ‡Faksimile-Ausg. /‡herausgegeben von Christoph
                             Wolff.
     IMP         ‡abaabc     ‡Leipzig :‡Edition Peters ;‡Frankfurt ;‡New York
                             :‡C.F. Peters,‡c1984.
     COL         ‡ac         ‡4 v. of music ;‡26 x 32 cm.
     SET-0       ‡a          ‡Musikwissenschaftliche Studienbibliothek Peters
     SERU        ‡a          ‡Peters reprints
     NOG         ‡a          ‡For harpsichord or organ.
     NOG         ‡a          ‡Second imprint from label on t.p.
     NOH         ‡a          ‡Reprint of works originally published 1731-
                             1741.
     NOG         ‡a          ‡Accompanied by: Johann Sebastian Bachs
                             Klavier"ubung : Kommentar zur Faksimile-Ausgabe
                             / Christoph Wolff (32 p. : facsims.) (in English
                             and German).
     NOCC        ‡a          ‡1. Sechs Partiten BWV 825-830 -- 2.
                             Italienisches Konzert : BWV 971 ; Franz"osische
                             Ouvert"ure : BWV 831 -- 3. Pr"aludium und Fuge
                             Es-Dur BWV 552 ; Orgelchor"ale BWV 669-689 ;
                             Duette BWV 802-805 -- 4. Goldberg-Variationen :
                             BWV 988.
     SUT-L       ‡a          ‡Harpsichord music.
     SUT-L       ‡a          ‡Organ music.
     AEPSA       ‡a          ‡Wolff, Christoph.
     CRO         ‡a          ‡v2v4
     FCC         ‡aaaaaa     ‡su‡ov‡pr‡fg‡cl‡vr
     PNMTR       ‡ab         ‡9314‡Edition Peters
     LAN         ‡gh         ‡engger‡ger
     IVC         ‡a          ‡kc01
     IVC         ‡a          ‡kb01
     CALL        ‡ab         ‡M3.1.B2‡K48 1984
FFD    DATE KY= r           DATE 1= 1984     DATE 2= 1731        LAN=
          COMP= mu            SCORE= z        PARTS=          ACC MAT= hi
       ME IN B=x             CNTRY= ge        REPRO=          MOD REC=
       INTEL LV=          LIT TEXT= n         CAT S=          CAT FORM= a
```

The Type of Date (DATE KY) and Dates fixed fields and the NOH note all indicate that this is a facsimile reprint of a published score. The edition statement includes a statement of responsibility. Note the presence of both traced and untraced series, a multiple imprint, and that accompanying material is described in the last NOG note.

Example 2

```
cm       88-751200
         CRD        ‡a        ‡/M
         MEPS       ‡a        ‡Bussotti, Sylvano.
         UTIA0      ‡ap       ‡Catalogo `e questo.‡Raragramma
         TILA3      ‡anpc     ‡Il catalogo `e questo.‡II,‡Raragramma /‡Sylvano
                              Bussotti.
         IMP        ‡abc      ‡Milano :‡Ricordi,‡1985, c1982.
         COL        ‡abc      ‡1 score (30 p.) :‡1 col. facsim. ;‡41 cm.
         SERD       ‡a        ‡Bussottioperaballet
         NOG        ‡a        ‡For flutes (1 player), violin, and orchestra.
         NOG        ‡a        ‡Reproduced from holograph.
         NOCC       ‡a        ‡Raragramma -- R. & R. -- Enfant prodige --
                              Paganini -- Calando symphony.
         SUT-L      ‡ax       ‡Flute and violin with orchestra‡Scores.
         SUT-L      ‡axx      ‡Music‡Manuscripts‡Facsimiles.
         SUPSL      ‡axx      ‡Bussotti, Sylvano‡Manuscripts‡Facsimiles.
         AED0S      ‡a        ‡Raragramma.
         SAPS       ‡at       ‡Bussotti, Sylvano.‡Selections.
         CROS       ‡b        ‡d19811121
         PNMPR      ‡ab       ‡133507‡Ricordi
         IVC        ‡bba      ‡wa01‡sa01‡oa
         CALL       ‡ab       ‡M1040.B94‡C37 1985
FFD   DATE KY= c            DATE 1= 1985     DATE 2= 1982        LAN=
          COMP= uu            SCORE= a         PARTS=          ACC MAT=
       ME IN B=x              CNTRY= it        REPRO=          MOD REC=
      INTEL LV=          LIT TEXT= n       CAT S=            CAT FORM= a
```

In this score for two solo instruments and orchestra, the dates of publication and copyright are both recorded in the IMP subfield ‡c and are reflected in the Type of Date (DATE KY) and Dates fixed field positions. The date in the CRO field derives from the date inscribed at the end of the holograph score. The single player on multiple flutes mentioned in the first NOG note is reflected in the IVC field. Subfields ‡n and ‡p are both found in the TIL field. Note the illustration statement in the COL subfield ‡b. A series traced in different form is found in the SER and its corresponding author/title SAP series field. A personal name as subject heading is found in the SUP field.

Example 3

```
cm          86-754683
      CRD         ‡a          ‡/M/r87
      MEU0        ‡a          ‡Nunc dimittis (Parr`oquia de Sant Pere de Canet
                              de Mar, Spain)
      TILN0       ‡ac         ‡Nunc dimittis a 11, s. XVII /‡an`onim ;
                              transcripci´o i estudi, Francesc Bonastre.
      IMP         ‡abc        ‡Barcelona :‡Institut Universitari de
                              Documentaci´o i Investigaci´o Musicol`ogica
                              "Josep Ricart i Matas",‡1983.
      COL         ‡ac         ‡1 score (22 p.) ;‡30 cm.
      SET-0       ‡av         ‡Quaderns de m´usica hist`orica catalana ;‡4
      NOG         ‡a          ‡For chorus (TipleA/TipleT/TipleATB), cobla
                              ensemble (2 xeremias, trombone), and continuo;
                              bass unrealized.
      NOG         ‡a          ‡Latin words.
      NOH         ‡a          ‡Edited from a ms. in the Arxiu Musical de la
                              Parr`oquia de Sant Pere de Carnet de Mar.
      NOG         ‡a          ‡Prefatory notes in Catalan and English.
      SUT-L       ‡a          ‡Choruses, Sacred (Mixed voices) with
                              instrumental ensemble.
      SUT-L       ‡a          ‡Nunc dimittis (Music)
      AEPSA       ‡a          Bonastre, Francesc.
      LAN         ‡ag         ‡lat‡cateng
      IVC         ‡aaaa       ‡ca08‡wy02‡bd01‡ke
      CALL        ‡ab         ‡M2021‡.N8 1983
FFD   DATE KY= s           DATE 1= 1983      DATE 2=               LAN= lat
         COMP= uu             SCORE= a         PARTS=          ACC MAT= i
      ME IN B=               CNTRY= sp         REPRO=          MOD REC=
      INTEL LV=         LIT TEXT= n            CAT S=          CAT FORM= a
```

In this record for an accompanied choral work, the prefatory notes mentioned in the final NOG note show up in the Accompanying Matter (ACC MAT) fixed field element as well as the LAN subfield ‡g. The IVC field corresponds to the first NOG field ("tiple" is a high voice; a cobla ensemble is a Catalan dance band; a xeremia is a Catalan wind instrument). Note the uniform title main entry (MEU) and the NOH note.

Example 4

```
cm1          82-771219
      CRD        ǂa          ǂ/M/r85
      TILN0      ǂac         ǂGaelic songs in Nova Scotia /ǂ[compiled by]
                             Helen Creighton and Calum MacLeod ; with a new
                             preface by Helen Creighton.
      IMP        ǂabc        ǂOttawa, Canada :ǂNational Museum of Man,
                             National Museums of Canada,ǂ1979.
      COL        ǂabc        ǂxi p., 308 p. of music :ǂill. ;ǂ25 cm.
      NOG        ǂa          ǂUnacc.
      NOG        ǂa          ǂWords in Gaelic with English translations.
      NIR        ǂpcf        ǂReprint. Originally published:ǂ1964.ǂ(Bulletin
                             / National Museum of Canada ; no. 196.
                             Anthropological series ; no. 66).
      NOB        ǂa          ǂBibliography: p. 298-300.
      NOG        ǂa          ǂIncludes index.
      NOG        ǂa          ǂCatalogue no.: NM93-198/1979.
      SUT-L      ǂaz         ǂFolk musicǂNova Scotia.
      SUT-L      ǂaz         ǂFolk-songs, GaelicǂNova Scotia.
      AEPSA      ǂa          ǂCreighton, Helen.
      AEPSA      ǂa          ǂMacLeod, Calum.
      SAU-0      ǂav         ǂBulletin (National Museum of Canada) ;ǂno. 196.
      SAU-0      ǂapv        ǂBulletin (National Museum of Canada).
                             ǂAnthropological series ;ǂno. 66.
      PNMTN      ǂab         ǂNM93-198/1979ǂNational Museum of Man
      GAC        ǂa          ǂn-cn-ns
      LANX       ǂaeh        ǂgaeǂengǂgae
      CALL       ǂab         ǂM1678ǂ.G144 1979
FFD   DATE KY= r           DATE 1= 1979    DATE 2= 1964        LAN= gae
          COMP= fm           SCORE= z      PARTS=         ACC MAT= b
       ME IN B=            CNTRY= onc      REPRO=         MOD REC=
       INTEL LV=      LIT TEXT= n        CAT S=         CAT FORM= a
```

The fact that this score is a reprint is noted in the Type of Date (DATE KY) and Dates fixed field positions, the NIR Note, and the two corresponding series uniform title added entries (SAU). The bibliography is noted in the NOB field and in the Accompanying Matter fixed field (ACC MAT).

Example 5

```
cm            87-751402
        CRD         ‡a        ‡/M/r88
        MEPM        ‡ad       ‡Mendelssohn-Bartholdy, Felix,‡1809-1847.
        UTIA0       ‡arl      ‡Kyrie,‡D minor.‡Greek
        TILN0       ‡ac       ‡Kyrie in d, f¨ur Chor und Orchester /‡[Felix
                              Mendelssohn Bartholdy].
        EDN         ‡ab       ‡Erstausg. /‡herausgegeben von R. Larry Todd.
        MPS         ‡a        ‡Partitur.
        IMP         ‡abc      ‡Stuttgart :‡Carus-Verlag,‡c1986.
        COL         ‡ac       ‡1 score (32 p.) ;‡30 cm.
        SERD        ‡a        ‡Ausgew¨ahlte Werke vokaler Kirchenmusik / Felix
                              Mendelssohn Bartholdy
        NOG         ‡a        ‡Chorus: SSATB.
        NOG         ‡a        ‡Duration: 10:00.
        SUT-L       ‡a        ‡Choruses, Sacred (Mixed voices) with orchestra.
        SUT-L       ‡a        ‡Kyrie eleison (Music)
        AEPSA       ‡a        ‡Todd, R. Larry.
        SAPM        ‡adtk     ‡Mendelssohn-Bartholdy, Felix,‡1809-1847.‡Vocal
                              music.‡Selections (Ausgew¨ahlte Werke vokaler
                              Kirchenmusik)
        CROS        ‡b        ‡d18250506
        PNMPR       ‡ab       ‡CV 40-482/01‡Carus-Verlag
        IVC         ‡aa       ‡ca05‡oa
        CALL        ‡ab       ‡M2020.M36‡K94 1986
        DSR         ‡a        ‡001000
FFD     DATE KY= s            DATE 1= 1986      DATE 2=            LAN= gre
            COMP= uu            SCORE= a         PARTS=          ACC MAT=
        ME IN B= x              CNTRY= gw        REPRO=          MOD REC=
        INTEL LV=           LIT TEXT= n          CAT S=          CAT FORM= a
```

A score with both an edition statement (EDN) and a musical presentation statement (MPS), this record has a SER/SAP combination as well. The Duration field (DSR) corresponds to the final NOG note. Mendelssohn-Bartholdy's compound surname requires appropriate first indicators in both the MEP and SAP fields.

Example 6

```
cm          85-750511
      CRD        ‡a       ‡/M/r86
      MEPS       ‡ad      ‡Mercadante, Saverio,‡1795-1870.
      UTIA0      ‡as      ‡Elena da Feltre.‡Vocal score
      TILA0      ‡ac      ‡Elena da Feltre /‡libretto by Salvatore
                          Cammarano ; music by Saverio Mercadante.
      EDN        ‡ab      ‡A facsim. ed. of the printed piano-vocal score
                          /‡with an introduction by Philip Gossett.
      IMP        ‡abc     ‡New York :‡Garland,‡1985.
      COL        ‡abc     ‡1 vocal score (237, 11 p.) :‡facsims. ;‡24 x 32
                          cm.
      SET-0      ‡av      ‡Italian opera, 1810-1840 ;‡v. 20
      NOG        ‡a       ‡Italian words.
      NOH        ‡pc      ‡Reprint. Originally published:‡Milano :
                          Ricordi, 1839.
      NOG        ‡a       ‡"Recito. e cavatina : 'Parmi che alfin
                          dimentica' : aggiunta all'opera Elena da
                          Feltre": p. 1-11 (2nd group).
      SUT-L      ‡ax      ‡Operas‡Vocal scores with piano.
      AEPSA      ‡ad      ‡Cammarano, Salvatore,‡1801-1852.
      CROS       ‡b       ‡d1838
      PNMPR      ‡ab      ‡H. 11231 H.‡Garland
      SBN        ‡ac      ‡0824065697 :‡$75.00
      CALL       ‡ab      ‡M1503.M553‡E4 1985
FFD   DATE KY= r          DATE 1= 1985      DATE 2= 1839        LAN= ita
          COMP= op          SCORE= c          PARTS=          ACC MAT=
       ME IN B= x           CNTRY= nyu        REPRO=          MOD REC=
      INTEL LV=          LIT TEXT= n          CAT S=          CAT FORM= a
```

The Type of Date (DATE KY) and Dates fixed field elements, the edition statement (EDN), and the NOH note all indicate that this is a facsimile edition of a previously published vocal score. The dates in the series statement (SET) are not separately subfielded, because they are considered an integral part of the series title.

Example 7

```
cm          86-754626
       CRD          ‡a          ‡/M
       MEPS         ‡a          ‡Kolb, Barbara.
       TILA0        ‡ac         ‡Time-- and again /‡Barbara Kolb.
       IMP          ‡abc        ‡New York, NY (24 W. 57th St., New York 10019)
                                :‡Boosey & Hawkes,‡c1985.
       COL          ‡ac         ‡1 score (18 p.) ;‡36 x 45 cm.
       NOG          ‡a          ‡Caption title.
       NOG          ‡a          ‡For computer, oboe, 2 violins, viola, and
                                violoncello.
       NOG          ‡a          ‡Reproduced from holograph.
       SUT-L        ‡ax         ‡Quintets (Oboe, violins (2), viola,
                                violoncello)‡Scores.
       SUT-L        ‡a          ‡Computer music.
       SUT-L        ‡axx        ‡Music‡Manuscripts‡Facsimiles.
       SUPSL        ‡axx        ‡Kolb, Barbara‡Manuscripts‡Facsimiles.
       CROS         ‡b          ‡d1985
       IVC          ‡aaaaa      ‡ec01‡wb01‡sa02‡sb01‡sc01
       CALL         ‡ab         ‡M562.K754‡T5 1985
FFD    DATE KY= s              DATE 1= 1985    DATE 2=            LAN=
           COMP= uu             SCORE= a       PARTS=       ACC MAT=
       ME IN B= x               CNTRY= nyu     REPRO=       MOD REC=
       INTEL LV=          LIT TEXT= n          CAT S=       CAT FORM= a
```

The title of this score features some out-of-the-ordinary punctuation. The publisher's address appears in the subfield ‡a of the IMP field. Formulation of the IVC field corresponds to the second NOG note.

Example 8

```
cm          86-753526
      CRD        ‡a         ‡/M
      MEPM       ‡aqd       ‡Eckhardt-Gramatt´e, S. C.‡(Sophie-
                            Carmen),‡1899-1974.
      UTIA0      ‡an        ‡Symphonies,‡no. 2
      TILN0      ‡abc       ‡Symphony II (E. 158) :‡Manitoba symphony
                            /‡[Eckhardt-Gramatt´e].
      EDN        ‡ab        ‡Restricted ed. for archival purposes only
                            /‡an[n]otations and corrections by the composer.
      MPS        ‡a         ‡Orchestra score & analysis.
      IMP        ‡abc       ‡Winnipeg, Canada :‡Estate S.C. Eckhardt-
                            Gramatt´e,‡1980, c1970.
      COL        ‡abc       ‡1 score (58, 62, 55, 67 p.) :‡port. ;‡29 cm.
      SERD       ‡av        ‡Selected works / S.C. Eckhardt-Gramatt´e ;‡v. 2
      NOG        ‡a         ‡Duration: 34:00.
      SUT-L      ‡ax        ‡Symphonies‡Scores.
      AED0S      ‡a         ‡Manitoba symphony.
      SAPM       ‡aqdtv     ‡Eckhardt-Gramatt´e, S. C.‡(Sophie-
                            Carmen),‡1899-1974.‡Selections (Selected works)
                            ;‡v. 2.
      CROS       ‡b         ‡d1970
      IVC        ‡a         ‡oa
      CALL       ‡aba       ‡M3.1.E27‡E8 1980 vol. 2‡M1001
      DSR        ‡a         ‡003400
```

FFD	DATE KY= c	DATE 1= 1980	DATE 2= 1970	LAN=
	COMP= sy	SCORE= a	PARTS=	ACC MAT=
	ME IN B= x	CNTRY= mbc	REPRO=	MOD REC=
	INTEL LV=	LIT TEXT= n	CAT S=	CAT FORM= a

The EDN field in this special edition of a score includes a statement of responsibility without a proper name. A musical presentation statement (MPS) also is present. Note the SER/SAP pair and the multiple surname in the MEP and SAP fields.

Example 9

```
cm      86-192870
     CRD          ‡a        ‡/M/r872
     TILN0        ‡ac       ‡Antolog´ia folkl´orica y musical de Tabasco
                            /‡[compilaci´on] Francisco J. Santamar´ia ;
                            arreglo y estudio musical de Ger´onimo Baqueiro
                            F´oster.
     EDN          ‡a        ‡2a ed.
     IMP          ‡abc      ‡Villahermosa :‡Gobierno del Estado de
                            Tabasco,‡1985.
     COL          ‡ac       ‡1 score (600 p.) ;‡21 cm.
     SET-0        ‡av       ‡Biblioteca b´asica tabasque~na ;‡1
     SERD         ‡a        ‡Serie antolog´ias
     NOG          ‡a        ‡Principally popular songs for voice and piano
                            and dances for piano.
     NOB          ‡a        ‡Bibliography: p. 89-91.
     NOG          ‡a        ‡Includes historical notes and biographies of
                            the composers.
     SUT-L        ‡azzy     ‡Popular music‡Mexico‡Tabasco (State)‡1981-
     SUT-L        ‡a        ‡Piano music.
     SUT-L        ‡azz      ‡Dance music‡Mexico‡Tabasco (State)
     AEPSA        ‡ad       ‡Santamar´ia, Francisco Javier,‡1889-
     AEPMA        ‡a4       ‡Baqueiro F´oster, Ger´onimo.‡arr
     SAU-0        ‡a        ‡Serie antolog´ias (Instituto de Cultura de
                            Tabasco)
     FCC          ‡aa       ‡pp‡df
     GAC          ‡a        ‡n-mx---
     IVC          ‡aa       ‡vn01‡ka01
     IVC          ‡a        ‡ka01
     SBN          ‡a        ‡9688890006
     CALL         ‡ab       ‡M1683.18‡A57 1985
FFD    DATE KY= s           DATE 1= 1985     DATE 2=              LAN= spa
            COMP= mu         SCORE= a         PARTS=          ACC MAT= bei
         ME IN B=            CNTRY= mx        REPRO=          MOD REC=
         INTEL LV=      LIT TEXT= n           CAT S=          CAT FORM= a
```

This score of ethnic popular and dance music has the code "mu" in the Form of Composition fixed field position (COMP), meaning that the FCC field must also be present. The Accompanying Matter fixed field element (ACC MAT) codes the information in both the NOB and the final NOG note. Two series statements (SET and SER) and one corresponding series uniform title added entry (SAU) are present. Note the edition statement (EDN) and the subfield ‡4 for the arranger in the last AEP field.

Example 10

```
dm1          82-770783
      CRD       ‡a        ‡/M/r85
      MEPS      ‡ad       ‡Liszt, Franz,‡1811-1886.
      TILA0     ‡abc      ‡Weinen, Klagen, Sorgen, Zagen :‡Praeludium
                          (nach J.S. Bach's Cantate) /‡von F. Liszt.
      IMPX      ‡c        ‡[1859]
      COL       ‡ac       ‡[4] p. of ms. music ;‡28 x 35 cm.
      NOG       ‡a        ‡Holograph, in ink.
      NOG       ‡a        ‡For piano.
      NOH       ‡a        ‡Based on a theme from the opening chorus of the
                          cantata.
      NOH       ‡a        ‡Published: Berlin : Schlesinger, 1863.
      SUT-L     ‡a        ‡Piano music.
      SUT-L     ‡ax       ‡Music‡Manuscripts.
      SUPSL     ‡adx      ‡Liszt, Franz,‡1811-1886‡Manuscripts.
      AEPSS     ‡adtp     ‡Bach, Johann Sebastian,‡1685-1750.‡Weinen,
                          Klagen, Sorgen, Zagen.‡Weinen, Klagen, Sorgen,
                          Zagen.
      CROS      ‡b        ‡d1859
      IVC       ‡a        ‡ka01
      CALL      ‡ab       ‡ML31‡.S4a No. 11
FFD   DATE KY= s          DATE 1= 1859    DATE 2=          LAN=
         COMP= pr          SCORE= z        PARTS=          ACC MAT=
      ME IN B= x           CNTRY= xx       REPRO=          MOD REC=
      INTEL LV=         LIT TEXT= n        CAT S=          CAT FORM= a
```

In this music manuscript (Type of record: d), note the two NOH notes (one explaining the work's derivation, the other its first publication), the IMP with only a date, and the formulation of the COL field. The author/title added entry for J.S. Bach formalizes the information found in the TIL and the first NOH field.

Example 11

```
dm          87-753561
       CRD          ‡a          ‡/M
       MEPS         ‡a          ‡Jolas, Betsy.
       TILA0        ‡abc        ‡O wall :‡op´era de poup´ee = a puppet opera :
                                1976 /‡Betsy Jolas.
       IMPX         ‡c          ‡1976 June 29.
       COL          ‡ac         ‡1 ms. score (12 leaves) ;‡44 cm.
       NOG          ‡a          ‡Holograph.
       NOG          ‡a          For flute, oboe, clarinet, horn, and bassoon.
       NOG          ‡a          ‡"For the Serge Koussevitzky Music Foundation in
                                the Library of Congress, and dedicated to the
                                memory of Serge and Natalie Koussevitzky."
       NOG          ‡a          ‡Duration: ca. 15:00.
       NOG          ‡a          ‡At end: Paris.
       NOG          ‡a          ‡In ink; on transparencies.
       NOG          ‡a          ‡Accompanied by photocopy (39 cm.) and sketches
                                ([2] p. ; 44 cm.).
       SUT-L        ‡ax         ‡Wind quintets (Bassoon, clarinet, flute, horn,
                                oboe)‡Scores.
       SUT-L        ‡a          ‡Musical sketches.
       AECNA        ‡ab         ‡Library of Congress.‡Serge Koussevitzky Music
                                Foundation.
       CROS         ‡b          ‡d19760629
       IVC          ‡aaaaa      ‡wa01‡wb01‡wc01‡ba01‡wd01
       CALL         ‡ab         ‡ML30.3c‡.J64 no. 1
       DSR          ‡a          ‡001500
FFD    DATE KY= s            DATE 1= 1976      DATE 2=              LAN=
         COMP= uu              SCORE= a         PARTS=          ACC MAT=
       ME IN B= x             CNTRY= dcu        REPRO=          MOD REC=
       INTEL LV=           LIT TEXT= n          CAT S=         CAT FORM= a
```

In this manuscript score (Type of Record: d), the date in the IMP field is derived from the date on the holograph and is coded in the CRO field. The quoted NOG note justifies the corporate added entry (AEC). Accompanying material is described in the final NOG note.

Example 12

```
cm7        88-953290
       MEPS         ‡ad        ‡Berlioz, Hector,‡1803-1869.
       UTIA0        ‡ak        ‡Songs.‡Selections
       TILA0        ‡ahc       ‡Ausgew¨ahlte Lieder‡[microform] /‡von Hector
                               Berlioz ; eingeleitet und herausgegeben von Karl
                               Blessinger.
       IMP          ‡abc       ‡M¨unchen :‡Drei Masken Verlag,‡1920.
       COL          ‡abc       ‡1 score (xii, 74 p.) :‡port. ;‡19 cm.
       SERU         ‡a         ‡Musikalische Stundenb¨ucher
       NOG          ‡a         ‡For voice and piano.
       NOG          ‡a         ‡French and German words.
       NOG          ‡a         ‡Call number of original: M2.M93B45.
       NOG          ‡a         ‡Master microform held by: DLC.
       NOX          ‡abcde     ‡Microfilm.‡Washington, D.C. :‡Library of
                               Congress Photoduplication Service,‡1988.‡1
                               microfilm reel : positive ; 35 mm.
       NOW          ‡a         ‡With: Quartetto e coro dei maggi / da H.
                               Berlioz.
       SUT-L        ‡a         ‡Songs with piano accompaniment.
       AEPSA        ‡ad        ‡Blessinger, Karl,‡1888-
       LANX         ‡ah        ‡gerfre‡fre
       IVC          ‡aa        ‡vu01‡ka01
       DFF          ‡a         ‡hd|afa—baca
       DFF          ‡a         ‡hd|bfa—baaa
FFD    DATE KY= r              DATE 1= 1988    DATE 2= 1920         LAN= ger
           COMP= sg            SCORE=          PARTS=           ACC MAT=
       ME IN B= x              CNTRY= dcu      REPRO= a         MOD REC=
       INTEL LV=          LIT TEXT= n          CAT S=           CAT FORM= a
```

This microform reproduction of a printed score has two microform DFF fields, the first for the positive item being cataloged, the second for the negative master mentioned in the final NOG field. Notice the GMD in the TIL field. The physical description of the positive microfilm appears in the NOX note. Another work filmed with this one is noted in the NOW field.

Example 13

Compact Disc

jm	89-751546		
	CRD	‡a	‡/R
	MEPM	‡ad	‡Jacquet de La Guerre, Elisabeth-Claude,‡ca. 1664-1729.
	UTIA0	‡a	‡Selections
	TILN0	‡ahc	‡Cantates & pi`eces vari´ees‡[sound recording] /‡Elisabeth Jacquet de La Guerre.
	IMP	‡abc	‡[France] :‡Arion,‡p1986.
	COL	‡abc	‡2 sound discs :‡digital ;‡4 3/4 in.
	SERU	‡a	‡Les Joyaux de votre discoth`eque
	NOG	‡a	‡Arion: ARN 268012 (ARN 268012--ARN 268013).
	NOG	‡a	‡Title on container: Cantates bibliques ; Pi`eces instrumentales.
	NOG	‡a	‡Title on spine of container: Cantates bibliques ; Pi`eces instrumentales et vocale[s].
	NOG	‡a	‡The 1st 4 works for soprano and continuo; the 5th for 2 sopranos and continuo; the 6th for 2 violins and continuo; the 7th and 9th for soprano, baritone, and continuo; the 8th for violin and harpsichord.
	NORG	‡a	‡Sophie Boulin, Isabelle Poulenard, sopranos ; Michel Verschaeve, baritone ; Bernadette Charbonnier, Catherine Giardelli, violins ; Francoise Bloch, viola da gamba ; Claire Giardelli, violoncello ; Guy Robert, theorbo ; Brigitte Haudebourg, harpsichord ; Georges Guillard, organ or harpsichord.
	CAN	‡a	‡Recorded in Mar. 1985.
	NOG	‡a	‡Compact disc.
	NOG	‡a	‡Analog recording.
	NOG	‡a	‡Program notes in French by Philippe Beaussant and words of the vocal works with English and German translations (32 p. : ill.) in container.
	NOCC	‡a	‡Suzanne -- Judith -- Esther -- Jacob et Rachel -- Jepth´e -- Sonate no 4 `a 2 viol. et violonc. -- Le D´eluge -- Les pi`eces de clavecin qui peuvent se jouer sur le violon -- Le raccommodement comique de Pierrot et de Nicole.
	SUT-L	‡a	‡Solo cantatas, Sacred (High voice)
	SUT-L	‡a	‡Cantatas, Sacred.
	SUT-L	‡a	‡Trio-sonatas (Violins (2), continuo)
	SUT-L	‡a	‡Violin and harpsichord music.
	SUT-L	‡a	‡Cantatas, Secular.
	AEPSA	‡a4	‡Boulin, Sophie.‡prf
	AEPSA	‡a4	‡Poulenard, Isabelle.‡prf
	AEPSA	‡a4	‡Verschaeve, Michel.‡prf

```
        AEPSA          ‡a4          ‡Charbonnier, Bernadette.‡prf
        AEPSA          ‡a4          ‡Giardelli, Catherine.‡prf
        AEPSA          ‡a4          ‡Bloch, Francoise.‡prf
        AEPSA          ‡a4          ‡Giardelli, Claire.‡prf
        AEPSA          ‡ad4         ‡Robert, Guy,‡1943- ‡prf
        AEPSA          ‡a4          ‡Haudebourg, Brigitte.‡prf
        AEPSA          ‡a4          ‡Guillard, Georges.‡prf
        AEPMN          ‡adtnkf      ‡Jacquet de La Guerre, Elisabeth-Claude,‡ca.
                                    1664-1729.‡Cantates fran coises sur des sujets
                                    tirez de l'Ecriture,‡bk. 1.‡Selections.‡1986.
        AEPMN          ‡adtnpf      ‡Jacquet de La Guerre, Elisabeth-Claude,‡ca.
                                    1664-1729.‡Cantates fran coises sur des sujets
                                    tirez de l'Ecriture,‡bk. 2.‡Jepht´e.‡1986.
        AEPMN          ‡adtnf       ‡Jacquet de La Guerre, Elisabeth-Claude,‡ca.
                                    1664-1729.‡Trio sonatas.‡No. 4.‡1986.
        AEPMN          ‡adtnpf      ‡Jacquet de La Guerre, Elisabeth-Claude,‡ca.
                                    1664-1729.‡Cantates fran coises sur des sujets
                                    tirez de l'Ecriture,‡bk. 2.‡D´eluge.‡1986.
        AEPMN          ‡adtkf       ‡Jacquet de La Guerre, Elisabeth-Claude,‡ca.
                                    1664-1729.‡Pi`eces de
                                    clavecin.‡Selections.‡1986.
        AEPMN          ‡adtnpf      ‡Jacquet de La Guerre, Elisabeth-Claude,‡ca.
                                    1664-1729.‡Cantates
                                    fran coises‡(1715).‡Raccommodement comique de
                                    Pierrot et de Nicole.‡1986.
        CAPS           ‡a           ‡198503--
        CROM           ‡bb          ‡d1695‡d1715
        FCC            ‡aa          ‡ct‡ts
        PNMIN          ‡ab          ‡ARN 268012‡Arion
        PNMIN          ‡ab          ‡ARN 268013‡Arion
        LAN            ‡dehgh       ‡fre‡freengger‡fre‡freengger‡fre
        IVC            ‡aa          ‡va01‡ke
        IVC            ‡aa          ‡va02‡ke
        IVC            ‡aa          ‡sa02‡ke
        IVC            ‡aaa         ‡va01‡ve01‡ke
        IVC            ‡aa          ‡sa01‡kc01
        DFF            ‡a           ‡sd|fsngnnmmnee
FFD  DATE KY= p          DATE 1= 1986    DATE 2= 1985        LAN= fre
        COMP= mu          SCORE= n        PARTS=          ACC MAT= defi
     ME IN B= x           CNTRY= fr       REPRO=          MOD REC=
     INTEL LV=         LIT TEXT=          CAT S=          CAT FORM= a
```

This digital compact disc derived from an analog recording. The Form of Composition fixed field element (COMP) has a corresponding FCC field. The Type of Date (DATE KY) and dates in the fixed field reflect the IMP subfield ‡c and the CAN note; the CAP field is derived from the CAN field. The item had no indication of stereo (hence, no mention in the COL field) but the cataloger surmised that it was stereo and coded the DFF position 5 as such. Note the complex LAN field and its relation to the last NOG note. Multiple music publisher's numbers result in multiple PNM fields and an explicitly input NOG note. Also note the multiple surname in the main and some of the added entries.

Example 14

Compact disc

```
jm      87-750942
        CRD         ‡a          ‡/R
        MEPS        ‡ad         ‡Smetana, Bedˇrich,‡1824-1884.
        UTIA0       ‡ak         ‡Prodanˊa nevˇesta.‡Selections
        TILA4       ‡apbhc      ‡The bartered bride.‡Overture and dances ; From
                                my life :‡string quartet in E minor‡[sound
                                recording] /‡Bedˇrich Smetana ; orchestral
                                version [of 2nd work] by George Szell.
        IMP         ‡abc        ‡London, England :‡Chandos,‡p1986.
        COL         ‡abc        ‡1 sound disc :‡digital, stereo. ;‡4 3/4 in.
        NORG        ‡a          ‡London Symphony Orchestra ; Geoffrey Simon,
                                conductor.
        CAN         ‡a          ‡Recorded Feb. 18-19, 1985, All Saints' Church,
                                Tooting, London.
        NOG         ‡a          ‡Compact disc.
        NOG         ‡a          ‡Durations: 24:23: 30:30.
        NOCP        ‡a          ‡The bartered bride. Overture (6:32) ; Dance of
                                the villagers (4:28) ; Polka (4:57) ; Furiant
                                (1:58) ; Fanfare (:41) ; Dance of the comedians
                                (5:32).
        SUT-L       ‡ax         ‡Operas‡Excerpts.
        SUT-L       ‡a          ‡Orchestral music, Arranged.
        AEPSA       ‡ad         ‡Simon, Geoffrey,‡1946-
        AEPSN       ‡adtmnro    ‡Smetana,
                                Bedˇrich,‡1824-1884.‡Quartets,‡strings,‡no. 1,‡E
                                minor;‡arr. 1986.
        AECNA       ‡a          ‡London Symphony Orchestra.
        AED0S       ‡a          ‡From my life.
        CAPM        ‡aabc       ‡19850218‡19850219‡5754‡L7
        CROM        ‡bb         ‡d1866‡d1941
        PNMIR       ‡ab         ‡CHAN 8412‡Chandos
        IVC         ‡a          ‡oa
        DFF         ‡a          ‡sd|fsngnnmmnee
        CALX        ‡a          ‡M1000
        DSR         ‡aa         ‡002423‡003030
FFD     DATE KY= p          DATE 1= 1986     DATE 2= 1985          LAN=
          COMP= op           SCORE= n         PARTS=          ACC MAT=
        ME IN B= x           CNTRY= enk       REPRO=          MOD REC=
        INTEL LV=          LIT TEXT=          CAT S=          CAT FORM= a
```

The Type of Date (DATE KY) and Dates fixed field elements are determined by information in the IMP subfield ‡c and the CAN field in this record for a digital compact disc. The TIL field includes a subfield ‡p and a GMD in subfield ‡h. The CAP field is derived from information in the CAN note. The NOC field first indicator is coded for "Partial contents" and the note is punctuated accordingly. Note also that in the second AEP field, the number of subfields exceeds seven; in cases such as this, WLN users are to remove the subfield codes and delimiters from the end of the field until only seven remain, leaving the text of any subsequent subfields as part of the seventh.

Example 15

Compact disc

```
jm          88-752942
      CRD         ‡a        ‡/R
      MEPS        ‡ad4      ‡Moretti, Isabelle,‡1964- ‡prf
      TILA0       ‡ah       ‡R´ecital de harpe‡[sound recording].
      IMP         ‡abc      ‡Arles :‡Harmonia Mundi France,‡p1987.
      COL         ‡abc      ‡1 sound disc :‡digital ;‡4 3/4 in.
      SERD        ‡a        ‡Cr´eations en val de Charente
      NORG        ‡a        ‡Isabelle Moretti, harp.
      CAN         ‡a        ‡Recorded Dec. 1986.
      NOG         ‡a        ‡Compact disc.
      NOCC        ‡a        ‡Sonate en sol majeur, Wotq 139 / Carl Philipp
                            Emanuel Bach (14:00) -- Sonate pour harpe /
                            Johann Ladislav Dussek (7:00) -- Sonate f¨ur
                            Harfe, 1939 / Paul Hindemith (11:00) -- Sonata
                            per arpa, op. 68 / Alfredo Casella (17:00) --
                            Sonate pour harpe / Germaine Tailleferre (9:00).
      SUT-L       ‡a        ‡Sonatas (Harp)
      AEPSN       ‡adtmnrf  ‡Bach, Carl Philipp
                            Emanuel,‡1714-1788.‡Solos,‡harp,‡H.
                            563,‡G major.‡1987.
      AEPSN       ‡adtmrf   ‡Dussek, Johann
                            Ladislaus,‡1760-1812.‡Sonatas,‡harp,‡C
                            minor.‡1987.
      AEPSN       ‡adtmf    ‡Hindemith,
                            Paul,‡1895-1963.‡Sonatas,‡harp.‡1987.
      AEPSN       ‡adtmnf   ‡Casella, Alfredo,‡1883-1947.‡Sonatas,‡harp,‡op.
                            68.‡1987.
      AEPSN       ‡adtmf    ‡Tailleferre,
                            Germaine,‡1892- ‡Sonatas,‡harp.‡1987.
      SAU-0       ‡a        ‡Cr´eations en val de Charente (Series)
      CAPS        ‡a        ‡198612--
      CROM        ‡bbb      ‡d1762‡d1939‡d1943
      PNMIR       ‡ab       ‡HMC 905184‡Harmonia Mundi France
      IVC         ‡a        ‡ta01
      DFF         ‡a        ‡sd|fsngnnmmnee
      CALX        ‡a        ‡M116
      DSR         ‡aaaaa    ‡001400‡000700‡001100‡001700‡000900
FFD   DATE KY= p           DATE 1= 1987      DATE 2= 1986          LAN=
         COMP= sn             SCORE= n          PARTS=          ACC MAT=
        ME IN B=              CNTRY= fr         REPRO=          MOD REC=
        INTEL LV=          LIT TEXT=            CAT S=          CAT FORM= a
```

This digital compact disc had no indication of stereo (hence, no mention in the COL field), but the cataloger surmised that it was stereo and coded the DFF fifth element as such. The Type of Date (DATE KY) and Dates fixed field elements are determined by information in the IMP subfield ‡c and the CAN field. The CAP field is derived from information in the CAN note. Note the subfield ‡4 for performer in the MEP field.

Example 16

Compact disc

```
jm          88-750309
        CRD         ‡a          ‡/R
        TILN0       ‡ah         ‡Brass bonanza‡[sound recording].
        IMP         ‡abc        ‡Sedro Woolley, WA :‡Crystal Records,‡p1986.
        COL         ‡abc        ‡1 sound disc :‡digital ;‡4 3/4 in.
        NOG         ‡a          ‡The 1st work originally for brass ensemble and
                                percussion.
        NORG        ‡a          ‡Metropolitan Brass Quintet (1st and 12th works)
                                ; Berlin Brass Quintet (2nd-4th works) ;
                                Annapolis Brass Quintet (5th-7th works) ; New
                                York Brass Quintet (8th work) ; Dallas Brass
                                Quintet (9th work) ; Saint Louis Brass Quintet
                                (10th work) ; I-5 Brass Quintet (11th work).
        NOH         ‡a          ‡Reissued from various Crystal Records albums.
        NOH         ‡a          ‡Eds. recorded: Atlantis Publications (5th-6th
                                works); Bruxelles : Editions Maurer (8th work);
                                C.F. Peters (9th work); Paterson's Publications
                                (10th work); Canada : Touch of Brass (11th
                                work); Novello (12th work).
        CAN         ‡a          ‡Recorded 1977-1984 in various locations.
        NOG         ‡a          ‡Compact disc.
        NOG         ‡a          ‡Analog recording.
        NOG         ‡a          ‡Program notes (4 folded p.) included.
        NOCC        ‡a          ‡Fanfares for the jubilee of Rimsky-Korsakov /
                                Liadov-Glazunov -- Allemande [i.e., Gaillard] /
                                William Brade -- Canzona per sonare : no. 1 /
                                Giovanni Gabrieli -- Sonata from Die
                                B¨ankels¨angerlieder : ca. 1648 / anon. [i.e.,
                                Daniel Speer] -- Sonata no. 4 ; Sonata no. 6 /
                                Daniel Speer -- Sonata no. 2 / Johann Kessel --
                                Par monts et par vaux / Michel Leclerc -- Six
                                dances / Alan Hovhaness -- Quintet / Malcolm
                                Arnold -- The carnival of Venice / Brent Dutton
                                -- Music hall suite / Joseph Horovitz.
        SUT-L       ‡a          ‡Brass quintets (Horn, trombone, trumpets (2),
                                tuba)
        SUT-L       ‡a          ‡Brass quintets (Horn, trombone, trumpets (2),
                                tuba), Arranged.
        AEPSN       ‡adtof      ‡Lyadov, Anatoly Konstantinovich,‡1855-1914.
                                ‡Slavleni͡i͡a;‡arr.‡1986.
        AEPSN       ‡adtpf      ‡Brade, William,‡1560-1630.‡Newe ausserlesene
                                Paduanen, Galliarden, Cantzonen, Allmand und
                                Coranten.‡Gaillard.‡1986.
        AEPSN       ‡adtf       ‡Gabrieli, Giovanni,‡1557-1612.‡Spiritata.‡1986.
        AEPSN       ‡adtkf      ‡Speer, Daniel,‡1636-1707.‡Musicalisch-
                                t¨urckischer Eulen-Spiegel.‡Selections.‡1986.
        AEPSN       ‡adtpnf     ‡Kessel, Johann,‡fl. 1657-1672.‡Symphonien,
Sonaten, ein Canzon, nebst Allmanden, Couranten, Balletten und
                                Sarabanden.‡Sonata,‡no. 2.‡1986.
```

AEPSN	‡adtf	‡Leclerc, Michel,‡1914- ‡Par monts et par vaux.‡1986.
AEPSN	‡adtmnf	‡Hovhaness, Alan,‡1911- ‡Dances,‡brasses,‡op. 79.‡1986.
AEPSN	‡atmf	‡Arnold, Malcolm.‡Quintets,‡trumpets, horn, trombone, tuba.‡1986.
AEPSN	‡adtf	‡Dutton, Brent,‡1950- ‡Carnival of Venice.‡1986.
AEPSN	‡adtf	‡Horovitz, Joseph,‡1926- ‡Music hall suite.‡1986.
AECNA	‡a4	‡Metropolitan Brass Quintet.‡prf
AECNA	‡a4	‡Berlin Brass Quintet.‡prf
AECNA	‡a4	‡Annapolis Brass Quintet.‡prf
AECNA	‡a4	‡New York Brass Quintet.‡prf
AECNA	‡a4	‡Dallas Brass Quintet.‡prf
AECNA	‡a4	‡Saint Louis Brass Quintet.‡prf
AECNA	‡a4	‡I-5 Brass Quintet.‡prf
CAPR	‡aa	‡1977----‡1984----
CROS	‡b	‡d1961
FCC	‡aaaa	‡df‡cz‡sn‡su
PNMIR	‡ab	‡CD200‡Crystal Records
IVC	‡aaaa	‡bb02‡ba01‡bd01‡be01
DFF	‡a	‡sd|fsngnnmmnee
CALX	‡a	‡M555

FFD	DATE KY= r	DATE 1= 1986	DATE 2=	LAN=
	COMP= mu	SCORE= n	PARTS=	ACC MAT= i
	ME IN B=	CNTRY= wau	REPRO=	MOD REC=
	INTEL LV=	LIT TEXT=	CAT S=	CAT FORM= a

Although this digital compact disc derived from an analog recording had no indication of stereo, and so no mention of it in the COL field, the cataloger surmised that it was stereo and coded the DFF fifth element as such. The Type of Date (DATE KY) fixed field is coded "r" (for reissue) but the Dates fixed field has only a single date because of the first NOH note, which mentions no original release date. Type of Date code "r" has precedence over "p", for which the recording dates in field CAN would be evidence. The CAP field is derived from information in the CAN note.

Example 17

Analog Disc

```
jm          86-750617
     CRD        ‡a      ‡/R/r87
     TILN0      ‡ah     ‡Mechanical music hall‡[sound recording].
     IMP        ‡abc    ‡Badminton, Glos. :‡Saydisc,‡[1972?]
     COL        ‡abc    ‡1 sound disc :‡analog, 33 1/3 rpm, stereo. ;‡12
                        in.
     SET-0      ‡av     ‡Golden age of mechanical music ;‡v. 10
     NOG        ‡a      ‡"Street, penny & player pianos, musical boxes &
                        other Victorian automata"--Container.
     NOG        ‡a      ‡Songs identified with various English music
                        hall performers.
     NOG        ‡a      ‡Instruments from the collection of Roy
                        Mickleburgh, Bristol.
     NOCC       ‡a      ‡Miscellany -- Florrie Ford songs -- Eugene
                        Stratton song -- Miscellany -- Tom Costello
                        songs -- Ellaline Terris song -- Harry Champion
                        songs -- Miscellany -- Albert Chevalier songs --
                        Marie Lloyd songs -- Lottie Collins song -- Leo
                        Dryden song -- Miscellany.
     SUT-L      ‡a      ‡Barrel-organ music.
     SUT-L      ‡a      ‡Player-piano music.
     SUT-L      ‡a      ‡Music box music.
     SUT-L      ‡az     ‡Popular instrumental music‡England.
     SUT-L      ‡ax     ‡Musical revues, comedies, etc.‡Excerpts,
                        Arranged.
     SUT-L      ‡a      ‡Musical instruments (Mechanical)
     AEPSA      ‡a      ‡Mickleburgh, Roy.
     PNMIR      ‡ab     ‡SDL 2232‡Saydisc
     GAC        ‡a      ‡e-uk-en
     DFF        ‡a      ‡sd|bsmennmplue
     CALX       ‡ab     ‡M175‡.B3
```

FFD	DATE KY= s	DATE 1= 1972	DATE 2=	LAN=
	COMP= pp	SCORE= n	PARTS=	ACC MAT=
	ME IN B=	CNTRY= enk	REPRO=	MOD REC=
	INTEL LV=	LIT TEXT=	CAT S=	CAT FORM= a

This is a record for an analog disc with title main entry.

Example 18

Analog disc

```
jm          86-753061
       CRD        ‡a         ‡/R
       TILN0      ‡ah        ‡1. Schweizerisches Drehorgel-Festival,
                             Arosa‡[sound recording].
       IMP        ‡abc       ‡Thun/Schweiz :‡Claves,‡p1979.
       COL        ‡abc       ‡1 sound disc :‡analog, 33 1/3 rpm, stereo. ;‡12
                             in.
       NOG        ‡a         ‡Claves: Cla D 907 (on container: D 907).
       NOG        ‡a         ‡Twenty barrel-organ pieces and "a dialogue
                             between a church organ and a barrel-organ,
                             played by Hannes Meyer and Heinrich Brechb¨uhl:
                             Variations on the theme 'God save the king'"--
                             Container.
       CAN        ‡a         ‡Recorded July 20-22, 1979, on the streets and
                             in the squares of Arosa, Switzerland.
       SUT-L      ‡a         ‡Barrel-organ music.
       SUT-L      ‡a         ‡Variations (Organ)
       AEPSA      ‡ad4       ‡Meyer, Hannes,‡1939- ‡prf
       AEPSA      ‡aq4       ‡Brechb¨uhl, H.‡(Heinrich)‡prf
       AEMNA      ‡andc      ‡Schweizerisches Drehorgel-Festival‡(1st :‡1979
                             :‡Arosa, Switzerland)
       AED0S      ‡a         ‡Erste Schweizerisches Drehorgel-Festival,
                             Arosa.
       CAPR       ‡aabc      ‡19790720‡19790722‡6044‡A87
       PNMIN      ‡ab        ‡Cla D 907‡Claves
       PNMIN      ‡ab        ‡D 907‡Claves
       IVC        ‡a         ‡zn01
       IVC        ‡aa        ‡kb01‡zn01
       DFF        ‡a         ‡sd|bsmennmplue
       CALX       ‡ab        ‡M175‡.B3
```

FFD	DATE KY= s		DATE 1= 1979	DATE 2=		LAN=
		COMP= vr	SCORE= n	PARTS=		ACC MAT=
	ME IN B=		CNTRY= sz	REPRO=		MOD REC=
	INTEL LV=		LIT TEXT=	CAT S=		CAT FORM= a

    Because two forms of the music publisher's number are found on this analog disc (see the first NOG field), two PNM fields are needed. Information in the CAP is derived from the CAN field. The AEM field is used for the name of the festival.

Example 19

Analog disc

jm		85-754264	
CRD	ǂa	ǂ/R/r872	
MEPS	ǂad	ǂHandel, George Frideric,ǂ1685-1759.	
UTIA0	ǂal	ǂGiulio Cesare.ǂEnglish	
TILA0	ǂahc	ǂJulius Caesarǂ[sound recording] /ǂHandel ; libretto by Haym ; transl. Trowell.	
IMP	ǂabc	ǂ[Hollywood, Calif.] :ǂAngel,ǂp1985.	
COL	ǂabc	ǂ3 sound discs :ǂanalog, 33 1/3 rpm, stereo. ;ǂ12 in.	
NOG	ǂa	ǂOpera; sung in English.	
NOH	ǂa	ǂ"Edition by Noel Davies and Sir Charles Mackerras"--Container.	
NORG	ǂa	ǂValerie Masterson, soprano ; Dame Janet Baker, Sarah Walker, Della Jones, mezzo-sopranos ; James Bowman, David James, countertenors ; Christopher Booth-Jones, baritone ; John Tomlinson, bass ; English National Opera Chorus & Orchestra ; Sir Charles Mackerras, conductor.	
CAN	ǂa	ǂ"Recorded at the Abbey Road Studios, London, in association with the Peter Moores Foundation"-- Booklet, p. 1.	
NOG	ǂa	ǂDigital recording.	
NOG	ǂa	ǂManual sequence.	
NOG	ǂa	ǂProgram notes by Brian Trowell in English and German and by Sir Charles Mackerras in English, synopsis in English and German, biographical notes on the singers and conductor in English, and English translation of the Italian libretto (24 p. : ill.) laid in container.	
SUT-L	ǂa	ǂOperas.	
SUPSL	ǂax	ǂCaesar, JuliusǂDrama.	
AEPSA	ǂa4	ǂHaym, Nicola Francesco.ǂlbt	
AEPSA	ǂa4	ǂTrowell, Brian.ǂtrl	
AEPSA	ǂa	ǂDavies, Noel.	
AEPSA	ǂacd4	ǂMackerras, Charles,ǂSir,ǂ1925- ǂcnd	
AEPSA	ǂa4	ǂMasterson, Valerie.ǂprf	
AEPSA	ǂa4	ǂBaker, Janet.ǂprf	
AEPSA	ǂa4	ǂWalker, Sarah.ǂprf	
AEPSA	ǂa4	ǂJones, Della.ǂprf	
AEPSA	ǂa4	ǂBowman, James.ǂprf	
AEPSA	ǂa4	ǂJames, David.ǂprf	
AEPMA	ǂa4	ǂBooth-Jones, Christopher.ǂprf	
AEPSA	ǂad4	ǂTomlinson, John,ǂ1946 Sept. 22- ǂprf	
AECNA	ǂa4	ǂEnglish National Opera.ǂprf	
SRNU	ǂa	ǂ7777339741	
CAP	ǂbc	ǂ5754ǂL7	
PNMIR	ǂab	ǂDSC-3974ǂAngel	
PNMIR	ǂab	ǂEX 27 0232 3ǂEMI	
LANX	ǂdhbehg	ǂengǂitaǂengǂengǂitaǂengger	

```
        DFF             ‡a          ‡sd|bsmennmplud
        CALX            ‡a          ‡M1500
FFD   DATE KY= s            DATE 1= 1985      DATE 2=              LAN= eng
        COMP= op             SCORE= n         PARTS=          ACC MAT= dfhz
      ME IN B= x             CNTRY= cau        REPRO=          MOD REC=
     INTEL LV=            LIT TEXT=            CAT S=          CAT FORM= a
```

The second NOG note and the DFF fourteenth element indicate that this analog disc was derived from a digital recording. The U.S. Universal Product Code for sound recordings is recorded in the SRN field. The second indicator of each PNM fields is set to print; both will generate notes in WLN. The LAN field is derived from the information found in the last NOG field.

Example 20

Analog disc

```
jm          88-751052
      CRD          ǂa          ǂ/R
      MEPS         ǂa4         ǂHawkins, Coleman.ǂprf
      TILA0        ǂahc        ǂBody and soulǂ[sound recording] /ǂ[performed
                               by] Coleman Hawkins.
      IMP          ǂabc        ǂNew York, N.Y. :ǂBluebird,ǂp1986.
      COL          ǂabc        ǂ2 sound discs :ǂanalog, 33 1/3 rpm, mono. ;ǂ12
                               in.
      NORG         ǂa          ǂColeman Hawkins, tenor saxophone, with various
                               jazz ensembles, big bands, and with strings.
      CAN          ǂa          ǂRecorded between Oct. 11, 1937, and Jan. 20,
                               1956, in New York City.
      NOG          ǂa          ǂBiographical notes on container.
      SUT-L        ǂa          ǂJazz ensembles.
      SUT-L        ǂa          ǂBig band music.
      SUT-L        ǂay         ǂPopular musicǂ1951-1960.
      SRNU         ǂa          ǂ7863556581
      CAPR         ǂaabc       ǂ19371011ǂ19560120ǂ3804ǂN4
      FCC          ǂaa         ǂjzǂpp
      PNMIR        ǂab         ǂ5658-1 RBǂBluebird
      GAC          ǂa          ǂn-us---
      DFF          ǂa          ǂsd|bmmennmplue
      CALX         ǂa          ǂM1366
```

FFD	DATE KY= p	DATE 1= 1986	DATE 2= 1939	LAN=
	COMP= mu	SCORE= n	PARTS=	ACC MAT= f
	ME IN B= x	CNTRY= nyu	REPRO=	MOD REC=
	INTEL LV=	LIT TEXT=	CAT S=	CAT FORM= a

The code in the Accompanying Matter fixed field (ACC MAT) reflects the last NOG note in this record for an analog disc. Information in the CAP is derived from the CAN field. The U.S. Universal Product Code for sound recordings is recorded in the SRN field. The gap between the dates of the original recordings and the date of this release is brought out in the Type of Date (DATE KY) and Dates fixed fields.

Example 21

Analog disc

```
im          85-755141
        CRD         ‡a          ‡/R
        TILNO       ‡ah         ‡Trains in trouble‡[sound recording].
        IMP         ‡ababc      ‡London :‡ASV Transacord ;‡Mitcham, Surrey
                                :‡Distributed by P.R.T. Records,‡p1979.
        COL         ‡abc        ‡1 sound disc :‡analog, 33 1/3 rpm, stereo. ;‡12
                                in.
        SET-0       ‡a          ‡Sounds of the steam age
        CAN         ‡a          ‡Recorded between 1957 and 1971 in Great
                                Britain, in 1970 in Yugoslavia, and in 1978 in
                                Austria.
        NOG         ‡a          ‡Notes on container.
        NOG         ‡a          ‡Issued also as cassette: ZC ATR 7016.
        NOA         ‡a          ‡Presents the sounds of steam trains in adverse
                                weather conditions and with mechanical
                                difficulties as they attempt to pull freight and
                                passenger trains.
        SUT-L       ‡a          ‡Locomotive sounds.
        SUT-L       ‡a          ‡Railroad sounds.
        CAPR        ‡aab        ‡1957----‡1971----‡5740
        CAPS        ‡ab         ‡1970----‡6840
        CAPS        ‡ab         ‡1978----‡6890
        PNMIR       ‡ab         ‡ATR 7016‡ASV Transacord
        PNMIN       ‡ab         ‡ZC ATR 7016‡ASV Transacord
        DFF         ‡a          ‡sd|bsmennmplue
        CALX        ‡a          ‡TJ608
FFD  DATE KY= p              DATE 1= 1979    DATE 2= 1957          LAN=
       COMP= nn                SCORE= n        PARTS=            ACC MAT=
     ME IN B=                  CNTRY= enk      REPRO=            MOD REC=
     INTEL LV=              LIT TEXT= s        CAT S=            CAT FORM= a
```

In this analog disc of nonmusical sounds (Type of Record: i), the Literary Text for Sound Recordings fixed field element (LIT TEXT) is coded for sounds. Multiple CAP fields correspond to the times and places of the recordings detailed in the CAN note. A second, nonprinting PNM field gives access to the item's publisher's number in another recording medium (cassette), cited in the last NOG note. Note both publisher and distributor in the IMP field. The gap between the original recording and the release dates is brought out in the Type of Date (DATE KY) and Dates fixed field elements.

Example 22

Analog Cassette Tape

```
jm      86-754808
        CRD         ‡a          ‡/R/r87
        MECN        ‡a4         ‡Marimba "Ind´igena Pura".‡prf
        TILA0       ‡ahc        ‡Sones nativos‡[sound recording] /‡[interpretado
                                por la] Marimba "Ind´igena Pura".
        IMP         ‡abc        ‡Guatemala :‡DYCSA,‡[198-?]
        COL         ‡ab         ‡1 sound cassette :‡analog.
        NOG         ‡a          ‡Popular Guatemalan instrumental music.
        NOG         ‡a          ‡Title on container: La ´unica chimalteca.
        NOCC        ‡a          ‡El xap -- Sal negra -- Maconaj -- Guarda
                                barranca -- El son de los bricadores --
                                Juventino -- San Rafael -- Cuando llora la malin
                                -- Tadeo Solares -- Frescas ma~nanitas --
                                Santiago -- El son de Mashico.
        SUT-L       ‡azy        ‡Popular instrumental music‡Guatemala‡1981-
        SUT-L       ‡a          ‡Marimba music.
        AED0S       ‡a          ‡´Unica chimalteca.
        PNMIR       ‡ab         ‡1001‡DYCSA
        GAC         ‡a          ‡ncgt---
        IVC         ‡a          ‡oy
        DFF         ‡a          ‡ss|lunjlcmnnuu
        CALX        ‡a          ‡M1685
```

FFD	DATE KY= q	DATE 1= 1980	DATE 2= 1986	LAN=
	COMP= pp	SCORE= n	PARTS=	ACC MAT=
	ME IN B= x	CNTRY= gt	REPRO=	MOD REC=
	INTEL LV=	LIT TEXT=	CAT S=	CAT FORM= a

The Type of Date (DATE KY) code "q" and the two dates in the fixed field are based on the uncertain date in the IMP subfield ‡c (this musical cassette tape was cataloged in 1986). The corporate name main entry (MEC) is the musical group, with a subfield ‡4 for performer.

Example 23

Analog Cassette Tape

```
im      88-740281
        CRD         ‡a          ‡/R
        MEPS        ‡ad         ‡Wiesel, Elie,‡1928-
        TILA0       ‡ah         ‡Elie Wiesel at the National Press Club‡[sound
                                recording].
        IMP         ‡abc        ‡Washington, D.C. :‡National Public
                                Radio,‡p1983.
        COL         ‡ab         ‡1 sound cassette (1 hr.) :‡analog.
        NOG         ‡a          ‡Publisher's catalog title: Elie Wiesel on
                                remembering.
        CAN         ‡a          ‡Recorded at a National Press Club luncheon held
                                in Washington, D.C.
        NOG         ‡a          ‡Broadcast Apr. 11, 1983, on National Public
                                Radio.
        NOA         ‡a          ‡Noted author, Holocaust survivor, and chairman
                                of the U.S. Holocaust Memorial Council Elie
                                Wiesel discusses attempts by journalists in
                                World War II to tell the world what was
                                happening in Germany and describes his own
                                mission to ensure that people will never forget
                                the Holocaust.
        SUT-L       ‡ax         ‡Holocaust, Jewish (1939-1945)‡Censorship.
        AECNA       ‡a          ‡National Press Club (U.S.)
        AECNA       ‡a          ‡National Public Radio (U.S.)
        AED0S       ‡a          ‡Elie Wiesel on remembering.
        CAP         ‡b          ‡3850
        PNMIR       ‡ab         ‡NP-830411‡National Public Radio
        DFF         ‡a          ‡ss|lunjlcmnnuu
        CALX        ‡a          ‡D804.3
        DSR         ‡a          ‡006000
FFD     DATE KY= s          DATE 1= 1983     DATE 2=              LAN= eng
            COMP= nn           SCORE= n       PARTS=          ACC MAT=
        ME IN B= x             CNTRY= dcu     REPRO=          MOD REC=
        INTEL LV=          LIT TEXT= 1        CAT S=          CAT FORM= a
```

The CAP field codifies the place of capture stated in the CAN field of this record for a spoken word cassette tape. A summary of the lecture appears in the NOA note. The Literary Text for Sound Recordings fixed field element (LIT TEXT) is coded for a lecture. Note that the dates in the SUT field are not separately subfielded and that the duration of one hour (COL) is coded in the DSR field.

Example 24

Analog Tape Reel

```
im          85-752880
        CRD         ‡a        ‡/R
        MEPS        ‡ad       ‡Eberhart, Richard,‡1904-
        UTIA0       ‡ak       ‡Florida poems.‡Selections
        TILA0       ‡ah       ‡Richard Eberhart‡[sound recording].
        IMP         ‡abc      ‡[Kansas City, Mo. :‡New Letters,‡1985]
        COL         ‡abc      ‡1 sound tape reel (29 min.) :‡analog, 7 1/2
                              ips, mono. ;‡7 in.
        CAN         ‡a        ‡Recorded at WUFT-FM in Gainesville, Fla.
        NOG         ‡a        ‡Broadcast Jan. 1985 on the radio program New
                              letters on the air.
        NOA         ‡a        ‡Pulitzer Prize winning poet Richard Eberhart
                              reads from his collection entitled Florida
                              poems.
        AEU0S       ‡a        ‡New letters.
        AEU0S       ‡a        ‡New letters on the air (Radio program)
        CAP         ‡bc       ‡3934‡G2
        DFF         ‡a        ‡st|omncmumnnue
        CALX        ‡ab       ‡PS3509‡.B456
        DSR         ‡a        ‡002900
FFD     DATE KY= s            DATE 1= 1985     DATE 2=              LAN= eng
            COMP= nn           SCORE= n         PARTS=          ACC MAT=
          ME IN B= x           CNTRY= mou       REPRO=          MOD REC=
          INTEL LV=          LIT TEXT= p        CAT S=          CAT FORM= a
```

The CAP field codifies information found in the CAN note of this record for a spoken word sound tape reel. Note the two uniform title added entries (AEU), one for the journal *New letters*, the other for the related radio program.

BIBLIOGRAPHY

Bibliography

Anglo-American Cataloguing Rules. 2d ed., 1988 rev. Ottawa: Canadian Library Association; Chicago: American Library Association, 1988.

Bratcher, Perry, and Jennifer Smith. *Music Subject Headings.* Lake Crystal, Minn.: Soldier Creek Press, 1988.

Crawford, Walt. *MARC for Library Use: Understanding Integrated USMARC.* 2d ed. Boston: G.K. Hall, 1989.

Format Integration and its Effect on the USMARC Bibliographic Format. Washington, D.C.: Cataloging Distribution Service, Library of Congress, 1988.

Holzberlein, Deanne, and Dolly Jones. *Cataloging Sound Recordings: A Manual with Examples.* New York: Haworth Press, 1988.

International Organization for Standardization. *Documentation—International Standard Recording Code (ISRC).* 1st ed. Switzerland: ISO, 1986.

ISBD(NBM): International Standard Bibliographic Description for Non-book Materials. Rev. ed. London: IFLA Universal Bibliographic Control and International MARC Programme, 1987.

ISBD(PM): International Standard Bibliographic Description for Printed Music. London: IFLA International Office for UBC, 1980.

Library of Congress. Processing Services. *Cataloging Service Bulletin.* Washington, D.C.: Library of Congress, 1978- Quarterly.

Library of Congress Rule Interpretations. 2d ed. Washington, D.C.: Cataloging Distribution Service, Library of Congress, 1989. With updates.

Library of Congress. Subject Cataloging Division. *Library of Congress Subject Headings.* 12th ed. Washington, D.C.: Cataloging Distribution Service, Library of Congress, 1989.

——. *Subject Cataloging Manual: Subject Headings.* 3d ed. Washington, D.C.: Cataloging Distribution Service, Library of Congress, 1988. With updates.

MARC Formats for Bibliographic Data. Washington, D.C.: Automated Systems Office, Library of Congress, 1980. With updates.

Music Cataloging Bulletin. Canton, Mass.: Music Library Association, 1970- Monthly. With index/ supplements.

Music OCLC Users Group. *MOUG Newsletter.* Madison, Wis.: MOUG, 1977- Irregular.

"Music Online Input Manual: Draft." Washington, D.C.: Library of Congress, 1982.

OCLC Online Computer Library Center. *Scores Format.* 2d ed. Dublin, Ohio: OCLC, 1986. With updates.

——. *Sound Recordings Format.* 2d ed. Dublin, Ohio: OCLC, 1986. With updates.

Olson, Nancy B. *Audiovisual Material Glossary.* Dublin, Ohio: OCLC, 1988.

Randel, Don Michael, ed. *The New Harvard Dictionary of Music*. Cambridge, Mass.: Harvard University Press, Belknap Press, 1986.

Research Libraries Group. *Cataloging in RLIN II: User's Manual*. 3d ed. Stanford, Calif.: RLG, 1987.

——. *RLIN Bibliographic Field Guide*. 1st ed. 2 vols. Stanford, Calif.: RLG, 1985. With updates.

Rogers, JoAnn V., and Jerry D. Saye. *Nonprint Cataloging for Multimedia Collections: A Guide Based on AACR 2*. 2d ed. Littleton, Colo.: Libraries Unlimited, 1987.

Sadie, Stanley, ed. *The New Grove Dictionary of Music and Musicians*. London: Macmillan Publishers; Washington, D.C.: Grove's Dictionaries of Music, 1980.

Seibert, Donald. *The MARC Music Format: From Inception to Publication*. Philadelphia, Pa.: Music Library Association, 1982.

Smiraglia, Richard P. *Cataloging Music: A Manual for Use with AACR 2*. 2d ed. Lake Crystal, Minn.: Soldier Creek Press, 1986.

——. *Music Cataloging: The Bibliographic Control of Printed and Recorded Music in Libraries*. Englewood, Colo.: Libraries Unlimited, 1989.

Thorin, Suzanne E., and Carole Franklin Vidali. *The Acquisition and Cataloging of Music and Sound Recordings: A Glossary*. [N.p.]: Music Library Association, 1984.

USMARC Format for Bibliographic Data. Washington, D.C.: Cataloging Distribution Service, Library of Congress, 1988. With updates.

Western Library Network. *WLN Data Preparation Manual*. 1st ed., rev. 2 vols. Olympia, Wash.: WLN, 1988. With updates.

INDEX

Index

finding, date and place of, 84-88; note, 187-88
fine groove, in 007, 46
first generation microforms, in 007, 41
flageolet, 102
fluegelhorn, 100
flute, 102
folk music, 13
folktales, nonmusical sound recordings, 30
forenames, as entries, 111, 112
form of composition
    fixed field, 12-18
    note, 182
form subheadings
    in corporate name headings, 123
    in meeting name headings, 129
    in personal name headings, 116
    in uniform title headings, 135
Format (OCLC), 19-26
format integration, xvii
format of music fixed field, 19-26
formatted contents note, 179, 184-86
FRM COMP (LC), 12-18
fugues, 14
full score, 19, 20
full track tapes, in 007, 48

G

gamelan, 101
GEN (RLIN), 41-42
general material designation
    microforms, in 007, 37
    sound recordings, in 007, 43
    in title statement, 157
    in uniform title headings, 135
general note, 181-83
generation, of microforms, 41-42
geographic
    classification
        area code, 86
        subarea code, 86-87
        subject headings, 145-52
GMD, See general material designation
gospel music, 14
graphic notation, works in, music format, 26, 28
groove width/pitch
    in 007, 46-47
    in physical description area, 168
GRV (RLIN), 46-47
guides, as accompanying material, 3
guitar, 102

H

half track tapes, in 007, 48
hardanger fiddle, 101
harmonium, 101
harp, 102
harpsichord, 101

high reduction ratio (microforms), in 007, 40
high voice, 102
hill-and-dale cutting (sound recordings), in 007, 50
historical information, as accompanying material, 3
history, nonmusical sound recordings, 30
horn, 100
host item entry, 5
hu ch'in, 101
hymnals
    format, 19
    type of record, 33
hymns, 14
hyphen, second, in Library of Congress control number, 58

I

IBM cards, See aperture cards
IMP (WLN), 163-65
imprint area, 163-65
imprint statement for sound recordings (pre-AACR 2), 195
incidental music, 16-17; with plays, type of record, 34
inclusive dates, in type of date, 7
incomplete contents note, 185-86
indeterminacy, music of, 13
indexes, thematic, as accompanying material, 3
indigenous music, 13
informal contents note, 181
instantaneous sound recordings, in 007, 49
instructional materials
    as accompanying material, 3
    instructional materials
    music, type of record, 33
    nonmusical sound recordings, 30
    scores, type of record, 33
    sound recordings, type of record, 34
instruments
    number of, code, 100-108
    solo, music format, 26
    technical/historical information on, as accompanying material, 3
interim card number system (Library of Congress), 59
International Standard Book Number, of original, 192
International Standard Recording Code, 64, 66
International Standard Serial Number
    of original, 192
    in series statement/added entry, 175
interviews, nonmusical sound recordings, 31
ISBD description, in descriptive cataloging form, 11
ISBN, See International Standard Book Number
ISRC, See International Standard Recording Code
ISSN, See International Standard Serial Number
issue
    date, in type of date, 8
    number, of sound recordings, 69
IVC (WLN), 100-108

X-Y-Z